SANTA ANA PUBLIC LIBRARY

VIDEO PRODUCTION TECHNIQUES

Theory and Practice from Concept to Screen

VIDEO PRODUCTION TECHNIQUES

Theory and Practice from Concept to Screen

DONALD L. DIEFENBACH

Routledge
Taylor & Francis Group
New York London

First published by
Lawrence Erlbaum Associates,
10 Industrial Avenue
Mahwah, New Jersey 07430

Reprinted 2011 by Routledge

Routledge
Taylor & Francis Group
711 Third Avenue
New York, NY 10017

Routledge
Taylor & Francis Group
2 Park Square
Milton Park, Abingdon
Oxon OX14 4RN

International Standard Book Number-13: 978-0-8058-3703-2 (Hardcover)

Library of Congress Cataloging-in-Publication Data

Diefenbach, Donald L., 1967-
Video production techniques : theory and practice from concept to screen / author, Donald L. Diefenbach.
p. cm. -- (Lea's communication series)
Includes bibliographical references and index.
ISBN-13: 978-0-8058-3703-2 (alk. paper)
1. Video recordings--Production and direction. I. Title.

PN1992.94.D54 2008
791.4502'32--dc22 2007016030

Visit the Taylor & Francis Web site at
http://www.taylorandfrancis.com

DEDICATION

FOR AIMEE AND JULIE

CONTENTS

UNIT III
ADVANCED APPLICATIONS

PREFACE

Video production is an art, a science, and a business. Learning to create successful video projects requires the integration of these three elements. There are excellent books that explore the technical craft of video production, and others that explore the foundations of film theory and aesthetics. Yet other texts concentrate on television and film business models.

Until now, however, students seeking to learn the essentials of video production were without a single resource that integrated these intrinsic elements. Instructors were forced to use a combination of texts or create reading packets to fill the gaps left by other books.

The primary mission of *Video Production Techniques* is to unify theory and practice in a single resource. Theory without practice is also without result. One must create art. Practice without theory is devoid of soul and purpose. At the end of the day, video projects have to be about something. Almost anyone can learn to run a camera and edit, but learning to be an effective storyteller is a challenging course of study that is as much about ideas and methods as it is about technology. This text goes beyond how the equipment works to include the rich history of production and to introduce the artists who have paved the way.

Video Production Techniques was created in the classroom. It is grounded in 15 years of production instruction, and written to meet the needs of introductory-level production students and instructors. *Video Production Techniques* puts technology into creative context, and addresses the questions students have about how the industry works and professional opportunities they can pursue in their own careers.

The text is structured to optimally meet the sequential needs of students and instructors. Many production books are formatted to follow the production process from beginning to end. Some books do not even introduce the tools of editing until the final unit. It is not useful to introduce editing at the end of a book or a course. Students need to know all of the basics early on so they can practice throughout their course of study.

This text is designed using a building-block approach. The basic skills of production are introduced in Unit I. Students explore writing, shooting, and editing right away. Unit II expands these basics skills with an introduction to short-form projects and in-depth explorations of lighting and sound. Unit II concludes with an exploration of documentaries, news, and other nonfiction forms. Unit III, the final unit, is dedicated to advanced applications, including the process of creating long-form projects, the elements of directing, and strategies for effective marketing and distribution. The book concludes with a chapter exploring professional opportunities in production and options for further study.

Video Production Techniques includes a companion DVD with professional examples, original demonstrations, and interviews with practitioners. You will not only read about making video projects, but will also review examples and hear from award-winning artists who make films and television for a living. The DVD is structured in parallel with the text. When a principle explored in the text is supported with an example on the DVD, this is indicated in the text with an icon in the margin. As you access optional DVD links, you will find illustrations and expansions of concepts that are discussed in the text.

Each chapter concludes with Sample Exercises to provide a foundation for practice and Recommended Readings to guide students wishing to explore each chapter topic in greater depth. Throughout the text, key terms are presented in bold, which indicates that they are defined in the glossary.

Additional ancillary materials for classroom support are available at our Web site (http://VideoProductionTechniques.com), including suggested syllabi, sample assignments with grading rubrics, and PowerPoint presentations for each chapter.

Video and film production are at a crossroads. Each year more and more professional content is captured with digital video technology; however, the foundations of motion picture theory and language are firmly grounded in the more traditional medium of film. This text unifies the technology of video and language of film. For consistency with evolving popular and professional usage, the terms "video" and "film" are used interchangeably when the context is not specific to one medium or the other. The practical focus of the text, however, assumes the student is shooting with digital video and not film.

Whether your primary goal is to better understand and appreciate the process and products of video and film production, or whether you wish to engage in making motion pictures for self-expression or as part of a professional career, this text will help you acquire a foundation in the far-reaching video production sphere of mass communication that will serve you for a lifetime. The text is designed as a resource for classroom education, and as a tool for the student studying on his or her own. Anyone with access to a basic camera, a video-editing system, and an imagination is invited to take the journey though these pages and through the video production process.

ACKNOWLEDGMENTS

Video and film production is a community activity; so, too, is creating a book about the process. I am indebted to many industry professionals and scholars who gave selflessly of their time, expertise, and films for the betterment of this educational resource.

Al Wilson, Richard Breyer, and Stan Alten served as mentors for me in my study of the theory and craft of video production. J. Chris Larson gave me opportunities in production practice that tested my resourcefulness and potential.

Innumerable students in my video production courses widened my concept of the production process. Many former students contributed directly to this project, including Erin Bereit, Apryl Blakeney, Chris Bubenik, Chris Carrerras, Chris Cantos, Jennifer Clickner, Michelle Dean, Andrea Desky, Jeffrey De Cristofaro, Ed Fickle, Brian Furr, Kenneth George, Jessica Green, Ann Grover, Colleen Hobe, Joanne Hughes, Daniel Judson, Clinton Lathinghouse, Ashley Lutterloh, Veronica Marshall, Dmitri Medvedev, Dianna Pitman, Jennie Picarella, Rebecca Rinas, Emily Sarkissian, Kevin Schaefer, Evan Schafer, Paul Schattel, Chanse Simpson, Kent Thompson, Chris Walker, and Alison Watson.

My family supported this project with their encouragement and editing, and I want to thank Mom, Dad, and Gretchen. Barry Weitz is a tremendous friend to education and this project. He was the first to offer his expertise and professional credits. Trenton McDevitt provided extensive professional resources and regular consultation. He contributed significantly to the review of this manuscript and to the content of Chapters 9, 10, and 11. I am particularly grateful to Trenton for sharing his expertise on the acting process. Chip Hackler contributed to Chapters 3, 6, 9, and 11. Judi Rivers worked closely with me to develop and refine the manuscript. Alan Hantz was the first person to share my enthusiasm for this project and its value to education. This book exists because of his vision, contribution, and contagious excitement.

Jesse Knight is a gifted filmmaker who applied his artistic vision to create many of the illustrations in this text. I want to thank Tom Anton, Brian Bain, Mike Berlin, Jerry Bledsoe, Paul Bonesteel, Walt Bost, Lee Brown, Leanne Campbell, John Clisham, Michael Cogdill, Aaton Cohen-Sitt, Frank Colin, Ron

Cutler, Gerry Donovan, Jenny Dunn, Charlie Geocaris, Laura Edwards, Merwin Gross, Don Henderson, John Hendon, Julie Hingle, Pat Hingle, Alexander Johnston, Elainie Johnston, Katie Kasben, Jim Knuth, Phyllis Lang, John Le, Susan Levitis, Kurt Mann, Hal Marienthal, Marc Norman, Sean O'Connell, Thomas Oliver, William Olsen, Larry Peerce, Chris Porter, Mary Rodman, Mark Ruppert, Sandi Russell, Tom Savini, Francis Shepherd, Bryan Sinclair, Travis Vaughn Skinner, Anne Slatton, Andy Still, Althea Sumpter, Adams Wood, and Angela Zarrella.

Amanda Edwards and Troy Scott Burnette created the companion DVD to this text, which I believe is as important to the value of this project as the book itself. As the scale and complexity of the DVD grew, so did their enthusiasm and dedication. I can never thank them enough for their achievement.

Many companies provided examples and consultation. I would like to thank The 48 Hour Film Project; Adobe Systems, Inc.; The Alpha Group; Angel Doll Productions, LLC; Anything For Love, LLC; Apple Computer, Inc.; Bclip Productions, Inc.; Blue Ridge Motion Pictures; Bonesteel Films; Filmaker's Library; Filmmakers, Inc.; Carolina Beverage Company; Final Draft, Inc.; Harrow Beauty; Ironwood Media Group; Jungle Software; Knight Productions; The Media Arts Project; Mole-Richardson Co.; Monarch Home Video; Mountain Eye Media; The Nevada Film Office; Oliver Media Services, LLC; ProComm Studio Services; RiverDream Productions; Shalom Y'all Films, LLC; Tabula Rasa Studios; UNCA Department of Mass Communication; UNCA Media Center; W&B Productions; WLOS-TV; WYFF-TV; and Wild Bunch Films, Inc.

Linda Bathgate and Lawrence Erlbaum Associates carried this project from idea to your hands today.

Tracy sacrificed our time together. For that I owe her much more than words here.

COMPANION DVD BIOGRAPHIES

Brian Bain is an Emmy Award-winning director. His credits include broadcast television and feature-length documentary works.

Richard Breyer specializes in international documentary production. His credits include *Esta Esperanza*, set in El Salvador, and *Kasturi*, produced in India.

Jenny Dunn is a reporter and anchor with ABC affiliate WFTW.

Trenton McDevitt is an award-winning film director and producer. He currently serves as president of Wild Bunch Films, Inc.

Marc Norman is a writer and producer. He won two Academy Awards in 1999 for Best Original Screenplay and Best Motion Picture of the Year for *Shakespeare in Love*.

Tom Savini is an actor, director, and special effects make-up artist. He created Jason of *Friday the 13th* and directed the 1990 interpretation of *Night of the Living Dead*.

Anne Slatton is a television producer and director. Her credits include award-winning documentary series for The National Geographic Channel and The Learning Channel.

Althea Sumpter is an Emmy-nominated producer, director, and editor. She focuses on ethnography and preserving cultural heritage.

UNIT I

THE BASICS

CHAPTER 1: INTRODUCTION TO VIDEO PRODUCTION
CHAPTER 2: THE LANGUAGE OF MOTION PICTURES
CHAPTER 3: CAMERAS
CHAPTER 4: EDITING

Getting started in video production requires four basic steps: (1) developing a story, (2) translating the story into the language of motion pictures, (3) recording the material with a camera, and (4) editing it all together into a final program. In this unit you will explore these sequential steps, and complete the unit with the basic knowledge needed to carry your projects from beginning to end.

In Chapter 1 you will examine the process of developing ideas for video programs and the tools used by screenwriters. Chapter 2 introduces techniques for translating screenplays into moving images. You will study options for composing images, and how a series of images is assembled to create a cohesive unit. Chapter 3 presents the motion picture camera, its features, and stylistic approaches to videography and cinematography so you can more effectively utilize the camera to tell a story. Unit I concludes with Chapter 4, which explores technical and creative processes of editing material into a final program. At the end of this first unit you will be able to produce your own motion picture programs from concept to screen.

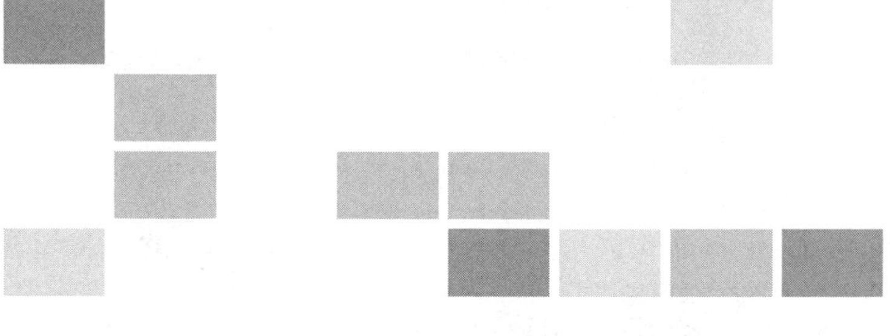

1

INTRODUCTION TO VIDEO PRODUCTION

CHAPTER OBJECTIVES

Motion pictures start out as ideas. Movies have extraordinary expressive potential, but you need to have something to say with the tools. This chapter focuses upon the inception and development of ideas for motion picture programs. You will survey the methods used by professional writers to inspire ideas, and the process of molding ideas into a creative concept for the screen. You will study the writing tools used for developing video and film projects, and explore the elements of the dramatic structure so you can organize your ideas to form a complete story. The objectives of this chapter are to:

- Introduce the three stages of video and film production: preproduction, production, and postproduction;
- Explore techniques for developing ideas and program concepts;
- Organize strategically for writing effective stories and treatments;
- Understand the dramatic structure;
- Survey the creative process of writing stories and scripts.

Creating video programs is a rewarding and complex process. There is a lot involved, from the writing of the script, to the challenges of shooting, to the range of choices that come in putting it all together in editing. When professionals talk about the process of creating motion pictures they usually break it up into three stages: preproduction, production, and postproduction.

THE THREE STAGES OF THE PRODUCTION PROCESS

Preproduction

The stage of preparing to shoot a visual program is referred to as **preproduction**. Preproduction is the most important phase of the process in many ways. It is a time to get everything in order and to plan for contingencies. It is also the time to make major creative decisions. Preproduction is the time to test production concepts and stories. Professionals do not move into production until they are convinced they are on the right track. Beware of moving into production too quickly before your script really works.

Wasted production time is expensive. It can cost thousands of dollars per hour to keep a crew on a large-scale professional shoot. The first *Project Greenlight* demonstrated the huge costs that can be incurred while trying to work things out in production. HBO's documentary series, *Project Greenlight* (2001), followed the making of the film *Stolen Summer* (2002) and captured the mistakes and overruns that resulted from poor preproduction planning. *Stolen Summer* ended up costing about $1.8 million to make and returned less than $200,000 in domestic box office sales. Shooting is not the time to start working out the details. All that needs to be planned in preproduction.

Once you have a script in hand, preproduction begins with a script **breakdown**. The breakdown translates the script into a list of elements needed for production, such as the number of actors, props to be used, and different locations where filming will take place. Other preproduction tasks include casting the actors, scouting for shooting locations, creating a budget, developing plans for renting equipment, hiring the crew, acquiring props and costumes, building sets, and rehearsing with the actors. With careful preparation in place, the project is ready to go into production.

Production

Production is the time frame of actually shooting the project. This is often the most expensive and highest-intensity phase of the process. Filmmakers should generally follow the plan developed in preproduction during shooting. Alfred Hitchcock was a strong believer in following his preproduction plan very carefully. For Hitchcock, the process of production was a somewhat mechanical one. His creative genius was pronouncedly expressed in the planning. The shooting, for Hitchcock, was a technical process of converting the plan to film.

Francis Ford Coppola, however, conducted a bold experiment in the production of *Apocalypse Now* (1979). Coppola allowed extensive improvisation on the set, and was actually unsure how the film would end halfway through shooting. This was a risky approach, which almost bankrupted Coppola and nearly ruined the production. Coppola's experiment was successful in the end,

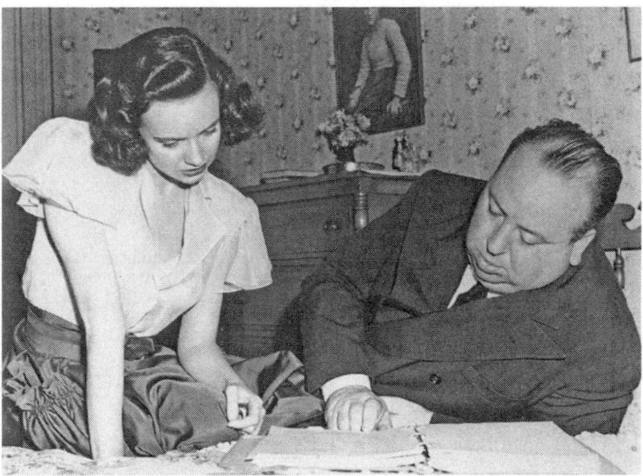

Figure 1.1 Hitchcock was known for his careful preproduction and for his meticulous execution of his plan in production. (Universal Pictures/Photofest; © Universal Pictures)

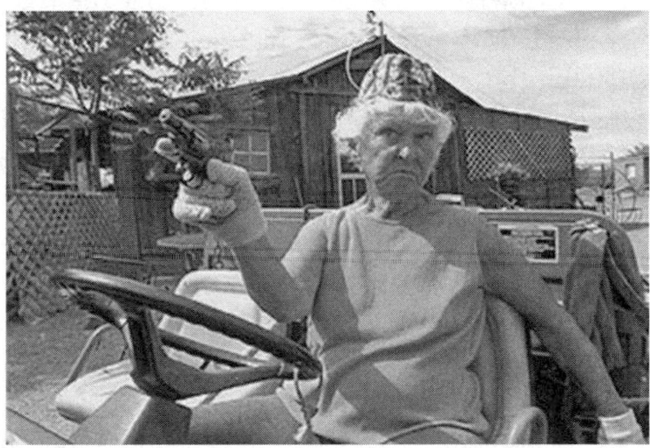

Figure 1.2 *Walking the Line* tells the story of vigilantes patrolling the U.S.-Mexican border. The dynamic subject required flexibility by the filmmakers to follow real and unpredictable events. (Courtesy of Filmaker's Library)

however, and *Apocalypse Now* is a benchmark of film history, winning the Palme d'Or at Cannes and two Academy Awards. It is important to note that this success story with such a free-form process is not the norm in fiction filmmaking. Nonfiction production, however, is often much more loose in the production process. It is not possible to predict what you will discover when your subject is real events in the world, and the nonfiction filmmaker needs to maintain flexibility to adapt as the story unfolds.

A lot of people work together on a set during production to contribute to the making of a video or film project. The **director** (in the case of fiction) or the **producer** (in the case of nonfiction) is the boss on the set and is responsible for the overall creative vision of the work. The **videographer** or **cinematographer** records the action with a camera. The **gaffer** is head of the electrical department and often designs the lighting plan. The **best**

boy is an assistant to the gaffer. There is often a **sound recordist** who captures the audio, and in many cases there is a **boom operator** who holds the microphone out of view of the camera. These are just a few of the roles you might encounter on a production. Professional shoots can have more than 100 people on the crew. Job titles on large-scale projects relate to areas as diverse as accounting, craft services (people who provide the food), and wranglers (people who provide and manage the animals used in making a film). The next time you go to the movies, watch the entire credit list and count all the credited names. You might be surprised at how many people work on a major project.

Postproduction

Postproduction is the phase that takes place after the material is shot. Generally, postproduction refers to the editing stage, but there are many other processes that go along with editing the picture. Music needs to be written and recorded to match the images. Sometimes audio needs to be rerecorded if it wasn't captured clearly on location. Postproduction is also the time when sound effects are added, and the time when marketing and promotion take off in full force to support a project's release.

While preproduction, production, and postproduction are often talked about as three separate stages of the process, it is important to recognize that there is inherently some overlap. A project might still be in the final planning stages as production begins, and it is not uncommon for a reduced crew to get **pick-up** shots during the postproduction phase. While there are inherent overlaps in phases, production is usually defined as the time from the first day of **principal photography** to the last day of shooting. Preproduction and postproduction come before and after that.

It takes hundreds of people and millions of dollars to make a big Hollywood feature, but visual stories can be created with a small-format video camera, a desktop editing system, a microphone, and a few lights. A handful of people working together can do amazing things.

The journey toward realizing your work on screen is a complex one. There are many steps in the process, many people to collaborate with, and many tools to work with along the way. The first step in the process, however, is very simple. You need an idea. It all comes from your idea.

THE IDEA

Ideas for visual programs often have their origins in the writer's experience and observation of the world. While science fiction, for example, seems like a fantastic vision of another world, the genre is mostly a commentary about the writer's own time and culture. Science fiction is not primarily about the future or about aliens. It is about today and it is about us.

Think of some of your favorite movies and television programs. Many of these films and television shows have fictional characters that are invented by the screenwriter. Some of these programs portray impossible events, such as time travel and interstellar transport. All visual programs, however, have elements grounded in the writer's experience and observations. You cannot write a script in a vacuum. Your experience and observations about the world direct your writing. Write about what is important to you. That is what gives a heart to your story, and it is what allows your audience to connect to your story.

Many young writers think that the world around them is not particularly interesting and seek to set their stories somewhere else, but keep in mind that what you take for granted is exotic to others. The prairie lands of middle America might seem mundane to the lifelong Nebraska resident, but this world, and the people who make their lives there, will be utterly fascinating to many on the East Coast. Learn to see what is around you, and think about how you can share your world with others through sound and pictures.

Filmmaker S. R. Bindler looked for stories to tell in his Texas community, and found an unusual competition in which the last person to take his or her hand off a pickup truck wins the truck. Bindler's documentary, *Hands on a Hard Body* (1997), does an amazing job of portraying the universal competitive spirit through this unconventional contest. The film went on to achieve national acclaim and it won the Audience Award at the AFI Fest. Be watchful for story ideas in your own backyard.

Personal experience is a valuable source of material for the writer. The things that happen to you directly can serve as scenes and isolated moments in your video projects. It is important to note that while personal experience is a valuable component, many writing coaches advise against developing an idea for a film that is too personal, especially for your early projects. If your characters reflect your own life too closely, you risk losing perspective in the writing process.

It is also important to beware of developing a story that is too far removed from your experience. For example, if you were to tell the story of a character in a distant land, from another time and another culture, there is a good chance that your story will be too abstract, and not very realistic unless you have done extensive research. A good foundation from which to develop your early projects is to stay grounded in a familiar context, but develop characters that do not mirror your own personal experiences too closely. While things that happen to you might make for a good dramatic moment or offer a creative line of dialogue, consider going beyond your own experience for program ideas. You can, of course, interject your values and concerns into your work, but avoid making your main character a loosely veiled portrayal of yourself.

There are many sources of ideas to be mined that lay outside of personal experience. Consider the people in your life: friends, relatives, and acquaintances. We all know people who have told us remarkable true stories that have caused us to think, "That should be in the movies." Create a work of fiction built around the lives of these people, or tell their stories through a documentary. Even if you do not know someone who is remarkable enough to form the basis of a character on his or her own, you can combine bits and pieces, and facts and stories, from a number of different people and attribute them to a single character. This is often done in fiction writing and is referred to as a **composite character**.

Keep the stories your hear and unique moments that you witness in mind. Take notes. Keep a journal. Collect stories and anecdotes. Many of these tales will find a home in your scripts as you develop your body of work as a screenwriter. Listen to how people speak. Listen to the actual words they use. Careful observation will help you to develop realistic stories and give personality to your characters.

Look at your world, too. Creating successful video productions requires seeing things a little differently than everyone else. In our day-to-day life we ignore and miss much of what is happening around us. This is primarily a matter of streamlining our experience for efficiency and saving our energy to process new information (Morris, Tarassenko, & Kenward, 2006). When we drive to work or walk to class we do not see as much as a tourist visiting for the first time. Once we habituate to our environment we generally tune it out. The filmmaker must always tune in. Study every scene you encounter with intention. Continually ask, "Can this image tell a story? Where can I put my camera? How can I compose this slice of the world in my viewfinder?" You will assess thousands of images per day. Most will never be recorded, but when you discover a setting for a scene or an image that conveys an idea about your story, the effect is magical.

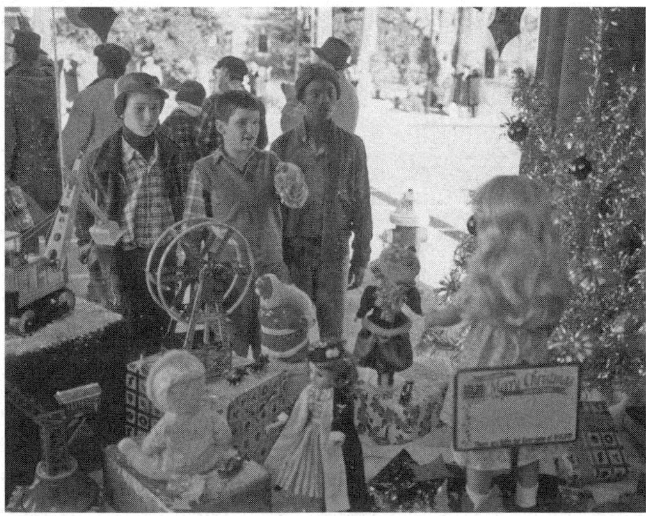

Figure 1.3 *The Angel Doll* is an example of an adaptation. The film is a screen translation of Jerry Bledsoe's award-winning novel of the same name. (Photo by Jim Bridges; Courtesy of Wild Bunch Films)

Monitor the news. Many successful programs, both fiction and nonfiction, reflect events happening in the world today. Scan Internet headlines, your local newspaper, and the evening news every day to see what is going on and ask yourself, "Is there a good idea for a motion picture here?"

In addition to the news, you can turn to literature, plays, and other artistic forms as sources of ideas for your productions. Novels and plays lend themselves to **adaptation**. It is common for books and plays to be translated for the screen, but this is not the only way literature can serve your writing objectives. Immersing yourself in literature will activate your imagination and inspire original ideas.

If you choose to adapt an existing work, you need to determine if the work is in the **public domain**. If it is, you can freely use and adapt it without permission. If it is a **copyrighted work**, you will need to obtain permission from the copyright owner to use the material. If you want to adapt a John Grisham novel into a film, you will need to get permission, and you will most likely have to pay a lot of money to get it. The works of Edgar Allen Poe, however, are in the public domain. You are as free to create and publish a film adaptation of Poe's *The Tell-Tale Heart* as any Hollywood studio.

History is a valuable resource for the writer. The more you study history, and the more you know about events of the past, the more options you will have as a writer. A background in history will ultimately yield a more sophisticated writing repertoire, which will make you more versatile and competitive in the writing market.

Ideas fly around all the time in an active mind. It takes some time and discipline to filter ideas, and to focus on ideas that are worthy of further development. There is an endless stream of ideas available to you if you pay attention. As director David Lynch (*Blue Velvet*, 1986; *Mulholland Drive*, 2001) says, "Ideas are the best things going. Somewhere there are all the ideas, and they're sitting there. And once in a while one will come bobbing up, and the idea is made known suddenly, from someplace it was, and now it's in your conscious mind. It's like a spark, and something is seen, and known, and felt all at once. And with it comes a burst of enthusiasm" (Lynch & Keeler, 1998). A major transition in the writing process takes place when you grab hold of ideas that impress you and distill these seemingly disconnected ideas into a creative concept.

THE CONCEPT

The **concept** is a formal articulation of ideas for a video project in a sentence or two. This is often called the **log line**. Consider the following example, which describes the origin of a creative concept for a feature film. Zachary Norman was studying Elizabethan drama in college. In a conversation with his father, Marc Norman, Zachary shared an interesting fact he learned in his studies. Shakespeare, it turns out, had a period of writer's block. From this fact, this

Figure 1.4 The concept for *Shakespeare in Love* came from a college history course. The film won seven Academy Awards including Best Motion Picture of the Year. (Photofest, Inc.)

idea grew a concept for a motion picture: "Shakespeare struggles to overcome his writer's block by seeking a muse and he discovers true love." If you have not guessed it already, this is the concept behind *Shakespeare in Love* (1998), and it all came from an idea that was discovered through the study of history.

Marc Norman went on to coauthor and coproduce *Shakespeare in Love* and won two Academy Awards for his achievements. *Shakespeare in Love* won seven Academy Awards, including Best Motion Picture of the Year. It all begins with ideas crafted into a creative concept.

Many times, program concepts are pitched to producers in a meeting and story development lives or dies based on this brief presentation. Shari Goodhartz brought her story concepts to the producer of *Star Trek: The Next Generation*. She pitched one concept that captured the producer entirely. "Data is kidnapped by a man who collects interesting things." Data, who is a human-like robot, is also an object. Goodhartz played upon this interesting dimension of Data's character and created a totally original concept. This one concept, one sentence, was the core of the **pitch**, and it was all that was needed to sell the story. She was hired to write the episode and brought on as a writer for the series. There are countless original concepts out there waiting to be discovered by you. Once you create a concept that inspires you, the next step is to develop the concept into a story.

THE EARLY STAGES OF WRITING AND STORY DEVELOPMENT

There are many writing formats and various software packages used in writing visual programs. Television commercial scripts look different than those for documentaries. Music video scripts are formatted differently than feature films. Television news packages have their own script conventions. We will explore each of these formats in turn throughout this text. Before composing a script most writers start with an outline.

The Outline

The **outline** is a universal and valuable writing tool. It is tempting sometimes to want to compose a script from beginning to end, word for word, just as a reader will experience it. A few writers work this way. Most writers, however, outline their programs first. Documentaries work primarily from an outline in most cases. Feature-length screenplays are often outlined scene by scene before the writing of dialogue and screen direction. How you use an outline will depend on your project and your writing style, but it is generally easier to compose with broad strokes and to fill in the details later than it is to start with word one and write straight through.

Outlines, by their very nature, can be customized to fit your needs. If you are writing a promotional video script for a manufacturing company, your first-draft outline might be very simple. It might read something like the following:

1. Interview with CEO
2. View of factory floor
3. Interviews with employees
4. Interviews with satisfied customers
5. Closing comments from the CEO

As your project becomes better formulated through research and pre-interviews, this outline might be altered and expanded to look something more like this:

Part I: Establishing the Company
- Exterior shots with CEO voiceover
- Transition to interior interview with the CEO
- Overlay manufacturing shots over CEO's description

Part II: Meeting the Employees
  Interview with Design Team leader (over images of team working)
  Interview with Production Manager (over images of factory floor)
  Interview with Quality Control representative (show inspection process)
  View of packaging and shipping process (with voiceover)
Part III: Meeting the Customers
  Interview with regional distributor
  Interviews with two or three retail customers
Part IV: Conclusions
  CEO reiterates major promotional points
  Montage of employees working and group shot at conclusion
  Contact information for product orders and plant tours

If you are developing a work of fiction, you might want to start by fleshing out a **scene outline**. A scene outline identifies each scene in the program in a few words. A scene outline often identifies the location of each scene, the time of day, and whether the scene takes place at an interior (INT.) or exterior (EXT.) location. This approach works for short films as well as feature-length projects.

When developing an outline for a program, start with what you know. In some cases you might know how your story begins and ends, but have very little idea about the dramatic journey that connects these two points in time. In this case, start by writing your first scene title and your last scene title and fill in the middle as you go through the developmental process.

In other cases, you might have a strong sense of the middle of your project. You might have a great idea for a turning-point scene in which the main character faces a huge challenge. Write that scene title on your outline and build around it forwards and backwards. You might be surprised how quickly your story grows when you break it down into manageable units.

The outline does not contain all of the information necessary for a production shoot. This is generally not the function of an outline. An outline is predominantly an internal working document to help structure the story. As your story becomes more developed, your outline will expand. When you feel the outline is adequately realized, you can convert these notes into a script.

Most outlines are composed on a computer, but some writers use pen and paper. The computer offers certain advantages. Word processing programs come with outlining features. These programs automatically indent and create hierarchical lists when working in outline mode. You can also opt to transfer a regularly formatted word processing document into an outline by selecting the "outline" option from the view menu.

Another advantage to composing outlines on the computer is that it is easy to cut and paste and to delete or insert new lines of text at any point in the document. Having your documents in digital form makes sharing your work and collaboration easier via e-mail. Also, having your outline in a computer-text format makes for easy importation and expansion of your outline into a script.

Mountain Justice
Scene Outline

1. INT. COFFE HOUSE — DAY
ARIEL meets KJRSTN and expresses discontent with her life.

2. EXT. MOUNTAIN ROAD — DAY
Kjrstn takes Ariel on a scenic drive and points out the things she has been missing.

3. EXT. WATERFALL — DAY
Kjrstn shows Ariel a hidden waterfall down a forgotten trail. Ariel lights up.

4. EXT. COFFEE SHOP — DAY
Kjrstn drops Ariel off at the parking lot. They make plans to meet again.

5. INT. ARIEL'S HOUSE — EVENING
Ariel reaches out to her husband, ROBERT, with simple conversation, but tension hangs in the air.

6. INT. COFFEE SHOP — DAY
Kjrstn and Ariel sit together at a table. Kjrstn asks Ariel if she thinks her husband is having an affair. Ariel admits doubt.

7. EXT. ARIEL'S HOUSE — NIGHT
Two cars creep down a suburban street. Ariel leads in the first car and shows Kjrstn, who follows, where she lives.

8. EXT. CITY STREETS — DAY
Kjrstn follows Robert to work and parks outside his office, watching the door.

9. EXT. ROBERT'S OFFICE — DAY
Kjrstn sinks into boredom from the lack of activity, and then springs up when Robert leaves with another woman.

10. INT. RESTAURANT — DAY
Kjrstn gives an account to Ariel of Robert's Day. She prepares Ariel and then tells the details of Robert holding hands and disappearing into a hotel with the mystery woman. Ariel is attentive and stoic.

11. INT. BAR — NIGHT
Kjrstn takes Ariel to a bar to shake off the horrible news. Ariel's mood evolves from shock to reckless abandon.

Figure 1.5 A scene outline is an effective way to develop a story before composing a screenplay.

Computer composition of your outline does have some limitations. You might not always have access to your computer when a brilliant idea strikes. For this reason, and for the sheer love of tactile composition, some writers prefer to compose their outlines with pen and paper, where handwriting and personal notes add inflection and reflect tone. A legal pad or a small pocket pad can be taken anywhere and kept by the bedside for spontaneous inspiration. Consider keeping pen and paper handy when you are away from your computer so a brilliant thought will not go unrecorded.

Notebooks and Bulletin Boards

Other options for organizing ideas and the early stage of writing include notebooks and bulletin boards. If you already keep a personal journal, you might prefer keeping a notebook to flesh out your ideas and concepts. The notebook approach requires significant editing and organization toward the end of the drafting process, but the ability to jot thoughts at random, to set aside a new page when a new line of thinking hits, and to draw pictures to give form to the visual components of your story can greatly enhance the creative process.

a

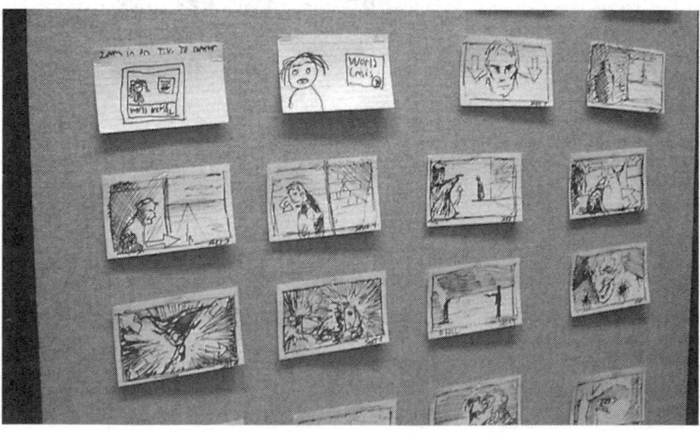

b

Figure 1.6 (a) Notebooks and (b) bulletin boards are popular options for developing and organizing story ideas. ([a] Jesse Knight; [b] Kenneth George)

Using a bulletin board, or simply dedicating space on an open wall, is another method of story development used by writers. With a bulletin board approach, you can organize your ideas, lines of dialogue and scenes on note cards, and affix these cards to the wall with tacks or tape. This provides the ability to see the big picture of your program graphically, and to reorder, remove, and insert scenes like a huge puzzle. It is a great form when working collaboratively so all contributing to the process can see the elements taking shape. Computers are powerful, and will be fundamental in the formal screenwriting process that we will explore later, but do not underestimate the value of these simple mechanical tools in the early stages of fleshing out your story.

THE TREATMENT

The **treatment** is one of the most valuable and widely used writing formats for developing visual programs. The writing tools discussed thus far (outline, notebooks, and bulletin boards) are mostly internal working tools. Writers use these documents to organize, develop, and expand ideas. They are generally not intended to be shared with others, except perhaps those collaborating in the development process. The treatment, however, is a document produced for circulation. It is used to share story ideas with potential financial backers, clients, and others involved in the process of producing programs. Learning how to write effective treatments is essential to getting your story ideas recognized and financed. The treatment is also a valuable tool that allows you to develop your story ideas without getting encumbered in the technical elements of formatting a screenplay. We will explore the elements of screenplay structure and formatting in Chapter 9, but for now you can do a great deal of story development by writing treatments.

A treatment is a narrative version of your visual program that reads somewhat like a short story, but a treatment is not simply a short story version of your motion picture concept. The objective of a treatment is to show the reader the story idea through words. Use visual and descriptive language in your treatment, and bring your visual program to life for the reader. A treatment does not contain all of the details of your story. That is the job of the screenplay. The treatment is a presentation of what your visual program is about. It is a synopsis and it presents highlights. It takes the reader through your story from beginning to end, but elements like dialogue and scene-by-scene detail are kept to a minimum. Think of the treatment as a sales tool. You want to get the reader as excited about your story idea as you are, so make sure to get the reader hooked and keep him engaged.

The treatment format can vary somewhat depending upon the audience and the type of visual program. Treatments can also vary considerably in length. Some treatments for promotional videos and short-subject films are only one page in length. A treatment for a theatrical motion picture might be 30 pages or more. The length of your treatment depends not only on the length of your

WEB OF DECEIT

Inspired by the Tina Yoder Story

Treatment for a Two-Hour Movie

By

Ron Cutler and Barry Weitz

RACHEL CLAYBORNE, 37, is a dedicated pediatrician working with seriously ill children and struggling to save a 5-year-old named LISA, who is ill with a serious blood disease. Rachel lives in Miami, with her husband CHANCE, 40, a dynamic and ambitious District Attorney. Though they have no children, Rachel's eight-year marriage appears both loving and fulfilling.

Rachel and Chance live in a dynamic atmosphere of financial and political power. Chance is the son of OGDEN CLAYBORNE, 70, an extremely wealthy businessman, landowner and developer as well as a powerful force in Miami's banking and social circles. Ogden is also the major force in his children's lives. He is a benevolent despot, who rules them with an iron hand. This has created internal rivalries within his family, as those around him vie for his attention and influence. Only Chance seems immune from his overbearing hand, due to Rachel's loving support and fierce oft demonstrated independence.

Though extremely vital, Ogden is deeply concerned about his legacy. His overriding ambition is for Chance to become a United States Senator and perhaps even a . . .

Figure 1.7 A treatment is often used to market a story idea. (Courtesy of Ron Cutler and Barry Weitz)

program, but also on your audience. Sometimes less is more. A treatment that gives too much detail might lose the interest of the reader before she gets to the meat of the story, where your original dramatic elements really take off.

Treatments are written in the present tense. You want the reader to experience your program as they read. Tell the reader what is happening right now. If your story has a romantic reunion, then the text should read, "Kelly runs across the room and embraces Michael," and not, "Kelly will run across the room and embrace Michael." Visually describe what is happening right now in time and place.

Treatments are generally presented in single-space format. Place several line breaks between sections to denote significant changes in time and location. This white space will help visually break up the document for the audience and make it more inviting for the reader. You want the reader to feel comfortable and not overwhelmed by a dense page of text. Each time you introduce a new character, put the character's name in all capitals, but only do this the first time the name is used. For example, "KELLY is locking the front door of the restaurant when the manager, MICHAEL, emerges from the kitchen, startling her."

There are several hints to consider for writing effective treatments that can help get your work noticed. First of all, make sure you capture the attention of the reader in the very beginning. It is essential that your treatment engages and draws the reader in, or else your treatment will most likely be set aside, and the busy producer will go to the next treatment in his huge stack of submissions. It is not uncommon for a professional producer to read dozens of treatments per day, so yours has to be unique to be noticed. Have a **hook**. Make sure your treatment has something special and original to make your story worth consideration.

It is common to put some detail into the first scene of a treatment. Portray the environment in which your story takes place, and give the reader a sense of the program's style through your use of language. As you introduce each major character, tell the reader some interesting fact about the character. Your goal here is to pique interest but you also need to be brief. It is okay to use dialogue in a treatment but do so sparingly. The lines of dialogue you choose to include should be central to the story or noteworthy in portraying the tone of the program. The body of the treatment can be somewhat condensed. You should not describe every scene of the program. Give the reader a general sense of the story's progression concentrating on the major **plot points**. A plot point is an incident that takes the story in a new direction. If two couples are having a dinner party and a character says something by accident that reveals an affair, the story will go in a new direction from that moment forward.

Finish your treatment as you would your program. Let the reader know the resolution and what happens in the end. Planning the progression of your story and the elements within it will be greatly enhanced by utilizing the dramatic structure.

THE DRAMATIC STRUCTURE

Understanding the elements of the **dramatic structure** is important for effective screenwriting. In its simplest form, drama, as defined by Aristotle, consists of three parts: a beginning, middle, and end. Gustav Freytag elaborated upon this basic model in the 19th century defining drama as a five-part structure, or five acts: exposition, rising action, climax (turning point), falling action, and resolution (either catastrophe in the case of tragedy or denouement in the case of comedy). Since then there have been further elaborations of the concept of dramatic structure but none that has been universally accepted across theater, novels, and screenplays as a standard. The following discussion of dramatic structure includes elements that professional screenwriters utilize in story development.

The beginning of a dramatic story usually involves **exposition**. Exposition is the background that the audience needs to know to be able to join the story. In effect, you "expose" the audience to the background information. Compared to forms such as novels, there is much less exposition in video programs. Television and movie audiences get bored with being fed a lot of preamble and background material before anything of significance happens. A good rule for screenwriting is to keep the front exposition as tight as possible, and to give exposition in creative ways. Do not spoon-feed the audience facts about the characters and the situation. Let the audience discover these facts visually through clues or through conflict. Consider using a conversation or an argument to reveal elements of a character's past. This can be an effective storytelling tool. In the case of *Star Wars* (1977), we join the story by seeing Luke working on his uncle's farm. We learn during an argument with his uncle that Luke has greater ambitions. He wants to be a Jedi like his dead father. Luke wants to leave and experience more than life on a farm, but his responsibilities keep him grounded.

Once we are introduced to the main character in a dramatic tale, there is an **inciting incident** that puts the dramatic quest of the character and dramatic question of the program on the table. Luke's farm is destroyed by Imperial troops while he is away. This is the inciting incident of *Star Wars*. There is nothing to keep Luke home any longer. In fact, he no longer has a home. He will join the resistance. Luke's quest in *Star Wars* is to train to be a Jedi warrior, and to help defeat the Imperial forces. The dramatic question for the audience is, "Will he be successful?"

Once the dramatic question is in place, and the hero begins his journey to achieve his quest, the character confronts a series of **complications**. Complications are the barriers that the hero faces and has to overcome in order to achieve his journey. Failure in any one of these circumstances could defeat the character. As the character faces and overcomes each complication he moves closer toward his goal. The number of complications, and their complexity, depend on the format of the program. A 30-minute television episode will be different in form and content than a 5-minute short, but the principle is the same. The successive cycle of facing and overcoming obstacles comprises the **rising and falling action** of the program. These complications give the program its tempo and mood and set the emotional tone for the audience as the tension builds and is diffused. For example, Luke, Han, and Princess Leia are thrown into the trash compactor by Darth Vader's henchmen. The mastering of this complication is necessary for their survival and the continuation of Luke's journey.

In the traditional dramatic structure, the complications become more severe until one of the complications is so monumental that it brings the hero to a point of **crisis**. This is the showdown that will determine the ultimate fate of the hero, and it sets up the scene that will definitively answer the question of whether the hero succeeds or fails in his quest. This crisis builds in intensity until the final outcome of the story is determined. Most visual programs have happy endings, and the hero is usually successful in prevailing in the crisis. This is the case in *Star Wars*. Luke is brought into the heat of battle to exploit the weakness discovered in the Death Star's defenses. If Luke is shot down, he dies and fails. If he misses the duct with his missiles he also fails, and the rebel base will be obliterated. Luke prevails, and the dramatic question of the film is answered. The moment when the dramatic question is answered is the **climax** of the story.

After this climax, visual programs have a brief **resolution**. It would be quite jarring for the audience of *Star Wars* if immediately after the Death Star exploded the final credits were to roll. It is valuable to allow the audience a chance to catch a breath and to come down off of the excitement with a brief segment that puts the resolution of the story into context. In the case of *Star Wars*, this resolution is offered in the form of the awards ceremony at which Luke and Han receive medals for their service to the resistance. A true hero's welcome is portrayed in this case.

Some visual programs have the hero failing in the end; others create complex endings where the hero achieves his objective but the victory rings hollow. We learn that what the hero thought he wanted was not really the important thing after all. It is valuable to drama that these exceptions exist. If we could always know the outcome, what fun would the journey be?

Think of your favorite movie of all time. You will probably find the elements of the dramatic structure in your favorite films. The dramatic structure is evident in the earliest tales of recorded history. It is still around because it is universal and effective. It is a time-tested method by which humans tell

Figure 1.8 *Star Wars* is a classic tale of good versus evil. Luke achieves his dramatic quest with the help of supporting characters. (Lucasfilm Ltd./Twentieth Century Fox Film Corp./Photofest; © Lucasfilm Ltd./Twentieth Century Fox Film Corp.)

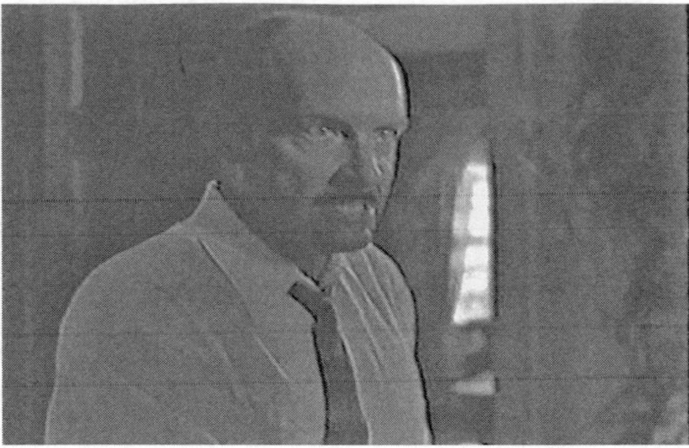

Figure 1.9 Drama is characters in conflict. (Courtesy of Barry Weitz)

stories. If written well, a story composed using the dramatic structure doesn't seem conventional. The audience gets so lost in the story that the structure becomes invisible. Keep the dramatic structure in mind, use its rules when appropriate, and you will have a solid foundation upon which to build your stories.

Even though this traditional format is called the dramatic structure, it applies to all types of narrative storytelling. Comedy and drama are, in fact, two sides of the same coin. An effective comedy has serious moments when the characters face important choices, and even the most intense dramas usually offer moments of comic relief to allow the audience to pause and regroup for the next wave of intensity. The dramatic structure can be applied across production formats. Documentaries, feature films, reality-TV shows, music videos, news packages, and even 30-second commercials all apply the dramatic structure to engage the audience.

Characters

All narrative stories involve **characters**. The hero of the program is the **protagonist**. He is often described as the main character, and it is the protagonist with whom the audience is generally supposed to identify. Luke Skywalker is the protagonist in the original *Star Wars*. We follow the story primarily from his point of view, and continue with his journey to the very end. A program need not have a single protagonist. Some stories take a buddy approach. *Butch Cassidy and the Sundance Kid* (1969) is an example of this type of story, but the careful observer will notice that these two characters are not of equal weight. Butch Cassidy is the one making the decisions and plotting the journey in the film. Other programs, such as Paul Thomas Anderson's *Magnolia* (1999) utilize an even more complex character structure by implementing an **ensemble cast**. In Anderson's film no single character is clearly identifiable as the protagonist. Instead a group of characters work independently and together

The Dramatic Structure

• Exposition

• Inciting Incident

• Complications (Rising and Falling Action)

• Crisis

• Climax

• Resolution

The Characters

• Protagonist (Hero)

• Antagonist (Villain)

• Supporting Characters

Figure 1.10 Elements of Drama

toward achieving the dramatic objectives of the story. This is an exception, however, and even though many stories have more than one character working together, and more than one heroic figure, the emphasis of the dramatic structure is usually in favor of one main character. For example, while Han Solo is clearly a hero in his own right in *Star Wars*, the film is about Luke and his journey. Han is a **supporting character** who helps Luke along the way.

Another major character type is the **antagonist**. The antagonist is the character responsible for creating obstacles for the protagonist. In the case of *Star Wars* the main antagonist is clearly Darth Vader. The antagonist in drama is often the "bad guy" or the villain, but the antagonist can play a role more subdued than that. The antagonist can be any character who is in competition with the protagonist, even if this competition is not violent and quite subtle.

The primary antagonist need not be a human being. *Jaws* (1975) demonstrates how a screen villain can be an animal. In the case of *Jaws*, however, the conflict between people is a central component of the story. The selfish mayor of the town, Vaughn, pressures Chief Brody to keep the beaches open and this leads to more shark attacks. While not a primary antagonist, Mayor Vaughn puts obstacles in place that impede the goals of the hero. Once out on the boat, tension causes Brody, Hooper, and Quint to argue and fight over how to proceed. *Jaws*, like all drama, is about characters in conflict.

All video formats have characters. In documentaries, the interview subjects are characters; in news packages, the reporter is a character. In *March of the Penguins* (2005), birds are the only characters. We experience their challenges and join them on their journey. No matter what your form or your story, make sure to define and develop your characters to create rich and interesting programs.

THE CREATIVE PROCESS OF WRITING

Writing can be defined as a technical process. Some of the tools and techniques discussed above are suggested to aid in the mechanical aspects of organizing ideas and writing. Writing, however, is more broadly defined as a creative process that includes elements of inspiration, insight, and the connection of seemingly unrelated ideas to form new concepts. It is these seemingly intangible elements of writing that give a story its soul. Your first writing effort will not be your best, but you will learn a great deal in the process. Write your ideas down on paper. Set them aside. Look at them again. How do they look after a few days? What do you like? What don't you like? Share your work with friends and with seasoned writers. Offer honest feedback to each other. This is how writers get to those intangible skills, improve the quality of their work, and find that spark of magic.

You might find that sitting at a computer or in front of a notebook staring at the blank page is a little intimidating. It is sometimes difficult to know how to begin. Sometimes writers get a good start, but then get stuck at a point when it is difficult to decide where to go next. If you experience this, know that it is not uncommon. A sense of pressure or forced effort can sometimes impede the creative process.

We have all had the experience of trying to remember someone's name but draw a total blank. Under pressure the name is illusive, but the moment you stop trying it pops right into your mind. Remember this example if you have trouble writing. Sometimes the best solution to promote the free flow of ideas is simply to step back and to activate the imagination in indirect ways. A study of some distinguished and successful writers demonstrates that the pathway to creativity is individual and sometimes quite odd. According to Diane Ackerman (1990), "[T]he poet Schiller used to keep rotten apples under the lid of his desk and inhale their pungent bouquet when he needed to find the right word. Then he would close the drawer, but the fragrance remained in his head" (p. 293). Ackerman reports that Robert Louis Stevenson, Mark Twain, and Truman Capote all preferred to lie down when they wrote, while Thomas Wolfe, Virginia Woolf, and Lewis Carroll all preferred to stand. Victor Hugo and Benjamin Franklin, among others, felt they did their best writing if they wrote in the nude.

This is not to suggest that any of these techniques are appropriate for you, but do pay attention to circumstances that facilitate your personal creative process. For some people the key to successful writing is discipline. Some writers set aside time each day for writing. If they have nothing to write, or no inspiration, they do nothing else but sit there. Eventually this discipline yields insight and writers who work this way reportedly can produce documents as fast as they can type once they get going. Like any skill, the process of writing requires practice. If you have a lousy experience the first time you attempt to write a visual program, the best thing to do is to try again sooner rather than later. Keep at it.

Research has demonstrated that music is a powerful tool for opening creative pathways in the mind (Bonny & Savary, 1973). Try playing your favorite music while you write. Some writers who work while listening to music play a variety of songs while others prefer to play the same CD or song over and over to serve as a sort of marching tune to drive their writing. Other writers demand absolute quiet. If you get stuck while writing, consider stepping back, taking a walk, smelling the air, and exploring your environment. Observe your thoughts. Keep that notebook with you. You might be surprised at the random thought or observation that puts you back on track with passion.

CONCLUSIONS

We have introduced the three main stages of the video production process: preproduction, production, and postproduction. You now know the basic tools and techniques for developing ideas and writing stories for visual programs. As you proceed, be mindful of major elements of the dramatic structure: exposition, inciting incident, complications (which comprise rising and falling action), crisis, climax, and resolution. Consciously identify and mold your characters as protagonist, antagonist, and supporting. Recall that drama in traditional narrative is characters in conflict and the journey of characters through the elements of the dramatic structure.

The most creative part of producing visual programs is arguably the writing. You have the luxury of time, privacy, and virtually no expenses involved while exploring and developing your ideas on paper. The tools required by the writer are a personal computer or a notebook, an imagination, and an eye to the world. You have the same access to these tools as any Hollywood screenwriter.

Turn on your computer and create a document on your desktop just for your story ideas. Add something to it every day. Review and edit your document when you have composed a few pages. Get a notebook and a favorite pen and start to record your concepts for visual programs. Tune into your environment and explore your world for stories you can tell. Edit, polish, and refine. Practice writing scene outlines and treatments until one captures your enthusiasm for development into a film. Converting words on paper into sound and images comes next. We will begin the process of this translation in chapter 2 by exploring the Language of Motion Pictures.

SAMPLE EXERCISES

1. Look at today's newspaper and write three concepts for stories based on news articles you see.
2. Write a two- to three-page treatment inspired by your own life's experience. How will you get the reader engaged? Who are the antagonists, and what complications do you face? How does the story end?
3. Choose one of your favorite films of all time. Identify the protagonist(s) and antagonist(s). What is the inciting incident? What is the dramatic question? What are some of the complications? Is the protagonist successful in his or her journey? What is the climax of the story?

RECOMMENDED READINGS

Armes, R. (1990). *Action and Image: Dramatic Structure in Cinema.* Manchester, NY: Manchester University Press.

Bishop, W. (1991). *Working Words: The Process of Creative Writing.* Mountain View, CA: Mayfield Publishing.

Wong, C., Atchity, K. J., Donatelle, R. J. (2003). *Writing Treatments That Sell: How to Create and Market Your Story Ideas to the Motion Picture and TV Industry.* New York: Owl Books.

REFERENCES

Ackerman, D. (1990). *A Natural History of the Senses.* New York: Random House.

Bonny, H. L., & Savary, L. M. (1973). *Music and Your Mind: Listening with a New Consciousness.* Oxford, England: Harper & Row.

Lynch, D., & Keeler, T. (1998). *Pretty as a Picture: The Art of David Lynch* (videorecording). Chatsworth, CA: Image Entertainment, Inc.

Morris, R., Tarassenko, L., & Kenward, M. (Eds.). (2006). *Cognitive Systems: Information Processing Meets Brain Science.* San Diego, CA: Elsevier Academic Press.

2

THE LANGUAGE OF MOTION PICTURES

CHAPTER OBJECTIVES

Movies have syntax. You can create more effective video projects if you understand and apply the rules of the visual language. You will recognize some elements of the visual language explored in this chapter from your own experience watching films and television. Other elements presented here will likely be new to you, as they come across almost invisibly when applied correctly. The objective of this chapter is to equip you with the tools of film language so you can take the ideas you develop and translate those ideas into images on screen. In this chapter we will:

- Explore the elements of visual composition;
- Examine the language elements of moving pictures;
- Acquire knowledge to compose an entire scene seamlessly;
- Learn how to maintain continuity and avoid common mistakes in building image sequences.

Motion pictures have unique language elements. Just as your treatments must use written language effectively to communicate your ideas, so too must your visual programs use the elements of motion picture language to tell your story effectively with images and sound. The language of film and video programs borrows elements from other art forms including theater (the dramatic structure) and painting (composition within the frame). The language of motion pictures contains elements unique to its form, too. For example, films are two-dimensional images, like photographs, but films also move forward in time, which make them more complex than still images, and require special consideration in composition and editing.

Motion pictures came into being in the 1880s. Sound was added in the 1920s. Before the advent of recorded sound, early filmmakers had to tell stories using only visual information presented on screen. Sometimes title cards were used to give essential narrative background or to convey a critical line of dialogue. Early filmmakers were required by the nature of their medium to develop a language through which all the elements of the story could be told with moving pictures. Many scholars consider the time before recorded sound as the "Golden Age" of film, and many filmmakers, such as Alfred Hitchcock, stayed with the philosophy of visual storytelling even after sound was widely available. Hitchcock believed that dialogue in a film should be kept to a minimum. Hitchcock didn't want a character to have to say anything that could be shown. Directors, such as Brian DePalma (*The Untouchables*, 1987; *The Black Dahlia*, 2006), continue this emphasis on visual storytelling, while other directors, such as Woody Allen (*Hannah and Her Sisters*, 1986; *Husbands and Wives*, 1992), choose to emphasize the development of story through spoken words, or **dialogue**.

Motion pictures can present a great deal of information without sound. A single frame of film can convey much to the audience. The power of the single image to communicate a story and to serve as a work of art has its foundations in painting and still photography. Motion picture has adapted some of its language from painting and photography. Among the greatest lessons of these traditional art forms are the elements and rules of composition.

COMPOSITION

One of the primary considerations for the visual artist is **composition**. The decision of what elements to include in the artwork, and the relationship between elements within the artwork, are central to creating aesthetically intriguing and informative images.

The Frame

The most basic parameter defining the image is its **frame**. The frame of an image refers to the outermost edge of the working area that is presented to the audience. In painting, some images are longer from side to side relative to their height. Horizontal frame orientations work well for the portrayal of landscapes, where the relationship of elements across a wide visual field is of primary interest. Other paintings choose to define the frame vertically. Human portraits often use vertical framing.

The width and height of the frame in painting can be customized for each work. Each canvas can be cut and stretched across a wooden frame to match the specific needs of the artist on an image-by-image basis. The relationship

a

b

Figure 2.1 Paintings generally utilize (a) horizontal orientations for landscapes while (b) vertical orientations are common for human subjects. (Courtesy of Mary Rodman)

between the width of the frame compared to its height is referred to as the **aspect ratio**.

The advent of still photography necessitated the mechanical definition of the aspect ratio as set by the size of the imaging surface. The standard 35mm frame size for still photography is approximately 3:2. This ratio of three units wide for every two units high allows you to make prints in the popular 4 by 6 inch size without **cropping**. Since each photographic image in still photography stands alone as an independent document, the still photographer has the option when using rectangular formats of turning the camera vertically for vertical compositions, and holding the camera horizontally for horizontally balanced compositions. As long as all of the essential information is recorded in the frame, the still photographer can later create any aspect ratio desired through the process of cropping. For example, 8 by 10 inch images made from 35mm negatives are cropped. The negative is designed to produce a full-frame image of 8 by 12 inches.

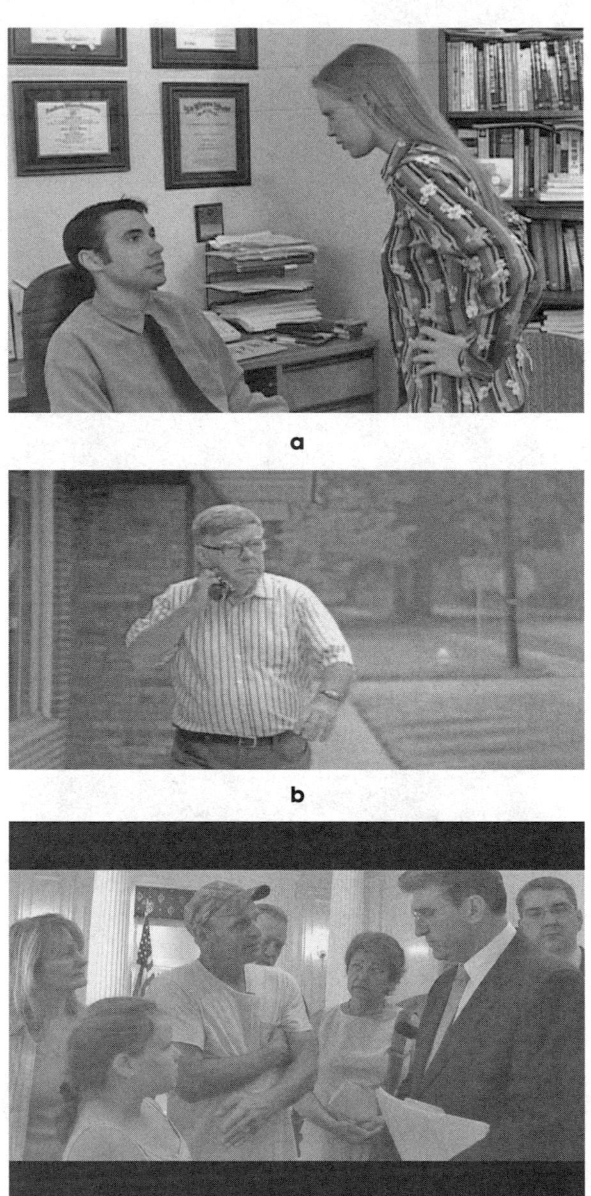

Figure 2.2 The aspect ratio of (a) standard television (4:3), (b) high-definition television (16:9), and (c) HDTV letterboxed for standard television. ([a] Courtesy of Ashley Lutterloh; [b] courtesy of Troy Scott Burnette; [c] courtesy of Mountain Eye Media)

Motion picture photography cannot readily change aspect ratios from one shot to the next. A unified frame size is generally selected for the entire program. All motion picture formats use a rectangular frame, and all frames are horizontal in orientation. The aspect ratio of standard film and television is approximately 4:3. This is the full frame recording area for standard 35mm motion picture photography, and it is the aspect ratio of standard video cameras and standard television screens. **High-Definition Television** (HDTV) is formatted in an aspect ratio of 16:9. Many video cameras allow the option of recording in standard (4:3) or HDTV (16:9). When the HDTV format is presented on a standard television screen it is letterboxed. **Letterboxing** masks the top and bottom of the screen with black bars to cover the portion of the screen not utilized.

There are a number of other different aspect ratios as well. **CinemaScope** (2.35:1), and **Academy Flat** (1.85:1) have unique frame sizes, which allow alternative emphases in visual composition. *Lawrence of Arabia* (1962) was shot in Super Panavision 70 with an aspect ratio of 2.2:1. This **wide-screen** presentation allowed F. A. Young, the cinematographer, to emphasize the barren landscapes of the desert and to visually explore the physical distance between characters in this tale of conflict and war.

Rule of Thirds

Defining the parameters of the frame is just the beginning. The content of the frame is what gives a composition most of its value. One of the most basic and valuable tools of visual composition is the **rule of thirds**. This principle, grounded in painting and classic two-dimensional design, is widely applied to the video frame as well.

Experiments in psychology and perception, as well as history, indicate that asymmetrical compositions are generally more interesting to viewers than symmetrical compositions (Krupinski & Locher, 1988). If you look through a camera viewfinder and put the subject right in the middle, with equal space and elements on all sides, you will create a balanced composition, but not necessarily the most dynamic and interesting one possible. Consider this alternative. Move the subject from the middle toward the left side of the frame. Now add a background element toward the right side of the frame that is not as dominant in visual weight as the main subject. You have now put together an asymmetrical composition and you are applying elements of the rule of thirds.

The rule of thirds works like this: Take your frame and divide it into thirds, vertically and horizontally, as if preparing for a game of tic-tac-toe. You now have a grid of nine spaces within the frame, similar to a checkerboard grid. When composing images, place elements of interest along or near the four lines in this grid. The two horizontal lines emphasize objects such as horizon lines, hills, city skylines, and clouds. Put your vertical elements of interest along or near the two vertical lines. These two lines emphasize objects such as people, trees, lampposts, and individual buildings. The four most powerful parts of the frame are the points where the vertical and horizontal lines intersect. These zones should generally hold the most significant elements of your compositions. The middle of the frame is not considered the most powerful or interesting part, which might go against your initial expectations. Amateur photographers often put the head of human subjects square in the middle of the frame without any regard for the surrounding elements. This is poor composition. Compositions can be strengthened by the rule of thirds.

This principle is applied across visual forms. Consider the example of Salvador Dali's *The Persistence of Memory* (1931), which is considered to be one of the greatest works of modern art. The rule of thirds is clearly evident when a reference grid is placed next to Dali's composition. Dali deliberately places most elements of interest on or near the four lines, and the intersection of lines in the upper-left corner is a particularly dynamic and interesting part of the composition.

Figure 2.3 Napoleon Dynamite utilizes a flat and highly balanced composition to create interest by exaggeration. (Fox Searchlight Pictures/Photofest; © 2004 Twentieth Century Fox)

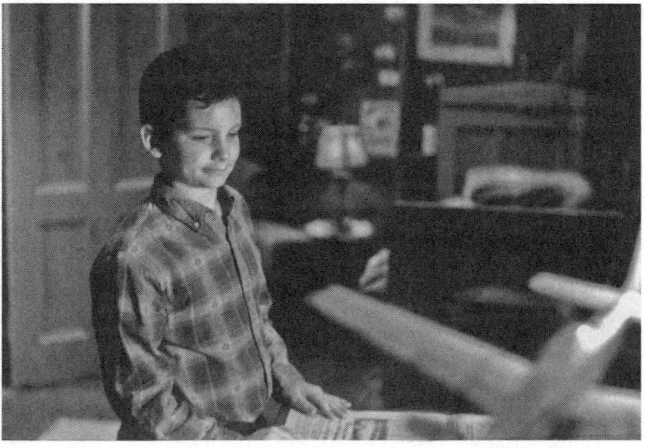

Figure 2.4 Unbalanced compositions are dynamic and can be used to emphasize depth. (Photo by Jim Bridges; courtesy of Wild Bunch Films)

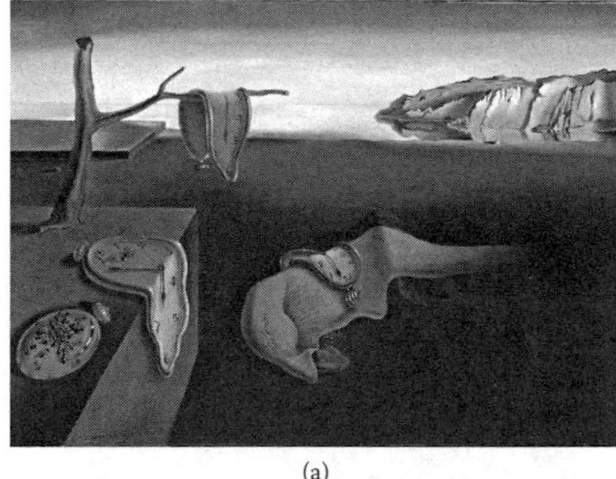

(a)

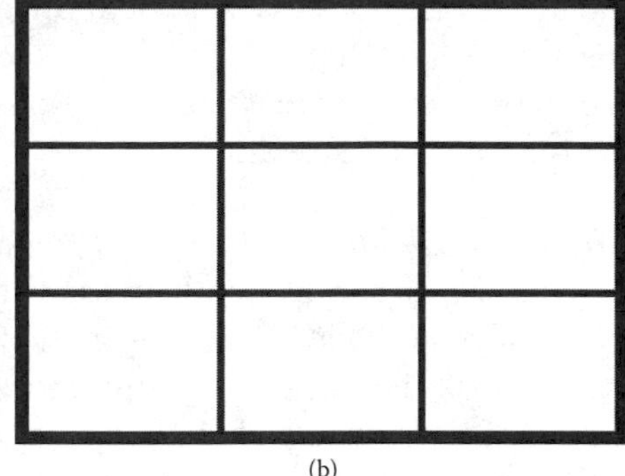

(b)

Figure 2.5 Salvador Dali's *The Persistence of Memory* (a) utilizes asymmetrical composition and the rule of thirds. Note the placement of elements in Dali's work using a reference grid (b). ([a] © 2006 Salvador Dali, Gala-Salvador Dali Foundation / Artists Rights Society (ARS), New York; Digital image © The Museum of Modern Art/Licensed by SCALA / Art Resource, NY)

Representing Three-Dimensional Space: Depth and Perspective

The video screen, like the painter's canvas, is a two-dimensional surface. The perception of depth, and the representation of three-dimensional space, must be accomplished by using tools that convey the illusion of depth.

Perspective Lines. When looking down a long hallway or a desert highway, the lines marking these pathways will eventually converge at a point in the distance. This point of convergence is called the vanishing point. Visual artists have systematically applied this perceptual tool since the 1400s. Artists use perspective lines to add realism and depth to two-dimensional images. In video production, you can emphasize depth by integrating elements that portray vanishing perspective. The use of diagonal lines in the frame generally adds to the sense of depth.

Scale. Manipulating scale creates a sense of depth in two-dimensional compositions. As objects of a fixed size are moved farther away from us, the image size of the object on our retina gets smaller. As we look at an image of many streetlamps, we get a sense that the lamps are receding in the distance because they get smaller and smaller. The relative size of the streetlamps tells us which ones are closer to us.

Foreground and Background. A simple but significant element of creating the illusion of depth is to apply principles of foreground and background. The scale of an object gives us a sense of how close it is, but there are other factors that define what is in the foreground and what is in the background. For instance, foreground elements block background elements. If one object obscures another object, it is perceived as existing in the foreground. This is obvious, but a conscious awareness of this simple fact will help you create compositions that emphasize certain elements and portray a sense of depth.

Light and Shadow. The most powerful tool for creating video programs with a rich sense of depth is to work effectively with light and shadow. Flooding the scene with illumination is not a sufficient approach for most creative applications in lighting motion pictures. It is the deliberate application of light and shadow that gives a composition depth and greater symbolic meaning. A maxim of cinematography is that the most important lights are the ones that you do not turn on. This saying illustrates the equal value of light and shadow in contributing to the creative process of making rich images.

Headroom and Noseroom. When composing a human subject for motion picture photography there are two additional rules to keep in mind. One important consideration is to frame the composition with a consideration of headroom. Headroom refers to the space between the top of the frame and top of the subject's head. There is no fixed amount of headroom that is considered correct, but a general rule is that it is appropriate to use more headroom as the frame captures more of the subject. For example, a full-body image might have a significant amount of headroom compared to an image that captures a subject from the chest up.

A similar consideration for composing a human subject is that of **noseroom**. When a subject is looking toward one side of the frame, it is generally advisable to allow the subject more space on the open side of the frame. Insufficient noseroom will make the composition feel confining, and will generally be awkward. Give a subject in partial or full profile sufficient noseroom.

Figure 2.6 Integrating perspective lines, manipulating scale, and using foreground and background elements helps emphasize depth. (Jesse Knight)

Figure 2.7 Headroom varies by the scale of the subject in the frame. (Emily Sarkissian)

a

b

Figure 2.8 (a) Sufficient and (b) insufficient noseroom

Mise en Scene

We have explored some ways of controlling composition. *Mise en scene* is a term borrowed from French meaning "putting into the scene." When filmmakers talk about *mise en scene* they are referring to the physical elements that contribute to making the entire visual scenario. This includes the elements we have discussed so far including framing, composition, depth, lighting, and also the physical elements within the composition such as actors, props, and how these elements are placed and moved. *Mise en scene* refers to the totality of making the image, or making the scene. The language of motion pictures also includes artistic impacts resulting from camera manipulation. A powerful way to manipulate the camera is through the selection of angle.

Angle

Angle refers to the position of the camera and the direction in which it is pointing. The choice of angle significantly affects the way the image is perceived by the audience, as well as the psychological effect of the composition.

Most camera positions for visual programs are set at approximately 3 feet to 6 feet off the ground. These limits approximate the range of view between

a

b

Figure 2.9 (a) Low angles emphasize dominance while (b) high angles convey vulnerability. (Courtesy of William Olsen)

a seated and a standing subject, and are considered standard angles of view. The audience generally perceives these angles as normal. This range, however, is only the starting point for considering the angle of view of your visual compositions. Angle is selected based on both the content of the composition and the context of the story. Consider that you are making a video project about a kid in the neighborhood, Steve, who is trying to overcome the taunting of a bully. This is the context of the story. The visual content of this particular shot is the bully, who you want to portray as a menacing character. One way to approach this composition is to show the bully (the antagonist) from Steve's (the protagonist's) point of view. In this way we put the audience in the same place and physical perspective as the main character. We invite the audience to identify with the main character and to vicariously experience his dilemma. The actor portraying the bully is much taller than the actor portraying Steve. You can set the camera at the level of Steve's eye, and tilt the camera up to see the menacing bully looking down at him. This is an example of a **low-angle shot**. Low-angle shots make the subject in the composition look powerful. The term *low-angle* refers to the position of the camera relative to the subject.

Low-angle shots can be severe and dramatic, as in the case of the bully, or they can be subtle. The camera positions of newscasts and talk shows are often set just below the eye level of the anchor or host. In this way we literally look up to them, and this communicates a sense of authority and credibility. Talk shows employ an additional psychological component in overall composition. The hosts on talk shows sometimes sit higher up than their guests. They get firm, raised desk chairs while their guests sink into comfy side chairs. This also reinforces a sense of authority. The comedian Andy Kaufman recognized this convention, and in a parody to make the point he hosted a mock talk show in which he sat 20 feet above his guests. Research demonstrates that the selection of camera angle influences viewers perceptions about the credibility of the subject, so there is good reason why news programs and talk shows portray their reporters and hosts with low angles. Subjects photographed with low angles are perceived as more credible (Tiemens, 1970). A **high-angle shot** is achieved by setting the camera position above the subject, thereby making the subject appear weak and vulnerable.

The placement of your camera position, and the angle of view of your camera can vary widely. You can portray an angle of view at ground level. Special mirror systems allow perspectives from the floor. Other equipment, such as cranes, can bring the camera way up high to give the audience the perspective of an observer over an entire landscape. Aerial videography can take your camera angle as high as you can fly. The important thing to remember is that you have a wide range to work with when composing a shot. Some videographers will lose sight of this and confine their camera positions to those that are comfortable for them, such as those that provide easy access to the viewfinder while standing or sitting in a chair. Remember to consider the full range of options you have to work with when making every composition. Choose the angle that is most interesting and supports the content and context

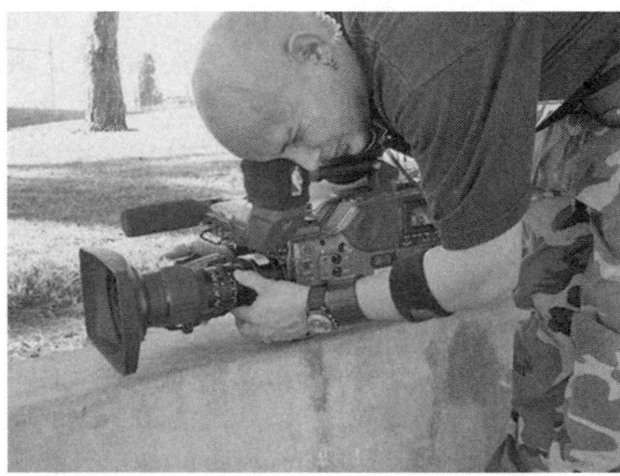

Figure 2.10 Be creative with camera position to achieve interesting angles. (Chris Walker)

Figure 2.11 Composition is often used to convey information about characters. What does this image say to you? (Photo by Jim Bridges; courtesy of Wild Bunch Films)

of the story most effectively. Try to make every composition a work of art. Sometimes the realities of time pressures and logistics will necessitate having to settle for a conventional or simple composition, but always be thinking of your options to create something interesting and meaningful when you have the opportunity.

The height of the camera (**y-axis**) is just one orientation to use when selecting angle. You are free to move the camera left and right as well (**x-axis**). You can also move the camera closer to or further from the subject (**z-axis**). To add even more choices, once you select the position of the camera you can change the direction in which the camera is pointing. You are free to combine directions as you move around the subject in a sphere of expanding distances. The permutations create a virtually infinite number of angles to choose from for each composition.

Moving the camera closer to, or farther away, from a subject changes the size of the subject in the frame. Changing the size of the subject in the frame changes the nature of the composition. In video production there are shot types defined by the size of the subject in the frame. These are referred to as long shots, medium shots, and close-ups.

SHOT TYPES

Basic Shot Types

There are standard shot names in video production that allow the creative team to communicate the nature of a composition with few words. If a director says to the videographer, "Give me a close-up," the videographer will have a good idea of how big the subject should appear within the frame. Although each individual director's interpretation of what a close-up is varies somewhat, the crew soon gets to know the director's interpretation, and communication about the visual elements can proceed much more efficiently from there. Although there is some degree of variation among artists, there are standard definitions of several shot types used in video and film production.

The area of coverage contained in a **long shot** (LS), sometimes also called a wide shot, can vary greatly depending on the context. A long shot usually gathers a wide view of a space. For example, a long shot of New York City could contain the entire skyline, comprising many miles of landscape. If we change the context, however, and are filming material in a living room, a long shot in this case will capture a significant view of the entire room. When referring to the composition of a human subject, a long shot is most often defined as a composition that contains all of the person's body in the frame, from head to feet, and the surrounding elements as required for the aesthetics of the shot and the context of the story.

A **medium shot** (MS) of a human subject generally captures all of the person's head, shoulders, and body from about the chest up. The exact cutoff

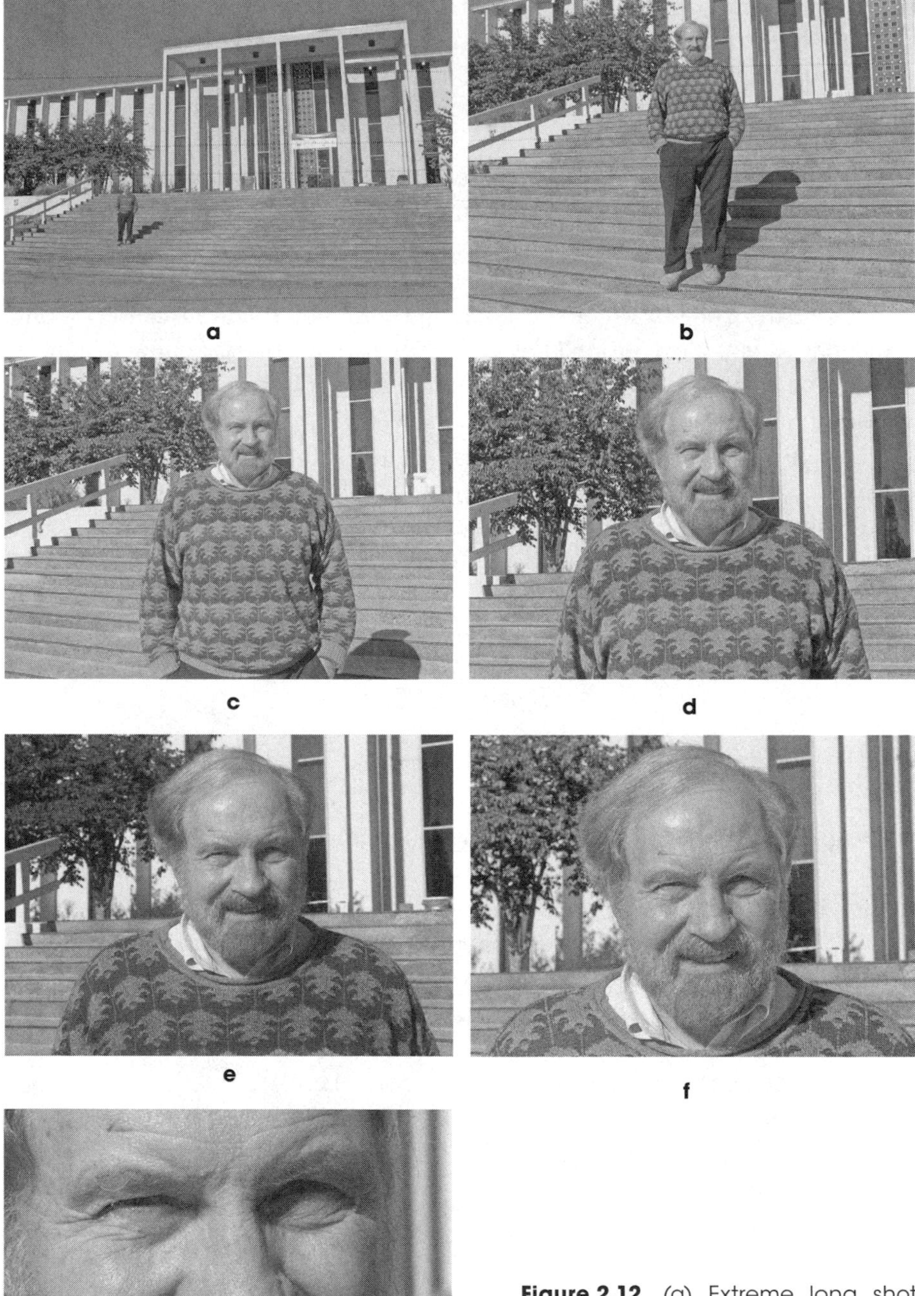

Figure 2.12 (a) Extreme long shot (ELS), (b) long shot (LS), (c) medium long shot (MSL), (d) medium shot (MS), (e) medium close-up (MCU), (f) close-up (CU), (g) extreme close-up (ECU).

marks for a medium shot vary depending on the artist and the content of the composition, but this is the basic area of coverage.

A **close-up** (CU) of a human subject generally covers the entire head, but the body might be excluded beyond that. The close-up emphasizes expression and facial characteristics. This shot type is frequently applied to inanimate objects. It is common for a director to call for a shot such as, "Give me a close-up of the flowers on the table."

These are the three main shot types, as defined by the scale of the objects in the frame. There are other shot types defined by scale such as the **extreme close-up** (ECU), which might feature a subject's eyes filling the frame. It is not uncommon for the top and bottom of a subject's head to be cropped in an extreme close-up. The extreme close-up isolates the details of a person or an object. A director might call for an extreme close-up to show a bead of sweat on a subject's forehead to communicate a sense of nervousness. Other shot types defined by scale include the **medium long shot** (MLS), which is longer than a medium shot but tighter than a long shot. Another variation of this type is the **medium close-up** (MCU). Sometimes shots are defined by the number of characters in the composition, such as a **two-shot** and a **three-shot**.

The selection of shot type creates varying levels of intimacy, which affects the meaning of the shot. For example, a close-up of a person portrays a feeling of intimacy, a medium shot signifies a personal relationship, a full-length body shot conveys a social relationship, and a long shot coveys a sense of social distance (Baggaley, 1980). Every time you compose a human subject you are making an optical commentary about that subject, and this commentary affects the audience's perception (Grabe, 1996).

Some shots are defined by their perspective. Most shots in motion pictures present an **objective perspective**. The goal of motion picture photography is often to give the viewer a sense of observing events. The audience is generally a witness to the story on screen. By contrast, some shots are designed to

Figure 2.13 Nonfiction production requires special attention to shot selection and optical commentary to portray people honestly. *In Gandhi's Footsteps* tells the story of prison reform in India. (Courtesy of Filmaker's Library)

present a **subjective perspective**. In this shot type the purpose is to give the audience the sense of participating in the action and the sense of being there. There is one shot type that is always subjective, the **point-of-view shot**. Recall the example of Steve and the bully. We introduced the option of portraying the bully using a low-angle shot. This shot was designed to be from Steve's point of view.

One of the most remarkable examples of subjective cinematography is in Steven Spielberg's portrayal of the landing at Omaha Beach in *Saving Private Ryan* (1998). The entire sequence on the beach is presented from a subjective point of view. Some of the shots are character point-of-view shots, while other shots are designed to look like handheld documentary footage, implying the point of view of a witness. Some shots are **over-the-shoulder** shots, such as the perspective from the enemy machine gun nest. The perspective in this sequence is always from within the action. A conventional way of constructing this scene would be to include an objective perspective once in a while, such as a wide shot from up high or far away to reorient the viewer, to give the viewer some emotional distance, and to give the audience the opportunity to break the psychological tension. Spielberg does not allow the viewer this retreat at any point during the entire battle scene because the soldiers who were at the real Omaha Beach did not have the ability to step out of the action. The director wants the audience to feel that experience as powerfully as the art of film can allow.

Another interesting shot type defined by its perspective is the **overhead shot**. This is an objective perspective, and arguably the most objective one possible. In the overhead shot the camera is directly above the action, pointing straight down. The overhead shot is sometimes referred to as the "point of view of God." It implies a detached and all-observing perspective, and it is often used in narrative film to foreshadow impending doom (*Psycho,* 1960) or to show the aftermath of a terrible event (*Taxi Driver,* 1976).

Figure 2.14 *Saving Private Ryan* conveys the unrelenting horror of the D-Day landing by trapping the audience in a subjective point of view. (Paramount/Photofest; © Paramount Pictures)

Moving Shot Types

The elements of visual image making discussed thus far emphasize the options available for **static shots**. In a static shot the camera stays in a fixed position and does not move once it is set. Motion picture, by its very definition, allows for movement. The element of movement exists because motion pictures utilize time as well as space. We have discussed the dimensions of composition that allow two-dimensional images to represent three-dimensional space. The video screen is defined by its width (x-axis) and its height (y-axis). The use of visual perspective, scale, and light and shadow allow this two-dimensional space to represent depth (z-axis). Since motion pictures are a succession of images moving through time, film and video also work in a fourth dimension, which is time (**t-axis**). An element in motion picture can be defined by its location in four dimensions: its place in width, height, depth, and time.

A moving camera actively explores the environment. There are two shots that are defined by the pivot of the camera on an axis during the shot. The **pan shot** pivots the camera from side to side on a fixed point, such as a tripod head, or perhaps on a shoulder in handheld recording. The pan is analogous to turning your head side to side as if saying no. The field of view is changed as the camera pivots on an axis, but the physical location of the camera does not change. Pans are often used to explore landscapes or to shift the viewer's attention from one part of a space to another. The **tilt** is similar, but the camera pivots on an axis to change the field of view up and down. This type of shot is most equivalent to moving your head up and down as if to indicate yes.

The **zoom shot** is an optical effect that magnifies part of a composition by adjusting the lens to make a portion of the field of view larger, thus highlighting it for the viewer. This can also work in reverse. A shot can start out tight and the shot might then zoom out to reveal the context of an element in the environment. Zooms magnify a part of the image, but the relationship of the elements in the composition stays exactly the same. To achieve the effect of changing the relationship between objects in your composition, the camera itself must be moved toward or away from the subject. This is called a dolly shot.

A **dolly shot** moves the camera forward or backward. In a dolly shot the perspective changes. The foreground elements part outwards in relationship to the background elements as the camera moves forward. A **tracking shot** (also

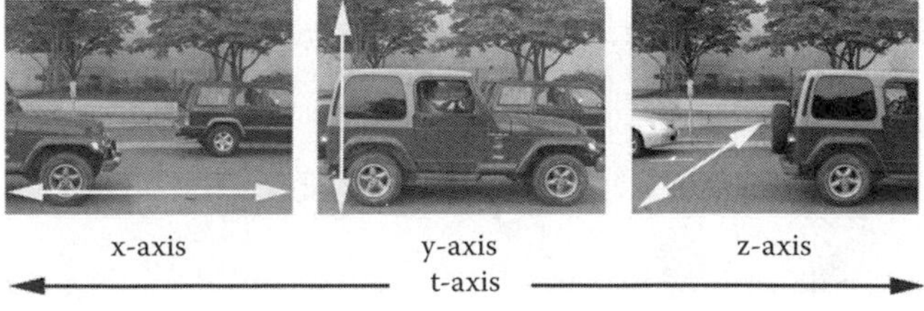

Figure 2.15 Motion pictures operate in four dimensions: width (x-axis), height (y-axis), depth (z-axis), and time (t-axis).

Zoom

Dolly

Figure 2.16 A zoom magnifies part of a composition while a dolly changes perspective. (Daniel Judson)

known as a **trucking shot**) moves the camera sideways to follow a moving subject or to visually explore an environment. Some people refer to all moving camera shots that are executed using a wheeled support as dolly shots, since this device is called a dolly. Just as it is important to allow sufficient noseroom for a subject in profile, it is important to allow sufficient **leadroom** as you track a moving subject. You don't want the audience to feel as though the camera is lagging, or as if the subject is about to smack into the side of the frame.

A **crane shot** emphasizes movement of the camera up and down. Unlike a tilt, which simply points the camera upward or downward to show the audience what is off in that direction, a crane shot physically moves the camera up or down to give the audience the sense of moving higher or lower through space. Crane shots are sometimes referred to as jib shots. These professional equipment options are explored further in chapter 3.

The most basic, and in some ways most universal, way to move a camera is to go handheld. This approach readily permits a wide range of creative movements. The handheld camera can travel down narrow halls and stairwells, which would be a problem for a dolly. Achieving effective handheld photography takes practice. Specialized equipment, such as the **Steadycam** (chapter 3), greatly reduces the amount of unwanted shake from handheld shots.

BUILDING BLOCKS OF VISUAL PROGRAMS

The smallest whole unit of measurement used to build motion pictures is the frame. The **frame**, in this context, is defined as a single image captured by the camera. Motion pictures are achieved by taking many individual pictures and

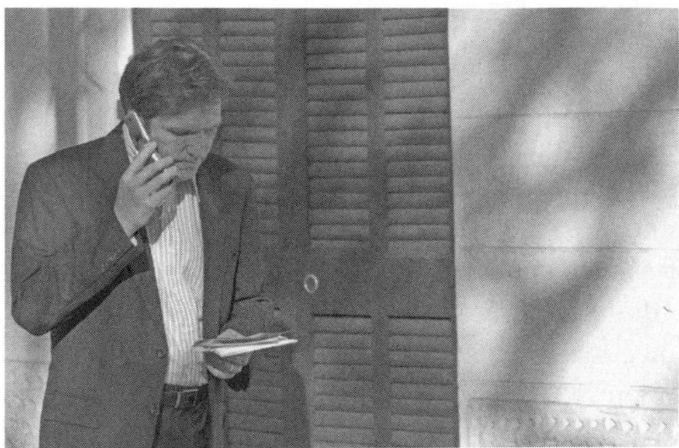

Figure 2.17 When tracking a moving subject make sure to provide sufficient leadroom. (Courtesy of RiverDream Productions)

stringing them together to create the illusion of movement. Motion pictures utilize generally 24 (film) to 30 (video) frames per second to create the sense of movement at normal speed.

A contiguous series of frames recorded from a single starting of the camera to the single stopping of the camera is called a **shot**. There can be anywhere from one frame to many thousands of frames in a single shot. Once the recording is stopped and then started again later in time, a new shot is defined. Once the visual program is edited, the shot as it appears in the final program might be shorter than the shot as originally recorded by the camera. Perhaps one shot will be cut up and appear as many separate shots in the final program. In the editing phase, the shot is defined the same way. It is a continuous series of frames without interruption.

A **scene** is a single shot, or a series of shots, that portrays events unified in time, location, and theme. For example, if two people are sitting in a diner talking intently about a plan to start a business, and then they change the subject to an extensive discussion about relationships, this would probably be defined as two separate scenes. These two conversations are not unified in theme, and therefore represent different scenes. Some films (*Rope*, 1948; *My Dinner With Andre*, 1981) take place at a single location and in a unified flow of time. It is therefore the content that will define the scene breaks in these cases. If the patrons of our diner get up and leave the restaurant, or if there is a change in time and we jump forward to another day, these changes will also define the start of a new scene.

The **sequence** is unified in theme, and takes place in contiguous **screen time**, but it might not be unified in either **dramatic time** or location. Dramatic time is the way time progresses in the program, which might be much faster than real time. For example, there might a sequence in a television program that shows someone rushing to clean up a home before a surprise party. We might see the person cleaning the living room, then vacuuming the bedroom, and so on. While it would take an hour to clean the house in reality, the show condenses this action to 30 seconds, thus defining the action as a sequence.

This series of shots is unified in theme, but disconnected in both time and location as the person moves from room to room. A classic example of a sequence is the dream sequence. Dreams often involve movement from one location to another, and a shift in content, but the dream itself is the unifying element, thus defining the sequence. Sequences that manipulate time, location, and/or theme to compress events are sometime referred to as a **montage**.

A series of scenes can be joined together to create **acts**. The acts taken together create the structure of the **feature**, **episode**, or **program**. The final program is not necessarily the largest unit of measurement in visual storytelling. Feature films might comprise components of a **trilogy**, such as *The Lord of the Rings* trilogy. George Lucas's *Star Wars* is an example of an even larger story structure, spanning six films to tell the story. Television episodes are units of the **season**, which are in turn units of the **series**.

Transitions

Transitions are used in video production to link shots, scenes, and acts together. Different transitions communicate different meanings, and when chosen thoughtfully, the creative use of transitions enhances your ability to communicate ideas and tell stories. The most common transition is the **cut**. A cut simply joins one shot to the next. The last frame of one shot is followed visually by the first frame of the next shot. It is that simple.

A **fade** is a shot that either appears gradually or disappears gradually. When a shot appears gradually it is called a **fade-in**. A shot that disappears gradually is a **fade-out**. Shots that fade are usually linked to black. For example, a program might start with a black screen and then the first shot will fade in. Many visual programs end the same way and the last shot will fade to black. In some cases a shot will fade to black, and then the next shot will fade in from black. This is called a dip to black, and it is used to designate act breaks or to signify a significant lapse in time, which is sometimes accompanied by a significant change in theme and physical location. The fade is considered a strong transition, and it is generally advised that it be used sparingly, especially in the body of a visual program.

A **dissolve** is a more technically complex transition than a fade, but a less dramatic one in terms of its meaning. In a dissolve, the end of one shot fades out while the beginning of the next shot simultaneously fades in. This creates a time during the transition when both shots are visible at the same time. For this reason, the dissolve is sometimes referred to as an **overlap dissolve**, or more simply a **lap dissolve**. Since the dissolve involves the simultaneous fading in and out of two shots, it is also sometimes called a **cross-fade**. Like the fade to black, the dissolve generally implies the passage of time, and this sometimes includes a change in location. A dissolve is likely to be used to express a shorter passage of time than a dip to black.

A **wipe** is a highly visible transition. Many viewers will not pay much conscious attention to a fade or a dissolve, but a wipe is likely to be noticed. A wipe is achieved when one image replaces another image by "wiping" it off the screen. Wipes can be vertical, horizontal, or can be created in a variety of shapes, including stars and circles. Wipes often signify a change in location, and sometimes a lapse in time. Often wipes are integrated into flashy montages, particularly in high-energy programs, such as promotional videos. There are many options for controlling the shape, texture, and timing of all transitions. We will explore these tools and options further in chapter 4.

CREATING A SCENE

Just as a single frame can constitute a shot, so too can a single shot constitute a scene. There are remarkable examples in film of complex interactions unfolding through a scene that is comprised of a single shot. Robert Altman's *The Player* (1991) begins with an eight-minute scene that is one continuous shot. Most scenes, however, are comprised of a variety of shots put into a logical order to move the audience through the scene and story. A scene often includes some long shots, and will predominantly be comprised of a mixture of medium shots and close-ups. You might see some of the specialized type shots we have explored, including over-the-shoulder and point-of-view shots. The use of multiple shots to construct a scene is especially significant for television, or other small-screen distribution, such as webcasting. Television is considered a close-up medium. Since the television screen is relatively small, it is not likely that a single shot will be used to convey information for a sustained period of time. For the audience to see the expression of characters and the details of environments it is necessary to use close-ups.

Crafting a scene requires recording a variety of shots and assembling them in an order to tell the story. There are many possible approaches to shooting and editing scenes, but to get started we will explore the standard method for creating scenes. This standard method is known as the **master scene method**. It is also sometimes referred to as the **master scene cut-in**. Since it is the industry standard for constructing scenes it is sometimes called the **Hollywood style of editing**.

Cut: Provides a change in perspective

Fade: Represents a significant lapse of time

Dissolve: Portrays a lapse of time

Wipe: Often used to signify a change in location

Figure 2.18 Basic transitions and their common meanings.

The Master Scene Method

The master scene method is used to construct scenes in a consistent and logical manner. The first shot of a scene is often an **establishing shot**. The establishing shot tells the audience where they are. The establishing shot might be an **exterior shot**, such as a city skyline or a restaurant storefront, or it might be an **interior shot**, such as the wide expanse of a hotel casino floor. A scene need not always include an establishing shot, particularly if it should be obvious to the audience where they are, or if you are returning to a location that you have already established in another scene earlier in the program.

The anchor of the master scene method is the **master shot**. The master shot captures the entire range of action in the scene. For example, a scene involving two people having a romantic dinner might begin with a master shot that includes the table and the two patrons sitting across from each other. The master shot is often a wide shot, but it does not always have to be. Often the master shot serves as the establishing shot, and often the master shot documents the entire length of a scene. The scene is constructed in editing by starting with the master shot and inserting other shots to direct the audience's attention to specific elements of interest. In the case of our romantic dinner, the scene might cross-cut between close-ups of the man and the woman as they talk. We might see the man from the woman's point of view, or we might see the woman from the man's perspective using an over-the-shoulder shot. The scene might show a close-up of the man's hands as he presents an engagement ring, and the next shot might be a **reaction shot** of the woman as she realizes what is happening.

Shooting a Master Scene

When filming a scene using the master scene method, the camera often records a master shot first to capture all of the relevant action. It is common for the actors to play the entire scene from this angle. It might require several **takes** to get it right. For long scenes, it is not unusual for the director to pick up the scene somewhere in the middle if there is a mistake. If the director feels that the first half of the scene was captured well, he might have the actors perform only the second half of the scene on later takes. This can work because the director knows that the editor will be able to seamlessly integrate elements from the first half of the master shot and elements from subsequent takes of the second half of the master shot.

After the crew captures the master shot of our couple sharing a romantic dinner, it is then time to gather other shots to cut into the master shot to provide shot variety and to direct the audience's attention. The director might order the camera to be moved to a position behind the woman's shoulder. From this position the camera operator can record shots of the man to be inserted in the

Figure 2.19 A scene is often constructed by inserting cut-ins within a master shot to reveal detail and to direct the audience's attention. (Photos courtesy of William Olsen; illustration by Jesse Knight)

scene. The crew might capture a shot from this angle of the man reaching into his pocket and pulling out the ring. They might record a close-up of the man saying the line, "Will you marry me?" and so on. Once all of the shots from this camera position are recorded, the crew moves the camera to another position, perhaps behind the man's shoulder. From this angle, the camera operator might record a close-up of the woman's reaction to the proposal. Sometimes it is appropriate to play the scene all the way through from many angles; other times only specific parts of the scene might be recorded from certain angles. The more coverage there is of a scene, the more options the editor will have.

Careful planning, however, is required to ensure against overshooting, which can waste valuable time and resources.

The director might use a **shot list** and **storyboards** to make sure that the scene is recorded according to plans, and to ensure that the editor has what she needs to compose the shots in postproduction. We will explore the process of creating shot lists and storyboards in chapter 5.

The shots of the man reaching into his pocket and the woman's reaction are called **cut-ins**. Cut-ins highlight details of the master shot. Another type of shot used in building a master scene is the **cutaway**. Cutaways show the audience detail outside of the master shot. For example, showing the reaction of a couple at a table across the room, or showing the kitchen door as a waiter emerges with a bottle of champagne are examples of cutaways that might be inserted into this scene.

A primary function of the master shot is to provide a reference for the editor to pace the construction of the scene. Editors often lay down the master shot first, and then replace parts of it, shot by shot, with various cut-ins. It is not unusual for a master shot to be almost completely removed by the end of the editing process.

CONTINUITY

Have you ever watched a film and seen someone's shirt collar change position from one shot to the next, or seen a glass of water magically get fuller when the camera changes angles? These are examples of **continuity errors**. When constructing a visual program, it is important to understand and observe issues of continuity.

Things like missing earrings or changing hairstyles are factors of **physical continuity**. Sometimes cut-ins recorded for a master scene will be shot much later than the original master shot. It is essential that the elements of these shots match up. Keeping track of continuity can be more difficult that you might imagine. It includes not only the clothes of the actors and the props, but also the way the light falls on the subjects, the exact position of each actors' arms, hands, and so on. Playing back previous recordings of master shots and cut-ins and taking still pictures are helpful in monitoring and maintaining continuity. Often it is valuable to assign the role of observing and maintaining physical continuity to a crew member. All major productions have at least one person whose exclusive task is maintaining continuity. This person is referred to as the **script supervisor**.

Overlapping Action

Temporal continuity is maintaining consistent use of time. One valuable way to maintain temporal continuity as you build a scene is to make sure to record

overlapping action from one camera angle to the next. Assume for example that your plan is to show a close-up of a person sitting in a chair as the phone rings, followed by a long shot of the character walking across the floor to answer the phone. Beginning filmmakers sometimes make the mistake of not overlapping the action between shots. The inexperienced director might have the person in the chair begin to stand up and then yell, "Cut!" After the camera is set to the new position for the long shot, the director then has the actor walk across the floor from the location of the chair. When the team gets into the editing process they learn that in neither the close-up nor the long shot did they record the action of the character standing up. There is no way to cut these two shots together without a break in continuity. If the editor tries to link these two shots, the actor will appear to be sitting, and then she will be instantly standing. This type of continuity error, when a person or object instantly moves from one location to another, is known as a **jump cut**, and it is a temporal continuity error as it breaks the realistic movement though time.

The solution to this potential problem is to make sure to overlap the action. In the close-up, the actor should execute the action of standing up, and then start to walk across the room. The director might want to keep the camera rolling even after the actor has walked out of the frame. To prepare for the long shot, the actor should sit back down, and the shot should include the entire action of standing up and walking across the room. Now the editor has several editing options, and can choose to make the cut between the close-up and the long shot before, during, or after the person stands. Overlapping action helps maintain continuity and provides more editing choices.

The Line

There is an imaginary line that exists in every scene, and knowing how to work with this line will help you maintain **spatial continuity**. Consider our dining couple. In this case the most standard way to define the location of **the line** is to imagine that a line passes between the two characters along their line of sight as they look at each other. The line is also known as the **axis of action**. Why do we need to have this imaginary line?

When you watch a play on stage your view of the actors is always from the same perspective. This keeps you oriented to what is happening on stage, but a motion picture changes perspective as the camera changes angles. The value of an imaginary line is illustrated in the flowing example. Typically, as you watch a football game on television, all of the cameras covering the game are set on one side of the field. The point of view never cuts from the 50-yard line of one side of the field to the 50-yard line of the other. Why not? If these two shots were placed in the program in succession it would appear as though the teams suddenly reversed direction, and that the offensive team is now running the wrong way. In this case the line exists between the two teams as they face each other. The line runs down the center of the field from end zone to end zone.

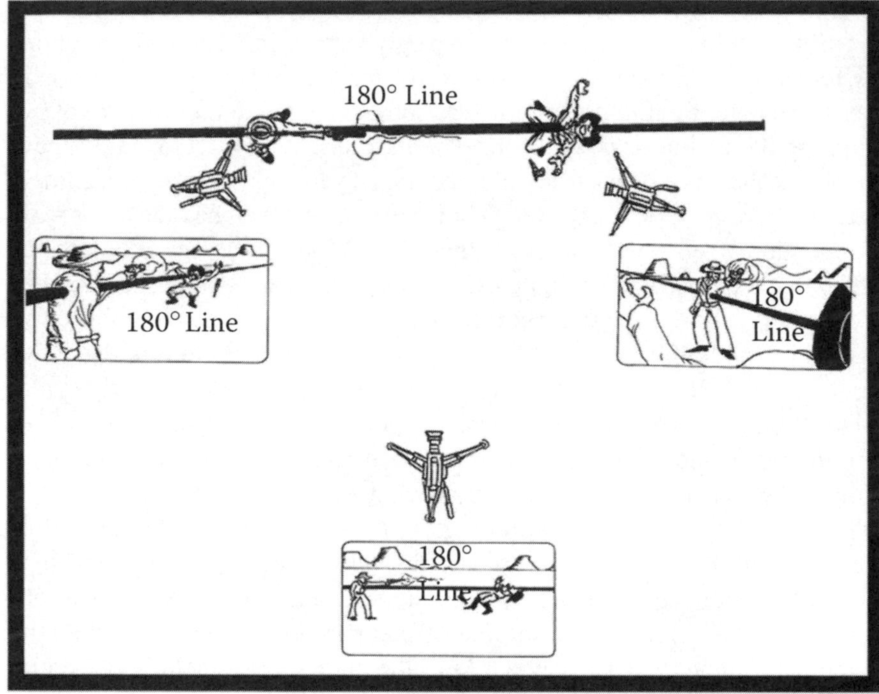

Figure 2.20 When shooting a scene you must be aware of the line (the axis of action). As a general rule you can place the camera within a 180-degree arc on one side of the line. (Jesse Knight)

The line defines the **180-degree rule**. Once you establish your imaginary line you are free to place your camera anywhere on one side of that line, thus you have 180 degrees of a semicircle to work in. Crossing the line puts you at risk of reversing screen direction, and disorienting the viewer. Experiments show that violating the 180-degree rule confuses and distracts the audience significantly (d'Ydewalle, 1998). There are circumstances in which crossing the line will not disorient the viewer. You can place the camera directly on the line. This will allow you the freedom to move to either side of the line in the next shot. You can move the camera across the line during a shot. If the audience has the experience of crossing the line during a shot with a moving camera, this will allow subsequent shots to take place on the other side of the line. Also, if the characters change their positions, or if a new character enters the scene, these factors can justify the establishment of a new line. A character exiting the scene can also serve as a justification for establishing a new line.

It is possible to cross the line without disorienting the viewer in circumstances other than the exceptions listed here, but such constructions require skill, practice, and an advanced understanding of the language of motion pictures and audience perception. In general, for your early projects, you should be aware of where your axis of action exists in a scene and keep your cameras on one side of that axis.

Eyelines

Closely related to the 180-degree rule are issues of **eyelines**. Some camera positions are placed close to the axis of action. In these circumstances it is important that the eyeline of the subject be cast on the proper side of the camera. Even if your camera position is placed on the correct side of the line, if the actor is looking on the wrong side of the camera, this will have the effect of reversing screen direction. It will look as though the character has jumped to the other side of the room, and it will no longer appear as if the characters are looking at each other as you cut back and forth. Make sure to maintain proper eyelines.

Position Jumps

Spatial continuity can be disrupted even if the camera is kept on the correct side of the line, and even if you keep your actors' eyelines in order. When composing cut-ins for a master scene it is important that the camera angle and the scale of the shots vary significantly. For example, if you have a long shot of a man and a woman sitting at a table, and then move the camera 70 degrees to record a medium shot of the man saying his lines, this will cut together

Figure 2.21 (a) Proper and (b) improper eyeline matching.

a Position Jump

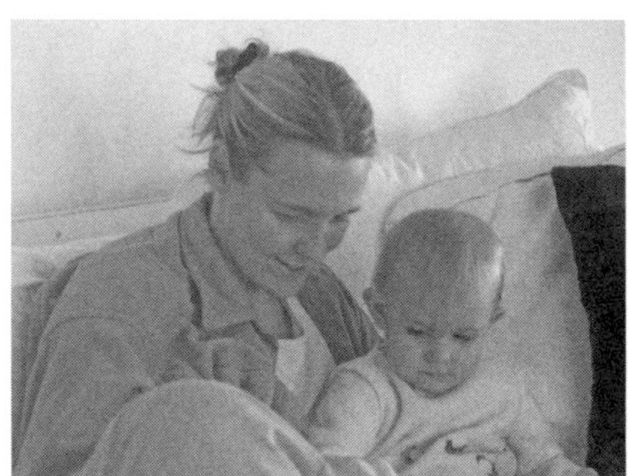

b Conventional Composition Change

Figure 2.22 A minor change in angle and focal length (a) can result in a position jump when one shot cuts to the next, while a significant change in angle and focal length (b) generally creates a smoother transition between shots.

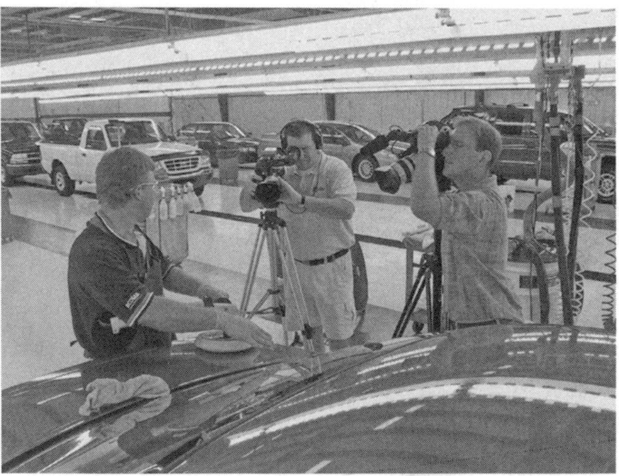

Figure 2.23 This industrial training film on auto detailing covers a scene with two cameras. This helps maintain continuity in editing by providing multiple angles of the demonstration. (Courtesy of Bclip Productions, Inc.)

well with the long shot. It is a significant change in angle and composition. If, however, you have a long shot of the man and the woman at the table, and then move the camera just 10 degrees to one side and keep the shot scale relatively long, it will look like the man has jumped from one part of the screen to another. These **position jumps** are disconcerting to the viewer and should be avoided unless intended for creative effect.

This discussion of continuity has focused primarily on staged scenes, but you must be conscious of continuity issues when working on nonfiction projects as well. News packages and documentary programs offer unique challenges for continuity. You might be recording live events with no opportunity for a second take. You must keep in mind maintaining your line and getting the angles and material your editor will need, often while working on the fly.

CONCLUSIONS

You now have an introduction to the unique language of motion pictures. You can experiment with the rule of thirds, scale, foreground and background, light and shadow, headroom and noseroom, and a creative variety of camera angles and perspectives to create *mise en scene*. Following the techniques of the master scene method, you can record an assortment of shots that will give you many creative options in editing your first scene.

In our next chapter you will explore the motion picture camera, and how to utilize its features to create images that best reflect the vision in your mind's eye. Most video cameras are user-friendly, and chances are that you can start recording visual programs right away. The digital video camera is a powerful tool. With knowledge of its functions and an understanding of how these functions can be applied, you will expand your creative range in visual storytelling. Chapter 3 introduces this remarkable storytelling tool.

SAMPLE EXERCISES

1. Select a classic painting. What is the story told in the painting? How would you adapt the painting into a scene for a motion picture?
2. Write an idea for an original scene that can be recorded using the master scene method. Construct the scene without sound or title cards. How will you communicate the story to the audience?
3. Using a still camera, take three pictures that demonstrate a change in a person's situation from happy to sad. How do angle, framing, and surrounding elements support your story?

RECOMMENDED READINGS

Krages, B. (2005). *Photography: The Art of Composition.* New York: Allworth Press.
Miller, P. P. (1999). *Script Supervising and Film Continuity.* Boston: Focal Press.
Zakia, R. D. (2002). *Perception and Imaging.* Boston: Focal Press.

REFERENCES

Baggaley, R. (1980). *Psychology of the TV image.* Westmead: Gower Publishing.

d'Ydewalle, G. (1998). Film perception: The processing of film cuts. In G. Underwood (Ed.), *Eye guidance in reading and scene perception* (pp. 357-367). Oxford, England: Elsevier Science Ltd.

Grabe, M. E. (1996). The South African Broadcasting Corporation's coverage of the 1987 and 1989 elections: The matter of visual bias. *Journal of Broadcasting and Electronic Media*, 40, 153-179.

Krupinski, E., & Locher, P. (1988). Skin conductance and aesthetic evaluative responses to nonrepresentational works of art varying in symmetry. *Bulletin of Psychonomic Society*, 26, 355-359.

Tiemens, R. (1970). Some relationships of camera angle to communicator credibility. *Journal of Broadcasting*, 14, 483-498.

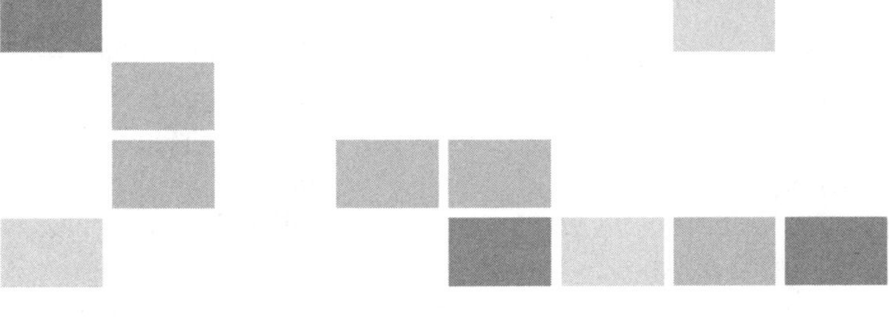

3

CAMERAS

CHAPTER OBJECTIVES

The core of the video production process is recording images with a camera. In this chapter we explore the history of cinematography and outline the available camera options. This chapter concentrates on the elements of video camera control that are consistent across formats and camera models. The small-format digital video camera is used as the foundation of the survey since this is the equipment most beginning students use to practice and learn the process of video production. This chapter concludes with an introduction to some stylistic approaches used in image making to provide options as you design your own visual programs. In this chapter you will:

- Explore the history of motion picture cameras;
- Gain an understanding of the technical equipment used for motion picture recording;
- Transcend basic functions to be able to manipulate the features of digital video equipment to create highly controlled images;
- Survey movements in the traditional arts that can be applied to video production.

The process used by a camera to record an image is similar to how we perceive visual images with our naked eye. Both the camera and the human eye operate by interpreting light in the visual spectrum. Light waves pass through the lens of our eye, which focuses this stream of light onto our retina. As the light passes through the lens of our eye it is reversed, and the image on our retina is actually backwards and upside down. Our brain makes an adjustment, and we perceive visual images oriented correctly.

The camera operates in much the same way. Light from the visible spectrum passes through a glass lens and is focused reversed and upside down on an imaging surface. This imaging surface records the picture for reproduction. In the earliest cameras used for still photography, the imaging surface was a plate of metal or glass treated with light-sensitive chemicals. Later, various formats of sheet and roll film were introduced. Today, most visual imaging is achieved by an electronic imaging surface, rather than film. When working with digital photography and digital video, the imaging surface is one or more **charge-coupled devices (CCDs)** or **complementary metal-oxide-semiconductors (CMOS)**. As light activates these image sensors, the camera records information for playback later in time.

Terms that describe the process of making motion pictures include photography, cinematography, and videography. Photography generally refers to the art of recording single images, one at a time. When many images are recorded in succession to create a motion picture, the process is called cinematography, which means to write in motion. Some people refer to the process of making motion pictures with video cameras as videography, and reserve the more traditional term of cinematography for the art of working with motion picture film. Whatever you choose to call it, today's state-of-the-art process of digital video production is the product of a rich history of scientific discovery and technological innovation.

HISTORY OF THE MOTION PICTURES

Pre-Cinema

Motion pictures work because of the way our eyes and brain work. There is a phenomenon called the **persistence of vision**. Ptolemy of Alexandria first documented this principle in 130 A.D. If you look at a bare light bulb and then close your eyes, you will see an afterimage. Once a visual stimulus is removed from our view it lingers in our mind. Our brain only processes about 10 to 12 images per second. If we could perceive exactly what was happening before us, motion pictures would not work. When a film is projected in a theater, the screen starts out black. The projector's shutter moves out of the way, revealing an image. This still image stays on the screen for approximately 1/48th of a second. The shutter moves across the image and the screen goes dark again. While the screen is dark, a claw in the projector quickly pulls down another frame of film using the sprocket holes and locks it into place with a registration pin. All of this happens while the screen is dark, in about another 1/48th of a second. This process is repeated over and over to project the film at 24 frames per second. We never see any of this mechanical action, nor are we aware of the fact that for every hour of motion picture projection the screen is actually black for 30 minutes. We sense fluid movement. The nature of human visual perception and the phenomenon of the persistence of vision make the illusion of seamless motion possible.

The **thaumatrope** of 1825 was a novelty device that utilized the persistence of vision. By placing two images on a paper disk and spinning it between one's thumb and fingers on a string, the illusion of a bird in a cage could be created when no such single image existed. The **zoetrope** of 1834 pushed this concept even further, allowing the illusion of an entire moving scene, such as a jester juggling three balls in the air. Francis Ford Coppola named his production company after this device with the advent of American Zoetrope.

The process of projecting images for entertainment goes back even farther than the Thaumatrope. The magic lantern can be traced back to the late 1600s. This device projects images painted on glass slides through a lens with lamplight. The magic lantern remained a popular form of home entertainment throughout the 19th century.

The ability to fix a photographic image was developed in the 1820s. Still photographs were adapted to work with the magic lantern, and the ability to project a photograph on a screen became possible. The advancement toward moving pictures, much like we know them today, developed quickly from there.

Figure 3.1 Zoetrope.

Figure 3.2 Magic lantern.

Series photography was a significant step in the evolution of movies. A camera with a revolver design allowed the capture of several images in fast succession. In 1878, Eadweard Muybridge conducted a landmark experiment in series photography by arming a racetrack with a number of cameras at equal intervals and attaching the shutter releases to trip wires. The experiment was designed to see whether a running horse ever has all four feet off the ground at the same time. The experiment proved that a horse does go airborne while running, and the photographic record produced a valuable dividend. When the photographs were flipped in quick succession it created the illusion of a running horse.

Film

Roll film allowed many pictures to be recorded every second, and when these pictures were played back the motion picture was born. The original film format for motion picture photography was 35mm film, and this is still the industry standard for production on film today. Early motion picture cameras and projectors were hand-cranked, so the rate of recording and playback was somewhat variable, but the rate for silent films was about 16 frames per second. This rate was standardized with the addition of the electric motor to the motion picture camera and projector. Sixteen frames became the standard because the rate was just fast enough to reduce the perception of flicker when the images were projected. It was important to stay as close to the **flicker fusion rate** as possible to avoid wasting film. Film uses silver as part of its chemical composition, and it is therefore expensive. Today it costs hundreds of dollars to shoot, process, and print just a few minutes of 35mm film.

With the advent of sound recording, and then sound film in the 1920s, 16 frames per second was too slow a rate for proper functioning of the sound track. The frame rate was increased to the minimum speed necessary for sound. This rate is 24 frames per second (fps), which is still the standard for American theatrical films today. Europe and select territories work in 25 fps.

While 35mm film is the industry standard, there are many other film formats including 16mm, 8mm, Super-16, Super-8, and 70mm. Sixteen-millimeter film was developed for the consumer market so people could shoot home

Figure 3.3 35mm film camera. (Courtesy of Bonesteel Films)

movies. While 16mm is about half the width of 35mm, the cost to produce it is actually about one fourth. That is because four images of 16mm can fit within the same area as one frame of 35mm film. Sixteen-millimeter film is still a popular format for students in traditional film schools and low-budget filmmaking, but in the 1930s it proved to be too expensive for most of the home movie market, and that is why 8mm film was born. Eight-millimeter film reduced the frame size to one fourth of that of 16mm and became a popular format for a large consumer market. For a few dollars, one could shoot and process a four-minute reel and capture important life events for posterity.

While 8mm film is relatively inexpensive, there is a significant trade-off for the savings. As the frame size gets smaller, the information recorded is less detailed. Eight-millimeter film is quite grainy when enlarged and therefore is not appropriate for professional applications. Picture quality across film and video formats can be compared in terms of horizontal lines of **resolution**. Thirty-five millimeter film has the equivalent of 4,000 horizontal lines of resolution. High-definition video captures 1,080 horizontal lines of resolution.

Super-8 and Super-16 are interesting variations. These film gauges are the exact same width as their respective 8mm and 16mm counterparts, but technicians noticed that a lot of good potential recording area was lost in traditional 8mm and 16mm cinematography because of the large sprocket holes. Super-8 and Super-16 use smaller sprocket holes, which significantly increases the recording area and resolution of the image. Super-8 and Super-16 film must be used with cameras and projectors specifically made for these formats.

Seventy-millimeter film was developed for projects striving to achieve even greater resolution than 35mm. With four times the recording area as the 35mm frame, 70mm offers unparalleled image quality for motion picture production. Seventy-millimeter achieved its peak of popularity in the 1950s and 60s as a competitive tool between rival studios. The major studios were fighting to produce the next blockbuster, and shooting in 70mm became an asset. Seventy-millimeter film is rarely used in initial capture today because of its expense.

Figure 3.4 Small-format film cameras.

Seventy-millimeter film has another significant disadvantage. To truly benefit from the improved resolution of shooting in 70mm, theaters must be equipped for 70mm projection, which is rarely the case. Most times the 70mm original is reduced to 35mm to work with standard theatrical equipment, so the expense and effort is generally not perceived as worth it.

The most advanced film format ever invented is IMAX. If you have experienced an IMAX film, you will likely remember the sense of how the screen appeared as a window to the actual scene. The level of resolution in IMAX film has never been paralleled since its introduction in 1970. IMAX works by modifying the highly detailed 70mm film format by increasing the effective frame size an additional threefold. This is achieved by running the film through the camera sideways to utilize a wide strip of film for each frame. The result is an awe-inspiring visual experience. If you have not seen an IMAX film, try to do so in order to experience the highest image resolution yet created for motion picture.

Video

Early electronic video systems focused light on an electronic tube. The tube translated the areas of light and darkness into an electronic signal. This signal was carried over an electric wire, and an image that could be viewed was reproduced on a second tube. John Baird made the first public demonstration of a rudimentary video system in Scotland in early 1926. In 1927, a video signal was transferred to a receiver over long distance using modulation of electromagnetic spectrum and television broadcasting was born.

Video Storage. In 1951 a system was developed for recording visual information on magnetic tape rather than film. A television camera translated an image into an electronic signal, and this signal was fed to a magnetic recording head. As a strip of magnetic tape passed over the record head, the particles on the tape were rearranged in the form of a wave that represented the image. This recording could be played back later and viewed on a screen. This was the birth of videotape. The first videotape format was 2-inch reel-to-reel.

The advent of videotape was revolutionary. It allowed the widespread archiving of television broadcasts. Before videotape, live television broadcasts had to be recorded on film through a **telecine**, and this expense meant that much content went unpreserved. With the advent of portable video recorders, and the low cost of videotape compared to film, television production became accessible to a wider range of producers. Videotape is also immediate. While film needs to be processed in a lab, videotape can be replayed right away. This technology also revolutionized television news, permitting faster news footage turn-around times.

The evolution of videotape produced a wide variety of formats. Two-inch videotape and 1-inch video were popular standards in broadcast television. U-

Figure 3.5 Videotape comes in a variety of formats and sizes.

Matic (also known as ¾-inch videotape) was popular for news and field production. VHS (Video Home System, which uses ½-inch tape) was introduced in 1976 and demonstrated remarkable longevity as the primary choice for home video use, while its rival, Betamax (also ½-inch), developed by Sony, faded quickly from the consumer marketplace because Sony's proprietary treatment of the format made it more expensive and less attractive to consumers. The Beta format survived for professional application in Betacam SP, which offers superior quality recording and high resolution.

In the mid-1990s, the method of recording information on videotape changed from **analog** (using a wave to represent the image) to **digital**. This resulted in superior recording quality and the ability to transfer information from one source to another without a loss in resolution. There are many digital videotape formats for professional and consumer applications. Sony's Digital Betacam and Panasonic's DVC-Pro are popular choices among professionals. For education and consumer use, Mini-DV, DVCam, Digital-S, and Digital-8 are widely used options. Other storage options for digital video cameras include memory cards, hard drives, and in-camera read-write media.

NTSC, HDTV, and PAL. There are a variety of video systems available. The two main options for production in the Americas are NTSC (National Television Systems Committee) and HDTV (high-definition television). **NTSC** is what we know as standard television. NTSC monitors utilize 525 horizontal lines of resolution and are formatted in a 4:3 aspect ratio. High-definition video systems utilize 1,080 lines of resolution, and are generally formatted in a widescreen 16:9 aspect ratio. Both systems utilize a rate of 30 frames per second*. A high-definition image can be translated to standard television and

* The frame rate of video is actually 29.97 frames per second, but for all practical intents and purposes video production is considered to be 30 fps.

shown in low resolution. Much broadcast television is produced in high definition, although many consumers watch these programs on a standard television. Conversely, a consumer can watch a standard television program on a high-definition monitor, but this program will be in the low resolution of the original format.

When working in standard video, it is important to note that NTSC is a format predominantly unique to the Americas. Most of the world uses a television system called PAL (phase-alternating line). **PAL** operates at 625 lines of horizontal resolution, and has a different visual texture than NTSC. You might have had the experience of flipping through the channels and noticed a program that was clearly a British comedy. There is something about the visual texture of PAL that is distinct, even after this signal has been translated into NTSC. Since PAL is a higher-resolution standard than NTSC, and the more popular world standard, many producers advocate production in PAL if the product is intended for the world marketplace.

24P. Film looks different than video. If you watch a daytime soap opera recorded on videotape and compare it to an evening drama that was produced on film, you will easily recognize the difference between film and video. Most people believe the film image looks superior. American television operates in 30 frames per second, but American film is produced in 24 frames per second. This is part of what makes images captured on film look different from images captured on video. What really contributes to the perceptual difference, however, is that standard video is produced using **interlace scanning**. Each frame of video is actually made up of two alternating fields. First the odd-numbered lines are scanned, and then the even-numbered lines. So there is never really a frame of video. Strictly speaking, we should talk about standard video as a process that occurs at 60 fields per second rather than 30 frames per second. Film cinematography and projection do not use a scanning process. The optical process of film records and projects a single frame all at once. 24P is a capture system that allows a video camera to closely mimic the perceptual phenomenon of film production. By recording in 24 frames per second, just like film, and recording the image using **progressive scanning** (the "P" in 24P is for "progressive") the look of 24P is remarkably close to that of film. Progressive scanning allows an entire frame to be created rather than a series of fields. 24P is a dramatic advancement in video technology, and is available in versions for both standard television and high-definition production.

The gap in quality between amateur and professional video recording equipment is narrower now than ever before, thanks to digital video technology. Only a decade ago, you would have had to spend tens of thousands of dollars to achieve the level of quality possible today for less than $1,000. This is an exciting and unprecedented time for video production. You have access to the tools to produce visual programs with professional quality. With the skills you will gain in your study and practice, you can enjoy the benefit of realizing your

Figure 3.6 High-definition video camera.

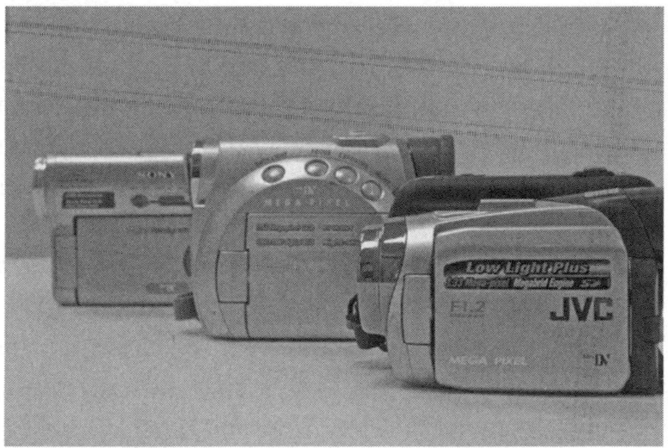

Figure 3.7 Small-format digital video cameras come in a range of designs but most share the same basic features. (Emily Sarkissian)

vision in high technical quality. It is up to you to exercise your imagination and to develop your skills to maximize the potential of these remarkable tools.

THE CAMERA TEAM

The camera crew on large-scale projects can include a director of photography, a camera operator, a focus puller, a clapper/loader, a dolly grip, and a number of assistants. The **director of photography (DP)** is both an artist and technician. On many projects, the director of photography gives significant direction to the crew. Some film directors concentrate on talent and performance, and rely on the director of photography for technical realization of the image.

Sometimes the DP not only supervises the camera crew, but also advises the **grip** crew, the electrical crew, the art department (suggesting use of color and set design), the sound team (suggesting microphone placement to avoid shadows and reflections), and even telling the transportation team where to park the trucks so they are not in the shot.

The rest of the camera team consists of a **camera operator**, who does the actual shooting of the scene. He is the one looking through the viewfinder. The **focus puller** uses a measuring tape, marks on the floor, and an external video monitor to make sure the focus is set exactly where it needs to be, even when people move during a shot. The **clapper/loader** holds the **slate** in front of the camera to identify each shot for the editor, and she will also load the film magazines and manage the videotapes or other digital storage systems. The **dolly grip** moves the wheeled camera support to create moving shots. The camera team works closely with the lighting crew. We will introduce the lighting crew and explore the art of lighting in chapter 6.

Some projects have a second camera unit. The **second unit** gathers additional footage for a program that does not require the main actors or the full crew. A second camera unit might get exterior shots in the mountains while the full crew is shooting in a cabin replica inside the studio.

On smaller projects there might be just one person in charge of all of the elements of videography, or perhaps a director of photography working with one or two multitasking camera assistants. The scale of the project, resources, and ingenuity will ultimately determine the size of the camera crew and their jobs.

DIGITAL VIDEO CAMERAS

The camera is the primary tool for bringing the constructs of your imagination to the screen. For most students, commercial, and independent production applications, the digital video camera is the option of choice. Its advantages are

Figure 3.8 A camera crew in action. (Photo by Jim Bridges; courtesy of Wild Bunch Films)

many. The technology is relatively inexpensive compared to shooting on film, and the picture quality is high. Digital video allows instant playback of material recorded to check for continuity, and to make sure there are no mistakes or unintended elements in the material. Learning to use a video camera is quite easy, but mastering all of its power and potential is a craft to be developed over many years.

Before taking your camera out into the field it is best to examine your camera closely and to shoot test footage. Study the manual of your particular camera model for direction on the exact features, and the location of the controls for each feature. If you do not have documentation, access the manufacturer's Web page. Virtually all camera manuals are available for download.

While the owner's manual will tell you about the features, technical specifications, and location of controls for your camera, the manual will not tell you how to apply these tools or the full range of effects that can be achieved. Understanding how to make a video camera really perform for you and to be comfortable with its features requires extensive exploration and practice. The goal of this section is to establish a foundation of advanced understanding.

An important step in making quality images using digital video is to understand the control options available to you, to know the functions and features of your equipment, and to know how to apply those functions and features to achieve your desired effects. Video cameras come in a number of formats and vary in their resolution and features. A basic camera can cost as little as a few hundred dollars, while a state-of-the-art professional digital video camera system can cost more than $100,000. We will explore the common components of digital video cameras and how you can make the most of their capabilities.

Figure 3.9 Shooting a television commercial on digital video. (Courtesy of Bonesteel Films)

Imaging for Digital Video

Like all cameras, a digital video camera focuses light with a lens onto an imaging surface. The charge-coupled devices (CCDs) or complementary metal-oxide-semiconductors (CMOS) of video cameras serve as the imaging surface and vary in the level of detail they are able to record. Basic digital video cameras record at resolutions of about 525 horizontal lines. Professional cameras used for standard broadcast television production capture images at a resolution of about 750 horizontal lines, and high-definition video cameras (HDV) capture 1,080 horizontal lines. When selecting a video camera for an application, pay attention to the lines of resolution recorded by the imaging device. It is an important property that will largely affect the final quality of your material.

Another major quality differentiator in video camera technology is based on the number of imaging surfaces used in the recording process. Basic video cameras have one imaging sensor, and all the visual information is recorded on this single imaging surface. More advanced video equipment has three imaging sensors, which record the red, blue, and green wavelengths of light separately. Red, blue, and green light can be combined in different ratios to create any color possible. When all three colors are added together equally, the result is white. The total absence of these three colors creates a black image. Recording the three **primary colors** (red, blue, and green) separately allows truer color reproduction and a sharper image. Three imaging sensors produce better quality images than a single imaging sensor.

Lens

Lenses control light coming into the camera in three significant ways. Lenses magnify, focus, and control the amount of light entering the camera.

Magnification. Lenses are classified in two categories: **prime lenses** (fixed **focal length** lenses) and **compound lenses** (a.k.a. variable focal length lenses and zoom lenses). A prime lens contains a single glass element, and its level of magnification cannot be changed. You cannot zoom in or out with a prime lens. Prime lenses generally require less light than compound lenses, and prime lenses generally produce a sharper image than compound lenses. Prime lenses were the standard in the early days of film and television, and because of their excellent quality and low-light benefits, prime lenses are preferred for many professional applications today. In all digital video cameras with permanent lenses, however, you will work with a compound lens. Some video cameras allow interchangeable lenses, and the mounting of either a prime or a compound lens.

A compound lens works by combining a number of glass elements within a lens housing. The elements within the lens housing can be moved to change its level of magnification. This is a valuable feature that adds much flexibility

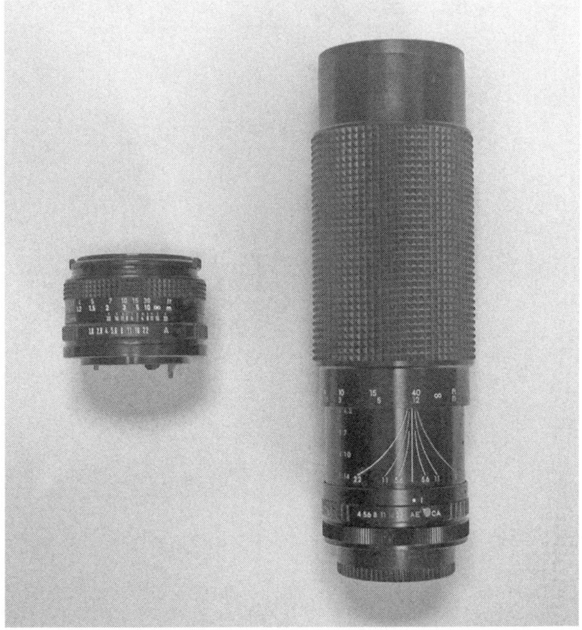

Figure 3.10 Prime and compound lenses.

for the camera operator working in the field. A composition made with a compound lens can be changed without physically moving the camera. For news and documentary coverage, the option of adjusting lens magnification quickly is crucial. A compound lens is often referred to as a **zoom lens**.

Lenses are defined by their focal length in millimeters. A 50mm lens is considered normal for 35mm cinematography. That is, a 50mm lens approximates the image size and field of view that you would perceive if looking from the camera position with your naked eye. When working in 35mm film, a lens shorter than 50mm, such as a 28mm lens, produces images in wide angle. A **wide-angle lens** produces a field of view that is wider than what would be perceived with the naked eye. Wide-angle lenses also exaggerate the actual distance between objects. A good way to remember this is to think of the side-view mirror of your car. This mirror is a wide-angle reflector to provide a wide field of view of what is around your car. We know it exaggerates distances because it says, "Objects in mirror are closer than they appear." Wide-angle lenses also exaggerate speed. Objects moving toward or away from the camera appear to move more quickly due to the rapid change in image size created by wide-angle lenses. Objects toward the edges will bend, and objects photographed very close to a wide-angle lens will appear rounded. An extreme wide-angle lens is referred to as a **fish eye**.

Conversely, a long lens, such as 120mm, is considered to be a **telephoto lens**. A telephoto lens magnifies the image more than the naked eye. Telephoto lenses are traditionally referred to as long lenses because, to work effectively, the lens element has to be moved farther away from the imaging device. This

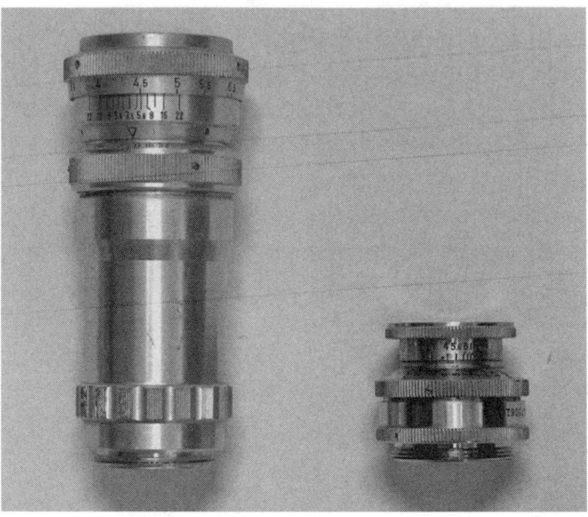

Figure 3.11 Long (telephoto) and short (wide-angle) prime lenses.

results in lens housings that are physically longer. Long lenses compress distances, and in general create an image that is considered to be flat.

The magnification power of a lens affects the way an image looks. It is important, therefore, not to set the focal length of your lens at a power of mere convenience to the position of the camera. If you want your shot to have a flat look and emphasize compression of depth, then move your camera farther away from the subject and set the magnification power higher.

In addition to describing lenses in terms of their focal length in millimeters, it is common to refer to lenses for video cameras in terms of their power. A compound lens for digital video might be called a 10X or a 12X. This refers to the level of magnification that can be achieved by the lens. Most consumer or **prosumer** video cameras have a lens that is close to normal at its widest setting, and this level of magnification increases from there to produce objects in the frame two times (2X) greater than actual size, 10 times (10X) greater than actual size, or more. In optical magnification, light is focused to create an enlarged appearance. This is the same principle used in simple microscopes, telescopes, and binoculars.

Most digital video cameras have an electronic control to change the level of lens magnification, often with a pivoting bidirectional button marked "T" for telephoto and "W" for wide-angle. This control is sometimes called a **rocker switch**. The telephoto control is generally forward of the wide-angle control. This allows for the thinking that to magnify the subject you push the button toward the subject, and to adjust the magnification away from the subject push the button away from the subject. It is important to know which direction to push for proper lens adjustment before your first big shoot. This operation should be second nature. A good videographer can control most major features of the camera without having to take an eye off the viewfinder.

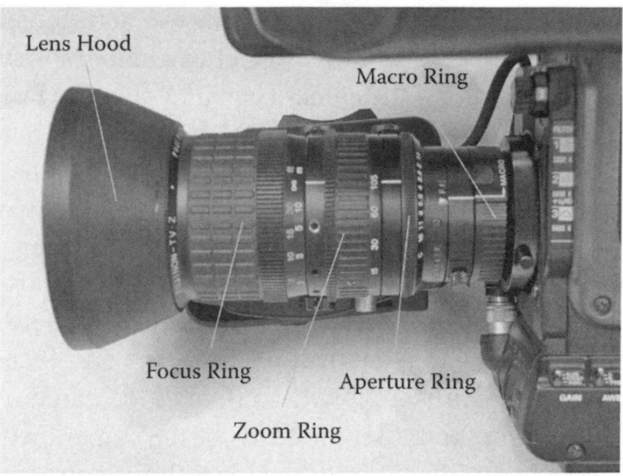

Figure 3.12 A zoom lens and its primary parts.

Some cameras only use one or two speeds for controlling the rate of lens magnification change. This can be limiting if you want to achieve an on-screen zoom effect and the change in magnification is a part of the shot itself. Other cameras use a **servo motor** to control lens magnification, which varies its rate of change depending on how much pressure is applied to the button.

High-end lenses have a zoom ring on the lens itself. A zoom ring allows precise and rapid changes in focal length, which can be valuable for special shots and documentary photography. A good videographer can make slight adjustments smoothly with a zoom ring.

Some video cameras offer the option of a **digital zoom**. This is not a feature of the lens at all, but rather an electronic processing of the video signal to magnify a portion of the image. This is generally not an effective feature because you can see the individual pixels that make up the image through magnification, and the effect is quite artificial. Do not use the digital zoom feature of a video camera unless working in a documentary situation in which it is absolutely necessary, or unless the pixilated effect is desired for aesthetic intent.

Focus. All lenses focus light. Our eyes have a lens, and we adjust the focus of this lens with the muscles of the eye. This process is fast and unconscious. As we shift our attention to a new object our eyes instantly and automatically adjust the lens of our eye to focus light on our retina.

Video camera lenses need to focus light as well. The **focal point** is defined as the fixed distance from the imaging surface at which light will converge with maximum sharpness. Most consumer and prosumer lenses have an **auto focus** feature, which usually operates by sending out an infrared signal and measuring the return of this signal to estimate the distance of objects from the camera. Auto focus systems can work quite well, and are appropriate in some circumstances. Auto focus can be a valuable tool in documentary photography, especially in circumstances where events are unfolding quickly, and the camera operator does not have the time to make careful focus adjustments. In most other creative applications in videography, however, auto focus should not be used. Professionals want to control this aspect of photography whenever possible. The auto-focus feature of the camera can only provide its best guess, and sometimes it will focus on the wrong element of a complex composition. It is better to manually control your focus whenever possible. Set the camera's focus control to manual override and control the focus of each shot yourself.

Setting Focus. There are some approaches to setting focus that will help you achieve your desired results. One of the basic rules for setting an accurate focus utilizes the lens magnification feature. To set the best focus, zoom all the way in as tight as the magnification will go. Direct the camera's field of view on the object you want in focus. Set the focus of the camera while zoomed in, and then zoom back out to the desired focal length for your composition. The process of zooming in not only magnifies the subject, but also magnifies any deviation from sharp focus. It is easier to set a sharp focus while zoomed in. When filming a human subject, use the person's eyes to set your focus. The audience is naturally drawn to the subject's eyes, and from a technical perspective the eyes are wet and glassy, which make them an ideal surface on which to check focus. When using this method it is important that your lens is calibrated correctly and that it holds focus. Lenses out of calibration will have a point of focus that drifts when zoomed in or out.

Some cameras have a **focal plane** indicated on the camera body. The focal plane symbol indicates the exact location of the imaging device within the camera. Knowing the location of the focal plane allows you to set focus using a measuring tape. Put one end of the tape at the focal plane, and pull the other end taut to the exact location of the object you want to have in focus. You can then set the focal point (in feet or meters) using the focal ring of the lens.

There is an additional approach for setting focus that can be valuable in many situations. You can use the auto-focus of the camera to your advantage without running the risk that the focus will shift and stray from your intended subject while shooting. For instance, assume that you are shooting an interview

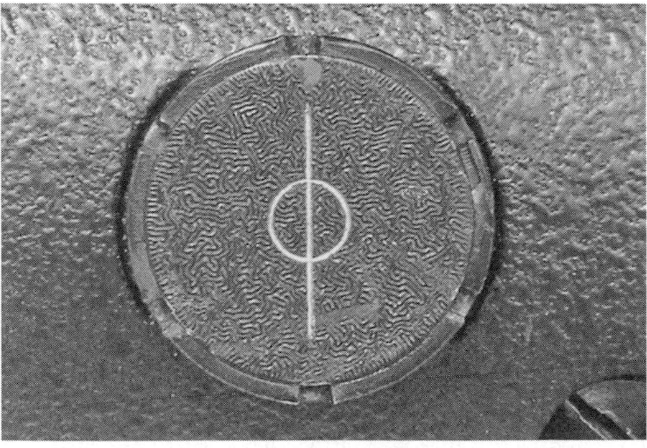

Figure 3.13 Focal plane. (Clinton Lathinghouse)

for a news segment or a documentary program. You have your composition set for an MLS (medium long shot) and the interview is going well. You had to set this up quickly, however, and you are not quite sure if the focus is perfectly sharp. You cannot zoom in to check the focus because the interview is in progress. One solution is to flip the camera to auto focus for just a moment or use the **push auto** control. This will allow the camera to make minor adjustments and to take an accurate focus reading on a stationary subject. You can then go back to manual focus and the focus point will stay locked on the last reading of the auto focus mode. This is good way to use auto-focus in a controlled manner.

The Aperture. The aperture setting controls how much lights passes through the lens to the imaging surface of the camera. While the aperture is part of the lens, the **aperture control** may or may not be on the lens itself. The aperture of a camera is sometimes called the **iris** as it operates much like the iris of the human eye, opening a hole wider or smaller to accommodate the intake of the proper amount of light. The camera's aperture is constructed with a series of overlapping plates that can be expanded or contracted to allow more or less light to pass through the lens.

It is important to be able to control the amount of light entering the camera because the imaging surface can only handle a fixed range of illumination to work properly. If too much light enters the camera, all that will be rendered is a white field. If too little light enters the camera, the audience will see only a black screen. Aperture control is needed for three main functions: proper exposure, creative exposure, and depth of field.

Proper Exposure. Not all environments have the same amount of light. Aperture control is needed to ensure proper exposure, as light levels vary from location to location. If you are filming outside on a sunny day, you'll have more light than you would inside during the late afternoon. To have each of these images exposed properly, the amount of light passing through the lens needs to be controlled. Generally, a small aperture setting is required for sunny days and a wider aperture setting is required to achieve proper exposure indoors at dusk. Adjusting the aperture to achieve proper exposure is only one of the aperture's functions. Proper exposure is not always the objective in videography.

Creative Exposure. A second utility of aperture control is that of creative exposure. You might wish to intentionally underexpose an image so that it looks dark and mysterious or you might have a composition that includes a wide range of shadows and highlights, and the aperture control allows you to choose which of these elements is set for an exposure that is consistent with your creative objectives. The aperture, therefore, is a powerful creative tool as well.

Video cameras contain an internal **light meter**, which measures how much light is entering the camera. When first working with a video camera you might not even be aware of the workings of the aperture. In automatic aperture mode, the camera itself determines the aperture setting. Be careful, however. Automatic aperture readings can serve as a reference, but ultimately the director of photography must make the final creative decision of how much light to let into the camera. You should be conscious of the light level and aperture setting for every shot, and override the automatic setting with a manual one to achieve your creative objectives.

Manual aperture overrides are often used to achieve proper exposure and to facilitate creative exposure. Sometimes the camera makes a mistake. Consider that your subject is standing in front of a bright window. The camera might think that you would like the light coming in from the window to be set at proper exposure, but this results in your foreground subject appearing very dark. You will need a manual override to correct for the camera's miscalculation. You can also use a manual override to achieve a specific creative effect. Perhaps you want to underexpose a scene to emphasize a sense of sadness, or perhaps you want to overexpose an image slightly to represent a dream or a vision of heaven. Manual aperture overrides help you achieve these effects in-camera.

When manually overexposing and underexposing images, it is important to consider a key factor of human perception. It is natural for people to see

a

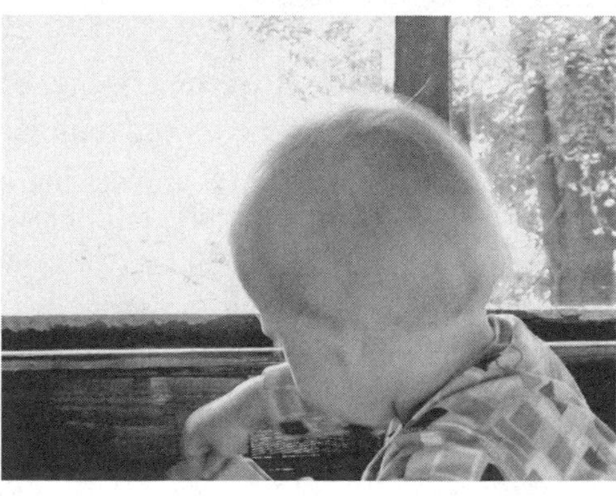

b

Figure 3.14 (a) A window in the composition can create a dark foreground. This might require a manual aperture override to achieve (b) proper foreground exposure.

images underexposed. When we walk outside in moonlight we see a world that is underexposed. We do not, however, see things overexposed. A video camera can produce an image where everything is blown out, but we do not see this way naturally. If there is too much light for our eyes to handle, we will squint and close our eyes. The human brain does not naturally create overexposed images. Therefore, when intentionally under- and overexposing images, remember that underexposure is an effect that represents natural experience while overexposure is not. Overexposure should therefore be used sparingly. It is not used frequently in video production, especially as an **in-camera effect**.

Most video cameras have a manual aperture control on the camera body or in the menu. You can select the manual override and adjust the amount of light entering the camera up and down. You might see this change in aperture setting represented with a bar scale, or you might see the setting represented using numerical values of the f-stop scale.

f-stops. Aperture settings are measured in f-stops. An **f-stop** is a mathematical ratio between the optical hole in the lens and the focal length of the lens. The normal f-stop scale reads as follows: 1, 1.4, 2, 2.8, 4, 5.6, 8, 11, 16, 22. As you can see, the numbers double at every other interval as you move up the scale. For example, look at the alternating f-stop numbers of this scale and you can see the doubling pattern 1, __, 2, __, 4, __, 8, __, 16, __. The same is true when we substitute the other half of the scale. __, 1.4, __, 2.8, __, 5.6, __, 11, __, 22. The only exception here is that a true doubling of 5.6 should yield a value of 11.2 and not 11, but the f-stop scale rounds this number down once the values reach double digits so that the scale does not need to be represented with three digits. If you are able to remember just a few numbers of the f-stop scale, you can fill in the rest easily. Complete the f-stop scale given here without looking at the examples above: 1, 1.4, 2, 2.8, __, __, __, __, __, 22. This is the normal range of the f-stop scale, but some lenses include values outside of this range. For example, there are some lenses that have f-stop values of 32 and above, and some with values less than 1. Other lenses contain an even narrower range of values than represented in this sample scale, and might begin at 2.8 or higher instead of 1.

The lower the f-value, or the numerical setting on the f-stop scale, the more light that is let into the lens. For example, an f-stop setting of 2 lets more light into the camera than an f-stop setting of 16. The f-stop scale works exponentially. Each time you raise or lower the f-stop setting one interval, you either

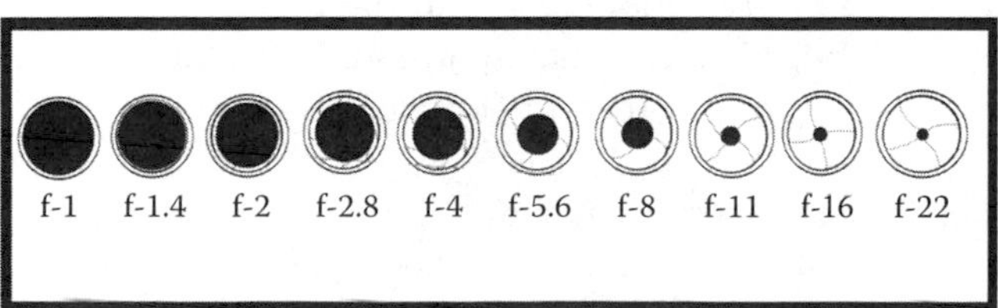

Figure 3.15 f-stop scale and aperture openings. (Jesse Knight)

halve or double the amount of light let into the camera. This is a little tricky. When you first consider the amount of light admitted to the camera between a setting of f/8 and f/4, you might be inclined to think that one of these settings lets in twice as much light as the other, but this is not the case. If you start at f/8 and move to f/5.6, you have doubled the amount of light entering the camera. If you move from f/5.6 to f/4, you have doubled the amount of light once again. Therefore the change in the amount of light passing through the lens from f/8 to f/4 is a four-fold increase. Similarly, any two-stop aperture adjustment, up or down the scale, will either decrease the light (quartering it) or increase the light (quadrupling it), which passes through the lens to the imaging surface.

The f-stop scale can handle a huge range of light values. Consider that your lens is set at f/22. You can lower the f-setting to f/16 and double the amount of light entering the lens. If you lower it again to f/11 you double the amount again for a four-fold increase over f/22. You can continue this process to f/8, f/5.6, f/4, f/2.8, f/2, f/1.4 and f/1. By the time you get to f/1 you are now allowing 512 times more light to pass into the camera than at f/22. Most lenses can handle a wide range of illumination.

It is possible to set your f-stop between two settings on many cameras, giving you even more control of the amount of light entering the lens. Sometimes a director of photography will say to the camera operator, "Set the lens between 4 and 5.6, closer to 4." The title of Federico Fellini's masterpiece, *8 1/2* (1963) derives a layer of meaning from the fact that 8 1/2 is a common f-stop setting between f/8 and f/11.

Sophisticated lenses have a physical **aperture ring** on the lens, and the camera operator can manually control the amount of light passing through the lens by rotating this ring and setting the f-stop setting to the corresponding hatch mark on the lens. When this type of lens is set for automatic light metering, you can see the aperture ring move on its own to make adjustments as light levels change.

t-stops. Some lenses measure the aperture setting with **t-stops** in addition to or instead of f-stops. This aperture measurement is more common on high-end lenses with powerful magnification and many glass elements. While the f-stop denotes the absolute size of the aperture opening in relation to the focal length, the t-stop takes into account the fact that some light is lost within the lens. Long lenses refract and absorb some of the light before it makes it to the aperture opening, so the t-stop is an adjusted measure that calculates the actual amount of light *transmitted* through the aperture. The "t" in t-stop is for transmission. T-stops are considered a more accurate guide for setting the aperture for correct exposure on compound lenses than f-stops.

Depth of Field. In addition to managing proper exposure and creative exposure, the aperture is also used to control **depth of field**. Depth of field refers to the range of distance that appears to be in focus. An image with a shallow depth of field only portrays a narrow range of depth in which objects appear in focus. An image with a deep depth of field might have all elements in the frame in focus including those just inches from the camera and others way off in the distance. Image-makers can use depth of field to direct the audience's attention and to support a creative objective. A shallow depth of field defines where the audience will direct their attention. The eye will naturally gravitate to the part of the image that is in focus, and therefore a shallow depth of field can be used to put the audience's attention where you want it.

Gregg Toland demonstrated unprecedented control of depth of field in Orson Welles's *Citizen Kane* (1941). *Citizen Kane* is considered by many to be the greatest film ever made, and should be studied by all students of film and video production for its technological and storytelling innovations.

Deep depth of field is often used in documentary production. In *Control Room* (2004), Jehane Noujaim takes the audience into the production center of Al-Jazeera television during the U.S. invasion of Iraq. As the viewer's eye explores the frantic control room, every part of the composition is in focus, which is how we would perceive the room if we were actually there. Deep depth of field is often used to convey realism.

To control depth of field you can change one or more of the following: lens focal length, aperture, focal point, and size of the imaging surface. Telephoto lenses have less depth of field than wide-angle lenses, so one way to control

b

Figure 3.16 (a) Shallow and (b) deep depth of field. (Courtesy of RiverDream Productions)

depth of field is to change the focal length of your lens. This adjustment might mean that you have to change the physical position of your camera. For example, if you want to achieve a shallow depth of field by using a telephoto lens, you might have to move the camera farther away from your subject to achieve a similar composition. The reverse applies for wide-angle lenses, which have a deep depth of field.

Depth of field can also be adjusted by manipulating the aperture. The narrower the aperture setting, the higher the f-stop number, and the deeper the depth of field will be. For instance, at an f-stop setting of f/22 the lens opening is small, creating a deep depth of field. Conversely, the wider the aperture setting (lower f-number), the shallower the depth of field will be. For instance, at an aperture setting of f/1 the lens opening is wide, causing a shallow depth of field.

To balance for proper exposure as you incrementally widen or narrow the aperture setting, you must correspondingly adjust the shutter speed. For example, if you open up the f-stop setting to create a shallow depth of field, you can compensate for the additional light by decreasing the shutter speed, which will lessen the amount of time each image is exposed to light. Doubling the amount of light entering the lens and cutting the exposure time in half will maintain consistent exposure. If you want a deep depth of field, slow down the shutter speed or add light to the set to allow for a small aperture setting.

A helpful tool for creating shallow depth of field is a **neutral density filter**. This filter reduces the overall level of light entering the camera without changing the color or the quality of the light. This can help create a shallow depth of field in a bright situation, such as shooting outdoors in full sunshine. The neutral density filter effectively reduces the amount of illumination entering the lens. This requires the camera operator to open up the aperture for proper exposure, which reduces depth of field.

In addition to focal length of the lens and aperture, focal point also affects depth of field. As the focal point of the lens is set farther from the camera, depth of field increases. A lens focused on a point 2 feet from the camera might have a depth of field of a few inches, while the same lens under the same conditions with the focal point set to 25 feet might have a depth of field that goes from 18 feet to infinity. Manipulating subject-to-camera distance is an effective way to alter depth of field in conjunction with the focal point setting. For a deep depth of field, put your subject away from the camera and focus accordingly. Moving the subject close to the camera and setting the focal point close will create less depth of field.

Depth of field is also affected by the size of the imaging surface. Smaller imaging surfaces create more depth of field. Eight-millimeter film cameras produce more depth of field than 35mm film cameras. Video cameras with small image sensors produce more depth of field than cameras with larger image sensors. A small imaging surface, however, also produces a lower quality picture than a larger imaging surface.

Maximum Sharpness Setting. Every lens has a **maximum sharpness setting**. This refers to the f-stop, or aperture setting, at which the point of focus is rendered with the best sharpness possible. While closing the aperture down increases depth of field (i.e., increases the total range of what appears to be in focus) the maximum sharpness at the point of focus is usually achieved with an aperture setting one or two stops from wide open. Therefore you must make choices when setting the f-stop. Do you want deep depth of field or maximum sharpness at the point of focus? They are each best achieved with different aperture settings. Since the setting for maximum sharpness varies for each lens, it is important to check the technical specifications of your lens to determine its maximum sharpness setting.

Macro Setting. Many compound lenses have a **macro setting**. By setting the camera's magnification level within the macro range, you can shoot extreme close-ups, such as filling the screen with a coin. This is achieved by placing the object very close to the camera lens, sometimes less than two inches away.

Lens Hood. Most lenses have a **lens hood** that helps keep out **light flares**. The lens hood also helps protect the lens by serving as a physical barrier around the glass surface. Lenses include a lens cap or a retractable door, which further protects the lens. Use it. Get in the habit of covering the lens whenever the camera is not in use. Dings and fingerprints easily damage lenses. Once a lens is damaged on a camera with a permanently attached lens, the camera is rendered virtually useless for professional applications.

Another valuable way to protect the lens is to cover it with a clear or UV (ultraviolet) filter. The outer parts of many lenses have screw threads, which allow the attachment of external filters. Check the size of your lens, measured in millimeters, and get a clear or **UV filter** of the matching size to protect the lens's outer element. If you do get debris or any marks, such as fingerprints, on your lens element, consult the manual for care instructions and leave any cleaning of severe marks to a professional. Cleaning with the wrong materials can make the damage worse and in some cases irreversible.

The Camera Body

The quality of your lens and how you control the lens is a large part of determining the final image that you capture with the camera. The camera body houses additional tools for image control and camera operation.

Power Switch. The first thing that needs to be done before recording is to turn the camera on. Most video cameras have power features beyond simple on and off. There is often a power-save mode, which works a lot like the standby on your computer by shutting down high-drain functions, such as powering the viewfinder, but keeping the internal components powered for quick operation.

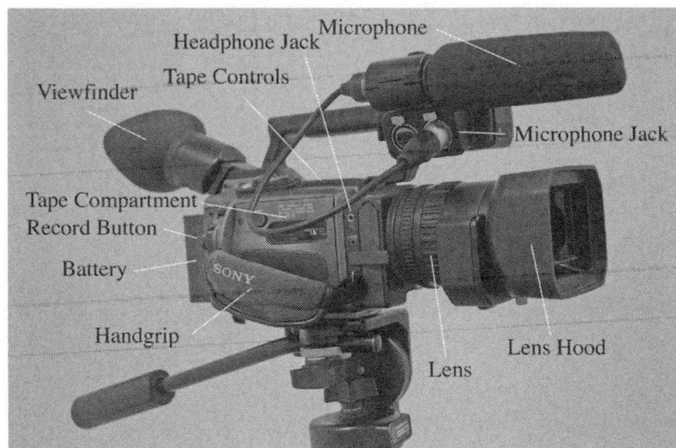

Figure 3.17 A digital video camera and its main features. (Emily Sarkissian)

Many cameras also have an automatic standby feature, which puts the camera into a power-saving mode if it has not been used for a fixed interval of time.

Batteries. Most cameras run under the power of a rechargeable battery, but it is also possible to run many camera models using A/C power. Make sure your batteries are fully charged before going out into the field, and that your batteries are charged according to the manufacturer's directions. Improperly charging batteries can damage them and shorten their life. When working in extreme conditions it is important to keep your equipment as evenly temperature regulated as possible. Cold will shorten the working time of your batteries and might make the camera motor and moving parts sluggish or inoperable. Heat can also damage batteries, cameras, tapes, and accessories. Dramatic changes in temperature and humidity can present other problems. Going from indoors where it is 65 degrees and low humidity to outdoors where it is 95 degrees and high humidity can cause instant condensation on the inside of your camera, making it inoperable until the condensation evaporates. This can take hours to finally resolve. Protect your gear.

Start/Stop Button. The camera's start/stop button controls the beginning and end of each shot. Some cameras have two start/stop buttons so you can easily reach one depending on whether you are working on a tripod or shooting handheld. The operation is simple. Press the button once and the camera starts recording; press it a second time and the camera stops recording. Make sure to verify that the camera is recording when you want it to by looking for the record indicator in the viewfinder. This may be a light in the margin of the visual display or a readout in the viewfinder such as REC. Get to know the sounds your camera makes and the subtle vibrations it gives off when it is running. Feeling this can be a great comfort when recording a critical shot. Beware of the "Uncle Bob syndrome." Uncle Bob is the one who shoots the family weddings and gets the start/stop control out of sync so that none of the events are recorded, but he gets all the footage of the floor in between.

Tally Light. The tally light is the little red light on the front of the camera that indicates the camera is recording. Some cameras do not have a tally light, and others allow you to disable this feature. If your camera has a **tally light** and does not have a disable option, you might want to cover the tally light in situations where it could be distracting rather than a benefit. Some interview subjects, for example, get nervous when they see the tally light come on and they freeze up.

Viewfinder. The viewfinder is your window through the lens. In addition to showing you exactly what the camera is recording, the **viewfinder** also displays other important information such as battery level and the amount of recording time remaining. Since the viewfinder is actually a miniature video monitor, it can be used for playback to check shots or to cue up a tape. If the image in the eyepiece viewfinder looks fuzzy, even after you focus the camera lens as best you can, check the **eyepiece focus** control, often found under the viewfinder. This control does not affect the image being recorded, but rather it adjusts the focus of the eyepiece itself for the eyesight of the camera operator. To set proper focus of the viewfinder, make sure the on-screen text in the viewfinder is in sharp focus. Most consumer and prosumer cameras also offer the option of a **view screen**, which can be opened from the side of the camera. This larger viewing area provides a picture of what is being recorded without having to keep your eye right up to the camera viewfinder. The disadvantages of using the view screen are that it drains power more rapidly than the smaller viewfinder, and since it is in the open environment it is vulnerable to glare from lights and the sun, making it difficult to see clearly under some conditions. Video cameras see differently from our naked eyes, so make sure to study each image in the camera's viewfinder or view screen to determine how the shot will look.

Microphone. Many cameras have a built-in **microphone (mic)**. The camera mic is usually stereo, which means that there are actually two microphones, each designed to pick up sound from a different direction. The sounds captured by each of these microphones are recorded on each of the two stereo audio tracks of the recording media, which results in stereo sound during playback. The camera microphone is rarely used in professional video production except to record ambient sound or perhaps as a back-up mic in some cases. The camera mic is often a relatively low-quality microphone, and it cannot pick up sound with optimum clarity in most situations because, in part, it is a fixed part of the camera. In fact, when the camera mic is used you can sometimes hear the camera motor on the soundtrack. This is not good. Most cameras, however, also have an external microphone jack that allows you to plug in any type of microphone that best serves the needs of each shooting situation. This feature also gives you the flexibility to place a microphone in the best location to gather the sounds that you need. Chapter 7 explores external microphone options and their applications for video production.

Headphone Jack. The headphone jack allows you to patch a set of **headphones** into the camera. Always use headphones to monitor all audio recording to make sure the sound is coming through in high quality. This will confirm that the microphone is working and the cables are connected properly. Headphones also allow you to monitor the audio tracks in playback after recording so you can confirm that the sound was captured properly, and there are no problems with the recording heads or the recording medium such as wrinkled tape or a bad drive sector.

Playback Control. The playback control buttons allow you to use the camera as a player for monitoring what you have recorded using the view screen and headsets. Playback reviews can also be done via an external video monitor and audio speakers by using the audio and video outputs of the camera.

Media Storage. The media storage compartment houses the videotape, memory card, hard drive, or optical media that records video and audio information. While videotape has the disadvantage of working in a linear form, it does have the advantage of good reliability. Sometimes a segment of videotape will fail due to a tape wrinkle or **dropout**, but it is rare that a tape failure results in the loss of all data on the tape. Even if videotape rips or snaps, professional repair can recover most of the content. This is not the case with hard-drive storage. When a computer hard drive is used to capture video directly from the camera and it fails, the result is often a loss of all data. For this reason, many productions that use direct computer storage for capture also simultaneously record the material on a tape for insurance. Another advantage of videotape is that it has a longer storage life than computer drives. All storage media will degenerate over time, but videotape is a good option for long-term archiving. Protect all stored media from extreme temperature and humidity.

Handgrip. The handgrip allows you to comfortably and securely hold and operate the camera. Shooting handheld is a favored approach in much documentary and news photography. It can also be an effective and dramatic technique in fiction filmmaking.

Time Code Indicator. Most video cameras generate and record **time code** on the storage media. Time code is a number generated to identify each frame of your material. This is a valuable tool for logging and editing your footage. When new storage media are put into a camera, some cameras start the time code at zero. Other cameras keep a memory of the last frame of time code recorded, and continue generating time code in succession, even if new media is inserted. Beware that having a blank or unrecorded interval when using linear videotape can cause a **time code break (TCB)**. This can happen when a shot is played back on location and the tape is not queued up correctly, which leaves a blank space on the tape. Many cameras will not know what to do and will start time code over from the beginning. Time code breaks can create problems in editing.

Time code is generally given in hours, minutes, seconds, and frames. The indicator might look like this: 01:23:46:18. Some systems also have an additional category for recording the tape, drive, or disk number. This is helpful for keeping track of the footage for large projects. Time code is usually displayed in the viewfinder or view screen, and sometimes on an external display window on the camera body. Get to know your camera's time code functions and how they are set and reset.

During shooting, it is valuable for a camera assistant to keep a **shot log** with reference to the time code indicator. The shot log documents key information about every shot recorded on location including the start and stop time of every shot according to the time code, the content of the shot, and notes about the quality of each shot. Write down what was good and bad about each shot, and make note of editing considerations or recommendations. This effort will provide guidance and save time in postproduction.

Shutter Speed. The **shutter speed** determines how long each image, or frame, is exposed to light by the camera. Since digital video cameras generally record 30 frames per second, the slowest shutter speed that can be used for normal motion is about 1/30th of a second. The standard shutter speed for digital video cameras is about 1/60th of a second depending on the model. Knowing the standard shutter speed of your camera is important to allow you to work with external light meters, which we will explore in chapter 6. You can adjust the shutter speed along a wide range of options, sometimes to rates as fast as 1/10,000th of a second.

Changing the shutter speed affects the amount of the light entering the camera for each frame, and therefore shutter speed can be used in conjunction with aperture to manipulate depth of field. Changing the shutter speed also affects the quality of the image, however, so shutter speed must be manipulated with consideration of the effects.

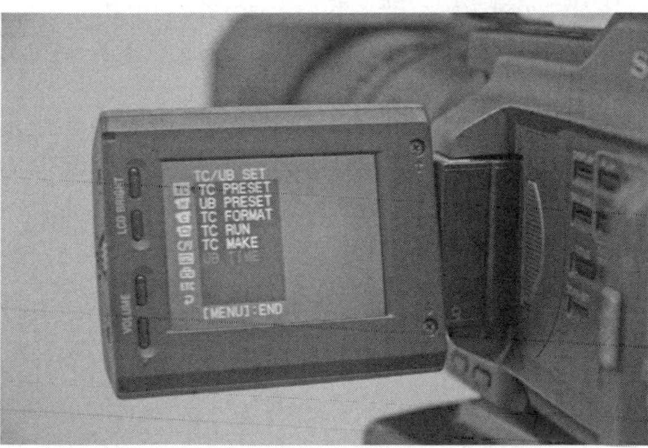

Figure 3.18 Time code settings in a camera's view screen menu. (Emily Sarkissian)

Since the human brain only processes about 10 to 12 images per second, we perceive a blurring and soft edges to quickly moving objects. Shutter speeds in motion picture of about 1/60 to 1/125 preserve this blurring in their exposure times. Moving objects actually blur slightly in each individual frame, thus preserving this perceptual phenomenon during playback. Faster shutter speeds, such as 1/500 to 1/10,000, freeze moving objects in place with great clarity. This can be an asset for video recordings to conduct motion analysis or for a creative objective, but the outcome in playback is an unrealistic effect. Since each frame is played back at about a rate of 1/30th of a second, a fast shutter speed can cause a strobing of moving objects, which is not how we normally see. When we see a puddle splash with our naked eye we see a blur of water. When we watch a playback of a splash of water in which each frame was recorded at 1/10,000th of a second we perceive individual water droplets frozen in the air, which strobe as they move from one frame to the next. Fast shutter speeds do not render moving objects realistically in playback.

Gain. The **video gain control** allows you to electronically boost the sensitivity of the imaging system to capture images in low-light situations. There is a trade-off for using this feature. Boosting the gain to render an image in low light creates a grainy image with interference (also referred to as noise). When boosting video gain, the blacks in the image turn to a grainy gray. The gain should not be boosted if you have the option to supplement the set with more light. High levels of gain should only be used when absolutely necessary. In general, keep the video gain control off or applied at a low level. Gain is measured in db. Boosting the image +3db will increase the camera's sensitivity slightly and produce little noise. Boosting the gain +18db will increase the camera's light sensitivity significantly, but also will create a noticeably grainy image. Many cameras have an **automatic gain control (AGC)**, which is used to adjust the level of video gain automatically to compensate for low-light conditions.

Aspect Ratio. Many camera models allow you to select either standard (4:3) or wide-screen (16:9) recording. The dual format is made possible by masking the unused portion of the frame.

Image Stabilization. The **image stabilizer** setting on your camera is a function that electronically processes the video signal to remove the shake from handheld videography by digitally sampling the image and taking these variations out. For the professional videographer this is a feature that should generally be avoided. If you want to avoid shake, use a tripod, shoot in wide angle, or practice keeping the camera steady. Any time you process the signal you lose quality, and this automatic feature sacrifices control.

Backlight Feature. Your camera has a setting that allows you to correct for a strong backlight, such as a person standing in front of a window. The light meter of the camera might take a reading for the bright window, and not your subject in the foreground. The **backlight setting** is merely a shortcut to force the camera to increase the size of the aperture opening. It can be useful in a pinch, but generally you should switch to manual aperture control in this situation and set the iris for the exact exposure that you want.

White Balance. Light color can vary and the video camera needs to correct for this variation. Digital video cameras generally do a good job of automatically color-balancing the image, but you should manually control this function whenever possible. The **white balance** feature allows this manual control. We will discuss light color and white balance in greater detail in chapter 6.

In addition to the parts and features listed above, most cameras include other functions such as a fade button, date and time indicators, and a multitude of display features and digital effects. Higher-end cameras contain additional controls for refined calibration and manual control. See the manual of the specific camera you will be using to learn all of its features and proper care. Keep in mind that some of the features on your camera are designed for people who will not have access to editing equipment. You, however, will want to add special effects in postproduction. Putting a fade or digital effect on a shot in the camera makes it permanent. If you capture the shot unaltered then you keep all your options available in editing.

TRIPODS

The **tripod** is the most basic and universal camera support available. It is efficient in its design. It can be lightweight or sturdy depending on the model. It provides stability, and it allows for careful compositions that can be locked down and recorded.

Tripods share some universal parts and functions, and the understanding of how one tripod works translates easily to an understanding of most available models. As its name suggests, the tripod has three legs. At the base of each of these legs is a foot where the tripod makes contact with the ground. The legs are usually adjustable, allowing the camera to be set within a variable range of height. Simple tripods have a rubber cup on the ends of the legs to protect floor surfaces. Other tripods have hinged feet, which pivot and add greater stability as the angle of the tripod legs is changed. Some tripods have pointed feet, which allow the tripod to be planted firmly on natural ground, but these types of tripods require a **spreader** when used on hard surfaces. A spreader serves as a flat base for the tripod legs to mount evenly. The spreader can be adjusted to allow the tripod legs to be lowered to various levels. Spreaders are also used for safety. They stabilize the tripod, making it less likely to fall or be knocked over.

Figure 3.19 Tripods come in models for working light and fast or solid and stable.

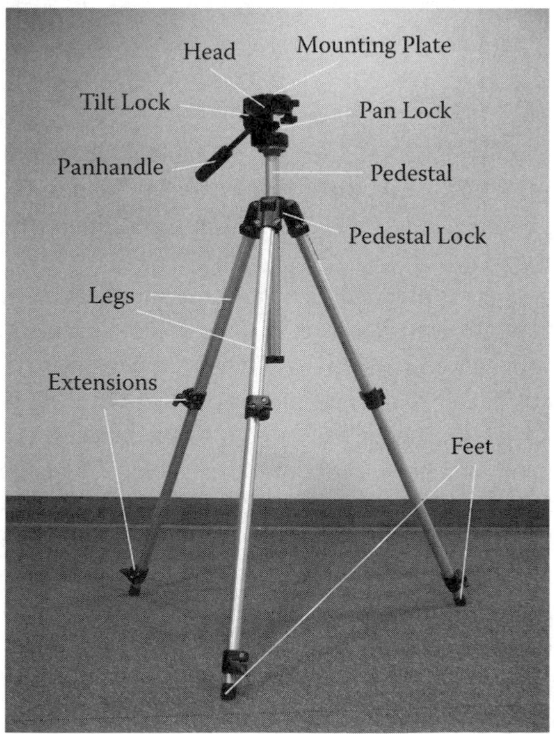

Figure 3.20 A basic tripod and its parts.

Above the legs on many models is a **pedestal**. The pedestal is a vertical post that can be raised or lowered. The **pedestal lock** keeps the pedestal from moving inadvertently, and the **pedestal crank** (found on more advanced models) allows the operator to make upward and downward adjustments. Operating a tripod at the top of its pedestal range can make the camera shaky when panning and tilting. A high pedestal shot is best recorded as a static shot.

Above the legs and pedestal of the tripod is the head. The tripod head is the foundation of much of its operation and function. Some tripod heads are permanently mounted to the pedestal. Other systems have interchangeable heads, which can be removed and reattached using a ball joint. The ball joint also serves as a leveling feature, which allows the camera operator to make fine adjustments to the position of the tripod head. This is helpful when the tripod is set up on an uneven surface. Some tripod heads have a built-in bubble level to aid in adjustment. Tripods that do not have a leveling head can be leveled by adjusting the extension of each of the legs, but this can be cumbersome for making minor adjustments, especially once the camera is mounted.

Additional parts and controls of the tripod head include the **panhandle**, the **pan lock,** and the **tilt lock**. These controls allow moving camera shots. By loosening the pan lock, you enable the tripod head to move from side to side, thus allowing the execution of pan shots. Loosening the tilt lock allows the tripod head to be tilted up and down. Advanced tripod systems include a separate control for **pan drag** and **tilt drag**. These controls fine-tune resistance in the tripod movement and are valuable for achieving smooth and steady camera moves.

It is important to tighten the tilt lock at the end of each shot series and to never leave a camera unattended on a tripod head. If a camera is left on the tripod head unattended and the tilt lock is loose, the camera can fall forward or backward under its own weight. The momentum of the flopping camera can bring the tripod and camera crashing down, creating a very bad situation. Always tighten the tilt lock before taking your hands off the equipment and remove the camera from the tripod head when it must be left unattended.

The **tripod plate** attaches and releases the camera from the tripod head. In fact, tripod plates are often referred to as **quick-release plates**. This term originated in contrast to older forms of tripod designs where the camera had to be directly screwed onto the tripod head. This was a cumbersome design. Fortunately, virtually all field tripods now include a quick-release design.

Each camera has a thread on the bottom to receive the bolt for mounting a tripod plate. Often tripod plates also have a pin, which fits into the camera bottom for a second point of contact. This keeps the camera from spinning inadvertently on the tripod. The plate is designed to snap into the tripod head and be released with the touch of a button or turn of a lever.

The panhandle moves the camera when panning or tilting. Its distance from the camera generally allows for better leverage and smoother movement than attempting to move the camera directly.

There are two main types of tripod head. **Spring heads** (or friction heads) pan and tilt against a spring or with the resistance of mechanical parts. A **fluid head** is far superior and contains viscous oil, which provides smoother movement.

ADVANCED CAMERA SUPPORT SYSTEMS

The tripod is the most basic and popular means of supporting a camera, but many other options exist. Advanced support systems allow even greater shot

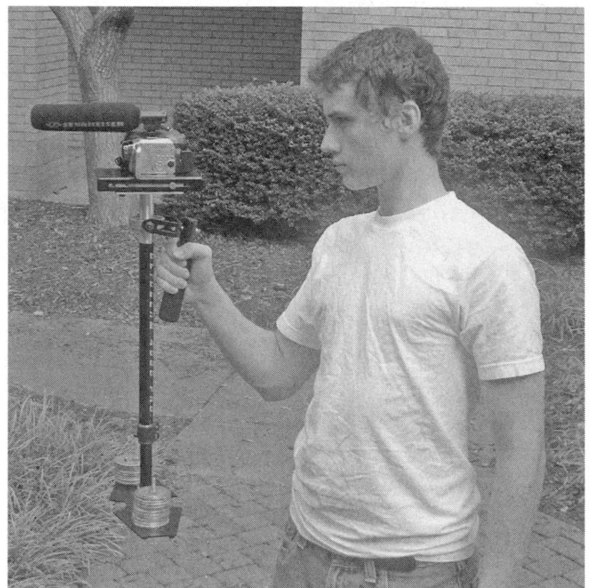

Figure 3.21 A Glidecam camera stabilizer for small-format video. (Kenneth George)

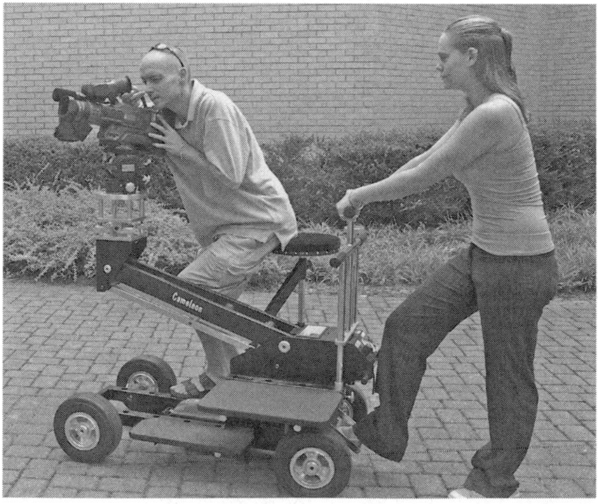

Figure 3.22 Camera dolly. (Emily Sarkissian)

variety and versatility. The **Steadycam** is a proprietary system that won an Academy Award for technical achievement. The Steadycam is worn over the shoulders and is designed to counterbalance the weight of a camera, which allows remarkably smooth movement in handheld cinematography. Other shake-reducing systems have since been introduced, including the **Glidecam.**

We discussed the term "dolly" in chapter 2 to describe a type of shot in which the camera moves either toward the subject or away from the subject. Dolly is also used to describe a piece of camera support equipment, which achieves this movement. A camera dolly is a wheeled mechanism that can roll on the floor, or on specially designed tracks, which moves the camera toward the subject, away from the subject, or tracking alongside the subject.

The **walk and talk** tracks characters with a dolly-mounted camera as they move and converse. This shooting method is utilized in many programs including *Annie Hall* (1977) and the television series *Lost*. This technique maintains the same coverage of the characters (a two-shot, for instance) while the back-

Figure 3.23 Camera jib. (Chris Walker)

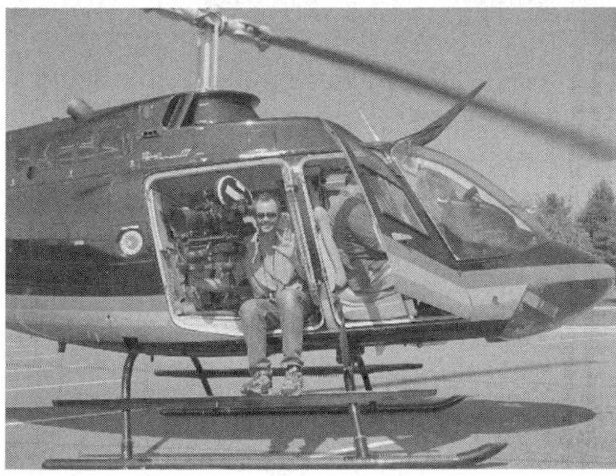

Figure 3.24 Helicopter mount. (Courtesy of Bonesteel Films)

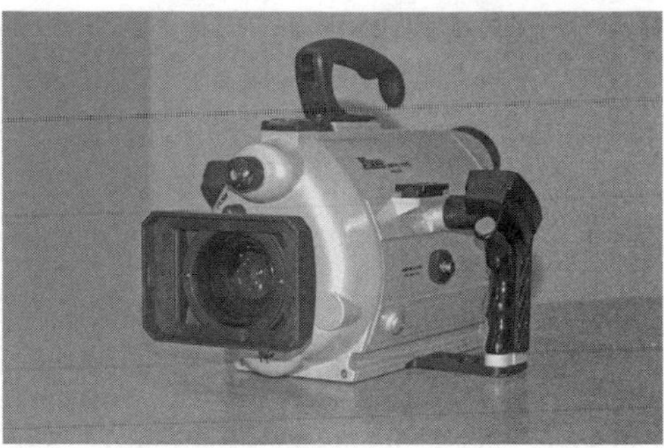

Figure 3.25 Marine housing. (Emily Sarkissian)

ground keeps changing. This makes the shot more visually interesting than a static shot of two people sitting.

Professional dollies often incorporate a hydraulic arm that can move up and down, thereby greatly increasing camera move options. While professional dollies are expensive, basic dolly moves can be achieved with a homemade system using small wheels attached to a platform.

Another camera support option is the **jib arm**. These systems can lower a camera to ground level or raise it 15 or 20 feet in the air. A crane takes the vertical movement of the jib and extends it to an even greater range. Professional **camera cranes** can lift the camera 50 feet or more into the air.

Other types of mounting systems and camera housings allow you to get innovative and unique shots. There are **vehicle mounts** that use heavy vacuum seals to attach a camera to a car or truck. Other vehicle mount systems use platforms attached to the bumper.

Helicopter mounts allow fantastic aerial photography. Some mounts are designed for operator control from the side door of a helicopter. In other cases, such as for television news production, gyroscopic mounts are permanently installed underneath a helicopter in a bubble housing and the camera is directed by remote control.

Bringing a camera high into the skies is not the only direction you can travel to achieve unique photography. A marine housing allows you to go deep underwater. Some marine housings are **universal housings** designed to hold a variety of camera models. Other marine housings are dedicated to work with a specific camera model. Professional marine housings can dive to tremendous depths well beyond the range of sport certification. With these additional tools the field is wide open for the types of shots that you can capture.

APPROACHES IN CINEMATOGRAPHY AND VIDEOGRAPHY

One of the first things a cinematographer or videographer must do before shooting begins is determine the look of a project. Some videographers have a distinct way of shooting and their work is often recognizable. Other videographers select a visual tone based on the content of the script. In other cases, the director might provide extensive guidance to cinematic orientation and parameters. There are many different visual approaches that can be applied to a script.

You have a world of stylistic choices in the visual arts. Just a few approaches in painting, for example, include realism, expressionism, impressionism, and surrealism. In realism, the goal of the artist is to represent objects in the painting as realistically as possible. You might have seen paintings in a gallery that are so realistic they look like photographs. This type of painting is sometimes called photorealism.

Expressionism has a different fundamental goal. In expressionism, the artist portrays objects, situations, and events in a style that evokes an emotional reaction about the subject. Impressionism, by contrast, strives to achieve a feeling of what it is like to have a sense of objects, events, or places. Impressionist images feel like a memory, or a mental afterimage, which captures the basic essence of the subject. Surrealism strives to present the world of dream logic and the unconscious mind.

Each of these artistic approaches, and many others not listed here, can be applied to motion pictures. Each approach has distinguishing use of light, focus, and camera angle. Your first impulse might be to approach your visual program with a highly realistic style. This is a good place to begin. It is valuable in any artistic training to master the tools of realism before applying more abstract forms. Even Picasso started with realistic paintings.

Realism

The film theorist Siegfried Kracauer (1960) believed that only realistic motion pictures are cinematic. He based his argument on the clarity of the image provided by film and the accuracy of perception of motion on film. Realistic pic-

Figure 3.26 Documentaries often utilize a naturalistic visual style with existing light and compositions that put elements into context. (*Kenya: Where Women Rule;* courtesy of Filmaker's Library)

tures, he argued, serve and pay homage to the material of the world. While other styles work to transcend the world, the realist filmmaker observes it; he does not escape it. Realist images are produced through the use of specific camera techniques.

To achieve a realistic look in film and video production, the focus of the camera must be sharp. Our eyes see real objects clearly, so the images on the screen must be sharp. The lighting must also look realistic. A good way to achieve realistic lighting is to start with **practical sources**. These are lights that exist in the environment before the filmmaker arrives and include windows, skylights, table lamps, fireplaces, and light fixtures. Rarely do the practical light sources provide light exactly where you need it, or provide enough light for a film or video camera to function properly. Filmmakers often move existing lights to accommodate the scene, and they often hide supplemental lights out of the frame to increase the overall level of illumination. It is important to make sure that supplemental lights look like they are coming from the table lamp, fireplace, or other practical source when striving for realism.

Documentary filmmaking, by its very nature, often utilizes a realistic visual approach. Fiction filmmakers borrow the tools of the documentarian to create dramatic fictional stories that feel real for the viewer. Many films, such as *Dog Day Afternoon* (1975), *Jaws* (1975), and *Man Bites Dog* (1992) use handheld cameras to give a documentary feel to these works. In *Dog Day Afternoon*, the audience feels like they are watching a hostage crisis on the news. The sea hunting sequences in *Jaws* look like they could be from a *National Geographic* special, and *Man Bites Dog* is a fictional story that is constructed to look like a documentary about an assassin. Television has adopted this technique as well. Virtually all prime-time police dramas integrate the use of a handheld camera. *Homicide: Life on the Street* (1993-1999) was filmed handheld exclusively. Even advertisers exploit the psychological association of this method. Sometimes interviews with satisfied customers in commercials are actually scripted performances by actors, but the subtle movement of the frame with a handheld camera is used to suggest to the audience that this is real.

Figure 3.27 Realism seeks to reproduce natural experience on film or video. (Courtesy of Paul Schattel)

Figure 3.28 Expressionism utilizes high contrast and exaggerated imagery to evoke a mood or feeling. (*The Cabinet of Dr. Caligari* [1920])

Expressionism and Film Noir

Expressionism is characterized by the control of images to create a mood or to convey a particular viewpoint. Expressionistic cinematography is sometimes called self-conscious because its dramatic techniques call attention to the fact that we are watching a staged image.

Expressionism was epitomized by the German expressionist movement in art, and was carried over into German films after World War I. The Germans felt a great deal of despair in the aftermath of the war and artists of all disciplines expressed this in their work. Filmmakers participated in this movement with works that were dark in visual tone, with stylized lighting cast from severe angles, and bizarre and fantastic stories. The expressionist movement in film was launched with Robert Wiene's *The Cabinet of Dr. Caligari* (1920) and is perhaps best exemplified by Fritz Lang's *Metropolis* (1927).

Hollywood adapted some of the techniques of the expressionists to create a new genre of entertainment programming called film noir. Film noir, French for "dark cinema" or "dark film," was first used to describe films coming out of Hollywood in the late 1930s. The label was widely applied to crime and detective films of the 1940s and early 50s. Film noir uses a distinct lighting style with single sources and images dominated by shadows and dark spaces. The feeling is raw, and the dark side of human nature is almost palpable on the screen.

Impressionism

Many films of the "Golden Age of Hollywood" exhibit characteristics of impressionism. Impressionist art uses diffused images to convey an idea about the subject that goes beyond the viewer's realistic assessment. In the black and white film era, images were softened using camera filters to convey an impression of some emotional state. For example, the lighting of main characters in many love stories creates a glow with an ethereal charm, suggesting that there is something magical between the two lovers. The soft, beautiful light, twinkling eyes, and foggy filtered images of actors portraying the rich and famous were not realistic, but they created a psychological and emotional impression of what it is like to live that lifestyle, or what a memory of that time would reflect. Just as Monet's "Water Lilies" paintings do not look like a pond, but rather a memory of a pond, so too does impressionist cinema convey a romantic memory.

Surrealism

Founded in Europe, Surrealism was a formal artistic movement of the 1920s and 30s. Surrealism means "beyond reality" or "above reality." The essence of surrealism is concrete irrationality. The surrealist image is often highly realistic, but also irrational. The elements within the frame do not match normal experience. We might see a woman with a fish's head or a lion leaping out of a pomegranate. Surrealism is based on psychoanalytic psychology, particularly dream analysis. Dreams are concrete but irrational. The Hollywood cliché for a dream sequence is to blur the image, but actual dreams are vivid. Alfred Hitchcock recognized this and hired the surrealist painter Salvador Dalí to design the dream sequences for his film *Spellbound* (1945). The surrealist image has been a part of motion pictures since the 1920s. Films such as *Un Chien Andalou* (1929), *Eraserhead* (1977), and *Naked Lunch* (1991) are dedicated to bringing our dreams and nightmares to life on the screen.

This is just a sampling of visual approaches to give you a reference as you plan your own creative approaches in videography. You need not conform to any one established style in designing your programs, but an understanding of different artistic approaches will expand your options as you face production choices.

CONCLUSIONS

You now have the tools to turn your script into a collection of images. You have surveyed the evolution of motion picture technology and know the available formats. As you advance in your practice and have the full range of options available, you can choose to record in standard (NTSC or PAL) or high-definition (HDTV) television. You can select an aspect ratio and compose your program in either standard (4:3) or widescreen (16:9). You might want to shoot in 24P to capture more of a "film look."

Regardless of the format of the equipment you use, the elements of successful videography are universal across platforms. By using the lens and adjusting the aperture, focal length, and focal point, you can control the light entering the camera. The camera functions including shutter speed, white balance, gain, and others will further define the final image. You have surveyed the different tools that can be used to support your camera including the range of professional high-end systems, and the workhorse basics, including the tripod and going handheld.

As you record your first scene, consider how it will look when put together and make sure you get all the shots you need. Check each shot using the view screen or an external monitor, and plan how the overall scene will look once it is edited. Consider what aesthetic approach you will take. For example, will your approach be realistic, expressionistic, impressionistic, or perhaps surrealistic? The next step will be to edit your shots together into a cohesive program. In the following chapter we explore the principles of editing and examine the tools for making it all come together.

SAMPLE EXERCISES

1. Design and shoot a two-minute master scene. Use the technical information in this chapter to realize the principles of the visual language you learned in chapter 2.
2. Shoot some camera tests. Can you create a shallow depth of field? How can you take that same composition and convert it into one with a deep depth of field? Practice handheld camera work. Describe how you could improvise a dolly shot with available resources.
3. Of the artistic approaches introduced in this chapter, which is your favorite artistic approach: realism, expressionism, impressionism, or surrealism? Write a scene in this style and outline how you would portray this approach visually.

RECOMMENDED READINGS

Grotticelli, M. (2001). *American Cinematographer Video Manual* (3rd ed.). Hollywood: ASC Press.

Malkiewicz, J. K., Mullen, M. D. (2005). *Cinematography: A Guide for Filmmakers and Film Teachers*. New York: Simon & Schuster.

Wheeler, P. (2001). *Digital Cinematography*. Boston: Focal Press.

REFERENCES

Kracauer, S. (1960). *Theory of Film: The Redemption of Physical Reality*. London: Oxford University Press.

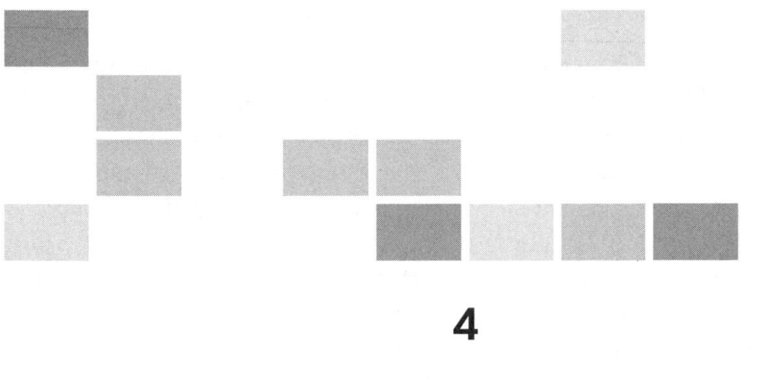

4

EDITING

CHAPTER OBJECTIVES

Without the editor there is no program. There is only a pile of tapes or disk drives. The editor creates the meaning of a program. The same raw footage can be cut together as comedy or tragedy depending on what the editor chooses to include and the timing and order of assembly. When people talk about films and video production they often talk about the wonderful acting, directing, writing, and camera work. The audience is less likely to discuss the editing. This is because successful editing is often invisible. Good editing allows other artists to shine. The editor is the unsung hero of the production process. Sitting in the dark, often alone, for days and weeks on end, poring over the material, the editor emerges with a unified work of art. In this chapter we explore the creative and technical processes of motion-picture editing. The goals of this chapter are to:

- Explore the theoretical foundations for editorial decisions;
- Gain an understanding of the universal features of computer-based video editing systems;
- Survey historical developments in editing techniques;
- Provide a skill base to build your first visual program in postproduction.

In video production, the term *editing* most commonly describes the process of assembling individual shots into a cohesive program. In a larger sense, however, the process of editing is a continual one. You edit your notes as you create story ideas. You make editorial decisions in choosing which shots to capture during your time on location. All of these decisions contribute to the formal process of editing in a postproduction suite.

On small projects there is usually one editor who rearranges pictures and sounds into the order of the final program. On larger projects the editor might have one or more assistants who help with routine tasks and technical implementation of creative decisions. Editing in the studio system is an apprenticeship craft. In Hollywood, assistant editors generally work their way up the creative hierarchy to the role of editor over many years.

In this chapter, you will learn how to assemble the material recorded in the field into a complete program. We will first examine practical and artistic considerations in editing; then we will examine the tools of the editor and explore the technical process of motion-picture editing.

EDITING IS SELECTING

The editor works with the director to make decisions about which images to include in a program and in what order to present those images. The editor's autonomy in this process varies. Some directors are known to give the editor wide latitude in making editorial choices, such as Woody Allen, who gave great creative freedom to Wendy Greene Bricmont and Ralph Rosenblum in the editing of *Annie Hall* (1977). Other directors, such as Martin Scorsese, are known to work closely with the editor in a creative partnership. In the process of editing *Raging Bull* (1980), Scorsese is reported to have looked over the shoulder of the editor throughout most of the editing process, conferring on virtually every decision. Generally, editing is not a group activity. Most professional directors and producers leave their editors alone while they organize their shots into scenes and scenes into programs; then these professionals have periodic meetings to give the editor feedback on his or her work.

Editing is being selective. You might have 15 minutes of footage for your first scene, which eventually might be cut down to 3 minutes. It is not uncommon for a feature-length project to begin as 50 hours of raw footage. The pro-

Figure 4.1 *Sunny Intervals and Showers* documents the life of a man with bipolar disorder over the course of a year. The editor had to condense this year into less than two hours of screen time. (Courtesy of Filmaker's Library)

Figure 4.2 The director meets with the editor to review progress and to suggest changes. (Apryl Blakeney).

portion of footage shot to the running time of the final program is called the **shooting ratio**. A two-hour film made from 50 hours of material has a shooting ratio of 25 to 1. A 15-minute tape that is reduced to a 3-minute scene has a shooting ratio of 5 to 1. Your job as an editor is to mine the gems from raw footage and to craft the material into a unified program.

The process of editing varies by project type. Nonfiction programs are often written in the editing process. In many cases, the documentary camera team scrambles to gather as much interesting material as possible while on location, and it is the job of the editor to distill a mountain of raw footage into a story. Fiction work is generally more structured than nonfiction in postproduction. Television commercials tend to be the most highly structured projects for the editor. In many cases, the script for a commercial is planned out to the very second to maximize the impact of this short form. Regardless of the form, all video editing is about making sense of raw material, and one of the tools the editor uses to begin this process is the shot log.

The **shot log** documents information about each shot recorded in the field, which helps the editor make choices. A good editor spends time with the material and allows options to circulate in his imagination. Some editors begin cutting in precise order; others lay down broad elements and experiment and refine from there.

Much of video editing is taking out the mistakes. You can eliminate a great deal of footage because of poor lighting, bad camera moves, and an actor's flubbed lines. Most of the editing process, however, is not so clearly defined. The editor needs to choose which reaction shot best fits the mood of the scene, when to cut to the hero, how long to hold the shot of the sunset, and whether to use the sunset at all. The permutations of constructing the order and duration of shots in a program are virtually infinite, and there is no single best way to build a visual program. Editing is making choices and realizing your vision. The audience seldom thinks of the editor's role, but the editor is the one who defines every moment in the final program and what the audience sees and feels.

Editing Styles

Just as there are styles that influence the way a videographer uses the camera, there are stylistic choices in editing as well. Many European filmmakers, including Sergei Eisenstein, Robert Bresson, and Alfred Hitchcock, believed the meaning of each individual shot is amplified and clarified based on how it is placed in relationship to other shots. Soviet filmmaker V. I. Pudovkin (1949) described film as a "plastic medium" because of its variability of achieving meaning through editing. Eisenstein (1949) took the point even further, arguing that the real meaning in motion pictures lies not at all in the content of individual shots but rather in the **juxtaposition** of shots. Meaning is created, he argued, when images collide into one another. He considered editing a dynamic process.

Eisenstein developed his theory of motion picture editing based on his study of Japanese language. Eisenstein was fascinated by the nature of Japanese ideograms, which represent words and ideas with pictures. In Japanese language there is a picture, or ideogram, that represents a knife. There is also an ideogram that represents a heart. When these two pictures are placed side

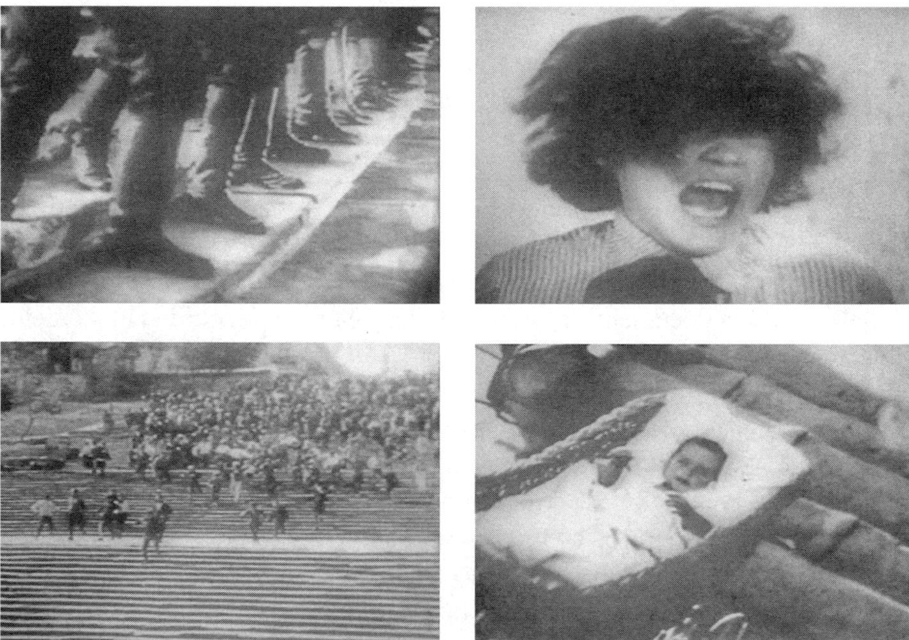

Figure 4.3 The Odessa Steps sequence of *The Battleship Potemkin* demonstrates many of Eisenstein's core editing principles including conflict of scale and conflict of direction in the juxtaposition of shots.

by side, their combined meaning is different from what you might expect. The combined word-picture does not mean violence of some sort, but sorrow. The combination of these two images creates a meaning both outside of and greater than the sum of their parts. In Eisenstein's algebra, A × B does not equal AB, but rather A × B equals C, a new concept totally different and greater than the product of the parts. Eisenstein's theory has been tested and supported in experimental studies (Zuckerman, 1990). As you edit your programs, put as much thought into the juxtaposition of shots as you do to the content of each individual shot.

Analytic and Synthetic Editing

The editor commonly constructs scenes in one of two stylistic directions. These two models include analytic and synthetic styles of editing.

Analytic Editing. In its most simple form, analytic editing starts wide and moves in closer. Visually speaking, this is **deductive scene construction**. This is the way scenes are created using the master scene method explored in chapter 2. When building a scene deductively, you present the audience with a wide view (or master shot) and then show the audience the details within that master shot with different cut-ins. This is the traditional way to build a scene, and the most conventional way to edit visual programs. The term *deductive* is borrowed from logic. If you are able to deduce something, you know that the conclusion must be true if the premises are true. If the master shot shows flowers on the table, then the close-up of the table will have flowers on it, too. It must be so in the logic of the scene.

Analytic editing is a more sophisticated concept than a simple visual progression of wide shot to assorted close-ups. The analytic editing approach begins with a whole idea, or global construct, and then breaks that whole down by examining the component parts individually. We see the whole, gain an impression of it, and then come to understand it as the artist fragments and analyzes its components. Eisenstein used this approach in his classic *The Battleship Potemkin* (1925). Many scenes in this feature begin with sweeping views of a situation. Through carefully composed and ordered close-ups, Eisenstein guides the audience to understand the significance of the wider perspective. We see an officer on the ship called to inspect meat at the request of discontented sailors. The inspection itself is not significant in long shot, but we see the sailors' tension and anger as they gather round the officer. As the scene progresses to closer views, revealing details, we learn that the meat is infested with maggots. The officer does not care, and the audience sympathizes with the crew of the Potemkin when mutiny erupts.

Synthetic Editing. Synthetic editing takes an approach opposite of that found in the analytic school. This style achieves meaning through the accumulation

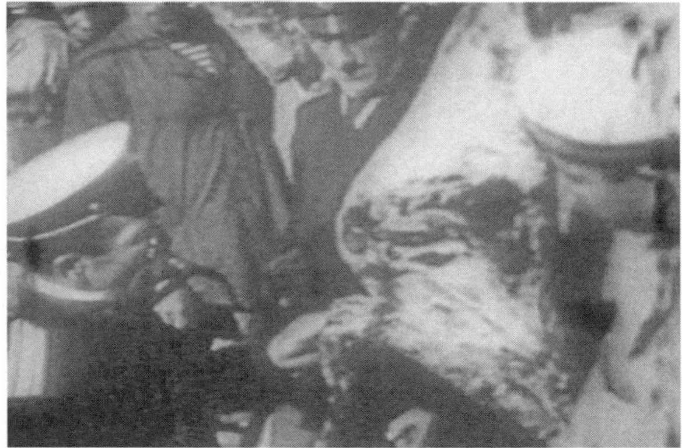

Figure 4.4 Analytic editing reveals the details of a concept the scene progresses. (*The Battleship Potemkin* [1925])

of detail. Visually, this is achieved by utilizing **inductive scene construction**. The editor presents the audience with details of a scene, and builds outward conceptually from there. The term *inductive*, like its deductive counterpart, is borrowed from the language of logic. If a conclusion is made inductively, it is based on evidence that suggests the facts, but the conclusion is only an inference. We might, in fact, find the large picture a little different from what we expect. Inductive scene construction is a less conventional way of presenting visual information. It challenges the audience, and for this reason, many artists find it a rewarding and interesting approach.

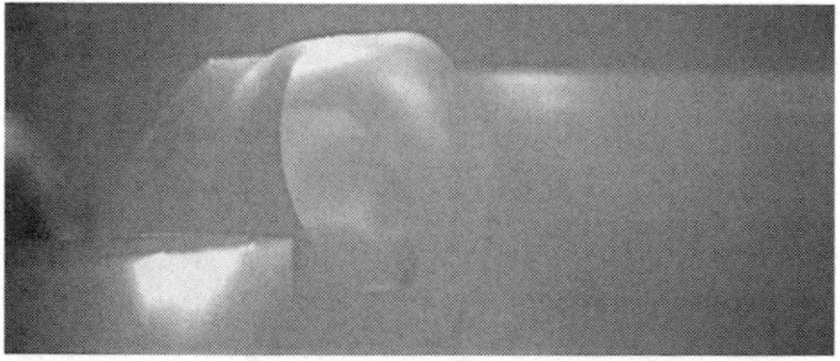

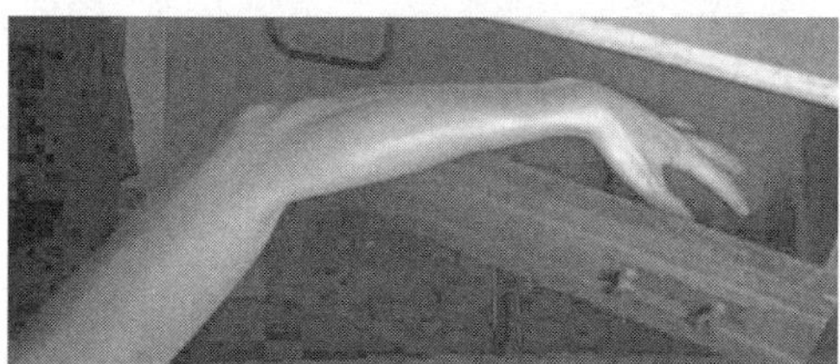

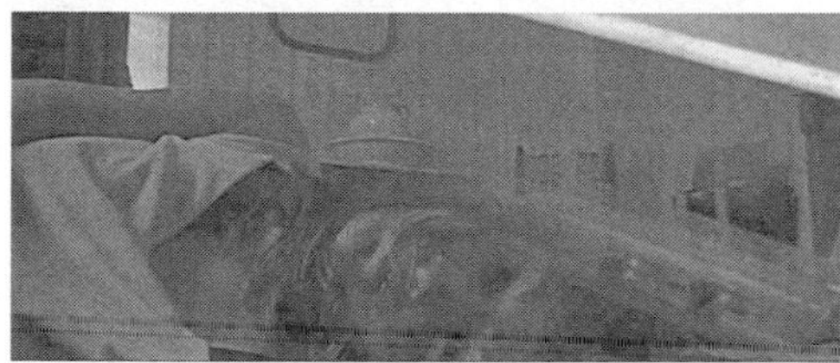

Figure 4.5 Synthetic editing creates meaning through the accumulation of detail. (Courtesy of Amanda Edwards)

Stanley Kubrick presents many scenes in *Barry Lyndon* (1975) using an inductive method. The scenes in this film often start with a detail in the form of a close-up, and the full context of the scene is slowly revealed as the perspective of the viewer widens over the course of successive shots.

Synthetic editing builds its concepts from details. Alfred Hitchcock knew when a synthetic approach was most effective. In *The Birds* (1963), Hitchcock and editor George Tomasini used a synthetic approach to build fear and suspense. Melanie, played by Tippi Hedren, arrives at the schoolhouse, concerned about the strange behavior of local birds. As she sits outside the schoolyard, the birds slowly gather behind her. The editor inserts point-of-view shots to reveal what Melanie sees. Each time the scene returns to an objective perspective more birds occupy the composition behind her. The tension, and the meaning of the scene, comes in the accumulation of details. When Melanie learns what has already been revealed to the audience, the threat is imminent.

Master Scene Method

The conventional way to construct a scene is to build it analytically and deductively using the master scene method. The editor selects a take of the master shot that is of the best technical quality of available options, and which best fits the mood, pace, and creative objectives of the program. This master shot is then broken up in editing, and parts of it are replaced with shots showing details within the master shot (cut-ins), and sometimes with various images that show things happening outside of the range of the master shot (cutaways). The editor might begin the scene with an establishing shot, such as a view of a building from outside, to help orient the viewer to where the scene takes place.

The master shot serves as a reference for setting the pace and for maintaining continuity, but the final version of the scene might contain very little of the master shot and may vary somewhat from its pace. For example, the editor can extend a scene for dramatic effect by holding a close-up longer than the moment occurred in the original master shot. Conversely, an editor can make the scene shorter or tighter by reducing pauses between lines of dialogue as close-ups of speaking characters are cut back and forth.

Continuity

The editor needs to maintain continuity. It is the editor's job to make sure the actors' movements and clothes match from one shot to the next in the final program, and to mask continuity errors made in shooting. The editor must also make sure there are not any jump cuts, position jumps, and that eyelines match for proper screen direction (see chapter 2). The classic view of motion-picture editing maintains that editing rules should be carefully followed to obtain smooth transitions between shots and to facilitate progressive movement through the narrative. Some researchers have found support for this approach by studying audience reactions to various editing conditions (d'Ydewalle & Vanderbeeken, 1990). More broadly defined, however, the editor is responsible for maintaining **holistic continuity**. That is, the program must make sense within the rules of its aesthetic and individual approach. A film can have jump cuts if they are part of the style. This might jolt the viewer, but sometimes disruption is a valid objective of the artist. The landmark film *Breathless* (1960) essentially ignores the traditional rules of editing and is filled with jump cuts. It works because jump cuts are presented as integral to the syntax of the film.

Likewise, a film can have position jumps if they are inserted deliberately to communicate something about the character or the story to the audience. Continuity is only broken when it is perceived as a mistake. Continuity is ultimately a function of perception and expectation.

Time

Motion pictures are images and sound in time, and the editor is in total control of this time. Movies do not generally take place in real time because much of life in real time would be pretty boring to watch on screen.

A few fictional programs make the pretense of happening in real time, but what they actually present is **dramatic time** acting like real time. In the television series *24*, the premise is that one hour of broadcast time captures one hour in the actual time of the story on screen. Agent Bauer, however, often does more

Figure 4.6 *Cancer Dreams* manipulates editing pace and chronology to portray a dream-like world in which characters experience an ever-changing environment. (Courtesy of Knight Productions)

in this hour than would be humanly possible. The audience does not notice this unrealistic advance through time. What the audience experiences is dramatic time, which is a compression and acceleration of events for entertainment.

The *War of the Worlds* radio broadcast of 1938 was similar in approach. This program dramatized events in the form of a news broadcast in real time, and many listeners thought it was real, but in just 45 minutes the Martians traveled millions of miles to earth, defeated our armies, and occupied much of the United States.

Dramatic time can expand events, too. The 10-second countdown to nuclear impact in *War Games* (1983) actually lasts longer than 10 seconds to build tension and anticipation. In Sam Peckinpah's *The Wild Bunch* (1969), time is slowed down when there is a death of a character so the audience has time to contemplate and meditate upon the violence.

The editor can also reorder time. Many films contain flashbacks and foreshadows. Some films, such as *Double Indemnity* (1944) and *Lolita* (1962), are told completely in the form of a flashback. Stanley Kubrick began the film version of *Lolita* with the murder of Quilty, which happens at the end of the story, to keep the audience engaged throughout the film with the question of, "What will happen to the killer?"

Memento (2000) completely revolutionized the possibilities of time manipulation through editing. Told in a brilliant structure, the film alternates scenes forward and backward and the story meets in the middle. It is at this point of convergence that the story makes sense for the first time. *Memento* tells the story of a man unable to form new memories, so the confusing structure of the film forces the audience to experience the character's frustration of living in isolated moments that do not make sense. *Eternal Sunshine of the Spotless Mind* (2004) also manipulates time in a confusing manner to reinforce audience empathy with a man whose memories have been erased. *21 Grams* (2003) is chopped up and reordered in such a manner that the film becomes a puzzle for the audience to decipher.

Pace

There are many ways to establish and vary pace in editing. If a scene contains a slow and deliberate conversation, the variation of shots can match this pace and point the audience to the element of the scene most important at that moment. A gunfight, by contrast, might command a faster editing pace to keep up with the frenetic action and chaos.

Editing pace can also be theoretically determined. **Metric editing** uses shots of equal length to set a pace and create a metronome-like drive. Metric editing can be set to music or any interval the editor chooses. Metric editing for long stretches is generally perceived as tedious, so it should be used in short doses or with a specific rationale.

Rhythmic editing assembles shots based on interval, but all the shots are not of equal length. A rhythmic montage might be based on shots that get progressively faster, or those that follow a short-short-long, short-short-long recurring structure. **Lyrical editing** is also interval-based, but even more complex, like the time progressions of a symphony. Lyrical editing is often used in conjunction with music.

Each of these pacing methods can be applied to music with the same time structure, but a more interesting approach in some cases is to use music against the pace of the visual editing. This creates dissonance and can be quite emotive.

Editing pace affects the audience. Experiments show that faster cutting rates in happy scenes cause the audience to judge characters as more pleasant (Heft, 1987). The energy of the faster editing pace is transferred to the characters in a positive way. Conversely, increasing the editing pace in angry scenes causes the audience to feel that the characters are less pleasant. The energy of the fast editing in this case increases audience anxiety, and this anxiety is transferred to the characters. Use editing pace to direct your audience and know that it affects the audience's mood, as well as feelings about your characters.

Space

The editor directs the audience through space. The master scene method directs the audience within a space. The editor establishes the parameters of the environment with the master shot, and then moves the audience within that defined space with subsequent shots. The 180-degree rule used by the camera crew on location carries over to the editor as well. It is a responsibility of the editor to make sure that the footage is cut together in a manner that keeps the audience oriented.

Directing an audience *within* a space is only one way to use space in film- and video-editing. The objective of sequential editing is to move the audience through space and to logically pass from one space to another. A chase sequence might start out in a room and then progress to the hallway, down the stairs, and out into the street.

Cutting Points

The editor has many options in selecting a cutting point. A cutting point can be determined by a need for a shift in attention. When watching a shot, determine when you want to move on and see something else. If the shot lingers too long, trim it. Generally, beginning editors like to linger on each shot too long. Tighter is almost always better.

Action can motivate the change from one shot to the next. When a character speaks or says something profound, that is often the time for a new shot. A character entering the room, a window blowing open, or a dog barking outside can all motivate a cut within the scene to a new image. There are three ways to cut around action: cutting on action, leading the action, and following the action. Cutting on the action, such as at the very moment that someone is handed a telephone, is the most conventional way to use action as a motivation for a cutting point. Leading the action with the cut, in anticipation of the phone receiver handoff, creates a slightly different effect. With this approach, you put the audience slightly ahead of the characters and create a moment of anticipation. Following the action is a way to catch the audience off guard. If a burglar were to burst through a doorway you could enhance the sense of surprise by cutting to the close-up just after the door is thrown open.

To ensure that the editor has creative options, it is essential that the production crew capture a variety of angles and that they overlap the action in each angle. It is imperative that the director makes sure there is enough coverage of each scene. If no close-up shot is recorded of the door swinging open, then the editor's options will be limited. During shooting, make sure every angle has the full range of action that might be included from that perspective. It will make the process of editing easier and your final product stronger.

Montage

Montage is the traditional term for the editing process. It has also been used to describe specific theories of editing (e.g., Eisenstein's theory of montage based on Japanese ideograms). Today, however, the term *montage* is used to denote a collection of images, usually with the intent of compression or elaboration. Film and video makers use montages to summarize a passage of time, to give the audience an idea of the scope of an action, and to examine the dreams or internal turmoil of an individual.

Fred Zinnemann's classic western *High Noon* (1952) contains a sequence known as the "11:58 Montage" that summarizes the narrative. Kane, the hero of the film, is preparing to confront the Miller Gang at high noon. The purpose of the montage is to show simultaneous events in the town in the two minutes before noon to build tension before the final showdown. Here are the shots in this two-minute montage:

1. Wide-angle shot of train tracks.
2. The church congregation at prayer.
3. Henderson at church.
4. Ezra (a defender of Kane) at church.
5. Men smoking at the bar in the Ramirez Saloon.
6. Jimmy drinking alone in the Ramirez Saloon.
7. The saloonkeeper in the Ramirez Saloon.
8. The pendulum of Kane's clock.
9. Kane writing his will.
10. Low angle of the deserted town street.
11. Another view of the deserted town street.
12. The train tracks.
13. The Miller Gang standing beside the tracks.
14. Two older townsmen watching.
15. Mildred and Sam Fuller looking at one another and then down.
16. Mart Howe looking up at the clock.
17. Helen Ramirez looking up at the clock.
18. Amy Kane looking up at the clock.
19. Kane's clock, side view, 11:59.
20. The pendulum.
21. The Miller Gang.
22. Kane writing.
23. The pendulum. The camera tilts up to show the clock at 12:00.
24. The chair in which Miller sat when he made his promise to return and kill Kane.
25. Amy Kane.
26. Kane.
27. Helen Ramirez.
28. The Miller Gang.
29. The train tracks.

This montage covers two minutes of both real time and screen time. The shots are cut metrically. Most of the shots are exactly the same length and cut on the beat of the musical score.

Tootsie (1982) uses a montage of magazine cover shots to chronicle the rise to fame of Dorothy, the film's lead character. A musical interlude accompanies a montage in *Butch Cassidy and the Sundance Kid* (1969) that elaborates the relationship between the heroine Etta Place, Butch, and Sundance.

Parallel Construction

Parallel construction can shift the viewer back and forth between two physical locations to portray events developing simultaneously. Also known as parallel development, this technique alternates images of two or more different scenes in order to heighten tension and portray layers of a program's simultaneous events.

Editors William Reynolds and Peter Zinner created an unforgettable parallel construction in Francis Ford Coppola's *The Godfather* (1972). The christening of Michael Corleone's son is intercut with images of Michael's soldiers murdering their business rivals. The juxtaposition of a newborn child in a church with grotesque violence tells us much about Michael's duality and invites audience interpretation.

Preparing to Edit

Before going into the editing room, it is essential to be prepared and get organized. The editor and director should start by reviewing the footage and becoming familiar with the material. One of the best ways to do this is to review copies of your material. These copies should be played back on a system that can display time code information or you can work with window dubs. A **window dub** is a copy of the footage that has time code numbers burned in the margin of the image on screen. This time code window allows effective logging from any location with a playback unit, even if the unit does not read time code information. Working with copies also protects your original source material. Start by watching all your material and carefully logging every shot. A log made from window dubs might look like this:

Shot	Take	Source I.D.	Time	Description	Notes
1	1	1	0:00:23 - 0:00:45	Opening door	No good
1	2	1	0:00:45 - 0:01:05	Opening door	Use this one

Using this list of notes, make an import log. An **import log** is a listing of the shots you intend to use and where they are located on your source materials. This allows you to import only material that you might potentially use and will save time and drive space. Your import log might be designed like this:

Shot	Description	Source I.D.	Location
1	Establishing shot of building	2	0:08:45-0:08:55
2	Master shot of guys at table	1	1:34:40-1:34-58
3	Close-up of bartender	1	1:25:30-1:25:37

When you enter the editing suite you should already be intimately familiar with your material and have a clear plan of action. You can change this plan, of course, once you see how the material really cuts together. Creative editing discoveries often happen through experimentation in the edit suite, but it is important to have an initial plan. If you do not begin making a plan until you are in the edit suite, you will likely have more stress and less time for experimentation and creative discovery. Preparing to edit before you enter the edit suite is absolutely crucial to success in an academic environment where there are many students competing for time on the computer. In the professional world, editing time is charged by the hour, and being ill-prepared costs money.

NONLINEAR COMPUTER-BASED EDITING

Computer-based editing is the standard for video production. The process is simple. The video source is connected to a computer. The editor selects the shots from the raw footage to be transferred to the computer. This transfer can be done with the assistance of the import log.

The shots are **digitized** (or **captured**) in the computer-based editing system at a resolution level selected by the editor. There is a mathematical game in choosing the resolution for digitizing. The higher the resolution, the better the image quality. Higher resolution, however, also requires more drive space. The level of resolution you select will be determined in part by your available drive space and the amount of footage you need to store for your particular project. Ten minutes of raw footage is no big deal to import in most cases, while 20 hours of footage requires enormous storage capacity.

Some editing systems offer the option of working in **draft mode**. This is a valuable function for large projects. Draft mode allows you to import footage at a low resolution, which is good enough for making editing decisions but not good enough for the final product. The computer keeps track of the time code of each shot and when you have made all of your editing decisions the computer then re-imports only the footage it needs at high resolution to create the final program.

Editing in draft mode is considered off-line editing. **Off-line editing** is the process of making creative editing decisions with equipment, or at a resolution, that is not sufficient quality for the final product. When a program is edited in high quality for final distribution, the process is referred to as **on-line editing**. If you edit off-line with the intent of mastering in higher resolution, it is crucial that you name each shot correctly and keep these labels consistent. This allows the computer to recognize the correct material on your original sources during the final mastering process.

Once the footage is imported into the computer it can be trimmed, reordered, and modified until you have the material composed just as you want it in the final program. The last step of the process is usually to export the final program to videotape or to burn the program onto DVD.

This editing process is called **nonlinear editing (NLE)** because once the material is in the computer it can be randomly accessed. Film and videotape are **linear media**. To access a shot made toward the end of a tape you need to wind all the way through the footage. Nonlinear systems, such as the computer-based editor, allow random access of any shot with the click of a button.

Figure 4.7 A nonlinear editing system with external video deck.

Nonlinear Editing User Interface

There are a number of different computer-based video-editing systems for both PC and Macintosh users. These systems vary in their range of features, power, speed, and price, but the fundamental interface is consistent across platforms. You first coordinate the importing of your material into the system. You then organize material by individual clips and identify each clip with a name and key frame. The key frame is a small picture that allows you to see an image from the clip in miniature to assist you in identifying the shot easily as you work. The default key frame is usually the first frame of the clip, but some systems allow you to set the key frame to any frame in the clip.

Once you have imported your material into the computer you refer to the segments of video as clips instead of shots. A shot, as you recall, represents the time period from when the camera starts to when the camera stops. A shot is also defined as a single uninterrupted piece of video footage in the final program. **Clips** can equal shots but they do not necessarily have to. You might import a clip that is actually three shots of original footage in a row. Perhaps it is three different takes of a reaction shot. The editor might feel it is easier to work with the collection of takes of this short video segment as a single clip. Clips can be trimmed down in the computer. You might import a 30-second clip, but only use five seconds of it in the final program. These five seconds then become the shot in the final program.

Some editing systems allow you to trim clips in a nondestructive way. With **nondestructive editing** you can cut a 30-second clip down to 10 seconds in the editing program and keep the whole clip in the computer memory. With a simple command you can expand the clip to 15, 20, or back to 30 seconds anytime you wish. Unless you erase the captured file from your hard drive, trimming a clip will not affect your source material or ability to make changes later. Other editing systems use **destructive editing**. If you cut a 30-second clip down to 10 seconds and save the changes with a destructive editing system, the remaining

20 seconds are erased, and you will need to reimport the shot from the source material if you wish to make it longer.

There are three primary interface windows used with nonlinear editing system: bins, preview window, and timeline. Clips imported into the computer are organized into bins. **Bins** are like folders that you use on your computer desktop to organize documents. On many systems, they can be used to sort clips by various topics. If you are working on a documentary, you might have a bin for each of your interviews. The term *bin* is carried over from traditional film editing where clips of film are hung on metal pins and stored in cloth-lined storage bins.

The bins can be organized into windows for easy access. In addition to bins to hold your clips, you need two other primary windows to build a program. The **preview window** is where you can watch an individual clip and trim the length of the clip. The third primary window is the **timeline** window, which contains tracks for video, audio, graphics, and effects. The timeline can be adjusted to a scale that works best for your needs. For example, if you are working on a two-hour feature, you might want one inch of your timeline to represent a minute of screen time. By contrast, if you are working on a 30-second commercial, you might prefer that an inch of the timeline be only one second of screen time. You build the program in the timeline with video, audio, titles, and special effects. The computer mouse, function keys, and drag menus allow you to play clips, reorder shots, and shape your visual program down to

Figure 4.8 Bins are used to organize your clips. Final Cut Pro organizes clips in the Browser window. (Screen shot reprinted with permission from Apple Computer, Inc.)

Figure 4.9 The preview window is called the canvas in Final Cut Pro. (Screen shot reprinted with permission from Apple Computer, Inc.)

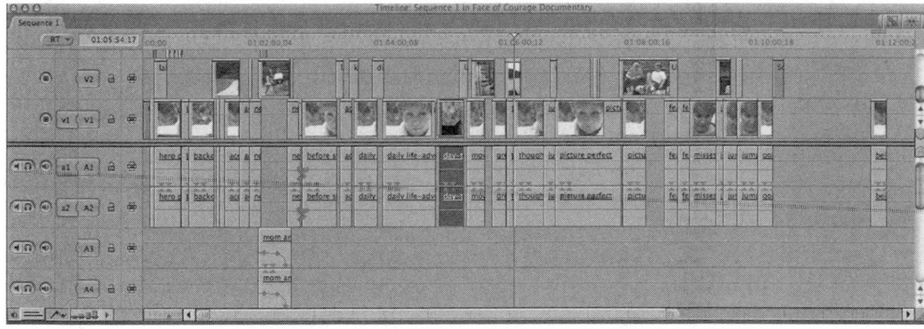

Figure 4.10 Timeline. (Screen shot reprinted with permission from Apple Computer, Inc.)

the exact frame. Some systems have proprietary names for each of the three primary interface windows, but the function is similar across systems. Final Cut Pro defines the bins that hold clips as the browser, and the preview window in Final Cut Pro is called the canvas. iMovie calls the bin the clips pane, and the preview window in iMovie is called the iMovie monitor.

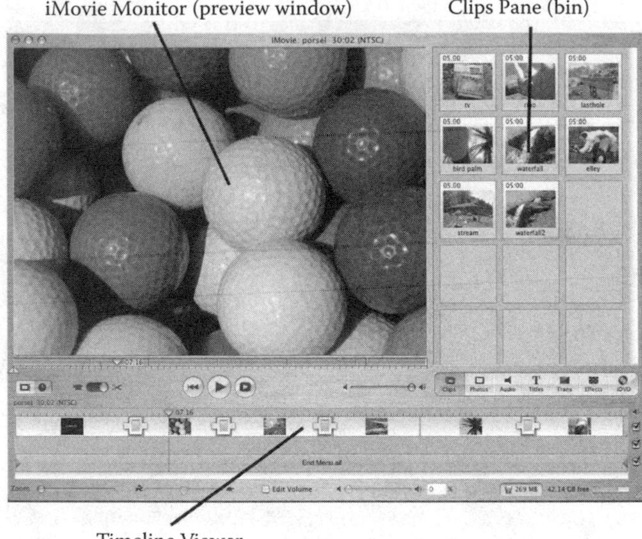

Figure 4.11 iMovie utilizes a single window divided into three primary user areas including the clips pane (bin), the iMovie monitor (preview window), and the timeline viewer. The clips pane can be replaced with other windows for control of audio, titles, transitions, and effects. (Screen shot reprinted with permission from Apple Computer, Inc.)

Transitions

You can incorporate transitions into your program during the editing process. The three primary types of transitions are fades, dissolves, and wipes.

Fade. You can build a **fade-in** or a **fade-out** using any shot in your program. You can set the length of the fade by choosing the start frame and the end frame. You can employ other fade options as well. For example, you might choose to fade to white instead of black.

Dissolves. A **dissolve** is also known as a **cross-fade**. This is an effect where one shot fades out as another shot fades in at the same time. You can have a dissolve take place wherever there is an overlap of two shots in the timeline.

Wipes. Computer-editing software offers many wipe options. Among the most popular wipes are across the screen from side to side, from top to bottom, and starting as a pinpoint in the center of the screen that opens up as an expanding circle. This latter type of wipe is sometimes called an iris.

In addition to traditional wipes, your editing system may offer a heart-shaped wipe, zigzag patterns, and other options. Some systems allow you to select a convergence point if you want a wipe to begin or end at a specific location on the screen. Beware that exotically shaped wipes are only rarely used in professional production and that overuse of wipes generally looks amateurish.

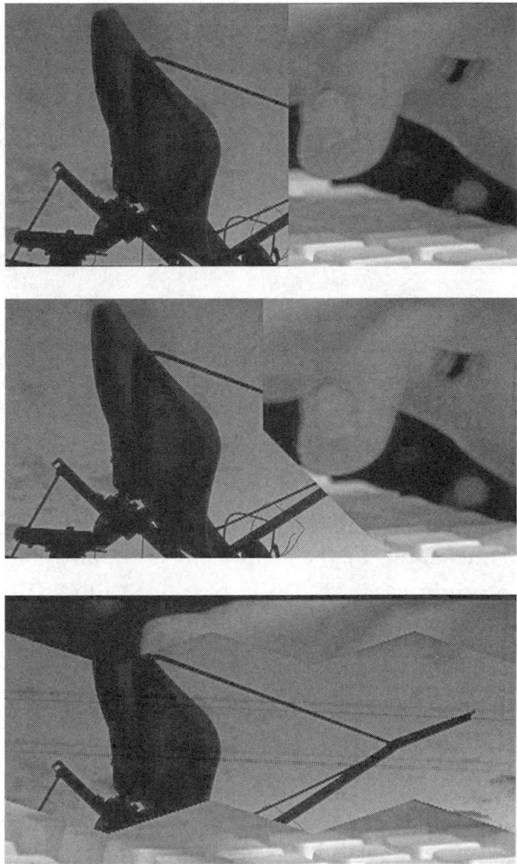

Figure 4.12 Many wipe options are available on computer-based editing systems.

Titles

You can compose titles, on-screen graphics, and credits for your program. You can select the font style, size, and color as well as motion effects and exact placement of the title on the screen. You can have credits scroll from bottom to top over black and adjust the speed of this **crawl**. You can have the name of an interview subject appear on the lower third of the frame with a fade-in and fade-out. You can choose to have the title of your program shadowed over the first scene or you might want to put a bold edge on your title. You can even choose to have a title fly in, letter by letter, from all directions in a variety of colors. Graphics programs for computer editing systems contain most effects and options that beginning and intermediate-level editors require. If greater power is needed, there are a number of stand-alone software packages for advanced graphics and title work.

When composing titles, make sure to include a **copyright notice** identifying the legal owner of the project. Legally protecting your work is easy. Simply

Figure 4.13 Title software helps put the finishing touches on a program. (Screen shot reprinted with permission from Apple Computer, Inc.)

publish the word *copyright*, or the copyright symbol (©) followed by the year of publication and the name of the person or company that owns the work. A copyright notice might read, "© 2008 Nancy Smith." Without a copyright notice in place, your work is subject to duplication and public use without payment or permission. You can further protect your work by mailing a copy of the project to yourself in a sealed envelope and keeping the seal intact. The postmark provides evidence of the copyright date in the event of a dispute of ownership. You can register a copyrighted work with the U.S. Government. This adds additional protection in the case of an ownership dispute, but there is a fee for copyright registration and it is not required for legal copyright protection. To legally protect your work from unauthorized reproduction all you need to do is include a copyright notice in your titles.

Special Effects

Computer-based editing systems can do a number of special effects. You can apply filters to create a fog effect, change the overall color, make slow motion, and so on. Advanced effects software can insert an object within a scene that did not exist before, add a sparkle to someone's eye, and remove the glare from a shiny object in the background. Computer editing programs sometimes include the option of creating **matte effects**, which composite two or more images together. Matte effects are often executed with the aid of a blue or green screen. The computer can be set to **key out** the color of the background screen, and replace this colored screen with any image you assign.

Your basic editing software might not be able to perform every special effect that you desire, but there are ancillary programs for specific effects that work in conjunction with editing systems to provide even more power in manipulating your material.

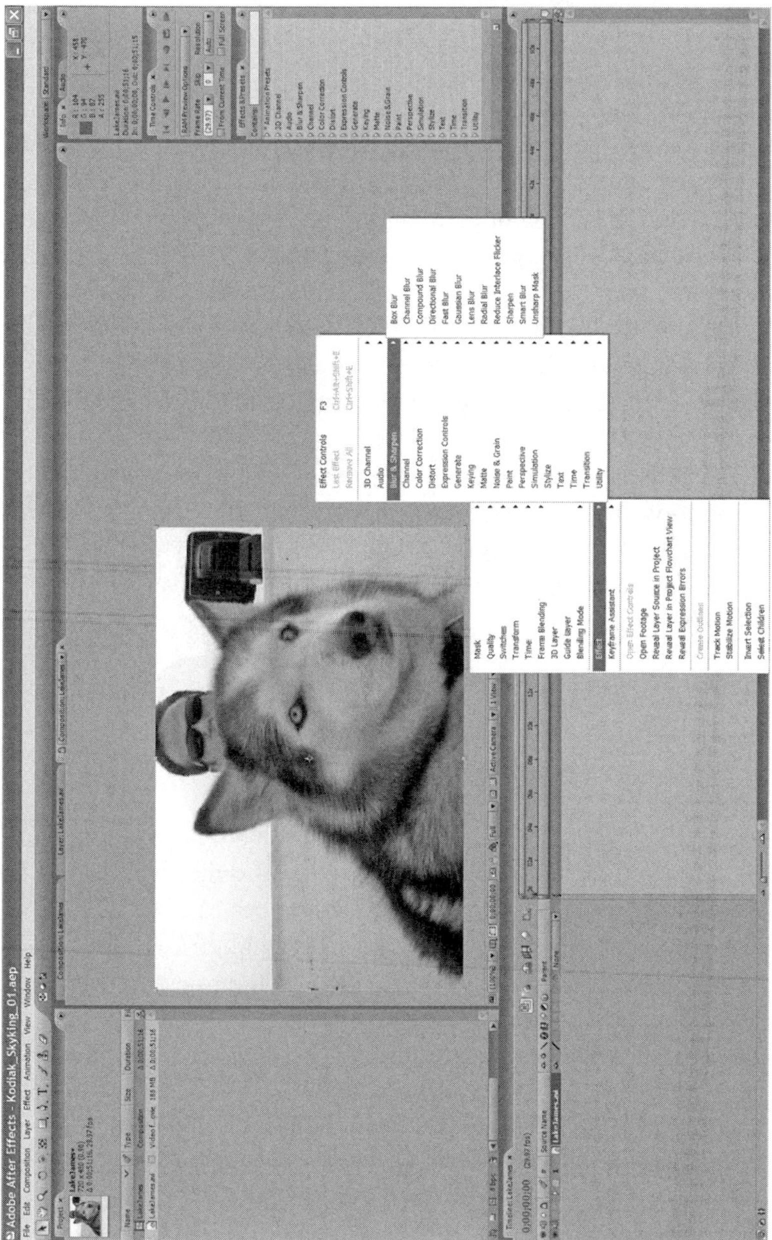

Figure 4.14 Supplemental software can be used to create special effects. (Adobe product screen shot reprinted with permission from Adobe Systems Incorporated)

Rendering

Any time you add a transition or effect to your program, you need to **render** that change. Rendering is the process of making a new file to portray the effect that you desire. When you add a dissolve, a fade, or a wipe into a program, the computer needs to create a file for this new segment of video. In most cases, the computer does not automatically render every transition that you place in the timeline. This is for two reasons. First, an editor often makes tentative decisions and then decides to change them. Also, the practice of rendering takes additional storage space and operating time on the computer. Rendering elaborate special effects can take hours on some systems.

For these reasons, many systems require that you tell the computer when you are ready to render each effect/transition. Or, if you wish to render all the effects you have put in the timeline at once, you can select "render all." This is a good time to take a break since the computer might have to work for a while to render the new files.

For each rendered file, the computer composes a new image frame by frame in full resolution from the different sources. Once the file is rendered, you can watch the video segment exactly as it will appear in the final program. You must be aware, however, that if you choose to make an adjustment to your transition or effect, the computer will often need to rerender the entire segment of video.

Audio

You can do rudimentary audio editing with a standard computer-based video editing system. When you digitize video clips, you can also digitize the matching soundtrack. You can import additional sound sources, too. For example, you can download sound effects and music from Internet libraries or load a CD file directly into the editing software. You can patch a microphone for voice-overs or import field audio from a disk-based recorder.

Your editing system will likely have an audio equalizer that allows you to emphasize or deemphasize certain frequency ranges (see chapter 7). You have multiple audio tracks to work with. Some systems contain only two channels of audio while others are unlimited. Multiple audio tracks allow the combination of sync sound, stereo music from multiple sources, voice-overs, and sound effects.

Just as there are supplemental video special effects software packages that can work with your editing system to enhance the image, there are also supplemental tools for advanced audio control. For most basic production applications, however, you will probably find all the power you need in a standard computer-based video-editing system. We will discuss sound and how to control, record, and manipulate audio in greater detail in chapter 7.

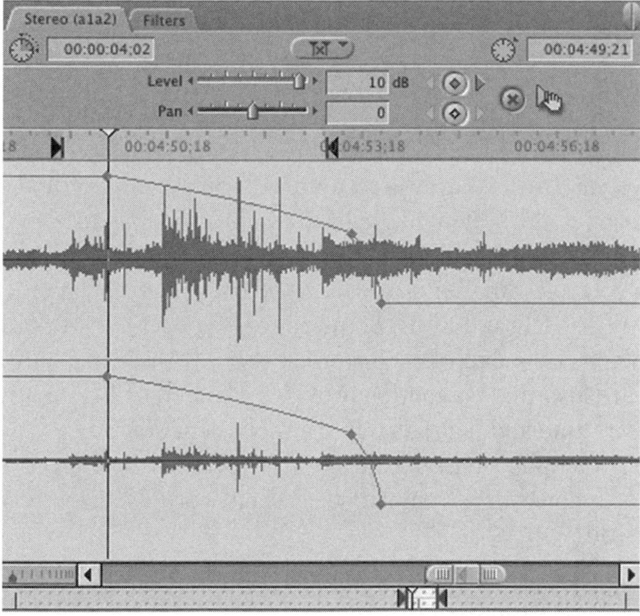

Figure 4.15 Editing systems allow control of audio as well as picture. (Screen shot repriinted with permission from Apple Computer, Inc.)

Peripherals

Your video-editing system requires some core components including the computer hardware, editing software, drive space for storing your media, a means for importing your material into the computer, and a way to master your final program when it is complete. In addition to a computer monitor, many editing suites also include an external television monitor, which allows review of the program in full resolution as it will appear for the audience. Make sure that your computer and external video monitors are calibrated correctly for color, brightness, and contrast. Reference your video editing software manual and the manuals of your computer and video monitors for specific information on calibration.

A good set of external audio speakers is a valuable addition to an editing suite. If you are working in a group lab, a pair of **circumaural headsets** will give you excellent sound reproduction and will not disturb those working around you.

Some nonlinear editing systems can fill a large room with a wide range of peripherals while other systems go miniature, building everything the editor needs into a laptop computer.

Backing Up Data

One disadvantage of computer-based nonlinear editing systems is the potential for lost data. Editing a video project can take dozens or sometimes hundreds of hours of work, and it is important to take precautions to protect your investment. If you are using an editing system that has multiple users, there is a greater chance of accidental erasure.

Password-protected drive sectors and servers and removable hard drives help protect data on systems with multiple users. These precautions cannot, however, save you from a hardware failure. If you are editing and storing your projects on a server, the system might have a built-in backup method. Check with your system administrator. In other cases you might be responsible for backing up your data yourself. Smaller projects can be backed up as data files on removable media, such as CD and DVD. Some editors export their work in progress to digital videotape at the end of each work session. If there is a hardware failure and all data are lost, this precaution provides a record of the creative decisions made and saves time and heartache in the reconstruction process.

Nonlinear computer-based editing is the standard of video postproduction. There are, however, circumstances when working directly from videotape is preferred.

LINEAR EDITING SYSTEMS

A disadvantage of nonlinear computer-based editing systems is the time it takes to import material into the computer. While some cameras with internal hard drives can transfer data quickly for editing, material recorded on videotape must be imported into the editing system in real-time playback before any editing begins. For most creative applications this is not a significant problem. The discipline and time it takes to carefully select the footage to import provides the editor with time to become familiar with the material and to contemplate options. Also, in cases such as batch digitization in draft mode, it can simply be a matter of allowing the computer to import the materials overnight.

There are applications, however, when an hour to digitize material is simply too much time. For this reason, broadcast news outlets platformed with videotape frequently use **linear editing systems**. Simply stated, a linear editing system works directly from the videotape source. Because the material has to be accessed in the order in which it was recorded on tape, it is referred to as a linear editing system. All the material is laid out on the tape in a line and must be accessed this way.

A basic linear editing system has a **source deck**, which plays back the footage shot in the field, and a **record deck**, which copies the selected shots in order of the final program. Between these two decks is a controller, which allows the exact timing of when a shot starts and when it stops. Some linear editing systems record onto a computer hard drive rather than another video tape.

A linear editing system requires a video monitor or computer windows so that you are able to see the material as you build your program. The controller allows you to select the **in-point** and **out-point** of source material that you

Figure 4.16 Linear editing systems are sometimes used in news production. (Joanne Hughes)

want to incorporate into your program. The selected material is then copied to your preferred location on the record deck or computer timeline.

The controller also allows you to select whether you want to record the video track, audio channel one, audio channel two, or any combination of these sources together. With this control, you can place a picture over existing audio or put music or a voice-over underneath existing picture. It also, of course, allows you to record the picture with sync sound.

In tape-to-tape editing, some controllers have a digital processor, which allows you to add transitions and effects between the playback deck and the record deck. The processor allows you to add fades, wipes, dissolves, and other special effects. The controller has a digital memory to hold a shot so that two shots can be manipulated simultaneously from a single playback source. This allows one shot to dissolve into another or one shot to replace another with a wipe.

The primary place you will still find linear editing systems is in broadcast news. A news team might shoot 10 or 15 minutes of material to create a 60-second news package. Working with a nonlinear editing system would require at least another 10 or 15 minutes in the editing studio just to import the material. With the fast turnaround requirements and deadlines of news production, this is often a luxury that cannot be afforded. Sometimes a news editor/photographer will only have an hour or less to cut a news package together. This is why a linear editing system is essential to some news professionals.

News photographers often edit their own material. As they are shooting they are gathering as much relevant footage as possible and making mental notes about how it will be cut together. When they get into the editing suite they know where they need to go on the tape to begin the editing process and how to build the package from there. A linear editing system allows a photographer/editor to create a package in a matter of minutes, if necessary. The edited package can then be physically carried or electronically transferred to the control room for broadcast.

Film Editing

Traditionally, films were edited in a mechanical and physical process. The original film negative, shot in the camera, was printed onto film stock to give the editor something to work with. This was called the **work print**. The sound track was recorded onto magnetic film stock and this was rolled in sync with the picture on a film-editing system called a **Moviola**. Anytime an editor removed a part of the picture from the work print reel the exact same length of sound had to be taken out on the sound reel so that everything stayed matched up. The editor pulled select takes from the work print and then trimmed these takes little by little. By reordering the shots the editor created a **rough cut** of the final program.

This process sounds cumbersome and it is. It is also expensive. For these reasons, mechanical editing of film has predominantly vanished from the industry. Virtually all films are edited on computer systems. A lab carefully handles the original camera negative and scans it into a computer frame by frame. The computer records a code from the film stock to provide a reference to the original camera negative. From there, professional editors make creative decisions about the ordering of shots and transitions in the same manner as you will on your desktop editing system.

For professional motion pictures, additional steps come into the process. A separate high-end audio facility will conduct sound rerecording and mix sophisticated, layered audio tracks. A film that requires special computer and optical effects will have these elements created by a lab for insertion into the final program.

Once the project is edited and mixed, the master program can be exported to videotape or DVD if it is designed for television or direct video distribution. If the film is intended for theatrical release then the editing decisions made in the computer have to be matched back up to the camera negative. In this case, an **edit decision list (EDL)** is generated from the creative decisions made in the computer. This list contains all of the code information to match up the cuts with the original camera negative. It is then the job of the **negative conformer** to take the film negative into a controlled environment and carefully cut the original negative and assemble it so it can be printed by a lab for theatrical distribution. Often the distribution prints are made from a copy of the negative, called an inter-negative, to protect the camera original in case the film is damaged at the lab.

It may be exciting and rewarding to recognize that when it comes right down to it, how you cut your first video project on a desktop computer is very similar to how creative decisions are made to edit features in Hollywood. As you learn how to edit your programs you are already developing the skills to work in the big leagues.

CONCLUSIONS

You have completed Unit I of the text: The Basics. You have explored the tools and techniques for taking an idea and molding it into a creative concept. You have the background to realize this concept on screen through planning and shooting. Now you can complete the production process through editing. You have developed the basic skills to make a complete visual program. With knowledge of film and video history, traditions and styles, you can proceed in the process of developing a style of your own.

The next unit of this text expands these basic skills with more advanced principles. You will learn the foundations of design for different program types. You will explore making television commercials and other short-form projects. You will expand your technical skills in video production with a detailed study of both lighting and sound, giving you greater power and options as an artist. Unit II concludes with a journey into the realm of nonfiction storytelling, the unique theories and methods for addressing documentary and news, and the challenges of bringing the real world to the big screen.

SAMPLE EXERCISES

1. Edit a two-minute scene. Take your characters on a dramatic journey. Illustrate either the analytic or synthetic editing approach.
2. Using a recording of your favorite television show, create a one-minute promotional segment that highlights the main themes of the program.
3. Edit a two-minute montage with a distinct visual rhythm.

RECOMMENDED READINGS

Button, B. (2002). *Nonlinear Editing: Storytelling, Aesthetics and Craft.* Lawrence, Kansas: CMP Books.

Dancyger, K. (2002). *The Technique of Film and Video Editing: History, Theory and Practice.* Boston: Focal Press.

Fairservice, D. (2001). *Film Editing: History, Theory, and Practice: Looking at the Invisible.* Manchester: Manchester University Press.

REFERENCES

d'Ydewalle, G., & Vanderbeeken, M. (1990). Perceptual and cognitive processing of editing rules in film. In G. Rudolf, G. d'Ydewalle, & R. Parham (Eds.), *From eye to mind: Information acquisition in perception, search, and reading* (pp. 129-139). Oxford, England: North-Holland.

Eisenstein, S. (1949). *Film Form: Essays in Film Theory* (J. Leyda Trans.). New York: Harcourt, Brace.

Heft, H., & Blondal, R. (1987). The influence of cutting rate on the evaluation of affective content of film. *Empirical Studies of the Arts, 5*, 1-14.

Pudovkin, V. I. (1949). *Film Technique and Film Acting.* New York: Lear.

Zuckerman, C. I. (1990). Rugged cigarettes and sexy soap: Brand images and the acquisition of meaning through associational juxtaposition of visual imagery. Unpublished master's thesis, The Annenberg School for Communication, University of Pennsylvania.

UNIT II

EXPANDING THE BASICS

CHAPTER 5: COMMERCIALS AND SHORT FORM
CHAPTER 6: LIGHTING
CHAPTER 7: SOUND
CHAPTER 8: NONFICTION

You now know the basics of producing video programs. You can develop story concepts and craft those concepts into a narrative using the dramatic structure. You can plan your production using the elements of visual language and take your plan into the field with your understanding of digital video cameras. Finally, you can bring these elements together into a cohesive structure through editing. In Unit II, you will expand these basic skills to increase your creative range.

You have explored the elements of crafting a scene, but scenes need to be composed into larger programs. Chapter 5 introduces short-format productions, including television commercials, public service announcements, music videos, and short films, to take your skills beyond practice scenes to the completion of a unified program. Unit II continues with an emphasis on expanding your technical skill base. Chapter 6 is dedicated to the control of light. Chapter 7 introduces advanced control of sound. Unit II concludes with chapter 8, which concentrates on nonfiction filmmaking and explores documentary and news production processes.

5

COMMERCIALS AND SHORT FORM

CHAPTER OBJECTIVES

One of the best ways to increase your skills as a visual storyteller is to practice by making short-form productions. This chapter introduces some of the most popular short forms including commercials, public service announcements, music videos, and short films. The logistics of production planning are elaborate. In this chapter you will explore the elements required for effective preproduction. This chapter also examines elements used in persuasive message design.

Video production is both a business and an art form. As you expand the scale and scope of your productions you will face resource realities that require attention to financing and budgeting. This chapter identifies some important business considerations that you must be aware of so you can take your skills beyond the classroom and into the marketplace. The objectives of this chapter are to:

- Introduce the business side of video production;
- Understand the process of designing and producing television commercials;
- Survey writing tools used in short-form production;
- Examine the psychological appeals used in designing persuasive visual programs.

The American television viewer watches hundreds of television commercials every week. Paid advertising is the engine that keeps broadcast television on the air. When asked, "What are television broadcasters selling?" very few people give the correct answer. Broadcasters do not sell television shows or commercials; they sell "eyeballs." The customers of television stations are not the viewers, but the advertisers. Advertisers pay broadcasters for access to viewers and paid advertising is what makes "free" broadcast television possible.

Upon first consideration it might appear that producing effective television commercials is easy. In part, this is because effective commercials make it appear easy. Much of advertising is common sense, yes, but there is more to it than that. You might find that grabbing the attention of your audience and persuading them to change their attitudes or behavior in just 30 seconds can be a tall order to fill.

Producing television commercials is a great way to gain practice in the art and skills of digital video production. The fixed and limited running time of commercials provides a manageable scale for practice. Also, because it is challenging to convey information in a short time frame, you will find that practicing the 30-second format will make the production of longer assignments and projects seem easier in significant ways.

There are opportunities in commercial production in every market. Many different types of companies produce television commercials including advertising agencies, television and film production houses, local television stations, cable providers, and freelancers. Even in small towns, businesses need to advertise. Small-market television commercial production is a great way to get started as a practitioner in video and film.

Producing practice commercials also provides material for your **show reel**. The show reel is a tool used to demonstrate your abilities in video production to potential clients and employers. Having a record of commercial production, even if just for practice, helps demonstrate what you are able to do. When it comes down to it, in most cases you will be hired based on the quality of your previous work, so it is important to build a record of what you can do. A collection of effective and creative practice ads might be what gets you your first paid job.

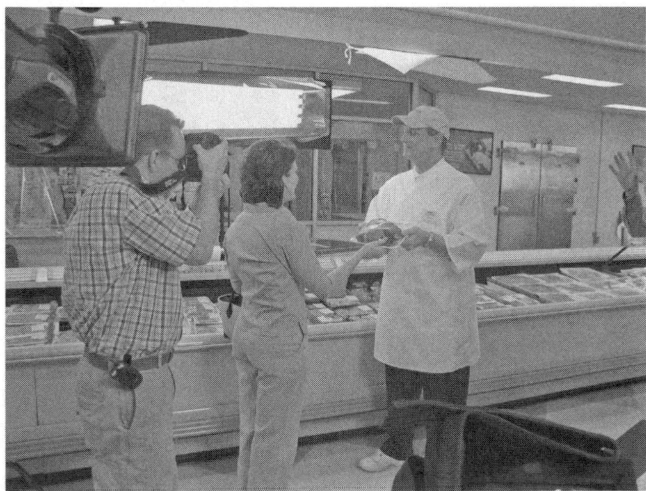

Figure 5.1 Shooting a supermarket commercial on location. (Courtesy of The Alpha Group)

TELEVISION ADVERTISING

Companies that make television commercials usually have clients approach them. In other cases commercial producers actively recruit clients. A commercial producer might conduct a study of the businesses in a community and their current advertising strategies in competitive media, such as newspaper and radio. The local cable company, for example, might approach businesses that are advertising on the radio to let them know what cable television advertising can do for them.

Broadcast television stations and cable television companies are able to offer a full-service advertising package to the client. The commercial department of a television station or cable provider can serve the client from creative development to production of the commercial, and then the same company can provide distribution of the commercial since they also have broadcast or cable channels to offer. When a client has a commercial produced with an advertising agency or a video production house, the client collaborates with the agency to make **media buys**, which is the strategic purchase of air time for the commercial to run. Media buys can offer diversified and targeted exposure.

Sometimes businesses that need a television ad meet with the creative teams of several agencies before making a decision of who will produce the ad. This shopping for producers is sometimes achieved through a formal bidding process. One of the key tools used in this approach is a **request for proposal (RFP)**. A business that needs an ad will sometimes put out an open call in the form of a written document that invites qualified service providers to bid on a pending project. Anyone with access to this call can respond and compete for the company's business. The request for proposal describes a project that a business wants to undertake, including project objectives, specifications, and a timeline. An RFP for a TV ad will usually ask for a show reel demonstrating the bidding company's previous commercial work, a written statement of the overall creative approach, philosophy of advertising, general information on the approach and strategy for developing an effective ad, and finally a bottom line of what the project is expected to cost.

An ad agency drafting a proposal for a potential client might indicate that based on their experience with similar projects, they expect a 30-second ad will cost $20,000 to produce on digital video and $24,000 on 35mm film. For that price the client gets one day of location time, a crew, and all the creative development to be approved by the client prior to shooting the ad.

The advertising production department of cable television providers can often present a fixed quote on the price of producing a commercial with little or no advance research. This is possible because creative development in local cable advertising is generally straightforward and the production approach formulaic. The **advertising copy** (or script) in cable advertising is often provided by the client, or generated quickly based on the producer's previous experience and some discussion with the client. The shoots for these commercials are often fast and without a lot of props or special effects. Cable companies concentrate on local stores, community professionals, and car dealers, and they are able to go in, shoot a commercial in one to four hours, and often have it edited the next day. In much of local cable advertising the client gets an inexpensive and verified bottom line, but the client also gets a straightforward product. A cable television provider can produce an ad and offer airtime for under $1,000 in some cases.

At the other end of the spectrum, a large New York advertising agency might coordinate a shoot with a production house lasting several days, using Hollywood actors, and a media buy on a national scale. For this level of service, the client can pay more than $1 million.

Often a television commercial is part of a comprehensive advertising campaign. An ad campaign might include contests, celebrity endorsements, and a coordinated series of advertisements across many media platforms.

Research

The first thing to do in developing a television advertisement is to gather a range of information about your client's business and the product or service they want to promote. In the case of researching a specific product, consider factors such as the product's history, its cost, market share over time, competitors, alternative products available, the ongoing customer base, target audience, and the factors that differentiate your client and its products from competitors. This information will assist you in better designing an advertisement that is effective in achieving your client's goals. Talk to the client about their motivation and objectives of the ad. Objectives can range from retaining existing customers to recruiting new customers to shifting market share away from competitors.

Some ads are designed to promote a company or organization rather than a specific product. In the case of a **public relations campaign** or **public service campaign** you need to establish what the client wants the public to gain from the ad. Is it to make the public more familiar with the company in general? Is it to make the public more aware of the service conducted by a nonprofit agency? Is the objective to change the public's behavior so that they will better protect the environment and their own health?

Perhaps the most important question in the research process is to ask, "Who is the audience?" You can not be all things to everyone. A commercial that tries to appeal to everyone or attempts to achieve too much usually ends up being less effective than an ad with specific, targeted objectives. If your client is a fast-food restaurant, you need to ask whether the ad is intended to reach teenagers or parents of small children. The creative approaches and ad design will vary greatly between these two audiences.

In addition to researching your client, the product, and your client's competitors, you need to conduct research on the **target audience**. The target audience is composed of the people the ad is intended to reach. Who are they? What do they like to do in their free time? How much money do they make, and how do they like to spend their disposable income? Is status important to them? What about value? Profile your audience as thoroughly as possible to better design an ad that connects with them.

Marketing and advertising research often utilizes professional research firms, databases, and scientific surveys. In the case of small-scale productions, however, you can learn a lot about your target audience through conversations with the client and its existing customers. Your client might have customer records and research that can provide additional background information.

Advertising Appeals

Once you have conducted research on the product or service to be promoted and have determined the target audience, you will have a better foundation to determine what type of advertising approach will best serve your client's objectives. There are four main types of advertising appeals: reason, emotion, humor, and fear.

Reason. You might choose an advertising approach that appeals to the audience's reason. Advertisements of this type frequently use logical arguments and relevant information to allow the consumer to make a decision based on selected facts. While this seems like an obvious component of effective advertising, in practice this approach represents only a percentage of ads and often it is not the dominant strategy. An insurance company that outlines the benefits of its coverage and value compared to a competitor is appealing to reason.

Emotion. An ad might appeal to the audience's emotions to sell a product or service. A diamond maker might attempt to make a husband feel like he is a bad person if he does not buy his wife a diamond necklace for their anniversary. An ad portraying an attractive person speeding down the road in an expensive sports car is designed to make people feel that they need this sports car if they want to be perceived as attractive and successful.

Humor. Humor is a popular form of television advertising (Weinberger, Spotts, Campbell, & Parsons, 1995). Humorous ads are entertaining and make the audience feel good. This feeling is then associated with the product or service the ads promote. When a humorous ad contains an element of surprise, the effect of the humor is often amplified (Alden, 2000). Humorous ads are also likely to be remembered and talked about, further promoting the campaign's objectives.

Fear. A public service announcement on disease might use fear to get the audience to protect their own health. An insurance company might use reason to appeal to the audience, but they might also try to increase sales with a fear-based campaign. A fear-based approach to insurance advertising could remind the viewer that he or she could be killed at any moment, and the surviving family will be financially ruined if a certain level of insurance is not in place.

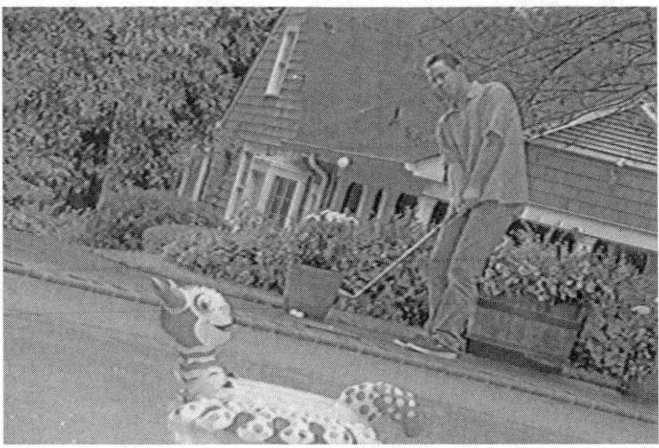

Figure 5.2 Television advertising utilizes a number of persuasive appeals. Humor is a popular tool for grabbing attention and creating positive associations. (Courtesy of The Alpha Group)

These are some basic advertising appeals used to persuade the audience. The best appeal to use in your first television ad will depend on the product, your client's objective, and the target audience. For example, antismoking ads often use humor when targeting a young audience and fear for reaching adults (Beaudoin, 2002).

These four common appeals are not unique to advertising. Documentaries, news packages, fiction programs, and music videos all use these methods to engage the viewer, affect his feelings, and hold his attention. All video production is, in a sense, advertising. You are always selling the viewer to stay with you for the next segment and the next scene. Tapping into the viewer's reason, emotions, sense of humor, and fear can be used to keep him engaged.

Advertising Styles

Each advertising appeal can be communicated through a number of styles. While the appeal (reason, emotion, humor, or fear) determines the tone of the ad, the style determines how the message is organized and communicated.

One of the oldest and most effective sales techniques is the **problem/solution format**. In this approach, a problem is portrayed to the audience and then the client's product or service is shown solving the problem. An ad might show someone embarrassed by bad breath, and then go on to show how the manufacturer's mints can remedy the problem.

Another popular advertising style is the **demonstration format**. Showing how a product or service works is a straightforward way to provide the audience with information and to let them know how this product is valuable to them. Many infomercials for kitchen appliances use the demonstration format.

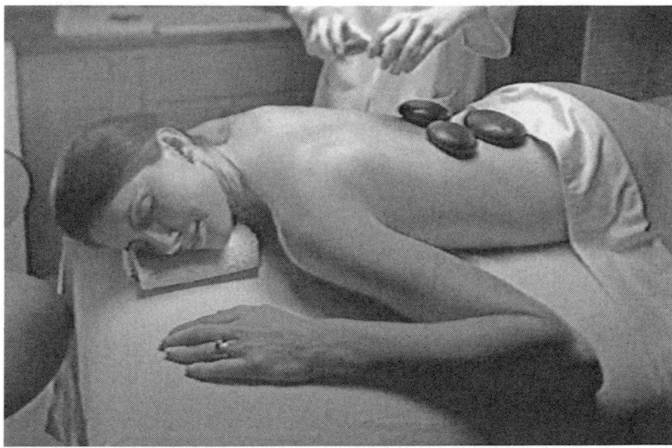

Figure 5.3 Commercials use a variety of styles. Shown here is an example of the demonstration format. (Courtesy of The Alpha Group)

Having a celebrity or expert **spokesperson** speak on behalf of a product can be memorable and persuasive. The product is then associated with a person whom the target audience finds attractive and trusts.

Allowing the audience to hear from satisfied customers can work effectively, too. These types of ads are called **testimonials**. Some testimonial ads portray actual customers, but since real customers are usually not strong actors, many ads of this type stage or reenact testimonials using professional actors. Some ads use **musical formats** and employ original scoring or a popular song to create a memorable impression and lasting association.

In other cases an ad will show many different people having a similar positive experience with a product, and this collection of quick images creates the impression that the product is universally successful. This is the montage applied to advertising.

Ads might use **symbolism** to convey an overall impression about a product. For example, you might see iron ore poured into a smelter, which then produces a hard-body pickup truck. Of course, trucks are not really made this way, but it symbolizes how strong and durable the truck is. Similarly, a sports car might be shown traveling faster than a fighter jet. The image emphasizes the car's speed.

Another effective approach is the **narrative commercial**. Narrative commercials tell a story. Taster's Choice coffee created a benchmark in advertising by running an effective campaign with miniature narratives. Some commercial campaigns tell an entire story in one ad; others stretch the narrative structure across several ads. This is a popular approach to Super Bowl advertising by major sponsors where an ad early in the game introduces characters and a complication; ads later in the broadcast show a resolution to the story.

These are just some of the basic formats and styles you can use to develop commercials. Your specific approach, however, will come from your original concept, which might be a hybrid of two or more of these styles, or your approach might not fit neatly into these classifications at all. What matters most is that your approach is effective.

Creative Design

The best commercial concepts and scripts are often developed through the process of brainstorming. This can be done alone but it sometimes works even more effectively in conjunction with a partner or in a small group. Start by free-associating. See what words come to mind when you think about the product and related elements about the company. Hold the product in your hand. Explore what comes to mind when you think about the target audience. Use your research to inspire and guide the brainstorming process. No idea is silly, worthless, or irrelevant. All ideas have value in that they move the process forward. A seemingly bad idea might ultimately lead to a good one. In looking back on the creative process you might be able to identify a "good bad idea." You might recall a specific unworkable concept that turned out to provide a major creative springboard for your project. Throw your ideas out there. Write them down on a white board. Most will ultimately get brushed aside but one will lead to the core of your concept.

Creative design in advertising works best when you do not hold back and let the ideas fly. Isolated words, concepts, and situations will start to take shape and lead to an approach to present to your client.

Once you have a winning concept on the table, you need to convert that concept into a presentation for the client's approval. Presentations (or pitches) for television commercials often use **presentation storyboards**. Using clip art or sketches, the creative team presents a single frame to represent each shot in the commercial using a PowerPoint presentation or poster boards. Many agencies prefer to use PowerPoint to pitch a concept to the client, while others value the intimacy of using physical poster boards. You can put narration, dialogue, and descriptive information about each shot underneath each image. This allows the client to "see the commercial" during your pitch. Practice your pitch. It is important to be familiar with your storyboards and enthusiastic about the concept.

If the client is not satisfied with the approach you present, it is important to understand why. Ask questions to determine why the client believes the ad concept is not effective. Based on this feedback it is sometimes possible to make refinements that meet the client's expectations and approval. Sometimes a client's preconceptions about what they think they want clouds their judgment, and although they do not like a pitch at first, with some discussion and encouragement they see the wisdom and potential of a creative concept.

In other cases, the client might decide to pull the plug entirely on the process after the pitch and the commercial is never produced. For this reason, the creative development of a commercial is billed separately. The client usually pays for the advertising agency's time and expertise, even if the commercial is never made.

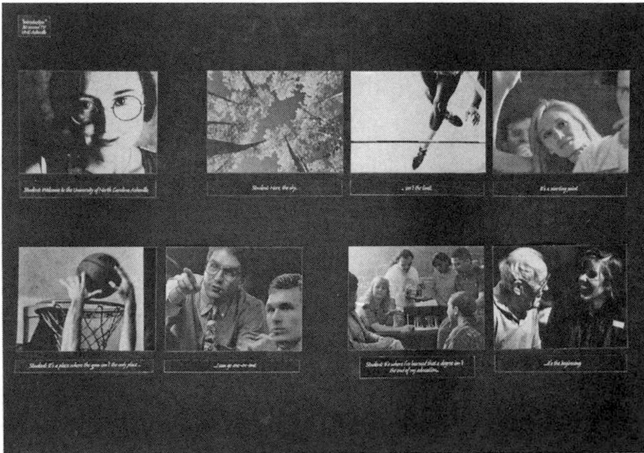

Figure 5.4 Presentation storyboards are often used to pitch an advertising concept to the client.

Market Testing

At each stage of the development process it is beneficial to test the commercial with an audience. Once you have developed a concept that you think will be effective, it is valuable to share the concept with a focus group. A **focus group** is a collection of individuals from the community who are paid for their time to come in and talk about their reactions to a commercial. A focus group should be composed of people sharing the same characteristics as a target audience. If the focus group does not like or understand a concept based on the storyboards, it is important to know this early in the process to avoid wasting limited project resources.

A focus group session usually begins with a presentation of the commercial in its most developed form. After the presentation of the ad, participants in the focus group fill out a questionnaire and provide some written open-ended comments. A professional focus group moderator then leads a discussion with the participants. The written survey before the discussion keeps the early comments offered in discussion from shaping the tone of the entire conversation, and it keeps conformists in the group from changing their opinions to meet the consensus. Discussion in a focus group often begins with each participant articulating some of their observations. Focus groups are frequently videotaped for presentation to the client as evidence of a concept's success or failure.

Focus group testing of a rough-cut of a commercial can indicate areas where more editing is needed, or it might alert the agency to the fact that an ad is a failure. In this case, a focus group can save significant money on media buys and the adverse effects on the client from a confusing or offensive ad.

Focus groups are common for large-budget commercials, but for smaller low-budget commercials focus groups are not usually done in a formal manner. It is still helpful, however, to get outside input for every ad. Share your concept with friends and ask them to give you honest feedback. Share your ideas with other people outside of the process to make sure that your perspective and expectations reasonably match those of your target audience.

Budgeting and Scheduling

Budgeting and scheduling ensure that everything you have planned to do can be paid for, and that everything you require will be exactly where it needs to be on the shooting days. On most projects, only part of the money paid by the client is budgeted for making the commercial. Part of the total budget goes to the advertising agency for overhead and creative development. Part of the budget might be reserved for research, media buys, and agency supervision of the ad throughout the production and testing process.

CLIENT: TWO PENNY FARM

PRODUCER: JOAN LEO
DIRECTOR: JUDITH AUSTIN
WRITER: CORY CARLSON

LOCATION: NEWTOWN, IL
SHOOT: 1 DAY
SHOOT DATE: FEBRUARY 27, 2007

BUDGET PREPARED BY: JOEL BOOTH

BUDGET DATE:

Acct#	Description	Amount	Units	X	Rate	Subtotal	Total
12-00	**PRODUCERS UNIT**						
12-01	Producer	1	flat fee		2,500	2,500	2,500
12-02	Producer's Expenses		allow		500	500	500
12-06	Office Support		allow		200	200	200
					Total for 12-00		**3,200**
12-00	**DIRECTION**						
12-01	Director						
	1 Day Shoot	1	day		1,000	1,000	
	1 Day Prep	1	day		700	700	1,700
					Total for 13-00		**1,700**
14-00	**TALENT**						
14-01	Actors						
	Inn Guest (female)	1	day		600	600	600
	Inn Guest (male)	1	day		600	600	600
14-06	Voice-Over		allow		800	800	800
					Total for 14-00		**2,000**
	ABOVE THE LINE TOTAL						**6,900**
20-00	**PRODUCTION STAFF**						
20-01	Unit Production Manager	1	day		450	450	450
20-12	Production Assistants (2)	1	day	2	100	200	200
					Total for 20-00		**650**
25-00	**SET OPERATIONS**						
25-07	Craft Services	1	day		400	400	400
					Total for 25-00		**400**
31-00	**MAKEUP & HAIRDRESSING**						
31-01	Make-up artist	1	day		400	400	400
					Total for 31-00		**400**
32-00	**LIGHTING**						
32-01	Equipment Rentals						
	Lighting Kit	2	kits		150	300	300
					Total for 32-00		**300**
33-00	**CAMERA**						
33-01	Director of Photography	1	day		500	500	500

Figure 5.5 Sample budget for a mid-priced, 30-second television ad produced on digital video.

33-05	Camera Assistant	1	day		200	200	200
33-11	Camera Package Rental	1	day		485	485	485
33-16	Videotape Stock	10	tapes		19	190	190
					Total for 33-00		**1,375**
34-00	**PRODUCTION SOUND**						
34-02	Boom Operator				300	300	300
34-09	Microphone Rentals	1	package		100	100	100
					Total for 34-00		**400**
	PRODUCTION PERIOD TOTAL						**3,525**
45-00	**EDITING**						
45-01	Editor	2	days		500	1,000	1,000
45-04	Editing Suite Rental	2	days		700	1,400	1,400
45-10	Tape Stock and Accessories		allow		150	150	150
					Total for 45-00		**2,550**
46-00	**MUSIC**						
46-06	License for Prerecorded Music		allow		250	250	250
					Total for 46-00		**250**
	TOTAL POSTPRODUCTION						**2,800**
	TOTAL OTHER						**0**
	TOTAL ABOVE-THE-LINE						**6,900**
	TOTAL BELOW-THE-LINE						**6,325**
	ABOVE & BELOW-THE-LINE						**13,225**
	CONTINGENCY (10%)						**1,322**
	GRAND TOTAL						**14,547**

Figure 5.5b (continued) Sample budget for a mid-priced, 30-second television ad produced on digital video.

The producer of the commercial is given a budget that is actually a subset of the total budget. For instance, if the client pays $20,000 for the full service, perhaps less than half of this, $8,000 or so, might go to the production house to make the commercial. With the approval of the script, it is the responsibility of the producer to itemize the production budget and to make sure that the specific concept can be executed with available resources. The production house needs to set aside some of the money for their operating overhead and to pay the people involved in making the commercial. Production equipment needs to be rented, or money set aside for depreciation, repair and replacement of equipment if the company owns its own gear. Film or videotape stock is needed, as well as actor fees, props, location and studio fees, transportation, accommodations, and food. The production must carry insurance for damages and injuries that might occur. Money is needed for editing facilities, voice-over talent, and tape stock or DVDs for mastering the final product. Finally, it is important to build in a contingency (usually 10%) in case there are unanticipated overruns. It is easy to see how an $8,000 budget can get used up quickly for even a small professional production.

A large-scale professional commercial may have a budget of $100,000 or more. It may have a crew of 15 or more people. A typical crew for making a high-budget television commercial includes a director, producer, associate producer, one or more production assistants, director of photography, camera operator, focus puller, clapper/loader, sound recordist, boom operator, gaffer (who is in charge of the lighting), one or more lighting assistants, camera grip, make-up artist, property master, and actors.

The producer, or an associate producer, works with each crew member who has responsibility for acquisitions and expenditures to make sure that all planning arrangements are in place. The director of photography, for example, has a list of equipment, materials, and personnel needed for the shoot, and the producer makes sure that everything is on budget, ordered, paid for, and on location when needed. The director works with the crew to transform the creative concept into a successful end-product. Such critical-path planning and organization is necessary to ensure success of a complicated project and to avoid delays and serious cost overruns. We will explore both the role of the producer and project budgeting in more detail in chapter 9. Directing is the topic of chapter 10.

Commercial Production Documents

Split-Page Script. Television commercials often use a **split-page script** format. Most commercial scripts can fit on a page or two. The split-page format divides the script into two columns. The left-hand column describes the visual information. The right-hand column presents the corresponding audio including voice-overs and dialogue. Some split-page scripts put time cues in the margin to help ensure that the entire script fits into the time window, which is usually 30 seconds, but there are 10-, 15-, and 60-second formats of video ads for various applications.

Since many advertising agencies do not do their own production, the split-page script is often a critical communication tool between the advertising agency and the production house. Not all advertising agencies use a split-page script format. Some agencies translate a concept directly into storyboards.

Storyboards. Presentation storyboards are a tool used to pitch an ad concept to the client and focus groups. **Production storyboards** are, however, different. The production team uses production storyboards to execute the making of a commercial. The general rule for storyboards is one storyboard frame for each shot in the program, but some complex camera moves require several storyboard frames to describe what takes place in a single shot.

The director often creates production storyboards to previsualize a shoot. Production storyboards are generally hand drawn. Since these are internal working documents, you need not worry about your artistic ability. Many effective storyboards are made with stick figures. What is important is that the storyboards clearly communicate the form of the program to the intended audience. Sometimes a director's storyboards are only for her use and can be informal. In other cases storyboards will be shared with the cinematographer, the production designer, and other crew members to aid in planning. Production storyboards are often composed on sheets of paper or individual index

Global Concept Advertising

CLIENT: Excursion Club
JOB NO: TV 103 - 002
TITLE: Excursion Club
DATE: September 17, 2008
MEDIUM: Television
LENGTH: 30 Seconds

IMAGE	**SOUND**
Alan Schwartz stands with a camera crew inside the main hall of the Excursion Club	
He turns, spots us and walks up to 'talk' to camera.	
	This is a very unique nightclub. The Excursion Club in Center City Philadelphia.
As he indicates features we see them ourselves	It's a photographers dream – the size of the place, and yet it's so elegant.
	The layout,
	…magnificent artwork, full bar and, as they say, this is where the stars come out at night.
Cut to 2 models posing	Lots of people to meet and greet….
Alan moves behind camera and peers through lens	…purely a professional interest on my part of course…
He laughs,	He laughs
Cut to Logo. Excursion Club	
	Excursion Club, Philadelphia Excellent!

Figure 5.6 Television commercials often use a split-page script format.

cards, which allow the reordering of shots as the production concept evolves. Some directors use a storyboard template. Template pages provide a frame for your sketches in the shape of a television screen and have room for dialogue, narration and descriptive information next to each frame. *Appendix B* contains storyboard templates for you to copy and use in both standard television (4:3) and HDTV (16:9) aspect ratios.

Direction arrows show character movement and camera moves in storyboards. These arrows bring life and energy to a static image. Well-illustrated storyboards can convey complex movements quite thoroughly.

While production storyboards are generally hand drawn, other options exist that are valuable for certain approaches. A series of still pictures with

Figure 5.7 Some commercials are written in storyboard form. (Jesse Knight)

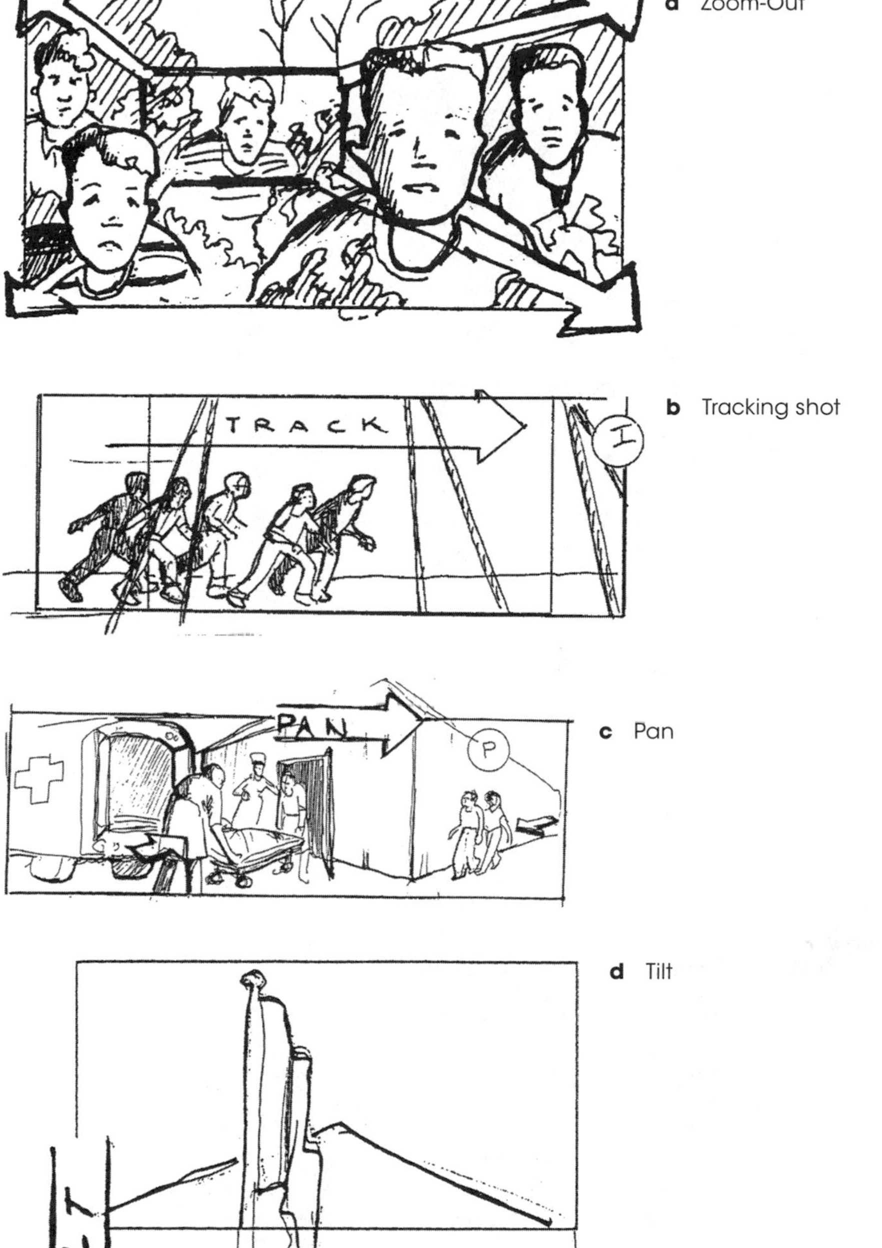

a Zoom-Out

b Tracking shot

c Pan

d Tilt

Figure 5.8 Production storyboards are used to plan a shoot. (Courtesy of Wild Bunch Films)

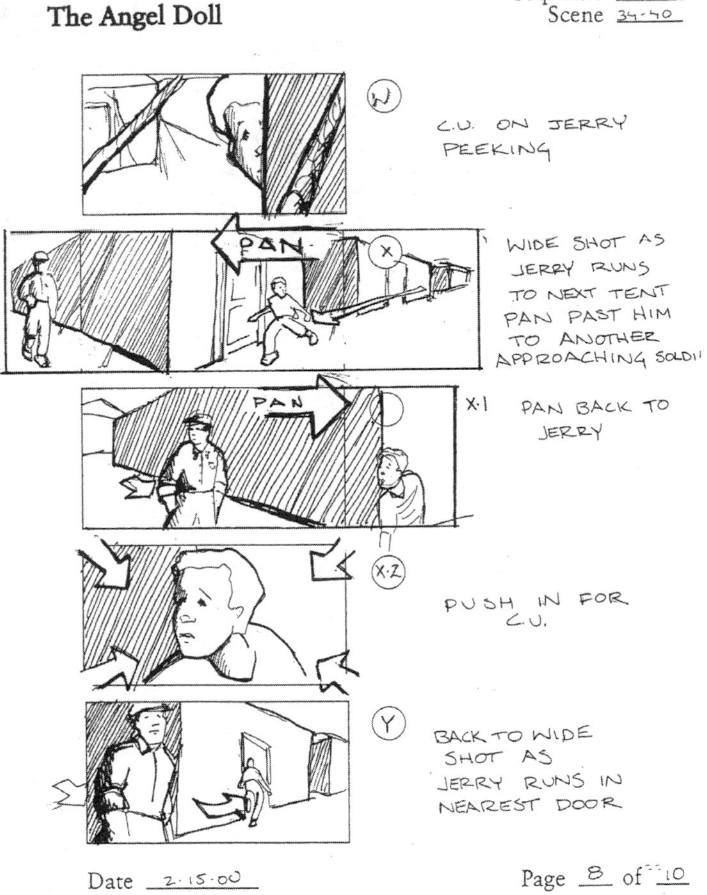

Figure 5.9 Storyboard templates allow the illustration of entire scenes and sequences in an organized manner. (Courtesy of Wild Bunch Films)

Figure 5.10 Direction arrows are used in storyboards to indicate movement. (Courtesy of Wild Bunch Films)

actors or stand-ins can be used to create a photographic storyboard. Clip art can be used for standard scenes and scenarios. For example, if a commercial has a shot of a person with a backpack standing on a mountaintop, followed by a shot of a waterfall, and then a shot of a field, clip art can approximate these images for planning purposes.

You can also produce moving storyboards. **Moving storyboards** aren't really storyboards at all, but rather simple movies to test out and plan a production. *Star Wars: Episode VI - Return of the Jedi* (1983) screen-tested the air scooter chase sequence using toy action figures moved with wire sticks on a primitive set, which was decorated with model train trees. This action was recorded using a home video camera and provided the filmmakers with a sense of the pacing and effective camera angles to plan the real sequence. Computer modeling can be used to create storyboard frames or fully animated representations in the computer.

Location Photos and Sketches. It is valuable to visit the location where you will be shooting ahead of time and record some digital video footage or still pictures so that you have a good sense of the space, and so that you are better able to accurately plan for the environment. Digital images can be used as a reference to create sketches for production planning. The director often creates an overhead floor plan for **blocking** cameras, props, and actors. Taking measurements of a space allows precise planning. Location sketches also serve as a foundation for planning the set design.

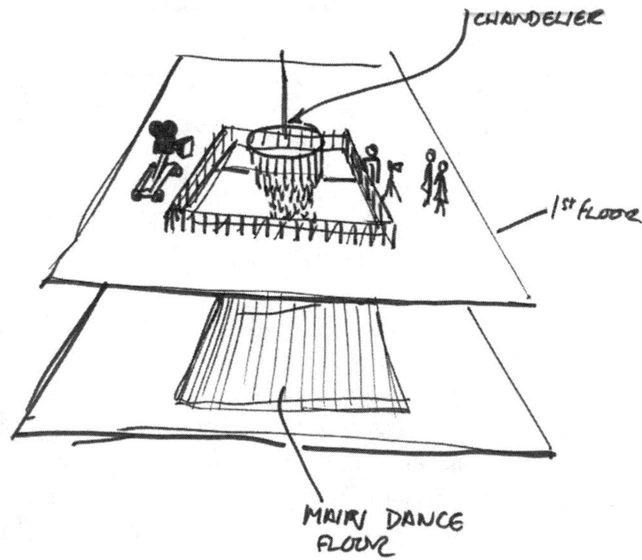

Figure 5.11 Location sketches are used to plan the placement of equipment, props, and actors.

Scene	Description	Location
Night 2300	MCU (level w/) machine (same as 2100) V.O.	Int. kitchen
Night 2400	Master - wide/long shot?	ext. yard
Night 2500	MCU machine (2100/2300) Seth passes by in bg.	INT. kitchen
Day/early 2600	- sunrise stock shot? Master - WS of dogs playing w/ house in b.g.	ext farmyard
2601	Pullin from wide shot to MCU of dog w/ rabbit	" "
2602	low angle shot (med.) of Seth stretching; smiling @ dogs	" "
Day 2700	High angle of Seth watering garden	ext farm
2701	Seth strolling	
Day 2800	Master - camera facing from house back; Seth comes out of barn; finds corpse	ext yard
2801	CU? of Snowball's corpse	
2802	High angle over Seth's shoulder	
2803	MCU Seth/rabbit	
2804	long shot Seth's POV of dogs	
2805	CU Seth	
2806	Seth stands up into frame, line, exits frame (tight shot)	
2900	CU Seth / sitting in kitchen	Int kitchen
2901	CU Fiona	EXT PORCH
2902	CU DAVID	

Figure 5.12 Shot list. (Courtesy of Anne Slatton)

Shot Lists. The director uses the script and production storyboards to generate a shot list. The **shot list** provides the most efficient order and the minimum number of setups required to capture all the images needed.

Production

As the date of a shoot approaches, a **call sheet** is distributed. On shoots lasting more than a day or two, a call sheet is generated for each day of shooting and is distributed in advance of each shoot. A call sheet provides important information that is circulated to every member of the cast and crew. It indicates the date, time, and location of the shoot, and contact information for any questions. In the case of a commercial, the call sheet provides a description of the product being promoted, the advertising agency in charge of creative development, and the company handling production. Call sheets itemize wardrobe and list the camera and accessories needed on location including a specific list of all lights, properties, film or tape stock to be used, the lab that will be doing postproduction work, and the hotel or other accommodations for the cast and crew.

Special Events Video

CALL SHEET

DATES:	THURSDAY SEPTEMBER 28 2008 FRIDAY SEPTEMBER 29 2008	: LOCATION SHOOT : LOCATION SHOOT
LOCATION;	EXCURSION CLUB PHILADELPHIA	215 965 xxxx
CONTACT	RUSSELL STONE -- MANAGER ANDY NUNCA	215 965 xxxx
CALL TIMES:	08:30 am 07:30 am LIGHTING	
PRODUCT:	EXCURSION CLUB	
AGENCY:	GLOBAL CONCEPT ADVERTISING 00 SPRUCE STREET PHILADELPHIA	215 965 xxxx
CONTACTS:	MARK GRIMES KENT THOMAS -- ART DIRECTOR SUSAN GRANT -- WRITER	215 965 xxxx
PROD NO:	FP980/30	
CREW		
DIRECTOR;	PAT SIMPSON	215 965 xxxx
PRODUCER:	NANCY WEST	215 965 xxxx
ASSOC. PRODUCER:	JEFF BUCK	215 965 xxxx
P.A.:	KEN KLESSEK	215 965 xxxx
PHOTOGRAPHY:	ROB NEUBAUER	215 965 xxxx
OPERATOR:	TRACY KREIDER	215 965 xxxx

Figure 5.13 The first page of a call sheet for a television commercial.

When making a commercial, the director often uses a stopwatch, especially if there is spoken dialogue. If an actor is reading lines too slowly, the director can get a sense that it will not be possible for the entire script to be delivered in 30 seconds. Using a stopwatch and having an intimate sense of the pace of the commercial will help ensure that the final program fits within the well-defined window of commercial television.

It is important to be open to a creative opportunity on location, but it is even more important to stay focused. Time is important on location and goes by quickly. It can sometimes take an hour to get the lighting for a particular shot just right. A 10- or 12-hour day can fly by, so it is absolutely important to stay on task and make sure there are no overages. If you are responsible for a crew on location and you run out of time, all those people are going to have to be paid overtime or the production will have to return for an additional day. If you prove your ability to deliver a creative product of high technical quality on budget, you will become a director in demand.

PUBLIC SERVICE ANNOUNCEMENTS

Television broadcasters use the public airwaves, and are entrusted by law to serve the "public interest, convenience and necessity."* **Public service announcements (PSAs)** are an important part of broadcasters' public service mission. Cable outlets also broadcast public service announcements as part of their mission. Producing public service announcements is a great way to practice your skills while helping a nonprofit agency or social cause.

If there is a nonprofit agency that you are interested in or have worked with before, see if they would like you to produce a public service announcement for them as a practice exercise. You can make the final product available to them, and if it is broadcast you will earn a production credit for your resume. The techniques used to produce PSAs are similar to those used for commercials. The main difference between a commercial and a PSA is simply the nature of the product or service that is promoted.

MUSIC VIDEOS

Music videos are another great area for gaining practice and experience in production. Their short format and the fact that they are based on matching original images to existing sound make them manageable projects with creative latitude. Young directors are often tested with music videos or commercials before mov-

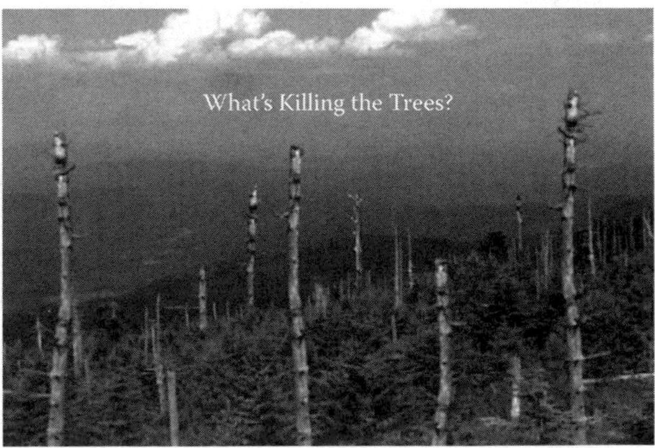

Figure 5.14 Public service announcements (PSAs) highlight issues of social importance. (Courtesy of Andrea Desky)

* Communications Act of 1934.

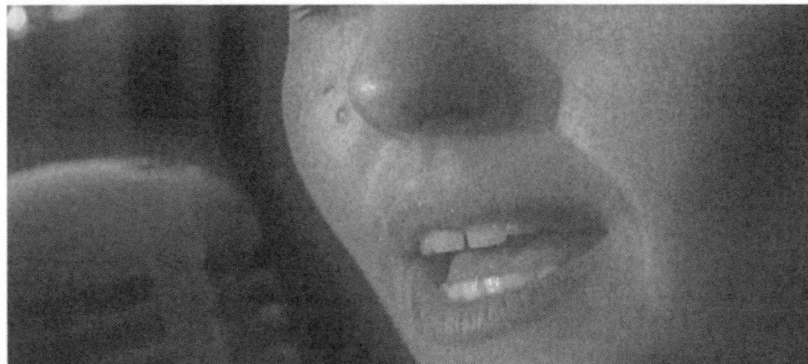

Figure 5.15 Music videos offer a broad platform for experimentation. (Courtesy of Troy Scott Burnette)

ing on to larger projects. Brett Ratner, director of *Red Dragon* (2002) and *After the Sunset* (2004), established his early career directing music videos.

Your imagination is the only limit with this form. Some music videos closely mirror the lyrical content of the song. Some work visually against the lyrics, while others tell a story completely different from the lyrics. Many music videos are not narratives at all, but rather collections of seemingly disconnected images or a record of a musical performance.

Perhaps the best way to begin creative development for a music video is to simply close your eyes, listen to the song, and see what appears before you. Make notes, let some time pass, and then do this again. Play the song over and allow yourself to wander from your original concept. See what occurs to you later with more understanding of the song and its progression and pacing. This was the creative method behind Walt Disney's classic *Fantasia* (1940).

Music videos are a powerful force in shaping youth culture and are used as a central method in marketing products and services to young people (Sherman, 1991). Music videos are essentially commercials, designed to promote artists and sell CDs. Like the commercial, music videos often use a split-page script. The longer running time of a song will likely require multiple script pages. The right-hand column, dedicated for audio, contains lyrical content and time queues for the song. The left-hand column is used to develop accompanying visual information. The budget, call sheet, and crew composition for a music video are often similar to those of a television commercial, although music videos often require more in the way of properties, special effects, and post-production work.

Some music videos include on-screen synchronous singing. This synchronization can be achieved by having playback of the song on location that is matched to the camera with time code. Many cameras are able to receive and record externally generated time code. Music videos that require images of singing and playing instruments in sync require that the song be played back on the set to guide the performance. The song playback has time code, and this time code is fed to the camera. The musical track can be played over and over, in whole or just in part for specific shots, and the time code at each point in the song will match perfectly every time it is played. This allows editing with perfect sync to the images in postproduction.

SHORT FILMS

The dramatic structure explored in chapter 1 can be applied to any program length. Making short films is the best way to practice the skills of narrative visual production and prepare for longer forms. The ability to tell stories succinctly is challenging and will demonstrate your effectiveness as an efficient communicator.

The very first films ever made were short films. Support of short film production and emerging filmmakers is critical to the advancement of film and video arts. This value is reflected in the numerous grant opportunities dedicated exclusively to short films. It is telling that the Academy of Motion Picture Arts and Sciences reserves several Oscars for the best short films of the year.

The production of short films provides the opportunity to experience all phases of production in a compressed time frame. The 48 Hour Film Project pushes this idea of time compression to an extreme. All participants in the festival have just 48 hours to write, shoot, edit, and submit a short film for competition. To make sure there is no cheating, the name of a character, a prop, genre, and line of dialogue are provided to each team just minutes before the contest begins. The companion DVD contains an award-winning film from this competition.

If things don't work out well with a short film the scale is small enough that you can take the lessons learned in the process and move on to another project without investing a great amount of time and resources.

The writing process for your first short film need not be formal. The most important thing is to get your ideas down on paper in a form that works for you. If you wish to use formal screenplay formatting, see chapter 9, which presents the screenwriting form.

Once you develop your creative concept and the script, sketch out production storyboards and make a shot list. Capture each scene using the master scene method and the rules of visual language. Assemble these scenes in post-production into a unified short film. The camera mic should be all you need for recording location audio on your first short film, but if you would like to study

Figure 5.16 Short films are a great way to practice production skills. The five-minute film *Detached* was written, shot, and edited in two days as part of the 48 Hour Film Project. (Courtesy of The 48 Hour Film Project and Paul Bonesteel)

advanced audio recording, see chapter 7, which offers a comprehensive range of options for location audio recording and sound design.

Short films are a wonderful way to express your ideas, experiment, and explore your potential as a visual artist. The most important way to become a great visual storyteller is to dedicate yourself completely to each individual project. Try to remain focused all the way through the process. After completing a short film and permitting some time to pass, return to your completed work and critique it. Imagine what you would do differently to improve the final product and then make another program. Practice and refinement allow you to improve your production skills. With each successive project, you should be able to increase the scale and complexity of your productions. Go from a two-minute short film to four minutes. When you feel comfortable that these short films are successful, then try making a 10-minute film. Over time the possibility of successfully completing a feature-length program will come within your reach.

CONCLUSIONS

Commercials offer one of the best entry-level business opportunities in video production. Whether you join one of the many organizations that produce television commercials or forge your own path as an independent, there are opportunities in virtually every market. Commercials and other short-form programs offer the best platforms to practice your skills.

Understanding the business side of video production will be helpful as you progress in your studies and career. You now have insights and knowledge of how television commercials are designed and produced. You are familiar with fundamental production planning tools including presentation storyboards, production storyboards, shot lists, location sketches, and the split-page script.

In the next chapter you will learn about light and lighting. Few effective programs are created without the careful control of light. You cannot expect to set up your camera and have the images look wonderful on their own. You often need to shape the light and control the image. Manipulating light is arguably the single most important technical element to master as a visual program creator.

SAMPLE EXERCISES

1. Select a product or service and design presentation storyboards for a 30-second advertisement, using research and brainstorming to develop your approach. Translate the presentation storyboards into production storyboards to plan the shoot.
2. Choose a song that you are not familiar with and study it. Get to know the musical structure and lyrics. Write a split-page music video script for this song.

3. Identify a nonprofit agency in your community. Visit their Web site and review their literature. Can you create an innovative approach to promote their services in a public service announcement?

RECOMMENDED READINGS

Adelman, K. (2004). *The Ultimate Filmmaker's Guide to Short Films: Making It Big in Shorts*. Studio City: M. Weise Productions.

Elin, L., Lapides, A. (2004). *Designing and Producing the Television Commercial*. Boston: Pearson.

Feineman, N., Reiss, S. (2000). *Thirty Frames per Second: The Visionary Art of the Music Video*. New York: Harry N. Abrams.

REFERENCES

Alden, D. L. (2000). Extending a contrast resolution model of humor in television advertising: The role of surprise. *Humor: International Journal of Humor Research, 13*, 193-217.

Beaudoin, C. E. (2002). Exploring antismoking ads: Appeals, themes, and consequences. *Journal of Health Communication*, 7, 123-137.

Sherman, B. L. (1991). Perceiving and processing music television. In J. Bryant & D. Zillmann (Eds.), *Responding to the screen: Reception and reaction processes* (pp. 373-388). Hillsdale, NJ: Lawrence Erlbaum Associates, Inc.

Weinberger, M. G., Spotts, H. E., Campbell, L., & Parsons, A. L. (1995). The use and effect of humor in different advertising media. *Journal of Advertising Research*, 35, 44-56.

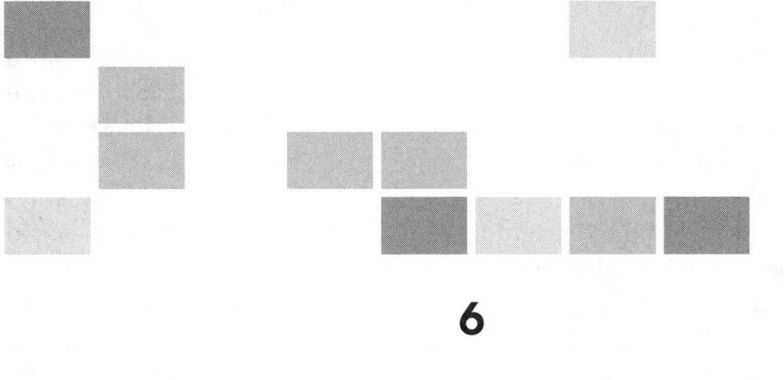

6

LIGHTING

CHAPTER OBJECTIVES

In chapter 3 we explored the process of controlling light with the camera. Proper setting of camera controls is crucial, but camera controls are only a small part of the lighting formula. The most challenging and essential elements of lighting happen in front of the camera. Lighting is primarily shaping and controlling the illumination on the set so the light reaching the camera lens carries your desired effects.

In this chapter you will explore the tools and methods for controlling light. A few fundamental strategies will allow you to control four important properties of light: amount, direction, quality, and color. You will study the factors that control each of these properties, the tools used by the cinematographer and lighting team, and the application of these tools to achieve lighting objectives. The chapter concludes with a survey of some basic creative approaches to lighting to provide a foundation for interpreting your own lighting designs. The goals of this chapter are to:

- Explore the properties of light;
- Understand the traditions and options for creative lighting design;
- Survey equipment used to supply and control light;
- Achieve a foundation to translate your concepts to screen through lighting design.

Motion pictures are light. The light that reaches the imaging surface in recording and the light that reaches the viewer's eye in playback define the movie. The visual component of creating motion pictures is all about controlling light. Look at how light behaves naturally in the environment. Study the light in the room you are in now. Are there windows? How is the light from the windows interacting with artificial lights inside the room? Observe a room with windows over time and see how the light changes throughout the day.

Watch films and television with the sound turned off. Analyze the images and the way light is used in every scene and shot. This is one of the best ways to heighten awareness of the range of lighting choices in video production and to build a repertoire of creative lighting options.

Understanding how light behaves naturally is an important foundation for learning to control light for video production in a way that meets your creative objectives. Controlling light is achieved by balancing four major lighting elements: amount, direction, quality, and color.

Elements of Lighting

Amount. Light control at its most basic level is determining the proper amount of light required for your creative objectives. Light quantity is traditionally measured in footcandles. One **footcandle** of light is the amount of light that is cast on one square foot by a light source of one candlepower of intensity from a distance of one foot away. A 150-watt household bulb produces more footcandles of light than a 40-watt household bulb. Some video equipment is rated in units of **lux** rather than footcandles. There are about 10.75 lux in one footcandle.

A primary way to control the amount of light is through the choice of lighting instruments used. Lighting instruments for video production vary in power consumption from a few watts for some LED camera-mounted units to 10,000 watts for large studio lighting instruments.

Placement affects light intensity. The light falling on a surface gets dimmer as the source of light is moved away. Light diffuses over distance. The reduction of light over distance follows an **inverse square rule**. As a lighting instrument is moved twice the distance from a surface, the intensity of the light is reduced to one fourth. Changing the physical distance of an instrument from the subject alters light intensity.

Light amount can also be controlled through scrimming the lights. A **scrim** is a metal screen placed over a lighting instrument, which is designed to reduce the amount of light emitted without changing its quality. Scrims allow you to reduce the intensity of light without having to physically move the lighting instrument away from the subject.

Light intensity can also be controlled by reflecting light. Light is scattered and partially absorbed through reflection, so another way to change light intensity is to bounce light off other surfaces.

Direction. The direction, sometimes called the throw of the light, is an important component in creative design. Light direction can be controlled

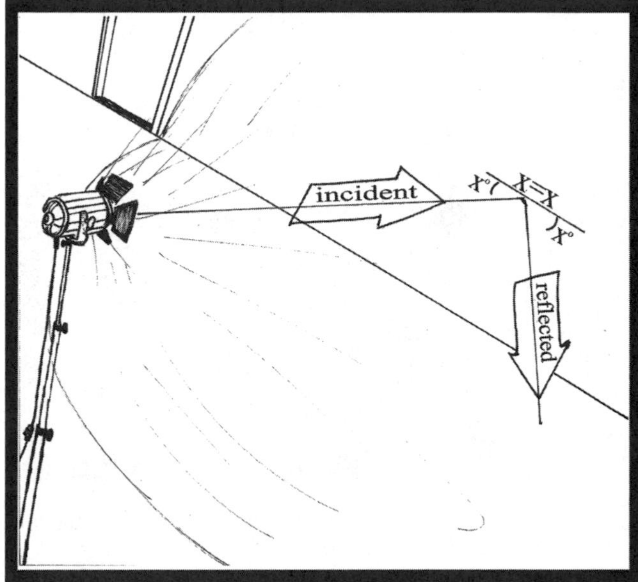

Figure 6.1 The angle of light incidence equals the angle of reflection. (Jesse Knight)

by the position and angle of the instruments. In a studio, you might have instruments mounted overhead on the ceiling. You might also work with lights on floor stands that can be adjusted to various heights. When working outside, the angle of the sun changes throughout the day, but even the angle of the sun can be controlled using reflectors.

Reflection allows you to change the angle of any lighting source. The angle of incidence equals the angle of reflection. For example, if light strikes a mirror at a 45-degree angle, it will be reflected off the mirror in an opposite 45-degree angle. Therefore, by positioning a reflecting surface between the lighting instrument and the subject, you can create almost any incoming angle.

Quality. Light also has a quality. Some light is described as hard, while another type is soft. Lighting that is hard is generally composed of **incident light** coming in a straight line from its source, whereas soft light has a lot of reflection, or **diffused light**, moving in different directions. Light coming directly through a window will be hard, whereas light passing through lace curtains will be much softer as the material diffuses the incoming light.

Reflecting light with different surfaces and using special filters over lighting instruments can change the quality of your light sources. A mirror reflects light wavelengths perfectly straight. A polished metal surface reflects light mostly straight. A white board, however, will scatter the light and soften it. Therefore, it is important to note that reflecting light not only changes the light's direction, but also changes its quality depending upon the nature of the reflecting surface.

Figure 6.2 Bounced light creates soft and even illumination. On this set, a large white screen is mounted overhead as a reflecting surface. (Courtesy of Bonesteel Films)

You can put filters over lighting instruments to change the quality. Filters designed for this purpose are referred to as **diffusion filters**. Two primary types of diffusion materials are frost and silk spun. **Frost materials** are sheets of plastic with varied patterns that affect the light in different ways. **Silk-spun materials** are woven sheets of thread in various patterns and densities. Since loosely woven silk-spun materials have holes in the weave, they retain some direct light. There are hundreds of options available among diffusion materials, which allows videographers to create the exact effect desired in shaping light quality.

Color. The color characteristics of light convey creative and emotional content. The color of the image in video production can be controlled by manipulating the color of the lighting source and objects in the composition, as well as through filtering.

Color filters can be used on the lights themselves and on the camera lens, or can be applied in postproduction. Controlling light quantity, direction, quality, and color are the primary ways to shape light for visual programs. The remainder of this chapter explores the tools and techniques for controlling light.

Lighting Instruments

Lighting instruments for video production come in a variety of sizes and shapes to meet different creative needs. The sun, too, is an option for lighting serving as the most plentiful and universal source available.

To get a sense of the basic parts and features of production lighting instruments we will examine the Fresnel light, which is a popular instrument used in video production. The **Fresnel lens**, named after its inventor, is designed to focus light without having a large and heavy lens. This is achieved by using varying concentric circles of glass.

Lighting instruments start with a housing. The housing protects the bulb and holds the electric circuitry. Some lights, like the Fresnel, contain a focusing knob that can move the lamp bulb closer to or further from the lens, thereby changing the pattern of the light emitted. A light set in a **spot setting** throws light in an intense narrow beam, whereas a light set in a **flood setting** casts the light over a wider area. Lighting instruments also contain mounting hardware attached to the housing so the light can be set on a floor stand or mounted on an overhead grid.

Most lights have a power cord. Field production lights generally plug into a regular wall outlet. Some high-intensity lights, however, require a special

Figure 6.3 A Fresnel lens uses concentric circles of glass to reduce size and weight. (Jennie Picarella)

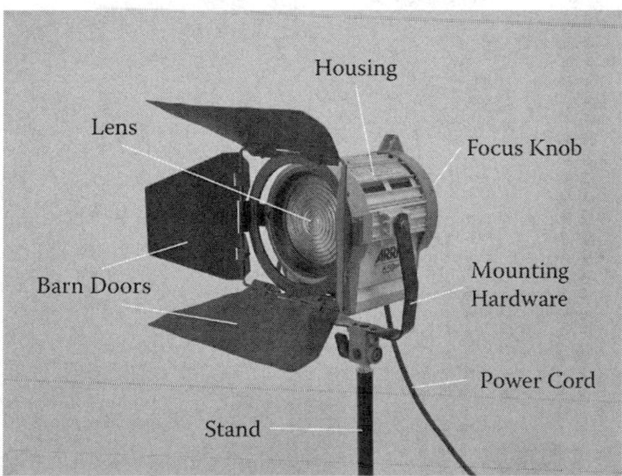

Figure 6.4 A lighting instrument and its parts.

high-power outlet or DC current. Many lighting instruments have barn doors. **Barn doors** allow you to block off light from certain parts of the set. Be careful when adjusting barn doors, or when touching any lighting instrument, as they can get very hot. It is important when working with lights to wear protective gloves.

Modeling Light

Three-Point Lighting. Three-point lighting is the model way to light a human subject in photography and cinematography. In a three-point lighting design, the main source of light is called the **key light**. The key light provides the primary illumination on the subject. The exact position of the key light varies depending on your creative objective, but generally the key light comes in at

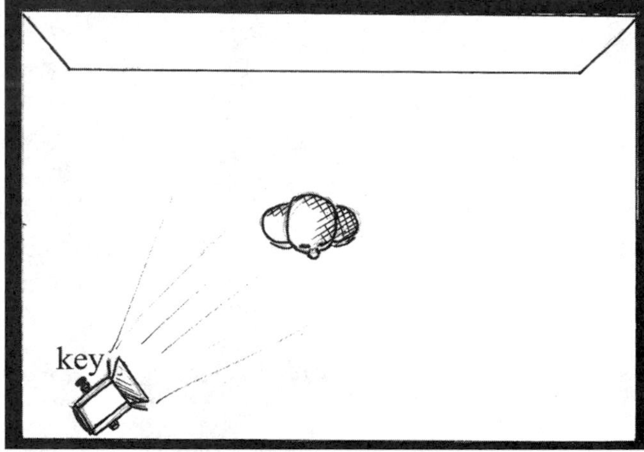

Figure 6.5 Key light. (Illustration by Jesse Knight)

about a 30- to 45-degree angle above the subject and about a 30- to 45-degree angle off-center from the subject's nose. The reason the key light is not pointed directly at the subject's face is that a direct light from the camera position creates a flat image.

Light that hits a subject head-on does not create a sense of depth. In video program design we strive to portray three-dimensional space on a two-dimensional screen. We must therefore use the tools from two-dimensional design introduced in chapter 2 to create the illusion of depth. When you move the key light off to the side it produces shadows across the subject's face. Shadows and light work together to create a sense of depth. You might notice, however, that the shadows on the subject's face are quite dramatic. Unless you are trying to create an image that is sinister or dark and depressing, this type of dramatic lighting might be inappropriate.

The second light in the three-point lighting design fills in shadows on the subject's face created by the key light. This second light, called the **fill light**, is placed on the opposite side of the subject from the key light, also at about a 30- to 45-degree height and about 30- to 45-degrees off the subject's nose. The fill light should not be the same intensity as the key light or the sum of the lights will be flat, and a three-dimensional effect will not be achieved. While the fill light eliminates the harshness of shadows from the key light, there should still be a sense that the key side of the subject's face is brighter.

Using a lower wattage light for the fill light than the key light will help achieve lower brightness on the fill side. Moving the instrument farther away from the subject, filtering it, or bouncing light off a reflecting surface can help get the key light and fill light in a balance that matches your concept.

The third light in the classic three-point modeling setup is the **back light**. The back light is designed to put a halo or rim of light around the subject's hair and shoulders to help separate her from the background. This creates greater definition and an increased sense of depth. Since the back light is behind the subject, it is often within the line of sight of the camera. This is not a problem in a studio setting where the instruments are mounted overhead, but in a field environment while working with light stands this can create challenges. You might have to move your back light to accommodate the composition or you can use special lighting attachments, which can help hide the back light out of frame. Often the back light is placed up high and off to the side so it will not be seen by the camera.

Four-Point Lighting. Four-point lighting is simply the three-point lighting setup with the addition of one more light. This additional light is called the **background light**. In some situations a background light enhances the composition by allowing the audience to see what is behind the subject. The background light is different from the back light. The back light is turned toward the back of the subject, while the background light illuminates the set and props behind the subject.

Figure 6.6 Fill light. (Illustration by Jesse Knight)

While the three- and four-point lighting designs are standard formulas for lighting subjects in studios, the fact is that much creative lighting for video production applies these principles indirectly. Location environments often have available light, such as a window, or the location might be a confined space that does not allow model lighting. Also, we do not go through life perfectly lit for model photography, so realistic setups should not always be three-point. If you wish to film a person looking in the mirror in a small bathroom, for example, you can see how three-point lighting would not only be unrealistic, but impractical to implement in this tiny space.

To create a truly effective lighting design on location, only use the three- and four-point lighting concepts as a loose reference. These lighting techniques can be applied as discussed above for interview subjects, or while working in a studio for classic compositions, but on location it is best to build your lighting setups one light at a time. This building of lights is the foundation of lighting design.

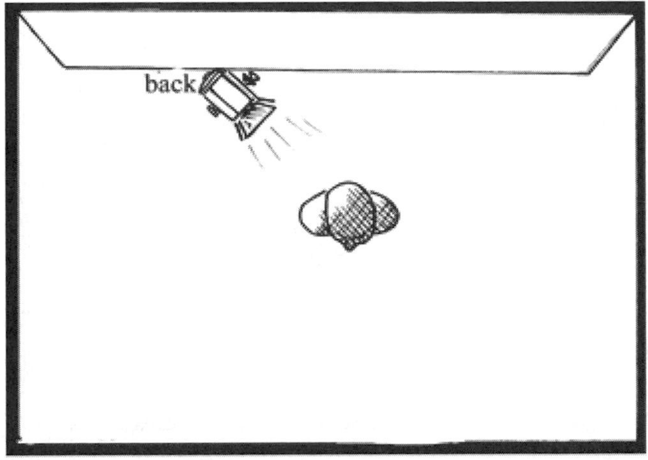

Figure 6.7 Back light. (Illustration by Jesse Knight)

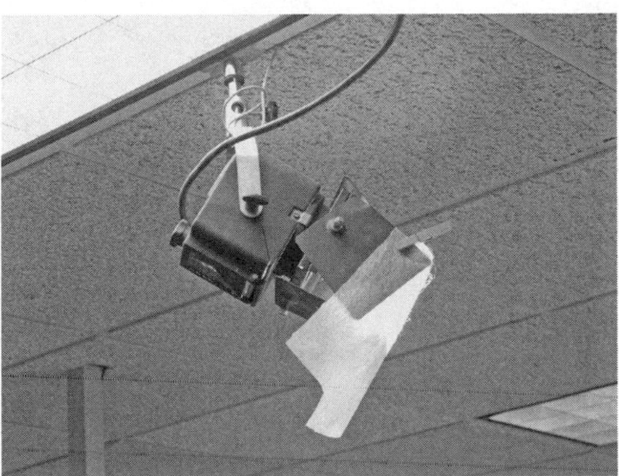

Figure 6.8 Special hardware can mount a back light out of view of the camera.

Figure 6.9 Background light. (Illustration by Jesse Knight)

Lighting Design

When planning the lighting for any scene, start by studying the available light and the practical lights. **Available light** refers to the light that exists naturally as part of the environment. Look for overhead lighting fixtures. Consider if you want to use them as a light source. Determine where the windows are and whether you want to use that light, too. Consider how you will address the changing window light as the day progresses. Available light is the light that is there before you show up.

Practical sources are the lighting sources that you see as part of the scene. If a campfire or table lamp is in the shot then it becomes a practical light source. For most creative applications it is important to consider the location and nature of practical lights to determine your plan for lighting the set.

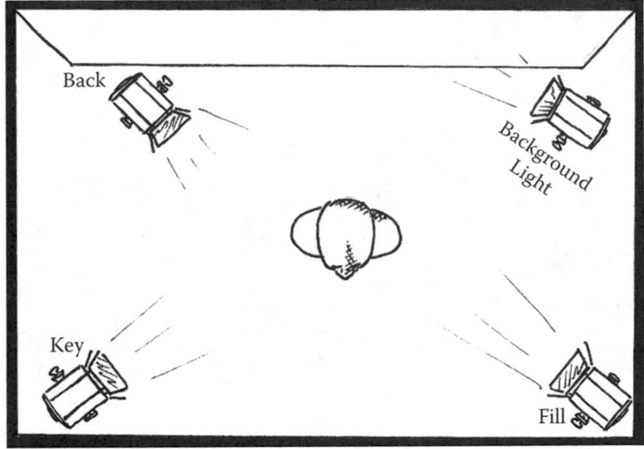

Figure 6.10 Four-point lighting design. Key + Fill + Back + Background. (Illustration by Jesse Knight)

In some cases, the use of available and practical light sources is adequate for achieving lighting objectives, but this is the exception. Usually available and practical lighting need to be supplemented either because there is not enough **base illumination** for the camera or because the available and practical lights leave shadows that are distracting or otherwise ineffective. If the issue is a matter of increasing light intensity, you can replace the bulb in a practical light with one of higher wattage, or you can put a production light out of view coming from the same direction as the practical light. You can put a 2000-watt light outside of a window to help boost the light coming into a room in a controlled way. Providing justification for artificial lights is called **motivating light**. If you light two people talking on a street corner, the overhead light and downward shadows that you create with a production light might be motivated by an overhead streetlamp, which you show to the audience in the establishing shot.

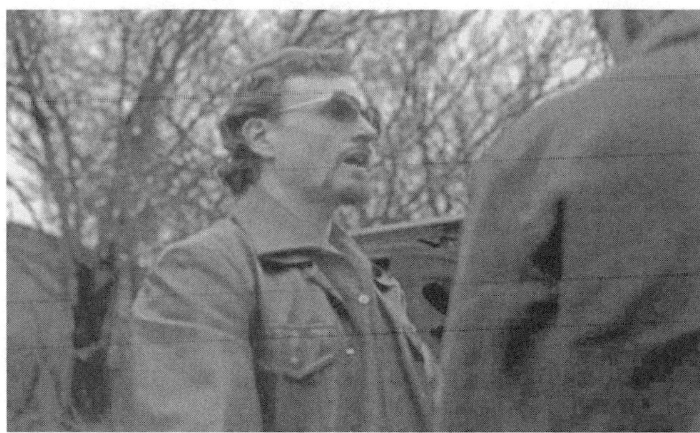

Figure 6.11 Sometimes available light is all you need. Before setting reflectors and instruments, conduct a detailed assessment of the existing light. This scene from *Sinkhole* was captured with available light only. (Courtesy of Paul Schattel)

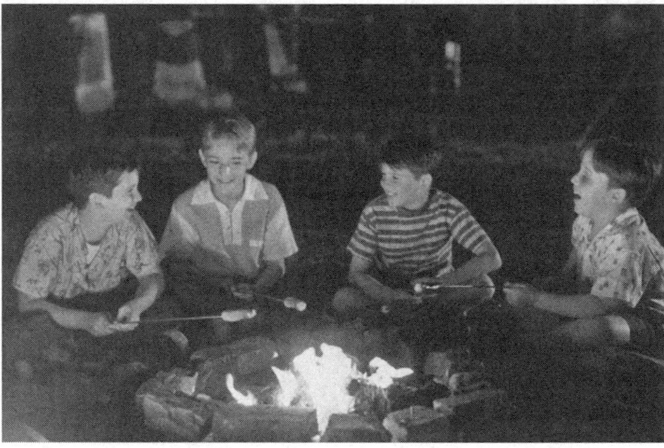

Figure 6.12 Practical lights provide motivation. The campfire justifies the artificial lighting used in this scene. (Photo by Jim Bridges; courtesy of Wild Bunch Films)

Build your lighting designs one light at a time. Start with the key light. Have the key light motivated by a practical source, if appropriate. Adjust its intensity by moving the light, filtering it, or using reflection. You might have to adjust the key light as you add more lights because the illumination level is sometimes affected by lighting spill. **Spill** refers to light leaking over into an unintended area. Determine from there if you need to make additional adjustments. Sometime a key light is all you need. If the shadows are too harsh for your objectives then bring in a fill light to soften them. You can have more than one fill light if the shadows of the key light need to be touched up in more than one spot.

Once you make these adjustments, decide if the light looks right. Check the camera monitor or a field monitor to see how your lighting looks on screen. Do you need a back light to create separation? Do you need one or more lights on the background?

Your subject might require an eye light. An **eye light** is a narrow beam of light that hits and highlights the subject's eyes for a glamorous or dramatic effect. You might need what is called a kicker light. A **kicker light** is a small light used to punch up a little part of a composition that is too dark. The important thing is to put lights where you need them to match your objectives, and not to strictly follow a textbook lighting design.

Using your lighting instruments, setting their positions, manipulating the barn doors, bouncing the light off surfaces such as the ceiling, walls, and bounce cards are only some of the available tools for control. We will explore additional filters and peripherals throughout this chapter. Lighting takes practice and experimentation, and interestingly, sometimes the simplest setups are the most effective.

Contrast Ratio

Contrast ratio refers to the range of illumination within a composition. An image on screen can be pure white, pure black, or any degree of illumination in between. A three-point modeling setup might have twice as much illumination on the key side of the actor's face as on the fill side. This is a 2:1 contrast ratio. A 2:1 contrast ratio is subtle and considered normal for many video applications. If a set has four times as much light on the key side than the fill side, this produces a 4:1 contrast ratio. This is a difference, as you will recall from chapter 3, of two f-stops. Each time you increase an f-stop you change the amount of light two-fold.

Practice lighting so that you know what a 4:1 and a 2:1 contrast ratio will look like in the final program. Set up a human subject in a chair, do a three-point lighting setup, and change the contrast ratio by altering the intensity difference between the key side and the fill side of the face. Many professionals use an external light meter to make these ratio measurements but the light meter in the camera can often be used effectively to check contrast ratios. Zoom in on each side of the actor's face and take a reading. The difference in these two readings can be used to estimate the contrast ratio. Make notes, play these images back, and you will start to get a sense of how contrast works in video production.

Manipulating the contrast ratio on human faces is only one small part of the contrast formula. You need to understand and control the effects of contrast within your entire scene. Light intensity is a major way of controlling the image, and contrast is a way of expanding that concept. You do not just control the overall amount of light falling on the scene, but the light amount in every single part of the scene.

Different media can handle different contrast ranges. The **contrast range** of any medium refers to the difference in the amount of light the medium can handle before an image will go from pure white to pure black. Consumer home video has a relatively narrow contrast range. Professional video equipment has a wider contrast range, allowing more creative latitude between highlights and shadows while still rendering the detail. Film has the widest contrast range of any motion picture option, approximately seven f-stops. This means that you can have 128 times as much light on one part of the scene than another and still render the details between white and black.

Human beings are susceptible to a visual phenomenon called **simultaneous brightness contrast** (Coren, Ward, & Enns, 2004). It is not possible to see pure black without having something light in our field of view at the same time. If you close your eyes and block out all light, you will not see black. Your brain will perceive a somewhat spotty dark gray field. We only perceive pure black when there is something white to contrast against it. This applies to viewing motion pictures as well. Putting highlights and dark areas together within the same composition stimulates the visual cortex, allowing the perception of pure blacks and whites.

Color

Visible light is a range of the electromagnetic spectrum that we can perceive with our eyes and brain to help us understand our environment. We perceive specific wavelengths within this visible spectrum as individual colors. The visual spectrum begins at about 700 **nanometers** and ends at 400 nanometers. It contains the following main colors that are visible in a rainbow: red, orange, yellow, green, blue, indigo, and violet. The first letter of each major color, in

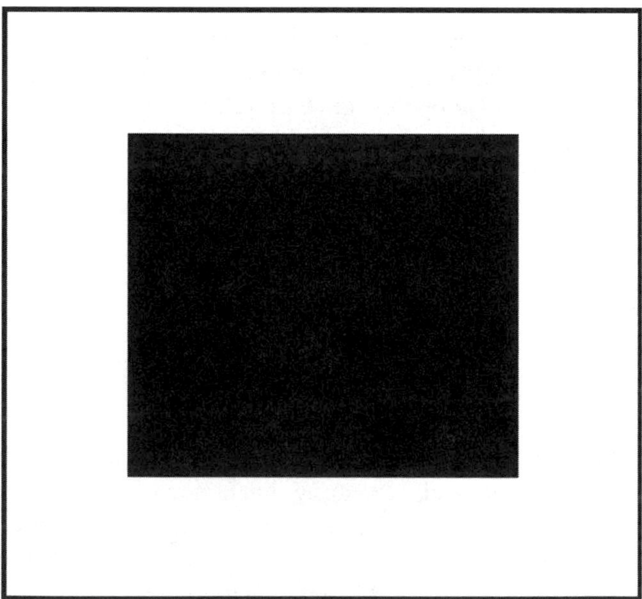

Figure 6.13 People perceive true black only when a dark area is contrasted against a bright one. To achieve rich blacks in your images it is best to have areas of white within the same composition. (Jesse Knight)

order across the spectrum, spells the name Roy G. Biv. That is a simple way of defining the visual spectrum. People can actually distinguish tens of thousands of individual colors within the color spectrum.

Color affects mood. Blue colors are considered cool while yellows are called warm. People who enter a blue room sometimes turn up the thermostat because the visual sensation of blue translates into a physical feeling of coolness (Boynton, 1971). Dark, saturated colors are associated with weight or heaviness (Alexander & Shansky, 1976), and red often indicates danger and violence, which is a primal reaction that may run as deep as the blood in our veins.

Color Theory. Colors interact in two main ways. We can work with subtractive color or additive color. **Subtractive color** manipulation is how printing is achieved. If you take the three **primary colors** of printer's ink (yellow, cyan, and magenta) and mix them together, you create black ink. You subtract color away until nothing is left but black.

Additive color manipulation is more relevant to our needs in video production. In additive color manipulation you use light instead of pigment. If you add the three primary colors in light (blue, red, and green), you create white light. Also, you can add different ratios of these three lights to create any color in the visual spectrum. If all three of these lights are turned off, you have black. If all three of these lights are turned on in equal amounts, you create white.

Color film stock has three light-sensitive layers, each layer sensitive to a different primary color. When the layers are exposed to light they are saturated in different amounts depending on the color of the object before them. When light is shown through the processed film later it reproduces these colors or, in the case of film negative, their complementary colors. The **complementary colors** are yellow for blue, cyan for red, and magenta for green. Using a filter of any color listed here will block its complementary. Therefore, if you wish to darken a blue sky, use a yellow filter over the lens. Video cameras with three image sensors have an image sensor for recording each of the primary colors of light.

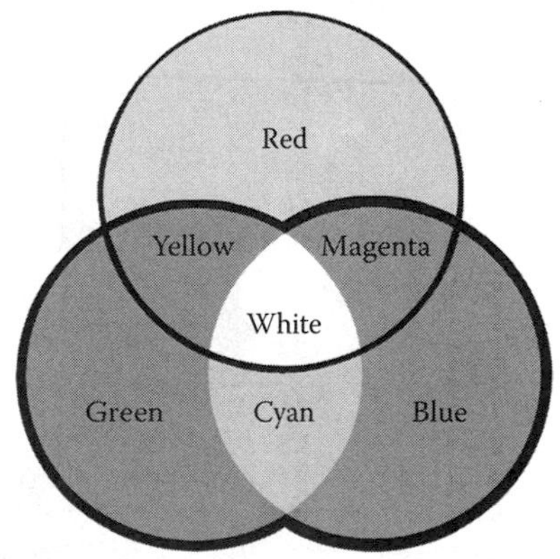

Figure 6.14 Additive color chart. Each color on the chart is opposite its complement. (Jesse Knight)

Color Temperature. Wavelength is only one way to describe the color of light. In video production we refer to the color of light in terms of its **color temperature**. The light we see is not usually white, but our brain perceives different light sources as white because of a phenomenon called **color constancy**. We recognize the color that objects should be and our brain makes an adjustment. The fact is, however, that objects outside in daylight are dramatically different in color from the same objects observed inside by a light bulb.

We measure color temperature for video in degrees Kelvin. The color temperature scale in Kelvin is determined by the color of light that would be emitted from a black box when heated to a given temperature. At the low end of the color temperature scale are the reds. A candle flame produces light at about 1,000 degrees Kelvin. An incandescent bulb and many instruments for film and video lighting use tungsten filaments, which produce light at about 3,200 degrees Kelvin. Tungsten light is orange. Daylight, by contrast, is much bluer. Average daylight at noon is about 5,500 degrees Kelvin. An overcast day can produce light of about 7,000 degrees Kelvin and reflected sunlight can reach 9,000 degrees Kelvin.

Film cameras cannot automatically adjust for changes in light color, so color correction filters are used over the lens to adjust incoming light to match the film's color rating. Digital video cameras can make electronic adjustments for color correction so that white objects appear white. This is achieved by white balancing. Video cameras do not always **white balance** correctly in automatic mode, however, so it is best to override the automatic white balancing feature of your camera and set the white balance manually for each lighting change.

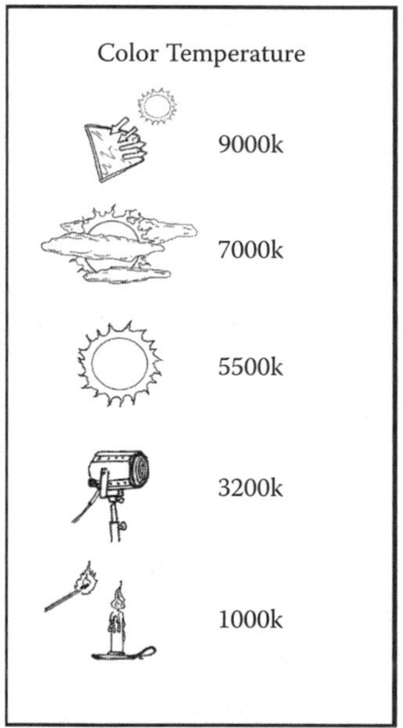

Figure 6.15 Color temperature scale. The most common color temperatures used in film and video production are 3,200 degrees Kelvin and 5,500 degrees Kelvin, which represent tungsten and daylight respectively. (Jesse Knight)

Manually setting the white balance of a camera is achieved by taking a white card, placing it in front of the lens in the light you wish to balance, and manually telling the camera to fix on the card as the white reference. All other colors will be rendered around that white reference. Check the manual of your specific camera for white balancing instructions.

White balancing the camera can only make an overall color correction. In some situations you will encounter mixed lighting. You might have light coming through a window (which is blue) as well as tungsten light indoors (which is orange) in the same shot. White balancing cannot correct for these two different colored light sources simultaneously, which need to both appear as white light. Solving this mixed lighting problem requires more sophisticated color correcting.

Mixed Lighting

One of the most common mixed lighting challenges that requires color correction is a scene that combines daylight and tungsten movie lights. Many scenes shot in interior environments utilize both natural daylight entering through windows and artificial electric lights. You will encounter situations where you will want to preserve the realistic and interesting look of a window and the directional light it casts on the scene, but you will find that you need to add supplemental artificial light to create the sculpted images you desire.

The challenge here is that these two light sources are dramatically different in color. Daylight, as we discussed, is blue in color, while tungsten light is orange. The camera can only white balance for one source or the other. If you set the white balance on the foreground and the subject's face under the tungsten light you will get a realistic color rendering of facial features, but the daylight backlighting her and the desk behind her will be a distracting and unrealistic blue. If you set the white balance for the daylight in the background, then the subject's face will turn to a troubling and deep jaundiced orange.

There are several solutions for correcting this mixed lighting situation. First, you can close the drapes or cover the windows with blankets, especially if the window itself is out of frame. This will allow total control of the lighting within the interior location using artificial lights. In many cases, however, you want to see the window and utilize the realistic quality of daylight entering through it.

The simplest filtering solution to preserve both light sources is to place blue filters on your tungsten lights to convert the 3,200 degree Kelvin light to 5,500 degrees Kelvin (daylight). The advantage of this filtering option is significant. This is a quick and easy way to make the color correction, requiring little time and materials. A few squares of blue filter and attachment clips or filter frames are all that is needed. For this reason, this is the preferred color-correction solution for most news, low-budget, and beginning-level student productions. The disadvantage of this approach, however, is noteworthy.

When a standard blue color-correction filter is placed on an artificial light to convert it to daylight, the effective transmission of the artificial light is reduced to just 36% of its original strength. A drawback of color correcting the artificial lights to match the daylight is the resulting discrepancy in intensity values between the light sources. Filtered foreground light cannot generally compete with the intensity of the sun.

An alternative solution, often preferred on higher-end productions, is to color correct the window light to match the artificial light indoors. The advantage here is this approach significantly shifts the brightness ratios of the mixed light sources as the tungsten lights can remain at full strength and the window light is reduced by filtering. The window light can be further reduced by using a special filter that is not only designed to change the light's color, but also to reduce its intensity by adding **neutral density** light-reducing properties.

Figure 6.16 Mixed lighting presents challenges for control of illumination levels and color temperature. (Photo by Jim Bridges; courtesy of Wild Bunch Films)

The disadvantage of this approach is the time for installation and expense. To cover a typical picture window can require 16 to 30 square feet of filtering material, and even normal-sized windows can consume a lot of filter material if several windows are within the composition. Unlike the small filters that are used to cover tungsten lights, the filter materials for covering a window need to be custom cut to size, particularly if the window is seen in the composition. The filter must have a tight seal on the window, without bubbles or wrinkles, to be invisible to the camera, and to allow light and heat to pass properly. If the resources are available, however, this is a superior and highly effective way to control mixed lighting.

A final approach to correcting this mixed lighting situation is to use artificial lights, factory balanced to give off the same color light as daylight. Hydrogen medium-arc-length iodide lights (**HMI lights**) use high voltage and therefore must use a **ballast box** for power conversion. These lights are expensive and hard to find on small-scale productions, but if you have these instruments available through your equipment supplier, consider this option for mixed indoor lighting or for supplementing daylight outdoors.

Light Meters

Video cameras come with a built-in light meter, which determines how much light to let into the camera for proper exposure. You can manually override the light meter in most cameras to create an effect of underexposure, overexposure, or to make a correction if the reading of the automatic light meter is inconsistent with your objective. All digital video camera light meters are **reflected light meters**. That is, they make their calculations based on the light

Figure 6.17 HMI lighting instruments produce daylight-colored illumination. The Mole-Richardson Daylight Par operates at 5,600 degrees Kelvin. (Courtesy of Mole-Richardson Co.)

reflecting off objects back to the camera. Most of these reflective light meters use an averaging system. If there are areas of light and darkness within the composition, the meter calculates an overall average to try to determine the best aperture setting for the total composition. Some cameras have a **zone metering system** that allows you to isolate particular parts of the frame and to set your exposure based on that individual zone.

External light meters are valuable for advanced lighting control in video production. A **spot meter** is an external reflected light meter that tells you the proper exposure for a specific point in a composition. A spot meter works like a riflescope. You look through a viewfinder and line the center spot on the part of the set you wish to meter. When you pull the trigger, the digital readout tells you the ideal aperture setting for that part of the composition. By taking many readings throughout a composition, you can get an excellent sense of the contrast ratio throughout the scene and can select your aperture setting based on that information.

An **incident light meter** measures the light falling on your subject. Rather than setting the light meter at the camera position, you put it at the subject's position. You might put the light meter up to a subject's face and take a reading of the key side and then the fill side. This is an effective way to determine the contrast ratio on the subject's face. Incident light meters often come with different reading element attachments. You can use a flat element for taking a general incident reading, or you can use a globe-shaped element, which

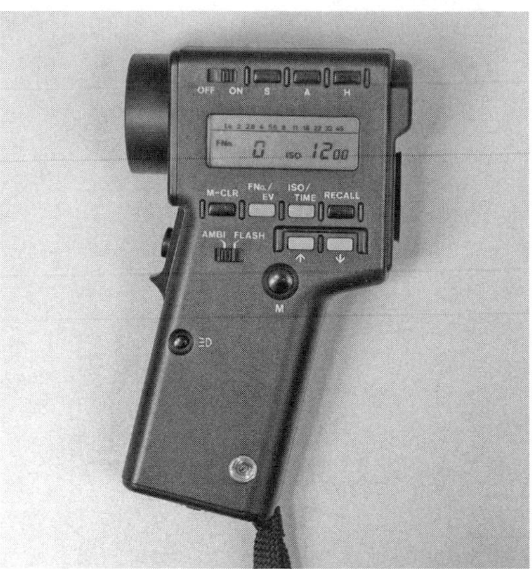

Figure 6.18 Spot meter.

reads the light wrapping around it, to more closely approximate the way light behaves on three-dimensional objects. External light meters are valuable tools for sophisticated lighting control.

Light meters need to be programmed with two pieces of information before they can give you a recommended f-stop setting. The light meter needs to know the shutter speed setting of the camera and the **exposure index (EI)** of the camera. Programming the shutter speed in the light meter tells the meter how much time each image is exposed to light. The exposure index refers to the sensitivity of the imaging system of a camera. In motion picture film cameras the exposure index is determined by the film stock used. This is the same for still picture film cameras as well. You might buy film with an exposure index of 100. One-hundred speed film requires a great deal of light to be properly exposed but it also has very fine detail. Film that requires a lot of light for exposure is called slow film because often a long exposure time is used to expose it. Eight-hundred speed film requires significantly less light than 100 speed film (three f-stops less) and is therefore a good choice for low-light situations and action photography. Film that requires low light for exposure is often called fast film since it can record an image with a short exposure time. The trade-off for using higher speed film is that it contains more grain. It is not as finely detailed as 100-speed film.

Digital video cameras also have an exposure index, or a sensitivity level, that can be translated into an exposure index number. Check the technical manuals or conduct a search online to determine the exposure index for your particular camera model. For consumer and prosumer cameras, tracking this information down sometimes requires research. Not all manufacturers publish the effective exposure index in the operator's manual.

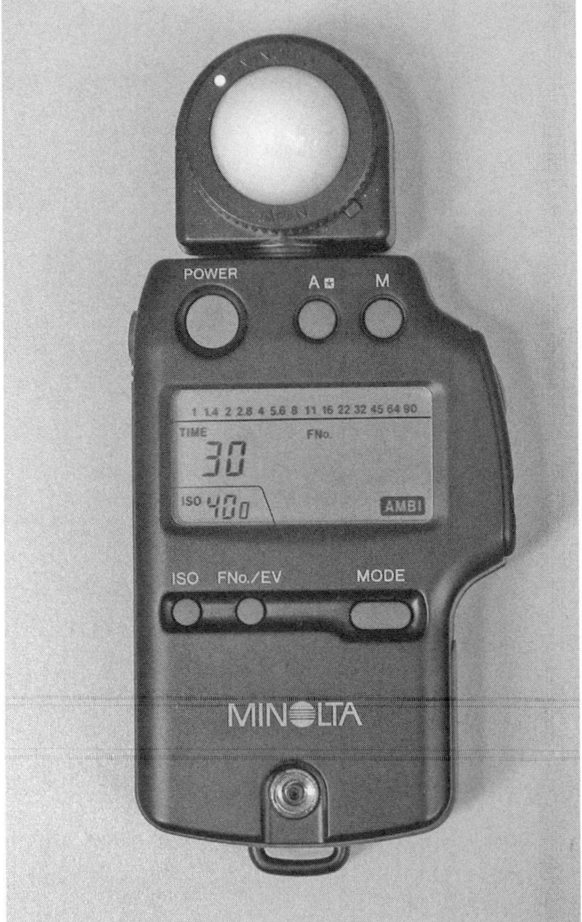

Figure 6.19 External incident light meter.

Once the light meter knows the camera's shutter speed and exposure index, the final piece of information it needs is the measurement of the amount of light on the set or on the subject. A light meter is a calculator. It reads the amount of light and can tell you, for example, that based on shooting at a shutter speed of 1/60th of a second with an exposure index (EI) of 100, you need to set the aperture at f/2.8 for proper exposure.

External Monitors

Using an external video monitor, known as a **field monitor**, allows you to check your material for lighting and composition. This takes a lot of the guesswork out of image control. A key to effective lighting in video production is to use the viewfinder or an external monitor to judge each lighting setup. Your eyes cannot properly judge the way a video camera will capture a scene. Your

Figure 6.20 Portable field monitor. (Clinton Lathinghouse)

camera might have a view screen in addition to its small viewfinder, but a larger external monitor, connected to the camera's video output, can give you even finer detail and easier viewing access for the director and crew.

Use a field monitor when appropriate and available. This can be more difficult to accommodate in settings that do not have electric power since an external video monitor can be a significant battery drain. When working outdoors or among bright lights it is helpful to have blinders on an external video monitor. Blinders allow you to see the true contrast of the image and color reproduction without glare. Make sure your field monitor is calibrated correctly. A professional field monitor is able to generate color bars. Make sure the color bars are set for proper brightness, contrast, and color information according to the manufacturer's instructions.

Professional video shoots often utilize a waveform monitor and vectorscope. A **waveform monitor** shows the luminance information of the video signal in graph form, while a **vectorscope** allows color calibration of a video signal using color bars in conjunction with a calibration scale.

Filters

Filters change the quality and characteristics of the light that passes through them. Filters can be used at three different points: over light sources, over the camera lens, and applied in postproduction.

Lighting Filters. We introduced two types of filters that can be placed over the lights. **Diffusion filters** are used to change the quality of light, and **color correction** filters are used to alter the color of light in mixed lighting situations. A third type of filter that can be used over a light is a **special effects**

color filter. While some color filters are used to correct light to make it appear natural, other color filters are used for a dramatic coloring of light. For example, you might use a deep blue filter to replicate moonlight, or green light in a dream sequence, or perhaps red light to mimic a neon sign in a bar.

Lighting filters for color correction and color effects are often referred to as **gels**. This is short for gelatin, which was historically used to make color filters. Lighting filters often come in small precut sheets and large rolls. Small sheets are nicely sized for use over lighting instruments, while rolls work well for windows. Some lighting professionals often purchase filters in roll form and cut it themselves, since filtering material is less expensive per square foot by the roll.

While lighting filters and other diffusion materials are heat-resistant, they are not fire- or burn-proof. It is important to allow air circulation on the inside of the filter or else they can overheat and melt. Also, do not use plastic clothespins to attach filters to barn doors as the plastic clothespins will melt.

Using a filter over a specific lighting source will, of course, only affect the light from that source. This allows you to create different textures, colors, and effects within the same composition. This is not the case with camera filters.

Camera Filters. Camera filters are usually made of glass and placed over the camera lens. These filters change the quality of all the light passing through the lens to the camera. Some camera filters are round and screw onto the outside of the lens. These filters must match the size of the lens or use an adaptor ring. Other camera filters are square, and are dropped into a filter holder mounted on the outside of the camera. This holder is often called a **matte box** since it can be used to hold mattes to mask the image as well, such as an outline in the shape of binoculars.

Camera filters can be used to achieve an overall color correction, to create an overall lighting effect, and to change the intensity of light. You should keep a clear protective glass filter over the lens of your camera. If the outer lens element of your camera is scratched, the lens is rendered useless for professional

Figure 6.21 Camera-mounted filters come in round versions that are screwed onto the lens, and square filters that are set in an external frame. (Clinton Lathinghouse)

applications. Lenses can be damaged easily, especially when working in the field. A clear glass filter adds a layer of protection to the lens. In a sense, if it is clear glass, then it is not really a filter, but any glass attachment for the lens is commonly referred to as such.

Even more popular than the clear glass option for lens protection is an **ultraviolet filter (UV)** on the lens. Ultraviolet light can cause a hazy and clouded image and can soften the edges of objects. Therefore, for outside photography, a UV filter can be quite valuable in making the image sharper. A UV filter is a valuable component of every professional's camera bag.

Another popular camera filter is the **neutral density filter**. Neutral density filters change the overall intensity of the light without changing its color or quality. These are good when shooting in bright situations where the overall intensity of the light needs to be reduced.

A **polarizing filter** only allows light from a certain angle to pass through. It is a good option for eliminating glare off windows or water sources. Some cinematographers utilize the polarizing filter as a neutral density filter. The polarizer reduces light intensity by about two f-stops. It can also be used to saturate colors, making skies bluer, clouds whiter, and grass greener. By reducing surface glare, the polarizing filter allows the true colors to come through.

There are also a number of **special effects filters** that can be used on a camera lens. Some of these create rainbow effects while others create starburst effects at pinpoints of light. Some create an overall fogging effect, and in other cases the filters are graduated. A **graduated filter** changes its level of filtering from one side of the filter to the other. Some graduated filters come half and half. You may have clear glass on half and a neutral density filter on the other half. This can be a useful tool to reduce the overall brightness of the sky by lining the filter up with the horizon. You might use a half-and-half filter that is green and orange to make a field of green pop with color, while making a sunset extra deep. There is a custom filter available for virtually every creative application.

Figure 6.22 Half-and-half filters are used to alter part of a composition.

Before purchasing filters for your camera it is important to determine the size of the filters you require. This can best be done by referring to the manufacturer's specifications or by taking your camera to a retail shop for fitting. Filter sizes are measured in millimeters.

Many camera filters have a number that indicates the **filter factor**. Since most filters absorb some light, you need to make exposure compensations when using a filter. If you are using the camera's internal light meter, this will be done for you, but if you are using an external light meter then you will need to refer to the filter factor to make the adjustment. A filter with a filter factor of 2 reduces the incoming light by 1 f-stop. A filter with a filter factor of 4 reduces the incoming light by 2 f-stops.

Day-for-night photography is a process in which scenes are shot during the day but on screen it appears like nighttime. Day-for-night photography can be achieved by using a dark blue camera filter and underexposing the image by two to three f-stops. It is important that day-for-night photography be done in high contrast lighting or else you will not see the detail and highlights in the final image. A famous day-for-night sequence was created for the opening of *Jaws* (1975). When the woman goes for a moonlight swim she is actually swimming at midday. If it were, in fact, late at night there is no way the audience would be able to see the horizon meet the water 20 miles out or the glistening of the "moonlight" on the waves.

There are applications for which camera filters are the best option. For applications such as neutral-density reduction, polarization, or ultraviolet light elimination, filtering must be done at the capture stage. There are, however, some types of filtering for which postproduction application of filters might be more appropriate. When you change the quality of the light in camera, that change is integrated into the image and it can be difficult or impossible to remove. For this reason, some filtering is best achieved in postproduction.

Postproduction Filtering. In chapter 4 we explored postproduction and editing options. Among these options are a number of filters that can be applied to the image in the computer. If you want to make a shot black and white, or if you wish to put a blue cast or a yellow warmth across an entire program, it might be best to apply this effect in postproduction at which time you can pick the exact degree of manipulation and change it if you are not happy with the result. The computer can also create other lighting effects. Starburst effects, highlights, fogging, and making an image appear like a painting can all be done in postproduction.

Lighting Instrument Options

Lighting instruments come in a wide variety of sizes, shapes, and powers. Many lighting instruments use lenses to focus light. There are other lights, referred to as open lights, that do not have lenses. **Open lights** create an overall softer light than those focused with lenses.

Location lighting often comes in kits. The Lowell mini-pro is an inexpensive and popular option for student productions, whereas the Arri Fresnel Kit is more advanced, more expensive, and seen often on professional field shoots.

Individual lighting instruments for studio and large-scale location work can be large and powerful. Mole-Richardson makes a 9,000-watt instrument that is actually comprised of nine individual lamps in a single housing. Interchangeable globes can be placed over the lamps to set their color temperature for either daylight or tungsten.

Some lights can be attached directly to the top of the camera. LED lights are often camera-mounted and require low power for their illumination. The LED is a good option for field shoots without access to plug-in power, but LED lighting is not very bright, so it can only be used in close proximity to the subject.

Keep in mind that a production light does not have to come from a professional lighting manufacturer. Sometimes a regular household lightbulb inside a hardware store work lamp can work just fine. Always be thinking about creative solutions. Who would have guessed that the key light in *The Shining* (1980) when Jack Nicholson is pounding to get out of the storage room was simply a household lightbulb taped to the camera operator's chest as he lay on the floor to shoot at a low angle? Visualize what you wish to create and follow the simplest path to achieving that effect.

It can be difficult to replicate dashboard lighting of a car realistically. Putting any sort of lighting in a car tends to come across as too bright and fake, but consider this effective and inexpensive option. For a few dollars you can purchase a string of white Christmas lights. Some short strings of holiday lights run on regular D- or C-cell batteries. If hidden out of the camera's view, just below the dash, these lights give a nice even illumination for digital video recording.

Figure 6.23 An open light does not contain a lens. (Jennie Picarella)

Figure 6.24 Lighting kits are often used in field production. Pictured here is a four-instrument Arri lighting kit.

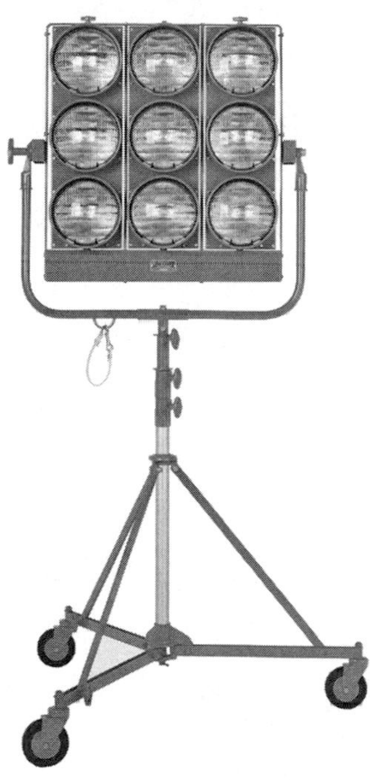

Figure 6.25 9,000-Watt Nine-Light. (Courtesy of Mole-Richardson Co.)

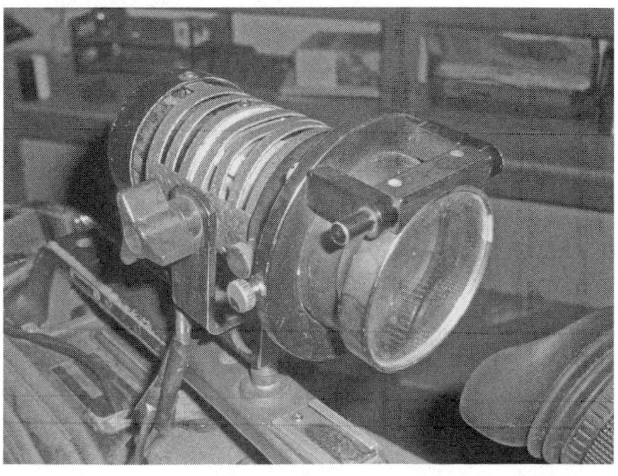

Figure 6.26 Camera-mounted lights are often used in news and documentary production. (Joanne Hughes)

Lighting Accessories

There are a variety of external accessories that can be used in conjunction with lighting instruments or available light to add additional control. Scrims are wire screens that reduce the overall intensity of light without changing its quality. Scrims come in different types. A **single scrim** reduces the overall amount of light by one half an f-stop and a **double scrim** reduces the amount of light a full f-stop. Some lighting systems allow layering of scrims so that you can reduce the light intensity by increments of one and a half f-stops, two stops, and so on. A **half scrim** only covers half of the light. This is a good option for a light that will hit both foreground and background objects. Since the light hitting the background will be reduced in intensity as it travels through space, the foreground will be brighter. A half scrim can compensate for this discrepancy by masking the part of the light that hits the foreground and reducing its intensity. Some lights have **filter frames**, which allow you to cut a piece of filtering

Figure 6.27 Wire scrims reduce the intensity of light without significantly affecting quality. (Clinton Lathinghouse)

Figure 6.28 Some lights have integrated frames to hold precut filtering material. (Clinton Lathinghouse)

material and place it in the metal frame. These frames can then be dropped into the scrim slot of a light.

Barn doors come standard with many lighting instruments, but there are other external accessories that help you control the shape of light. **Snoots** are tubes placed over lighting instruments that keep the light narrowly focused in a specific direction. **Flags** are pieces of black framed material that can be manipulated on wire rods and mounted on light stands and grip stands to block light from certain parts of the set. **Dots** are similar to flags but are very small and are designed to cut the light out of just a pinpoint on a set. A **cucoloris**, also known as a cookie, is designed to cast a pattern of light. Cookies come in different shapes, including abstract ones, and also realistic light patterns, such as Venetian blinds. **Umbrellas**, **reflector boards**, and **bounce cards** are available to change the quality of light through reflection. The equipment used to position lighting accessories is collectively called "grip," which is rooted in the simple fact that it holds things. **Grip stands** and special clamps called **gator grips** are used to keep bounce cards, flags, and other accessories in place. The accessories for professional lighting provide a solution for virtually every lighting challenge.

Gaffer tape is valuable on every set. Gaffer tape is cloth tape that is very strong and does not leave a sticky residue, so it will not damage furniture, walls, and floors. Gaffer tape can be easily removed and is used for affixing cords out of view, to tape cords down to the floor, and for many other applications. Gaffer tape comes in a variety of colors for easy coding. It can be used to mark the location of furniture, lighting instruments, props, and other equipment so these items can be reset in the exact same spot if moved.

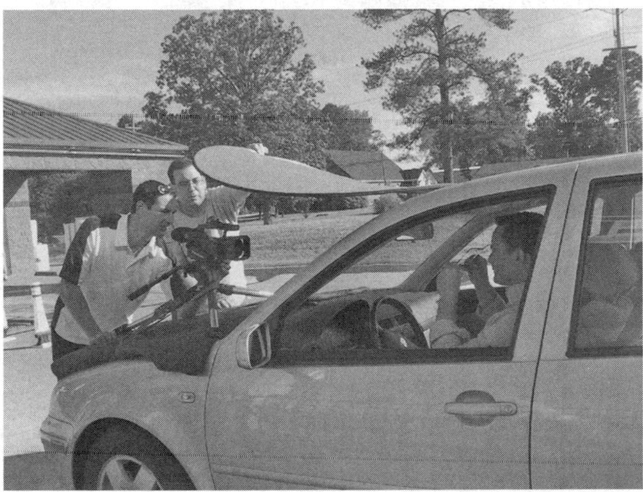

Figure 6.29 A flag is used to block incoming light while making a TV commercial for a regional car wash. (Courtesy of Bclip Productions, Inc.)

Figure 6.30 A cucoloris is used to create light patterns such as simulating Venetian blinds.

Figure 6.31 An umbrella reflector. (Dmitri Medvedev)

Power and Safety

Working with lighting equipment involves critical safety considerations. Unless your lighting is based solely upon available light and supplemented only with reflectors, you will need to use electricity to power lighting instruments. The three primary sources of power for field production are A/C current outlets, generators, and batteries.

A/C current from existing outlets is the most common source of lighting power for small-scale field productions. Do not assume that a location will have outlets where you need them or the proper circuit capacity to support your lighting needs. Visit a location ahead of time and note the location of outlets. Get as much information as possible on the wiring and circuit capacity of each location.

If your lighting needs are modest, say less than 1,000 watts total, then a detailed schematic of the location wiring will most likely not be necessary. If,

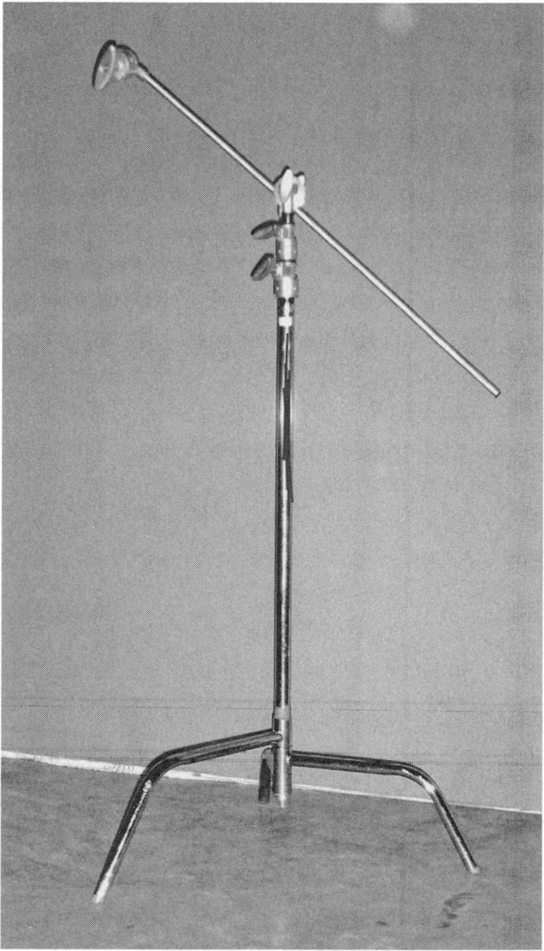

Figure 6.32 Grip stands and accessories help control light. (Jesse Knight)

however, you anticipate a complex lighting design with several thousand watts, then more research is necessary. Visit the breaker box before a shoot and test the circuits to determine which outlets are matched with each circuit. Make a schematic. Always get permission of the property owner before using electric instruments. This is an important consideration for three reasons. First, the use of electricity involves expense, and this expense can be considerable for a long shoot using thousands of watts of power. Second, it is a safety concern. You want to make sure there is nothing extraordinary about the location that could cause harm to you, your crew, your equipment, or the property. Finally, the property owner's insurance might not allow you to be using lighting equipment. For these reasons (and common courtesy), it is important to ask permission before plugging in.

If you do access a breaker box, it is important to only touch the door handle used to open the box and the circuit switches. Ask an authority with knowledge of the specific system if it is in safe working order, and have supervision of the property owner when checking or resetting circuits.

A typical 15-amp circuit running 120 volts can safely power about 1,440 watts. If you exceed this load on the circuit, you risk tripping the safety mechanisms of the system, which will result in a disconnection of power to all outlets on the overloaded circuit. If you require a high load of power using existing A/C outlets, you might need to design your lighting scheme to be distributed across several circuits, being careful not to exceed the maximum load of any individual circuit. This might require running extra extension cords, which must also be rated to handle the load of wattage you intend to use over the length of the run needed. Study the ratings for extension cords before using them in the field. It is not acceptable to use cheap extension cords for movie lights or to string several extension cords together. These two practices can create a significant fire hazard.

If you trip a breaker during production, do not attempt to reset the breaker with the existing power arrangement. The tripping is a warning that the load on the breaker is too high, so reduce the load to a capacity below the maximum rating for the breaker before attempting to reset and continue.

If you are working in an older building, you might encounter a fuse box rather than a breaker box as a safety system to regulate the electricity distribution. If

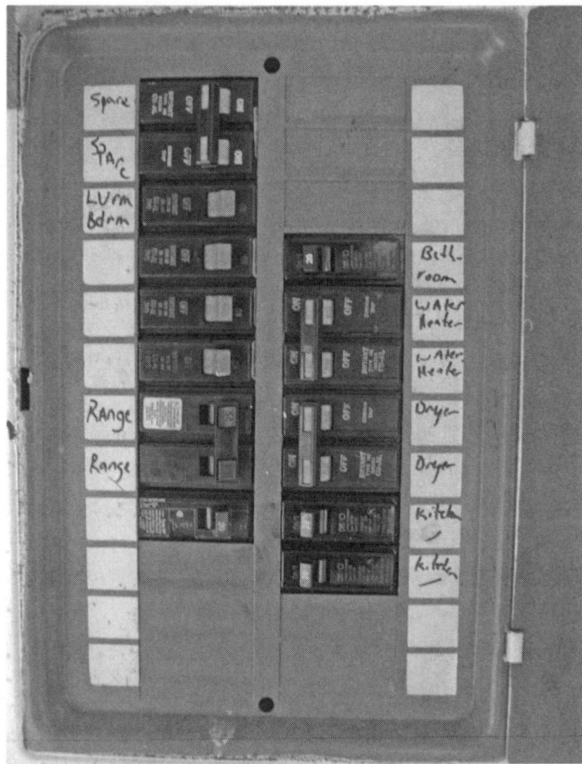

Figure 6.33 Know where the breaker box is and use it safely. (Emily Sarkissian)

you blow a fuse on a location, you will not be able to use the circuit until the fuse is replaced with a new one. Do research ahead of time and purchase replacement fuses of the type used at the location. Fuses are inexpensive, but the time lost in running out to buy some while the crew waits can be costly. Electrical connections and boxes are dangerous. Always use caution and never open an electrical box without permission and supervision of the property owner.

Generators

Another power source for lights and other equipment is the portable generator. Small gasoline-powered generators produce A/C power in the range of 1,000 to 6,500 watts. These small generators are good for providing modest supporting power at locations where wall current is not available or practical. These generators, which can be rented at many equipment supply facilities, are quite loud and heavy and are often impractical where sound quality and rapid mobility are important.

Professional productions often use large trailer-mounted or truck-mounted generators to supply power for location production. These generators are quite large but are installed in soundproof, wheeled housings. The advantages of generators are significant. With a generator you are not dependent on the power you find at a location. The production crew is self-contained when they come with their own generator, and they know the exact circuit capacity in advance. A lighting scheme can be designed ahead of time and replicated on location with known equipment.

Figure 6.34 Portable generators allow a production to go virtually anywhere.

Batteries

You can run low-wattage lighting equipment on battery power. Most battery configurations will not run thousands of watts of power for a sustained time. Many production situations, however, simply need a little kicker light, fill light, or a camera-mounted light for an interview.

There are battery packs that run A/C power for short durations, but most battery systems are designed to support low-voltage D/C equipment. High-efficiency fluorescent lighting and LED options provide a good illumination to power consumption ratio, which can be supported with battery power. When using fluorescent and LED lights in the field, make sure to set your camera white balance for these sources as they have unique color temperatures.

The electricity itself is only one element of safety when working with lighting and other powered equipment. Cables, light stands, and bounce cards can all be accidents waiting to happen. Make sure all cables are out of the line of foot traffic. Line cables along walls and securely tape all cables down with gaffer tape or cover them with an approved cable threshold device in any doorway or where people need to cross. When using overhead lights, make sure that a safety chain is attached to both the lighting instrument and a stable area of support in the ceiling or overhead lighting grid. Use sand bags to weigh down equipment stands, especially if working outdoors in windy conditions. It is impossible to put every piece of equipment totally out of potential traffic, but by thinking about potential accidents while you set up, taking prudent steps to secure cables, and keeping light stands and production gear secure and out of tripping range, you will create a much safer working environment for your cast and crew.

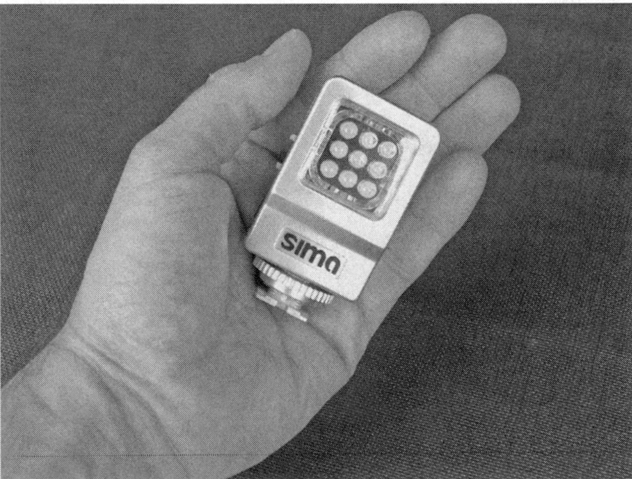

Figure 6.35 Battery-powered LED camera light.

Exterior Lighting

When you move outside to shoot a project you surrender a degree of control. You can watch the forecast and have a back-up location to cover other scenes indoors if there is bad weather, but once you get to a location it is impossible to know for sure how the weather will behave. The film industry flourished in Southern California in part because of the consistent weather conditions that allow shooting schedules to proceed with great reliability. It only rains about 27 days a year in Los Angeles.

A bright sunny day is actually not the ideal condition for maximum lighting control outdoors. If you want to see the vista of a blue sky then you want it to be clear and sunny, but if you are shooting without the sky or expansive scenery in the shot then a cloudy day is the cinematographer's best friend. On a cloudy day you can use the existing flat and even lighting as a base light and use artificial lights to fit the needs of each scene. In fact, on some exterior locations lighting crews often install a giant screen over the set to create an even base light so they can control its exact direction and quality.

Most small-scale video projects use the sun as the main source of light when shooting outdoors, and with a few tricks you can control exterior lighting to create some varied and marvelous effects.

It is helpful to scout each exterior location in advance. Take photographs and make notes about where the sun is in the sky at various times during the day, and plan your shoot to make use of the sun in a preferred position for your objectives.

When shooting landscapes and buildings it is generally more effective to shoot during the early morning hours and the late afternoon, rather than midday. When the sun is low on the horizon it casts long shadows, which help accentuate the dimension of buildings and natural features. Also, the sunlight at this time of day is warm and can create a pleasing and serene image. When shooting midday, the light comes straight down in a flat and even wash and ultraviolet light reflecting in every direction can create a hazy image.

Regardless of whether you are shooting large-scale landscapes or a subject for an interview, you can choose how to use the sun in your lighting scheme. When shooting a landscape, the effect and mood is radically shifted when comparing a shot taken with the sun behind the camera to one where the sun is in the frame serving as a subject of the shot.

When shooting with human subjects outdoors you can bounce cards to direct sunlight on your subject. By using a single reflector you can use the direct light from the sun as a key light, and the reflected light as fill light. The success of this technique depends on the sun's position in the sky and its intensity because this setup requires direct sunlight on the subject's face, which can be too intense in many situations. You can avoid all direct sunlight on a subject's face, and add a backlight to the formula for a full three-point lighting setup by adding a second bounce card to the design. In this approach, use the sun as the backlight and the two bounce cards as a key and fill light. You can control the brightness and contrast ratio by moving the cards in proximity to the subject.

If your project requires both interior and exterior shoots, schedule the exterior shoots first. In the event of poor weather you can then utilize the day by changing the plan and shooting indoors. If you complete all of your interiors first and the weather turns against you, then the production will be delayed.

Working outdoors requires an alert eye to lighting continuity. As the sun changes position, trying to match a shot recorded first thing in the morning with one shot at noon can be a challenge. Be aware of the moving sun and how this affects your exposure settings, continuity, and color temperature. The color temperature of daylight changes throughout the day. Daylight at noon is about 5,500 degrees Kelvin, but at sunrise and sunset it can drop to 2,000 degrees Kelvin. Reflected sunlight can read at 9,000 degrees Kelvin.

One of the most rewarding things about shooting outdoors is the opportunity to film during "magic hour." **Magic hour** is the brief window of time between sunset and dusk when the light is ethereal with a beautiful evenness, and has the presence of blue and orange hues that are nearly impossible to create any other way. Fantastic images can be gathered during magic hour, but this special time really only lasts about 20 minutes per day and then only when the atmospheric conditions are just right.

Full Metal Jacket (1987) utilizes magic hour during the climatic scene of the confrontation with the sniper. Terrence Malick directed *Days of Heaven* (1978), which is filmed predominantly during magic hour. This is a bold experiment in filmmaking. Malick chose to create a feature-length motion picture in which much of the shooting could only take place in a 20-minute window each day.

The Lighting Team

The **director of photography** is responsible for the overall creative vision of the lighting. The **gaffer** is in charge of the physical placement of lights on a set. The term gaffer comes from the old days of studio production when lights were permanently affixed to an overhead lighting grid. The professional in charge of setting lights moved them around with a big stick that looked much like a fishing gaff. The gaffer usually directs the electrical and lighting crews under the supervision of the director of photography.

The **best boy** is an odd title you might recall from film credits. This is also a member of the lighting team. The best boy is the gaffer's primary assistant. Depending on the scale of the project, the gaffer might supervise a crew of many people in the actual placement and adjustment of lights and accessories. On a small project a single person might assume the responsibilities of the director of photography, camera operator, and gaffer.

Creative Approaches

With the wide range of lighting tools available, you can create any mood and scenario. Two primary approaches in creative lighting are high-key and low-key lighting.

High-key lighting is bright overall. There are not a lot of shadows in high-key lighting and therefore, in some ways, there is not a lot of depth. The primary objective in high-key lighting is to illuminate the scene. High-key lighting is often used in fashion photography. It is frequently used in advertising and situation comedies where characters move around the set without lighting changes, so every part of the set needs to have illumination. High-key lighting generally transmits an energetic and upbeat mood, excitement, and happiness.

Low-key lighting, by contrast, contains significant darkness and shadows and typically has a high-contrast ratio. Low-key lighting can portray a sense of isolation, loneliness, despair, and ill will. Low-key lighting is indicative of film noir and horror.

In addition to these two styles, there are other methods that can be used to create interesting designs. One tool for the lighting technician is to work with **pools of light**. If you have a large space and break that space up with pools of light—areas of brightness and shadow—then the audience gets a greater sense of depth. **Shafts of light** are another great tool for creative lighting. By shaping the barn doors of a light, or using grip accessories, you can throw a shaft of light on a subject, scene, or background for an interesting effect.

Darkness is not necessarily a bad thing in videography. Anybody can flood a scene with light, but only an artist can put the lights and shadows in just the right places to create something interesting. Do not think of darkness as negative space, but as elements as important as those which are illuminated. We discussed some creative approaches to cinematography in chapter 3 including realism, expressionism, film noir, impressionism, and surrealism. Think

Figure 6.36 High-key lighting is characterized by overall bright illumination. It is typical of light and happy scenes. (Photo by Jim Bridges; courtesy of Wild Bunch Films)

Figure 6.37 Low-key lighting is defined by high contrast and directional lighting. It is often used for dramatic and ominous scenes. (Photos by Jim Bridges; courtesy of Wild Bunch Films)

about how you can use the tools of lighting to realize each of these artistic approaches on screen.

When designing your lighting, consider your audience and the script. Consult with the director on her vision. What is your interpretation of how the script will be translated into pictures? Consider not only the global lighting approach, but also how that approach will be broken down into each individual setup. Do you want to do something that is highly realistic or psychologically expressionistic? Do you want to create a lighting design that is experimental and use light in a way that draws attention to the filmmaking process or do you want the lighting to be natural and invisible?

Study light. Most people take the light around them for granted, but light creates everything we see. Exterior light changes with the movement of the sun and rhythms of the atmosphere. No two moments in time ever look exactly the same.

Take a light meter into the natural environment. Measure it. See what the natural contrast ranges are in the world, and then experiment with contrast ranges using your lights and camera. Look at the results. Practice lighting rooms. Create moods. Play with light and manipulate light. Light is what makes motion picture possible.

Figure 6.38 Shafts and pools of light create interest and emphasize depth.

CONCLUSIONS

By controlling the amount, direction, quality, and color of light you can sculpt images to achieve your creative objectives. When available light and practical lights need to be supplemented, you have a range of lighting instruments to use including focusable instruments and open lights. You can employ the wide range of lighting accessories including scrims, flags, clamps, barn doors, and reflector cards to further refine your lighting designs.

You now understand the studio modeling techniques for three- and four-point lighting. You can implement these designs and use their general concepts to guide your original lighting approaches. When planning for light, make sure you have adequate power and that cords, instruments, accessories, and electricity are all handled safely. Lights can become hot quickly and remain hot after they are turned off. Be aware, and take care not to burn yourself or others.

You now have a more advanced foundation for image control. Getting the light just right, however, is only part of the complex equation of video production. An effective program must also utilize the power of sound. Exploring sound elements and sound design are the goals of our next chapter.

SAMPLE EXERCISES

1. Try a three-point lighting setup and record the design on videotape. Add a background light to expand the experiment to a four-point lighting scheme.
2. Light a human subject three different ways. For each of the three setups try to achieve a feeling that matches the artistic styles of realism, expressionism, and impressionism.
3. Spend a day shooting test footage of an outdoor environment. Document how the light changes throughout the day.

RECOMMENDED READINGS

Alton, J. (1995). *Painting With Light.* Berkley: University of California Press.

Box, H. (2003). *Set Lighting Technician's Handbook: Film Lighting Equipment, Practice, and Electrical Distribution.* Boston: Focal Press.

Jackman, J. (2002). *Lighting for Digital Video and Television.* Lawrence, Kansas: CMP Books.

REFERENCES

Alexander, J. B., & Shansky, M. S. (1976). Influence of hue, value, and chroma on the perceived heaviness of colours. *Perception and Psychophysics*, 19, 72-74.

Boynton, R. M. (1971). *Human color vision.* New York: Holt, Rinehart & Winston.

Coren, S., Ward, L. M., & Enns, J. T. (2004). *Sensation and Perception.* Hoboken, NJ: J. Wiley & Sons.

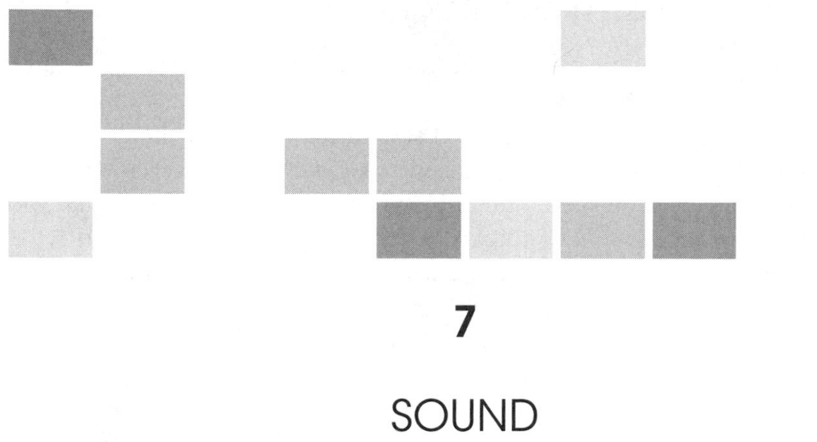

7

SOUND

CHAPTER OBJECTIVES

If you go to see a scary movie you can always close your eyes. It is much harder to hide from the soundtrack. The screeching music, fists of a serial killer pounding on the door, and screams in the dark house are likely to create screams in the theater.

The sound team makes a silent movie screen come to life. Recording sound is challenging. It requires an ear for the environment and knowledge of the range of tools that can achieve each creative objective. The sound recordist ensures that ideal audio capture is achieved during production.

The sound designer brings the audio elements together in postproduction. She creates new worlds and guides the audience through remarkable experiences by crafting location sound, rerecorded dialogue, music, and sound effects. In this chapter we explore the tools and techniques of sound recording and sound design. The goals of this chapter are to:

- Examine the role of sound in video production;
- Survey the tools for sound recording and design;
- Explore the process of selecting the proper audio equipment to achieve creative objectives;
- Build a foundation for managing the complex audio requirements of field and studio production.

Over the decades, some practitioners have argued that the image is paramount in film and video, claiming that the Golden Age of motion pictures came before the advent of recorded sound. Other practitioners argue that sound is a critical synergetic component of movies, which has elevated the medium to creative heights that far exceed the potential of either image or sound by themselves.

Since its introduction in the late 1920s, sound has greatly intensified the motion picture experience, creating sensory and emotional layers that move visual images into entirely new dramatic spheres. The information that the soundtrack communicates is significant. Dialogue informs us through what is said and how it is said. Intonation and inflection are as important as the words in communicating mood and subtext. Silences give the audience the opportunity for contemplation (Olsen, 1994). Music is a universal language that impacts impressions and emotions. In fact, evidence indicates that humans are hardwired to process music (Peretz, 2006). Natural background sounds and special sound effects add even more to the aural experience. Take a DVD you have not played before. Play a part of the disc without looking at the screen. Play another segment with the sound turned off as you are viewing the screen. Which experience is more rich and informative? What information does the sound provide that the picture does not?

We perceive layers of sound more effectively than layers of pictures. If someone is shown one moving image superimposed over another and asked to attend to both images simultaneously, most people can only comprehend one layer of the picture at a time (Neisser & Becklin, 1975). The viewer can switch attention back and forth, attending to one image and then the next, but most cannot attend to multiple visual layers at once. Visuals are not layered in our natural experience. When we superimpose one image over another, we create an artificial experience. In reality, we experience pictures sequentially. Sound is both sequential and simultaneous. With sound perception the mind is more nimble and dynamic. Think about how complex the perceptual layers of sound are that you encounter every day. If you walk down a city street, just a few of the layers you might encounter include car engines, horns, jackhammers, cranes, footsteps on the sidewalk, wind, pigeons, people on cell phones, and so on. Our aural world is rich, and taking some time to really listen to your world will open your perception to sounds you never noticed before.

Our brain sorts and streamlines experiences so we can direct our attention to perceptions and decisions that really matter to the achievement of goals, objectives, and purposeful behavior. We habituate to familiar elements in our environment. Force yourself outside of habituation to experience your world of sound. Let the background become the foreground. You will hear the hum of fluorescent lights and the rumble of the air circulation system in the walls. You will hear birds off in the distance. Learning to listen to your world is the first step in learning to design realistic and fantastic worlds of sound for video productions.

Just as we never experience true black when we close our eyes, we never experience true silence either. We hear a tone in our ears even when the environment is quiet. This tone is the product of a high-pitched sound of our nervous system and a low-pitched sound of our circulatory system.

Sound experience is more omnipresent than visual experience. We can close our eyes and effectively lock out the images around us, but we cannot close our ears in a similar way. Without using some sort of headsets to block out the sound we are always exposed to the aural environment.

Sound can be more realistically reproduced than visuals. We have **stereoscopic** vision and **binaural** hearing. The ability to see in stereo allows us to judge depth and to determine an object's position in space. We generally cannot reproduce this effect with movies. There are 3-D motion picture systems, but these are generally novelty programs that require special glasses for the effect to work. We experience our visual environment in stereo, but visual programs are flattened out to two dimensions and the illusion of depth must be approximated.

Our binaural hearing allows us to judge the direction from which a sound originates. This perception is the result of both the intensity and the time difference at which a sound arrives at each of our two ears. We can recreate a highly realistic sound experience for a theatrical audience by controlling the direction and intensity of all sound elements in the way the sound is recorded and played back on multiple speakers. When audience members experienced the opening battle sequence of *Saving Private Ryan* (1998), many ducked to avoid the ricocheting bullets they heard bouncing all around them. This is the power of good sound.

How We Perceive Sound

We hear sound because movements in the environment cause changes in the air pressure around us. As vibrations disturb the air (or liquid in the case of underwater sound) they cause the air disturbance to travel outward in the shape of a wave. These waves travel through the air at about 1,130 feet per second. When sound waves reach our ears, this change in air pressure causes movement in our eardrum. The physical movement of our eardrum moves a small bone in our inner ear called the cochlea. The cochlea then transfers the vibrations to tiny hairs in our inner ear. These hairs convert the vibrations to an electrical signal, which our brain translates into the perception of sound.

Protect Your Hearing

Take precautions to protect your hearing. Your ability to design sound is only as good as your ability to perceive sound. While the range of human hearing is approximately 20 **Hertz (Hz)** to 20,000 Hertz, this range degenerates over time. Our hearing range can be greatly limited due to **cumulative noise damage (CND)** and exposure to loud onset sounds. In addition to frequency range, cumulative noise damage also affects the perception of amplitude as well. People with CND cannot hear quiet sounds well or at all.

Cumulative noise damage fatigues and injures the delicate hairs of the inner ear over time through exposure to loud, repetitive frequencies. Lawnmowers and similar equipment are notoriously bad for your ears. Cumulative loud noises should be avoided and precautions taken to protect your hearing. Sudden onset noises damage your ears because your ear is designed to close up to some extent to protect itself, but a loud sudden onset sound reaches your inner ear before this protective measure can take effect. Gunfire and fireworks can be particularly damaging. Sounds above 90 decibels present a significant threat to hearing. A lawn mower produces about 90 decibels. A jet airplane at takeoff is about 140 decibels.

If you have ever left a concert or other event with your ears ringing then you probably have suffered some damage to your hearing. It is never too late to work to protect your hearing, however, and the sooner you begin the better it will serve you and your ability to do effective sound recording and design in the future.

The simple solution is to use hearing protection in any potentially harmful situation. Hearing protection is available in the form of circumaural headsets and also in small, soft, disposable earplugs. These form-fitting plugs can cut 30 decibels from incoming sounds, which offers a significant degree of protection over an open ear.

If you are interested in sound recording and sound design at a professional level, consider having your hearing checked to establish a baseline of your effective hearing range. This can be a valuable reference. A sound recordist's ears are the most important tools he brings to any shoot.

Microphones

Microphones are the ears of the audio-recording process. Just as the camera is closely modeled after the structure of the human eye, the **microphone** borrows its structure from our ears.

Microphones come in a wide variety of sizes, shapes, and types. There is an ideal microphone made to match virtually every recording need. There are many different classification types, but three basic characteristics will help you to identify a particular microphone: pick-up element (dynamic or capacitor), directionality, and frequency response.

Dynamic and Capacitor Microphones. Microphones are broadly classified as one of two primary types: dynamic and capacitor. **Dynamic microphones**, as the name suggests, function by movement. Dynamic microphones are magnetic induction microphones. They use a moving coil, which is affected by changes in air pressure. The dynamic force of air pressure is what causes the coil to oscillate. This oscillation is translated into an electric signal, which can be recorded and translated back into sound using an amplifier and a speaker.

Dynamic microphones have inherent advantages and disadvantages. On the upside, these microphones are rugged. They are a good choice for working in hostile or fast-moving circumstances where a microphone might not receive optimal care. These are also relatively inexpensive compared to their capacitor counterparts. Also, they do not require any electrical outlet or batteries to work, which the capacitor **mic** (pronounced "mike") does. Air pressure is all that is needed to activate the dynamic microphone and to make it work. On the downside, because the dynamic microphone uses air pressure to function, it is not a sensitive microphone. If a sound is quiet or distant, the dynamic mic might not have enough air pressure at its location to record the sound properly. The human ear is more sensitive than the typical dynamic mic. The dynamic mic is not able to record every sound that you can hear. It is for recording strong sources in close proximity.

Capacitor microphones use an electrically charged plate as the sound-receiving element instead of a moving coil. Capacitor microphones, by virtue of this charged plate, are sensitive. They can pick up sounds that are much more subtle than the dynamic mic. The electrical charge aids in the mic's function. The capacitor mic is not dependent on the force of air pressure moving a coil. These are high-quality microphones, and are a superior option for achieving the best possible sound recording.

There are some disadvantages to the capacitor mic. These mics are generally more expensive than their dynamic counterparts and more fragile. A capacitor mic must be handled with care. This fragility makes its superior recording ability worth sacrificing in some rugged shooting situations, such as some field news and documentary work. Another potential disadvantage to the capacitor microphone is that it requires electric power to function. This puts another variable in the process and failed microphone batteries will quickly bring a shoot to a halt. It is essential that the person in charge of the mics put fresh batteries in all capacitor mics before a shoot and that she has more than enough replacement batteries on hand for the shoot's duration.

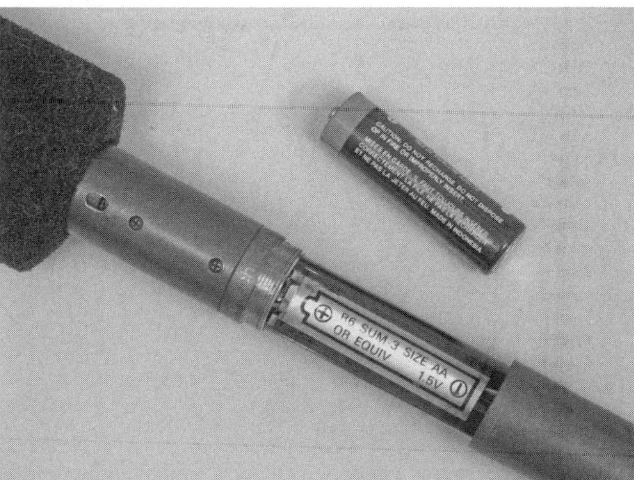

Figure 7.1 Capacitor microphones require electricity to function and often use batteries.

Batteries for capacitor microphones come in a variety of sizes. Some mics use standard AA batteries; others use special watch or photo batteries. The batteries are sometimes loaded into the microphone while other equipment configurations locate the battery compartment on the mic's cable.

Capacitor mics can also function with phantom power. **Phantom power** works by sending a mild electric current to the microphone on its connection cable. Phantom power is generated by equipment that mics are frequently connected to, such as cameras and audio-mixing boards, but not all cameras and mixers have this ability. It is important to know the configuration of your equipment in advance and to plan for batteries as needed. It is always good to have spare batteries. If you are using phantom power from a mixer and it fails in the field, or if you do not have A/C power to run the mixer, the prudent technician will be able to load batteries into the microphone, bypass the mixer, and plug the mic directly into the camera. Problem solved.

Directionality. Another way to classify microphones is by directionality. Some microphones are engineered to pick up sounds from all around. Other mics are designed to pick up sound from only one direction depending on where the mic is pointed.

Microphones that pick up sound from all directions are called **omnidirectional microphones**. These microphones are a good choice when a general reproduction of the environment is desired or if it might be difficult to control the microphone placement. Say, for example, you have the opportunity to record a press conference and attach a microphone to the podium. Two speakers will be at the podium to make a joint announcement. You cannot run up to the podium to adjust your mic during the event. You do not know if the speakers will take turns at the podium or stand side by side. In this unpredictable scenario the omnidirectional mic gives you the best chance of uniform coverage.

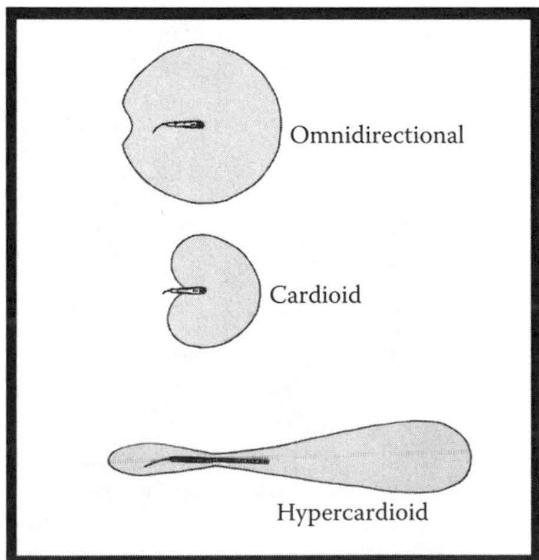

Figure 7.2 Pick-up patterns for omnidirectional, cardioid, and hypercardioid microphones. (Jesse Knight)

Cardioid microphones are **unidirectional microphones** that have a pick up pattern that looks like a valentine heart; thus the name cardioid, which is taken from the Greek root *cardia* for heart. Cardioid microphones are a good option when you prefer some latitude in the pick-up range and have control of the microphone's placement in relationship to the desired sound source to be recorded. Cardioid mics record what they are pointed toward well and include some **side rejection**. That is, a sound source that is not directly in front of the mic will not be recorded as strongly. This makes the cardioid mic a good choice for stand-up interviews in the field. A handheld cardioid mic has a slightly different physical shape from a handheld omnidirectional mic. The head on the cardioid mic is generally elongated, and this mic also has vents on the side. These vents allow sound cancellation, which affects the mic's directionality.

Cardioid microphones are further classified into **supercardioid**, **hypercardioid**, and **ultracardioid** types. Each has an increasingly narrower pick-up pattern and a longer interference tube. Generally, as the microphone gets physically longer, the pickup pattern gets narrower. The hypercardioid is longer and narrower than the supercardioid. The ultracardioid mic is the longest and most directional mic option. Some highly focused ultracardioid microphones are more than 3 feet in length. Microphones of these three classes are commonly referred to as shotgun microphones.

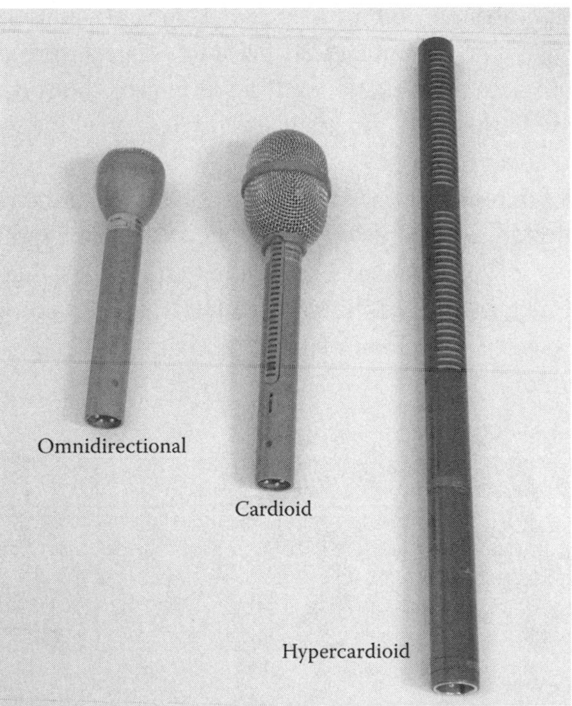

Figure 7.3 An omnidirectional, cardioid, and hypercardioid microphone. As the pick-up pattern becomes narrower, each microphone is physically longer. Directional microphones have a longer interference tube with cancellation vents.

Shotgun microphones can register sound targeted from a greater distance more clearly than omnidirectional microphones, which makes the shotgun mic a good choice for circumstances when the microphone should not be included in the picture. Shotgun mics are often mounted in a pistol grip or on a boom pole, which allows them to be held steady at various heights and angles out of frame.

Frequency Response. A third general way to classify microphones is in terms of frequency response. Sound travels through the air in waves. As the frequency of a sound wave gets shorter, the pitch of the sound gets higher. The frequency of sound waves, and thus their pitch, is measured in Hertz. Hertz refers to the number of cycles of a wave each second from crest to crest of the wave. A sound at 20 Hertz is perceived as low rumble, such as the sound of the earth moving due to a tremor. The pitch of a sound at 20,000 Hertz is at the highest end of the range of human hearing and only some people can actually hear it. The human voice generally occurs in the range of 300 to 3,000 Hertz. At 300 Hz you will experience a low male voice somewhat in the family of James Earl Jones portraying Darth Vader. At 3,000 Hertz you will experience a high-pitched female voice.

Because human speech occurs within a specific range, many microphones are designed to optimize the reproduction of frequencies in that range. A general voice mic, for example, will pick up sounds lower than 300 Hz and greater than 3,000 Hz, but many manufacturers build in a **speech bump**, which boosts performance for vocal reproduction. All good microphones come with a frequency response chart so that you know exactly how well the microphone will perform for any given frequency.

General speech reproduction is a popular objective in microphone design, but there are other frequency response designs for specific applications. There are microphones made to record bass drums and others that are better for strings. The ability to fully utilize these specialized microphones requires advance study beyond the scope of this text, but it is valuable to know that these options exist.

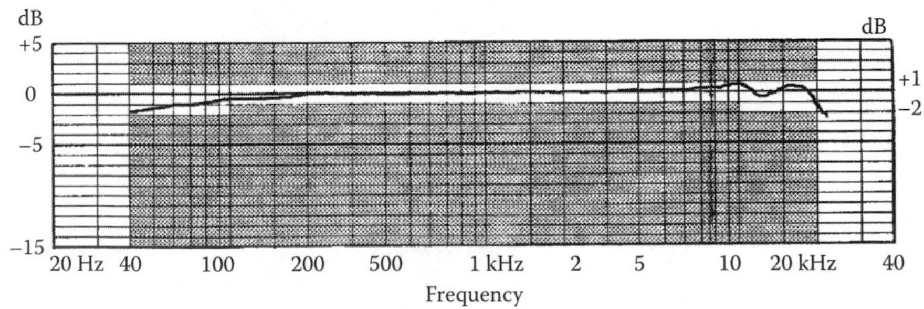

Figure 7.4 A frequency response chart illustrates the exact recording characteristics of each microphone.

As you imagine your required audio recording needs, consider the ideal microphone type (dynamic or capacitor), directionality, and frequency response to select the best microphone for the job.

Sizes and Shapes. Microphones come in a wide variety of sizes and shapes to further expand your options. There are tiny microphones that can be hidden under a lapel. There are handheld mics for field interviews. There are mics designed to be mounted on a support pole, and there are special microphone systems that can pick up a voice from 50 feet away.

The **lavaliere microphone** (or tie clip mic) is a staple that should be in any core sound-recording kit. These mics can be used for miking performers in a studio and for subjects and reporters for sit-down interviews. Their small size and effective range allows them to be hidden under a top layer of clothing so they can be used for fiction work and other situations where it is essential that the microphone be hidden. These microphones are available in wired and wireless variations, further enhancing their versatility.

Handheld microphones are a staple for news and many documentary applications. If time is of the essence, and control of the environment is limited, a handheld mic is clear and effective. This is a good mic to select only if the circumstances permit the mic to be seen in the frame. Because of its size and need to be close to the sound source, the handheld mic is not a good option to try to hide within or keep outside of the frame while miking a person speaking on camera. For these purposes another option will be superior, but necessity is the mother of all invention. A handheld mic can be hidden behind a flower arrangement, or suspended above the frame secured to a broom handle. Creative filmmakers can often solve a problem using the materials at hand.

A **boundary microphone** looks like a flat plate and is usually placed on a flat surface. The boundary mic is unique in how it works and is effective

Figure 7.5 A lavaliere microphone is sometimes called a tie clip mic.

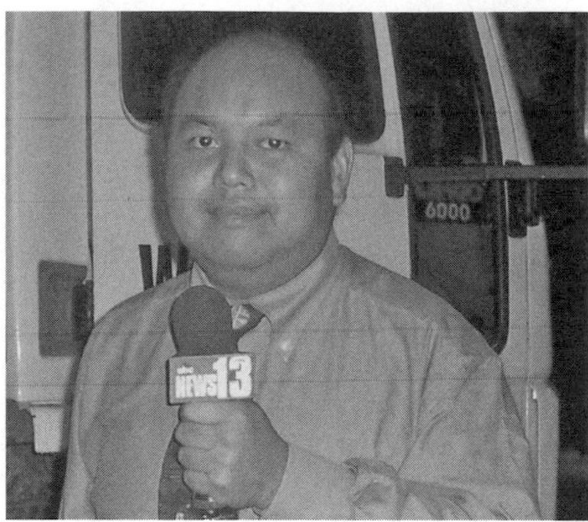

Figure 7.6 Handheld mics are often used in news and other situations where the mic can be seen in the frame. (Apryl Blakeney)

when applied in the right situation. The boundary mic turns the surface it is in contact with into a giant pick-up element. If you put a boundary mic on a table, the sounds in the room vibrating the table are picked up by virtue of physical contact with the microphone. A pair of boundary microphones was used to **mike*** a Thanksgiving dinner scene in an episode of *M*A*S*H*. The producers wanted to execute a 360-degree camera pan in the mess tent. It would have been difficult to otherwise mike the talent in this revealing composition, so two boundary microphones were placed on the tables hidden by turkeys. The boundary microphone picks up knocks quite readily, and since it only records indirect sounds its effect is a little unnatural. The boundary mic is not used often in video production, but can be valuable for special circumstances.

You might have seen people standing on the sidelines of sporting events holding what looks like a giant Plexiglas salad bowl toward the field. This is a **parabolic microphone**. A parabolic mic gathers sound using a parabolic reflector and focuses this sound on a microphone mounted in front of the dish, much like a satellite dish receiver. This design allows the amplification of sound from far away, which is why you can hear the voices and collisions of the players on the field from many yards away. The parabolic mic is a good example of how a creative microphone design and application can be used to achieve a desired effect.

Accessories. Popular accessories for microphones include **shock mounts**, which suspend the microphone in a cushion of rubber bands and help to reduce the capture of unwanted sound from the jarring of the microphone. Most microphones have a **windscreen** accessory that can be placed over the mic element. The windscreen is also known as a **pop filter**, as it can remove the popping

* "Mic" is generally used as an abbreviation of the noun "microphone," while "mike" is often used as a verb meaning to position a microphone to record a sound.

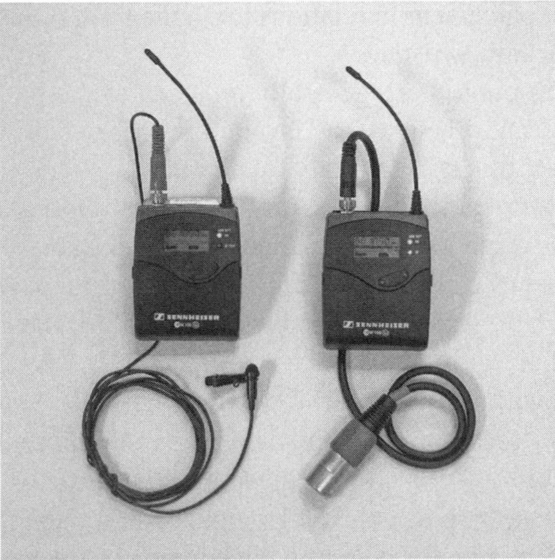

Figure 7.7 Wireless microphone transmitter and receiver.

sound made by the breath on a mic when creating hard sounds (such as words that begin with "P"). Some mics have a pop filter integrated into the design.

It is generally advisable to use a microphone's windscreen in most situations, especially if you will be working outdoors on a windy day of if a subject will be close enough to a microphone that the wind of their breath will hit the microphone as they speak. Microphones are designed to record changes in sound pressure, so wind affects microphones significantly and creates a distracting effect.

Some microphone systems are wireless and use a transmitter attached to or located within the microphone. This transmitter is battery-powered and sends the audio information on a radio frequency to a nearby receiver, which is attached to an input device such as a camera or mixing board. The receiver can be either battery-operated or A/C-powered. Battery-powered receivers offer more versatility for moving the camera.

Positioning the Microphone. How a microphone is positioned affects the quality of the sound recorded. Microphones need to be positioned correctly for proper technical function. A microphone that is too close to a sound source can be distorted by the wind from a person's breath or by the **proximity effect**. The proximity effect occurs when a sound source close to the microphone causes an increase in the low-frequency sensitivity. A microphone that is too far away from a desired sound source can be overwhelmed with interfering sounds from contaminating sources or it might simply be too far away to register the sound of the source at all. This can result in a poor **signal-to-noise ratio**.

Another issue of sound quality and microphone positioning is related to the perspective of the sound, which changes as the microphone is moved closer or farther away from a sound source. If the visuals present a train miles off in the distance, then producing a realistic presence of the whistle requires a different microphone placement in relationship to the train than if the image were a close-up of the train's whistle.

Lavaliere microphones are generally attached to the outside of a person's attire at about mid-chest height. The lavaliere mic is versatile. This versatility comes from the fact that it is an omnidirectional mic so the sound source need not come from any specific direction, as long as it is close enough for the mic to register the sound clearly. The lavaliere mic works surprisingly well when placed under a layer of clothing so it can be hidden from view when necessary. The disadvantage here is that there is more potential for the rustling of clothes to be recorded when the subject moves. If a person is wearing a sweater that contrasts strongly with the color of the microphone cable, you might opt to run the mic cord under the subject's shirt, and place the microphone close to the subject's collar. Even under a chin the lavaliere mic works very well.

A **boom pole** is a support pole used to hold a microphone out of view of the camera. When using a boom pole it is important to work in conjunction with the camera operator and director to make sure that your recording approach is well integrated into the blocking of the scene and that the mic is not in the shot. A good way to determine the safe range within which you can lower the boom is to start with the mic at a low level, within the frame, and then ask the camera operator to look through the viewfinder and tell you when you are out of the frame. Lift the mic slowly and wait for the cue, "Out." You now have a sense of the minimum height you need to maintain for the composition. Since it is impossible to hold a mic overhead for a long time without some movement, it is best to add some extra safety space above the minimum height level so you will not stray into the frame during the shot.

Some boom poles have a mic cable integrated inside the pole; some are telescopic for easier transport, storage, and length adjustment for the needs of each shot. Boom systems often have an integrated shock mount for reducing microphone vibration. Boom poles can be held overhead and they can just as easily be brought in underneath depending on the framing of the shot. An important factor to consider when deciding whether to mike a subject from above or below with a boom pole is other sound sources that lie within the path of the microphone. A unidirectional microphone picks up sounds in its path quite clearly, even those at considerable distance from the microphone.

Some boom operators are tempted to mike a shot from below when possible, as this requires less physical effort than holding a mic overhead. Sound is generally recorded better when miked from above rather than below. Also, when you mike a voice from underneath you point the microphone at the ceiling. Many buildings have air circulation systems with registers in the ceiling; in the case of large office buildings and other institutional settings, these systems cannot be turned off for your shoot. If you are working in such an environment, then miking from below can essentially mean miking the air register. This air circulation system might be virtually invisible to the untrained ear, but on the soundtrack of your program it can sound like a train coming through.

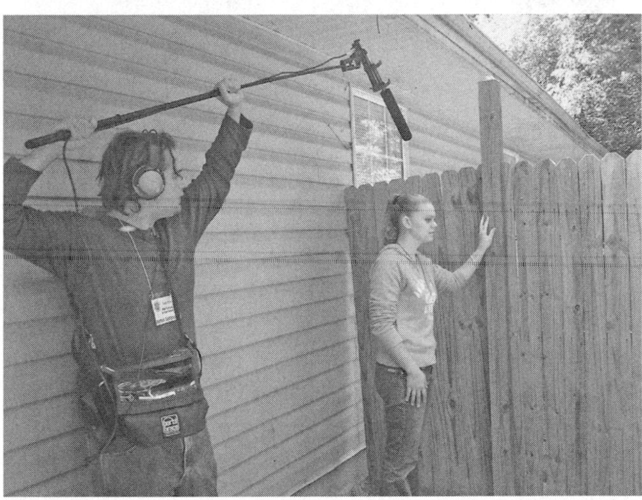

Figure 7.8 Boom miking can be achieved from above or below to meet the needs of the composition and to minimize external sound elements. (Dmitri Medvedev)

Microphones that are frequently used with booms can also be used with a **pistol grip**. A pistol grip has shock-mounting hardware and is a good option in situations where the sound recordist can be out of the frame while close to the sound source, such as in the case of interviews composed in a medium shot. The pistol grip is also good for operator comfort and ease of use for gathering sound to be added to the picture later.

You can position a microphone to either record a subject on-axis or off-axis. Recording a sound **on-axis** simply means having the microphone pointed directly at the source. Recording a subject **off-axis** occurs when the microphone is turned somewhat to one side from the direction of the sound source. This distinction is irrelevant for omnidirectional microphones, which record sound from all directions equally. For all other pick-up patterns of microphones, how-

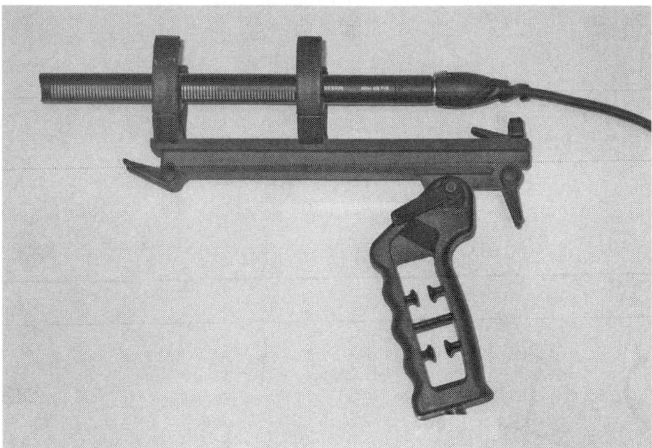

Figure 7.9 A pistol grip can be used to mike subjects. It is also a good option for operator comfort while gathering wild track and effects.

ever, the variation will make a significant qualitative difference. Generally you want to record sources on-axis, but there are circumstances, such as recording two different sound sources simultaneously with one microphone, when you will elect to deliberately record a sound source off-axis.

The Process of Sound Recording

Monitoring Sound. The ability to monitor audio while recording is essential. This is done primarily with the use of headsets. Many small-format digital video cameras have a 1/8" connection (also called a mini-plug) for headsets. This is the same sized plug used for personal stereo headsets, so you can use your personal headset for location audio monitoring in a pinch. The best way to monitor audio, however, is with **circumaural headsets**, which completely cover your ears and block out external noise. With circumaural headsets you can know what the microphone is really picking up.

Keep in mind that monitoring audio during the recording process is only part of the quality-control process. Monitoring audio while recording tells you if the microphone is capturing the sound the way you want it to. It also tells you if there is a problem with the microphone, such as dead batteries, or with the audio cable, such as crackling from a bad connection or hum from an adjacent electrical cord. Monitoring audio during the recording process will not, however, confirm whether the sound is being clearly recorded on storage media. To verify this you need to play the audio back and **spot check** the recording before **striking** the set and moving on. Clogged recording heads can result in no audio captured to tape and a failed drive sector can ruin audio captured to disk.

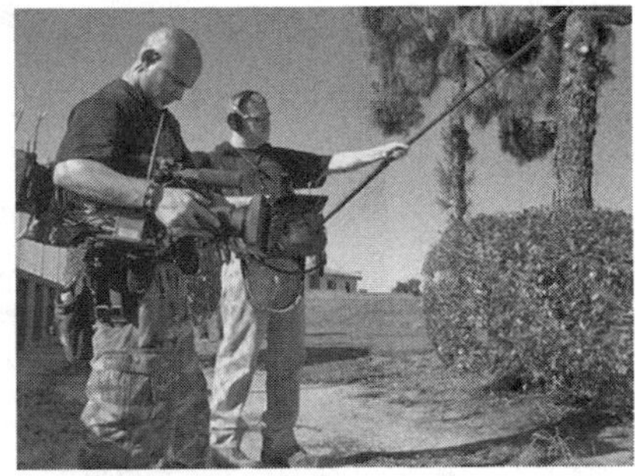

Figure 7.10 A separate sound recordist often works in conjunction with the camera operator. (Chris Walker)

On a small-scale shoot, the camera operator will likely monitor the sound. If there is a boom operator, both the boom operator and the camera operator should monitor the audio. This can be achieved by tapping a signal splitter into the audio monitor of the camera. In this dual monitoring situation each technician is listening for different things. The boom operator is listening to make sure that the microphone position is ideal for clean recording and proper perspective of the source. The camera operator monitors overall levels and makes adjustments to the recording levels as needed using the camera's audio input controls.

On larger-scale shoots the role of sound recording is more clearly differentiated from the role of camera operator. A separate **sound recordist** monitors the recording levels of the microphones and controls these levels using a **field mixer**. In this case, the camera operator does not monitor the sound at all. The camera input level for audio is set at a fixed level using a reference tone, and the sound recordist feeds levels to the camera based on this reference level.

 ***Controlling Sound Levels.*** A primary objective in audio recording is to control the loudness of sounds. The **amplitude** of a sound wave refers to how high the wave is from crest to trough. Two sound waves can be the exact same frequency but different amplitudes. The sound wave with the higher amplitude is louder.

In audio recording and design, the loudness of sound is frequently measured in **volume units (VU)**. This reading is often displayed on a VU meter. The zero point on the VU meter is considered the ideal level for fully saturated recording. Recording a sound at zero VU offers the highest quality and the most options for manipulation in postproduction.

Sound that is recorded significantly below the zero point on the VU meter is considered to be in the mud. When sound is recorded significantly below the zero point, valuable information is lost and background noise becomes a significant part of the signal. This creates a poor signal-to-noise ratio and produces a signal with a lot of hiss.

Sounds that are recorded significantly above the zero point on the VU meter are considered to be riding hot. If an analog recording goes 8 to 12 units above the zero point, it can go beyond the recording capability of the equipment and cause distortion. In digital audio recording there is no headroom. There is no room to spare above zero VU in digital recording. If a digital signal is recorded above zero VU, it will be clipped. Sounds that are clipped

Figure 7.11 A VU meter monitors audio levels.

are distorted and produce a grating effect when played back. In extreme cases, distortion can make a recording indecipherable.

VU meters are located on cameras, on mixing boards, and in postproduction equipment. Many pieces of production equipment can generate a **reference tone**. This fixed frequency tone allows equipment to communicate with other components so they can be set at the exact same level for clean communication and quality recording at every stage. That tone you hear when you see color bars is an audio reference tone.

The VU meter presents its scale in universal volume units. Zero VU, as mentioned, is the ideal point for full saturation. Above the zero point, the VU meter measures units above the ideal level in db (+2db, +4db, etc). Below zero it measures units recorded under the ideal level (-10db; pronounced "minus ten dee bee").

Audio-recording systems can handle significantly lower db levels than ideal and still provide adequate playback. For example, a signal recorded at minus 20db can often be salvaged in a pinch. Once you get any degree above zero VU in digital recording, or 8 to 12 units above the zero point in analog recording, you will encounter distortion that can render an audio signal unusable. Your VU meter will warn you of potential distortion by showing that your signal is in the red.

Many cameras and audio-recording devices have an audio limiter control and an audio automatic gain control. The **audio limiter** prevents a recording from becoming distorted by setting the maximum recording level at a certain point that is below the point of distortion. The audio **automatic gain control (AGC)** is more complex in its operation. AGC seeks to constantly record all incoming audio at the ideal level of saturation (zero db on the VU meter). This can be an asset in fast-moving documentary and news situations, but a liability in other creative applications. The disadvantage of using the audio automatic gain control is that quiet moments will be amplified so they are at full saturation. This can result in a dramatic pause in dialogue turning into a loud hiss of amplified background noise. Beware of using the audio AGC.

Figure 7.12 Camera audio inputs.

Recording Multiple Sources. Cameras generally have two channels of audio, which allow stereo recording of location sound. In fact, the integrated camera mic on many digital video cameras is actually two microphones within the same housing, designed to capture sound from the left and right side of the camera. Each of these microphones is dedicated to the left and right channels of the recorded soundtrack, respectively. Most cameras have audio inputs, which allow you to connect external microphones to the camera. Using two external microphones, one for each audio channel, is quite common. You might mike an interview subject and a reporter each with a lavaliere for a sit-down interview.

Figure 7.13 External audio mixer.

You might do the same with two actors in a dramatic scene. You can have a boom mic covering a scene while using the camera mic on the second channel as a backup. The camera mic can offer reference audio if the boom mic cuts out or fails.

It is possible to use more than two microphones even if your camera only has two audio channels, but to do this you will need to insert an audio mixer into the signal flow between the microphones and the camera. An **audio mixer** can take 8, 10, 12 microphones or more and mix them down to two stereo channels. This is a good option for complex audio setups including musical concerts.

Some specialized microphones offer remarkable stereo and surround sound recording in a single unit. The Holophone is a specialized microphone for recording sound for playback in surround sound, and the Kunstkopf is a head-shaped unit with the microphones in the ears that produces a perfect binaural sound experience when the sound is later played back through headsets.

Phasing. When working with multiple microphones that are fed to a common recording track, the audio recordist needs to be aware of the potential of microphone phase cancellation. **Phasing** takes place when the sound from a source reaches one microphone at a slightly different time from a second microphone. The combined audio signals can be slightly out of phase and the skewed audio waves create a reduction in stereo imaging and loudness. To reduce the danger of phase cancellation it is best to have microphones a considerable distance from each other in relationship to their distance from the audio sources. A good rule of thumb is that each microphone should be three times as far from each other as they are from the sound source.

Another way to avoid phase cancellation is to use a **head-to-head method**. If you want to record sound from two different directions for mixing down to one track, one option is to put the microphones head-to-head pointed in differ-

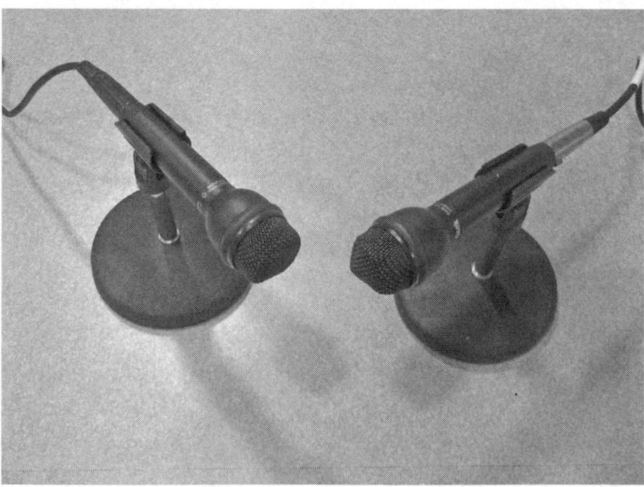

Figure 7.14 Head-to-head miking helps minimize phase cancellation.

ent directions. This will ensure that the sound spilling from one microphone to the other arrives at the exact same time, which will prevent phasing.

Audio Cables and Connectors. Microphones and audio components are linked together using cables. Audio cables come in both balanced and unbalanced types. Balanced cables are superior: they transmit a signal more clearly, are less likely to experience signal degeneration over the length of the cable, and are less vulnerable to interference from outside signals in the environment. Balanced cables have a three-pin connection, which includes an independent positive pole, negative pole, and ground wire. This configuration provides better signal transfer. This type of audio cable and connection is called an **XLR**, which identifies each of the three independent wires in the system. XLR connectors come in both socket and plug configurations, which are sometimes referred to as female and male connectors. Microphones wired for XLR connectors always have a plug connector, while cameras wired for XLR audio inputs have socket connectors. This allows microphones to be connected to a camera using an XLR cable with a plug connector on one end and socket connector on the other. This is the standard configuration of stock audio cable.

There may be circumstances where the existing connections do not match the specific configuration that you need. The solution to this problem is simple. XLR adapters allow the bridging of a plug-to-plug or socket-to-socket connection.

XLR audio cables vary in quality. Some cables are shielded, while others are unshielded. Shielded cables cost more, but offer more insulation from interference and help preserve the integrity of the signal. Length of an audio cable also affects the quality of the signal preservation. It is a common mistake of beginning filmmakers to take the longest run of microphone cable available for a shoot. The reasoning behind this common mistake is that this option offers

Figure 7.15 Plug and socket XLR connectors on an XLR cable.

the most flexibility for microphone placement relative to camera position. You can always use less than the maximum run. This is good reasoning if you do not know the circumstances you will encounter on location and if you can truly only take one mic cable. With some advanced research, however, and careful equipment selection, you can have options available on location that minimize the unnecessary use of extra cable length. Keep in mind, too, that every connection is a new opportunity for signal loss and interference. For this reason it is better to use a 20-foot audio cable rather than linking two 10-foot audio cables together.

XLR cables have a positive lock, which keeps the cables connected until a release button is pressed. You should take care to avoid stress on audio cables, especially at the connection location where the cable can be damaged over time at the base of the connector. The XLR is a single-signal cable, which is sometimes called a mono cable.

While the XLR is the professional choice for audio cables and connections, there are other audio cords and connectors. Some microphones, headsets, and component connections use 1/4" plugs. This is called a **phono plug**. A 1/8"connector, or **mini-plug**, is used for personal headsets and some microphones. A 1/8" connector is a common connection type for consumer digital video cameras due to its small size and wide compatibility with consumer-line mics and headsets. One-quarter inch and 1/8" connectors come in both mono and stereo types. You can tell the difference between mono and stereo 1/4" and 1/8" plugs by the number of contact rings on the plug. Stereo plugs have two rings, while mono plugs have only one. Another common type of audio connector is the RCA. **RCA cables** are generally used for line-level signals (see below), and are not commonly used to connect microphones.

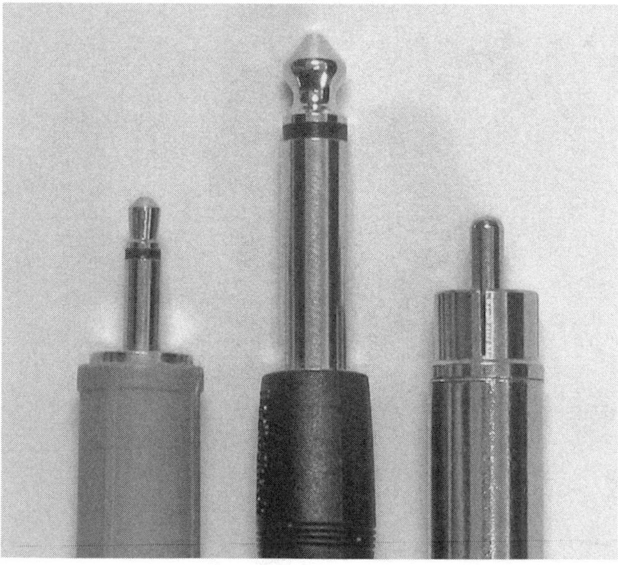

Figure 7.16 1/8" (mini plug), 1/4" (phono plug), and RCA audio connectors.

It is important to take care of your audio cables. One of the primary ways to do this is to coil your audio cables and other production cords correctly. Many people wind cables by locking their elbow 90 degrees and wrapping the cord around their open hand and elbow. This will kink the cords and damage them over time. It will also promote tangling. Instead, lay the cable open on the ground and bring it into coils. Velcro cable ties can be affixed to the cables to bind them after winding and are well worth the investment.

Mic Levels and Line Levels. What is the difference between mic levels and line levels? As one audio engineer puts it, "Line levels are about 1,000 times louder." This is an exaggeration but it makes the point.

You will work with two different types of audio signals. **Microphone-level signals** are weak. When microphone-level signals are input into cameras and mixing boards they are amplified. **Line-level signals** are used by components, such as CD players and mixing board outputs. Line-level signals are already amplified. If you put a mic-level signal into a port that is made for a line level, you will barely be able to hear a thing. If you put a line level signal into a mic level input it will be loud and distorted.

Single-System and Double-System Sound Recording. The most common approach for recording **synchronous sound (sync sound)** is a **single-system** approach. In single-system recording, the sound and the picture are recorded together. This is the method for most small-format digital video applications. Film production, however, uses **double-system** recording. Motion picture film does not have a sound track. A film camera only captures the picture. The sound for film must be gathered separately.

Have you ever wondered why they put the slate in the frame and say, "Scene one, shot one," and then close the clapperboard? The picture of the clapperboard closing provides a visual reference for the camera and the sound

Figure 7.17 Digital audiotape (DAT) is sometimes used in double-system recording.

Figure 7.18 A scene slate allows sound and film images to be matched up in postproduction. (Jesse Knight)

of the clapperboard closing provides a reference for the audio track. This allows sound and picture to be put in sync in double-system recording.

The necessity for the clapperboard is reduced with the advent of time code. Time code can be matched to the film stock **edge numbers** and can be recorded on the audio media as well. This allows electronic matching of sound and picture sources in postproduction.

Creative Approaches to Sound Recording and Design

Voice and **dialogue** are important components of sound recording and design. Often voices are recorded in sync on location but many times **voice-over** is added later. Voice-over can be constructed in two primary ways. Sometimes the picture is edited first and the voice-over talent reads a script to match the images. In other cases the talent reads the script first, and the editor puts the pictures and other elements in place to match the pacing of the voice-over track.

Another major sound element is **sound effects**. Sound effects add texture to the aural experience. Sound effects elicit audience attention and increase information retrieval in educational content (Schwartz, 2006). Sound effects come in two categories: hard and soft. **Hard effects** are in sync with the picture. Hard effects might be recorded in sync or added in postproduction to appear as though they happened in sync with the picture. For example, we might see a gunshot and muzzle flash on screen, but the sound that was gathered at the time of the shooting was not quite the texture that the director wanted. This hard sound effect might be added later with a different gunshot sound. Hard effects are in sync with the picture, but need not be recorded at the same time.

Figure 7.19 Professional sound studio. (Courtesy of ProComm Studio Services)

Soft effects are not in sync with the picture. If we see a person walking down the street and we hear a jackhammer off in the distance, but never see the jackhammer operator, this would be an example of a soft sound effect.

Wild sounds or **wild track** refer to audio not recorded in sync with the picture. In fact, the camera does not even need to be present to gather wild track. You can take a **disk-based audio recorder** into the woods and gather nature sounds. These sounds can be added to a project in postproduction. You can also use a camera for gathering wild track. Most digital video cameras have excellent sound-recording capability, so use this tool to gather your wild track even if you do not care about the picture that happens to be in the frame at the time.

Music is another important element of sound design. Music is one of the strongest sources of emotion in film (Cohen, 2001). In some cases music is originally composed for a production. This is often the case for professional programs and is not uncommon for student productions. As your skills and video projects become more advanced, you might find it valuable to work in collaboration with colleagues in your school's music department or a friend with a band to add original music to your programs. Original music adds production value and does away with the concerns of copyright permission and fees to use published music.

Using popular music in your programs can be expensive. To avoid overexposure, which would diminish the commercial value of the song, copyright owners generally charge a substantial fee for permission to use a popular song in a film or television program. It is not uncommon for use of a song to cost thousands of dollars. It is possible in some cases to obtain a **festival release** to use a copyrighted song for the limited application of entering a work into film and video festivals. A sample letter for requesting permission to use copyrighted music can be found in *Appendix A*.

Many sound designers prefer to record their own sound effects. To have a sound element in your program that nobody has ever heard before has some real value. In many cases, however, it is not possible to personally gather every single sound effect that you want to use. It is common for sound professionals to use sound effects and music libraries to build sound elements for their programs.

Sound effects and music libraries come in a number of different forms. Some provide a **blanket license**. In this case you pay for permission to use the music or sound effects as often and in as many programs as you want. Some music sources are provided on a **per-use license**. In these cases you may pay as little as a few dollars to use a song once, but be careful to sample the content before paying a license fee to use any music. Often library music is generic in tone. Use of poorly produced music libraries can decrease the value of your program.

Music resources and libraries, as well as sound effects resources and libraries, can be obtained on compact discs and many are available online. You might find, particularly in the case of sound effects, that there are license-free options available for download. You can import the files directly into your editing software to supplement your programs.

Managing A Location

A true **sound stage** blocks all external sound from within the working environment. This allows the sound recordist to design a perfectly controlled sound setup. In most recording situations, however, particularly on location, there are a number of challenges for audio control.

Exterior sounds often spill into the recording environment; while some of these sounds can be controlled, others cannot. For example, if someone is mowing their lawn, you might ask them in a friendly manner if they would wait half an hour because you are about to record an important interview. Other external sound sources might be something you cannot shut off. If you are shooting in a building right next to a busy highway, that noise is going to be

Figure 7.20 Sound stage. (Courtesy of The Alpha Group)

present. In that case, you need to work to minimize the external sound. How you position the actors and microphones and the placement of filtering materials can help to minimize external sound spill. Examples of other contaminating sounds include air circulation systems and refrigerators. Generally it is best to dampen or remove as much extraneous sound as possible.

Hard and Soft Environments. Some environments are hard while others are soft. A room with bare walls and wood floors is an extremely hard environment for sound. The sound will bounce around, reverberate, or echo. Some level of reverberation is natural, realistic, and desired. In fact, sound studios often have some hard surfaces so there is a more realistic sound quality. An overly hard environment can, however, sound unpleasant, like a high school gym.

Other environments are soft. A room with hanging quilts and wall-to-wall carpeting is a dead space. The sound will be absorbed by these surfaces and not reverberate. One of the things you want to do as a sound designer is to control the amount of reflection in a space. You can brighten a room and make it harder and more reverberant by removing area rugs and adding reflective surfaces. Conversely, you can soften a hard environment by bringing in blankets and area rugs.

Mic Cables and Power Cords. When working with microphone cables, it is important to note how they lay in relationship to power cords. In most situations you will work in conjunction with lighting, and there can be a number of electrical cords on the set in addition to your audio lines. If your audio cables run in parallel to an electrical cord, there is a good chance, even with a shielded cable, that you will pick up a 60-Hertz buzz on your sound track (electric cur-

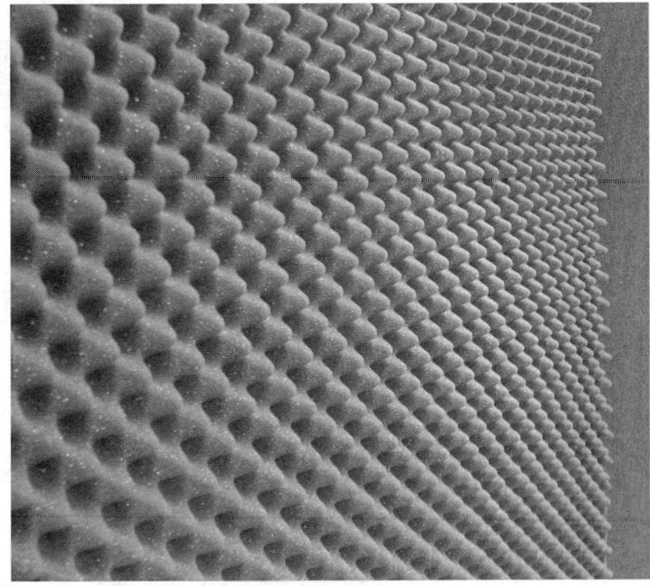

Figure 7.21 Sound baffle prevents reflection and is used to help soften a hard environment.

rent runs at 60 cycles per second). This can ruin your material. If you need to cross a power cord with an audio cord, it is best to do so at a sharp angle. If an audio line does need to cross a power cord, it is best to avoid contact by using an insulating material between the cables such as wood or cloth. Do not run audio and electric lines in parallel. Keep distance between them whenever possible.

Blimping. Video cameras are generally quiet, but their mechanisms can create a significant sound if the microphone is in direct contact. Keep this in mind, and keep your microphone away from the camera if possible. Film cameras have a mechanical shutter and are generally louder than digital video cameras. Film cameras often use a **blimp**, which is a cover made specifically for reducing camera noise.

Designing Sound Layers. When recording sound, beginning filmmakers often try to create the entire aural environment on location. For example, when recording a conversation at a cocktail party, a new sound recordist might have the background conversation taking place while the primary actors converse in the foreground. If a phone rings in the scene, he might have somebody call in from a cell phone to get the sound of the phone ringing during the scene. This is not the best approach. What you want to do is totally isolate every sound element and control it. When recording a conversation at a cocktail party, have the background guests merely mouth their conversation. You can then gather the audio of the main actors with perfect clarity and this will greatly enhance the sound quality and your options in editing. You should record the background elements and sound effects separately and mix these elements together in post-production when you can control the levels and balance between the sound elements exactly the way you want them.

Continuity. We discussed image continuity in chapter 2. Audio has its own elements of continuity. Sound levels and sound perspective must be consistent from shot to shot. The sound must also be in sync with the picture. The sound presence must be realistic and the balance of audio elements must match the picture. When recording and editing sound keep in mind that sounds, too, must remain in continuity.

Equalization. An audio **equalizer (EQ)** electronically manipulates sound waves to enhance or reduce specific frequency ranges. The bass and treble control on a standard consumer stereo is a simple audio equalizer. By boosting the bass you add strength to the low-end frequencies. By cutting the treble you reduce the strength of the high-end frequencies.

Professional audio equalizers offer more control. At minimum, professional equalizers have three frequency ranges: low, medium, and high. Most audio equalizers have even more frequency ranges. A parametric equalizer allows the isolation of an exact frequency bandwidth for manipulation. A **parametric equalizer** has two controls that work together. One control sets the frequency

Figure 7.22 An equalizer (EQ) allows the boosting or reduction of certain frequency ranges in an audio signal.

bandwidth to be manipulated; the second control adjusts the level of either reducing or increasing the strength of that bandwidth. If you forgot to move an audio cable away from a power cord and ended up with a 60-Hertz buzz on the audio track, a parametric equalizer will allow you to isolate the frequency window at 60 cycles per second and reduce that buzz significantly.

If you are putting music behind a narrator's voice-over in a documentary, you might find that the music competes with the vocal frequencies. A parametric equalizer allows you to isolate the frequency range of the narrator's voice and boost it. You can also cut a window on the music track and reduce the strength of the exact same frequency range there. This will often eliminate a sense of competition between two audio elements.

Equalizers offer a lot of power for both repairing poorly recorded audio and making creative enhancements in audio design. It is important, however, not to rely on an equalizer to create miracles. Poorly recorded audio simply cannot be rescued in every case.

Room Tone. No space is really quiet. There are always atmospheric sounds or a **room tone**. Record the sound of each environment to give the editor a background track to bridge shots and provide audio continuity across a scene. Usually room tone is recorded at the end of a shoot at each location. This way the crew is certain that everything critical with the actors is taken care of first.

The sound recordist will often announce after the last setup is captured that he or she needs to grab room tone. At that point everyone will be still and quiet and the recording will be identified as room tone (or sometimes as an **atmospheric track** when working outside). This will usually run for 60 seconds. If the scene is longer than 60 seconds, the track can be looped and used more than once.

When gathering room tone, it is important to do so before the production lights in the space are turned off. This is important for two reasons. First, the lights can create electronic noise when operating and you want the sound of your room tone track to match the sound at the time of shooting as closely as possible. Secondly, when some lights cool down they click, and this creates interference that contaminates a room tone recording.

Automated Dialogue Replacement (ADR). Many productions replace some or all of the actors' lines in postproduction. The actors watch themselves perform the scene on a playback screen and redo their lines, in perfect sync, one by one. This is the process of **automated dialogue replacement (ADR)**. This process is also called looping. This term came from the days when film and audiotape were actually put on a loop so that takes could be attempted over and over until they were hit just right.

Figure 7.23 Automated dialogue replacement (ADR). (Courtesy of ProComm Studio Services)

Figure 7.24 Foley stage. (Walt Bost)

Foley. Foley is the process of creating sound effects in a studio to match visuals on the screen. If you need to represent somebody running down a sidewalk and then falling into a parked car, this can be created with **Foley**. The Foley technician has different surfaces to work with and will run in place across some concrete at just the right pacing and using just the right shoes. He can then replicate the sound of hitting the car with his wide range of studio props, which can include a car door. The process of Foley recording is named after Jack Foley, who developed the technique.

Sound Editing

Working with sound editing can be extremely rewarding. Most editing software offers numerous audio tracks. While you might only have two audio channels to work with in the field, you can build 10, 12, or 20 layers of audio in postproduction depending on your needs and the complexity of your design. This allows you to integrate synchronous sound from multiple channels, stereo music tracks that overlap, and a rich palate of special effects.

Editing is the time when you really make sound design come to life. In the field and the recording studio, your objective is to isolate sounds and record them cleanly at full saturation. In editing, you change the relative balance of the sounds. You can change their texture through equalization and digital processing effects. If you have a phone conversation in your program, you will want

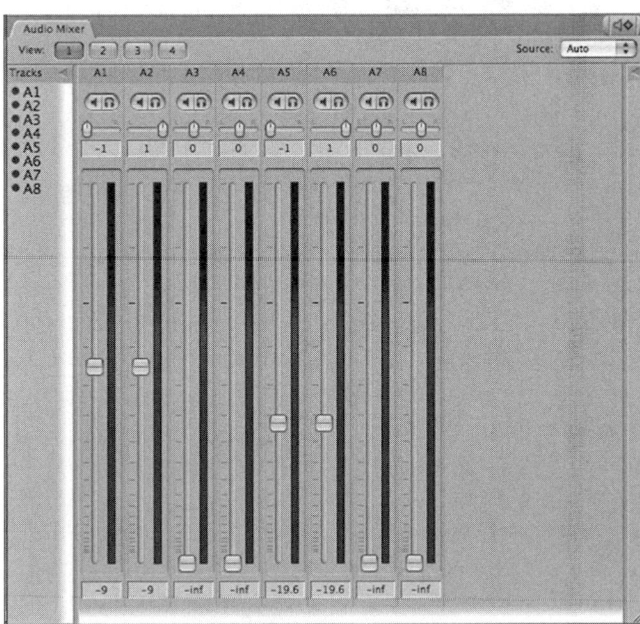

Figure 7.25 Audio level sliders in a nonlinear editing program. (Screen shot reprinted with permission from Apple Computer, Inc.)

to record the conversation with perfect clarity, but by using an audio filter in postproduction you can make it sound like the voice is coming over a standard phone line or a cell phone. Equalization generally takes place in postproduction. It is best to leave a signal unprocessed while recording and preserve your options for postproduction. You can add audio transitions, which allow you to go between scenes with creativity and smooth flow.

One popular audio transition is the **cross-fade**. An audio cross-fade overlaps sounds as a scene changes. As one sound source gets quieter, another one rises in intensity at the point of the scene's transition. Another effective way of designing audio transitions is to lead with the audio. As you are approaching the end of a scene you might show a character on screen thinking about a critical decision while we hear the sound from the next scene. The audio lead motivates the visual cut to the next scene, which reveals the consequences of his decision.

You can build audio montages in postproduction. A documentary might have dozens of interviews. Editing together a series of short quotes in quick succession can get the audience hooked and foreshadow the story of an entire documentary in a few moments.

When creating your final sound mix, you need to control how the audio tracks you constructed are exported for playback. Very simple audio mixes are in **mono**. In mono audio mastering, all the different sound layers are combined and exported to a single channel. A more common approach is to create a **stereo mix**. In a stereo mix, the different audio sources are adjusted so certain sounds are emphasized on the left side, while others are emphasized on the right. Sounds that have equal balance on both sides create the aural illusion that they are coming from the center.

Music libraries are generally recorded in stereo. When building your tracks, keep the left and right music channels isolated in editing so that you maintain stereo reproduction when your program is edited and exported.

If a character is featured in the center of the screen, you generally want to maintain equal balance of vocals on the left and right channels when creating a stereo mix. If you have a conversation taking place with one character screen-left and one character screen-right, slightly emphasize the left channel for the character on the left and the right channel for the character on the right. This gives a more realistic presence to the sound during playback. Keep in mind that this effect only works if the scene stays in long shot. If the visuals cut to a close-up and the audio is panned left or right, this will be dislocating. Since most visual programs contain close-ups and significant shot variety within scenes, most vocals are centered in mastering.

You can apply stereo separation to sound effects to build additional creative textures. If a car passes from left to right, you can start the sound effect on the left channel and then pan it over so it crosses completely to the right channel. This can be a dramatic effect.

Other audio designs are even more complex than stereo. **Surround sound** offers the capability of assigning the left and right channels, a center channel,

Figure 7.26 Mixing studio. (Walt Bost)

one or more rear channels, and a sub-woofer or bass channel. Surround sound systems come in a number of formats. Surround sound 5.1 has five main speakers as well as the sub-woofer, whereas Surround sound 7.1 has seven speakers and a sub-woofer. As you can imagine, the sound design for these systems can be extremely complex and offers tremendous creative potential for the sound artist.

CONCLUSIONS

You now have the technical foundation for controlling sound in video production. When planning a shoot, consider the best microphones for each application. Does the scene require a rugged dynamic mic or is the more sensitive capacitor mic a better option? Choose the best microphone pick-up pattern and frequency response range for the job. Select microphone placement for optimal audio recording while maintaining proper presence and perspective.

When recording audio make sure to monitor the sound using headsets, and spot check the recording afterwards through playback. Keep sound levels at proper saturation, and avoid recording a signal in the mud or one that is riding hot. When using multiple microphones, take precautions to avoid phase cancellation. Make sure you have the proper cables and connectors to do the job and extra batteries for all capacitor mics.

When working in the field, listen for contaminating sounds and work to minimize unwanted sound spill. Bring blankets to soften a hard space, and remember to remove area rugs and add reflective surfaces in a space that is too soft.

Many people visualize a script when they read it. The sound designer listens to the script. Imagine what the world of the script sounds like. Determine how you will use the elements of synchronous and rerecorded sounds, sound effects, music, and sound mixing and editing to create that world.

One of the most remarkable and rewarding areas of production is the art of presenting real events and allowing people to tell their story. Our next chapter explores these nonfiction forms.

SAMPLE EXERCISES

1. Create a two-minute story told only with sound.
2. Take an assortment of microphones into the field and do comparative tests to see how these mics record sounds differently.
3. Import the video of a scene from one of your favorite movies. Totally build the sound track to this scene using original audio and library music and effects.

RECOMMENDED READINGS

Alten, S. (2005). *Audio in Media*. Belmont: Thompson Wadsworth.
Holman, T. (2002). *Sound for Film and Television*. Boston: Focal Press.
Rose, J. (2003). *Producing Great Sound for Digital Video*. San Francisco: CMP Books.

REFERENCES

Cohen, A. J. (2001). Music as a source of emotion in film. In P. Juslin (Ed.), *Music and Emotion: Theory and Research* (pp. 249-272). New York: Oxford University Press.

Neisser, U., & Becklin, R. (1975). Selective looking: Attending to visually specified events. *Cognitive Psychology, 7*, 480-494.

Olsen, G. D. (1994). Observations: The sounds of silence: Functions and use of silence in television advertising. *Journal of Advertising Research, 34*, 89-95.

Peretz, I. (2006). The nature of music from a biological perspective. *Cognition, 100*, 1-32.

Schwartz, N. C. (2006). Integral or irrelevant? The impact of animation and sound effects on attention and memory in multimedia. *Dissertation Abstracts International Section A: Humanities and Social Sciences, 66*, 2899.

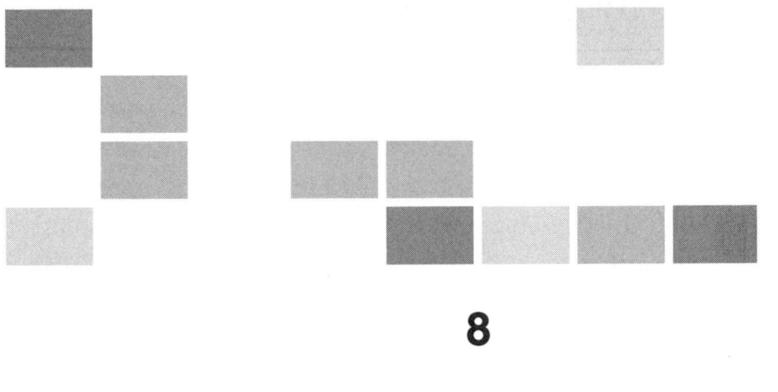

8

NONFICTION

CHAPTER OBJECTIVES

Fiction programming often invites the audience to escape from the real world. Nonfiction works challenge the audience to engage the real world.

While documentary filmmaking is rarely a lucrative business, these filmmakers spend their days exploring the issues of the world that matter most to them, expanding knowledge, and creating a priceless record for posterity. Nonfiction filmmaking is often described as a calling. Those who have the passion to tell true stories that make a difference and affect change report that there are few creative methods as powerful and far-reaching as the documentary form.

In this chapter you will explore the history and some unique elements of the documentary and other nonfiction forms including news, industrial films, instructional programs, and reality TV. The goals of this chapter are to:

- Survey the history and varied philosophies of nonfiction filmmaking;
- Examine popular nonfiction approaches, styles, and formats;
- Introduce documentary research, writing, financing, and production;
- Explore the process of planning and recording effective on-camera interviews.

Documentary filmmaking is experiencing a renaissance. Since the beginning of the 1990s, documentaries and other nonfiction forms have grown in popular success and critical recognition. In 2004, the documentary feature *Fahrenheit 9/11* was the No. 1 film its opening weekend. That was the first time in history a documentary was the top-grossing film at the box office. With *Super Size Me* (2004), *Grizzly Man* (2005), and *An Inconvenient Truth* (2006), audiences are familiar with nonfiction films in a theatrical context.

This was not always the case. For decades documentary exhibition was mostly limited to educational settings and public television. Documentaries used to be synonymous with a narrator talking about a technical subject in a dry tone, but now nonfiction programs are more innovative in their production techniques, bold in their subject matter, and mass audiences are more receptive and supportive of these works.

Reality television might have a lot to do with the current success of documentary features. The reality TV genre has made audiences comfortable with storytelling that is set in a real-life context, and the conventions invented by reality television have pushed the artists of all nonfiction storytelling to be more aware of the wider range of tools and techniques available to engage an audience.

The dramatic structure discussed in chapter 1 applies to nonfiction as well. You need dynamic and interesting characters to propel your story forward. You need to keep the elements of the dramatic structure in place to make your nonfiction work compelling. It is up to your subjects to present the facts, but it is how you structure the facts that tells the story.

APPROACHES TO NONFICTION PROGRAMS

On December 28, 1895, Paris residents entered a small makeshift theater and were amazed by a new innovation. On this day motion pictures were projected for a paying audience for the first time. Auguste and Louis Lumiere, inventors and businessmen, exhibited their first two films, *Leaving the Lumiere Factory* and *The Arrival of a Train at La Ciotat.*

The titles are straightforward and descriptive. The techniques used in these early films were also straightforward. Both films are a single shot in duration. The camera is mounted on a tripod, which captures the action with a fairly wide-angle view. The camera does not pan, tilt, or zoom. Both works exhibited that day were nonfiction. The Lumiere brothers placed a camera outside of their factory and on a train platform to capture a slice of reality as it unfolded before them. It is said that the power of this new medium was so intense that people cowered when the train approached the platform on screen.

The Lumieres attributed great power to this new medium on another level. Philosophically, they maintained that the motion picture is not an imitation of reality, but a record of people that is true to their inherent nature.

That might be hard to agree with more than 100 years later, but the birth of motion pictures as a tool for representing reality introduced a debate and a diversity of approaches that continues to evolve today.

Figure 8.1 The first film ever projected for a paying audience was a work of nonfiction. (*The Arrival of a Train at La Ciotat* [1895])

The First Documentary

Robert Flaherty, an American filmmaker, created the first film to be called a documentary: *Nanook of the North* (1922). The film, Flaherty's most famous, portrays the life of the Inuit people by following Nanook and his family through their day-to-day activities. We watch Nanook build an igloo, we see his children at play, we see his family waking up in the morning, and we follow a hunt on the tundra. Many praise Flaherty for his documentary, which provides greater understanding of a culture few have visited firsthand. Others, however, criticize Flaherty's documentary for ignoring many crucial facets of culture including religion, marriage, and political structure.

There are several circumstances behind Flaherty's film that raise questions about honesty and ethics in nonfiction filmmaking. Since there would normally not be enough light inside an igloo for early cameras, Nanook helped construct a special igloo that was, in fact, missing a large part of its side to serve as a set with adequate lighting for making the film. Also, the film was sponsored by the fur industry, which stood to gain by romanticizing and personalizing the life of fur hunters. Furthermore, Flaherty paid his subjects for appearing in the film and staged most of the action for the camera. A conversation between Flaherty and Nanook is reported in Flaherty's writings. Flaherty asks:

"Suppose we go," said I, "do you know that you and your men may have to give up making a kill, if it interferes with my film? Will you remember it is the picture of you hunting the iviuk [walrus] that I want and not their meat?"

"Yes, yes, the aggie [motion picture] will come first," earnestly he assured me. "Not a man will stir, not a harpoon will be thrown until you give the sign. It is my word" (Flaherty, 1924).

Figure 8.2 *Nanook of the North* (1922) is the first film to be widely labeled a documentary.

Some people argue that staging action for the camera is more real than not staging action. The logic behind this argument can be illustrated with an example: If you wish to create a documentary about a family interaction during dinner, you could capture an actual family eating dinner, but the presence of the camera in the room is likely to alter the behavior of everyone there. If you conduct unobtrusive research, however, to study how the family interacts during dinner, and subsequently stage a dinner with actors, this might actually be more real for the audience. This is the reasoning used by John Grierson.

The British School

John Grierson was a liberal and a humanist who believed that art should be a force of social good. He supervised hundreds of films as director of The General Post Office Film Unit in the 1930s. Grierson developed an approach highly influential to the documentary movement in Britain. Grierson's films were often designed to achieve practical objectives. He introduced the problem-solution format. Grierson used recreations in his films and even actors to better express the psychic reality of events. Grierson was also the first filmmaker to portray the British working class in serious and heroic roles rather than comic ones.

Cinema Verite

French filmmaker Jean Rouch's work is in the style of Cinema Verite (true cinema). **Cinema Verite** acknowledges that the presence of the camera does alter the event, but Rouch argued that altering the event brings to the surface a deeper reality that is normally hidden. In his film *Chronicle of a Summer*

Figure 8.3 *Chronicle of a Summer* (1961) is a pioneer film of the Cinema Verite movement. Jean Rouch employs interviews to explore a deeper reality normally hidden by everyday life. (Courtesy of First Run/Icarus Films)

(1961), Rouch asked people, "Are you happy?" The introduction of the filmmaker, the camera, and the question altered the event, but by approaching a person with a camera and asking this question, the audience is introduced to the deeper reality of the interview subject's character.

Direct Cinema

Robert Drew of Time Life was a formative figure in the American movement of Direct Cinema in the 1960s. Drew believed that the camera could capture reality. Drew used rigid rules to help ensure objectivity and fidelity to reality. Unlike any approach before, only **Direct Cinema** limited content to real events as they unfold with no recreations. Editing is only done in chronology. There is also a frequent use of subjective camera—often handheld—to give the viewer the sense of being there. One of Drew's most significant works is his documentary *Primary* (1960), which covered the Humphrey-Kennedy primary. The contemporary news approach grew out of the Direct Cinema movement.

Consider the philosophical choices made by each of these artists. You might find some approaches that you agree with more than others. You might also conclude there is not one single approach that will best apply to all situations. It is not important that you stick to any single ideological approach, but rather that you are honest with your audience. If you feel deep down that you are presenting something out of context, or portraying something that does not represent the events and facts as you understand them, then it is time to stop and reassess.

NONFICTION FORMATS

Documentary

The **documentary** can take many forms and tell many types of stories. It can vary in running time from a few minutes to a series of many hours. Regardless of length or subject, the form has some universal elements.

The documentary form is grounded in real-world events. These events can be global in scale, the story of a community, or the life experience of one person. These might be events that happened a long time ago or they are unfolding right now. Historical documentaries, which examine events of the past, present unique challenges. When studying the past it is not possible to record events directly. You need to rely on other tools to bring the story to life including reenactments, photographs, paintings, archival footage, or new footage of the location where events took place. Interviews can help support historical documentaries by presenting the point of view and voice of experts who have studied the topic in great detail or, in cases of recent history, experiences and memories of those who were there at the time of an event. The use of a **narrator** is also a valuable way to provide the audience with background information, since it is often not possible in historical documentaries to hear from the people who were actually there.

A documentary about contemporary events offers some additional options. The filmmaker can capture actual events as they unfold. The filmmaker can speak with participants in the process and the people who are central to the story.

In its most standard form, the documentary story is told by recording interviews, which are considered to be the **A-roll** material, and then inserting various images over top of the interviews to further convey and dramatize what the subject is saying. The visuals that are inserted are called the **B-roll**. Many interesting and compelling documentaries take this basic concept and add other elements, while some do away with the interview element altogether.

Ken Burns' series *The Civil War* (1990) brilliantly integrates voice-over readings of historical letters. These methodic readings are set to visuals that show the locations where events took place. Shots of locations only show the subtle movements of water and wind. Period photographs and historic documents fill the screen and transport the viewer to this earlier time.

The Private Life of Plants (1995) demonstrates the remarkable world of plants with the aid of **time-lapse** photography. We witness the change of a landscape over the course of an entire year in just a few seconds. The stories of plants around the world are told by narrator/host David Attenborough. Sometimes he enters the frame in the plant's natural habitat to tell us where we are and what we are experiencing. In other moments, a close-up of the plant tells the story.

Michael Moore (*Bowling for Columbine,* 2002; *Fahrenheit 9/11*, 2004) chooses to be a central character in his documentary films. He is seen on screen interacting with his subjects. Moore made this his signature approach

Figure 8.4 Historical documentaries often use reenactments to take the audience to another time and place. (Courtesy of Phyllis Lang and Chanse Simpson)

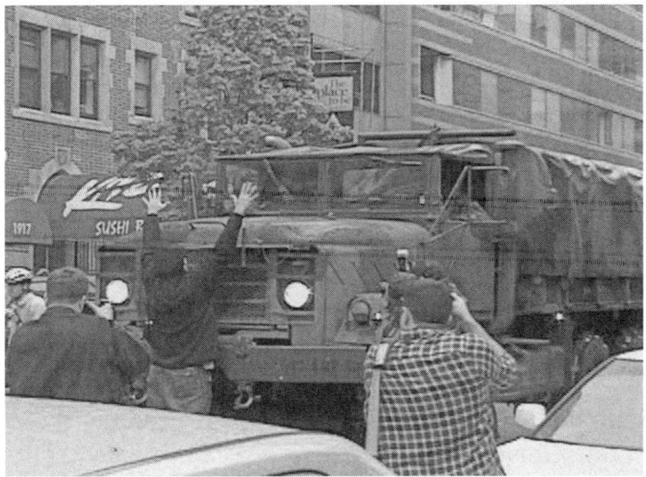

Figure 8.5 Contemporary documentaries direct the audience to important issues. (Courtesy of Alison Watson)

in his first documentary feature, *Roger and Me* (1989). Errol Morris (*The Thin Blue Line*, 1988; *The Fog of War: Eleven Lessons From the Life of Robert S. McNamara,* 2003*),* by contrast, is a much more low-key presence as a filmmaker. There are some interactive moments in Morris's films, when we hear his voice off camera asking a question in an interview, but for the most part Morris allows the visuals and the words of his subjects to tell the story.

Some remarkable documentaries stray from the conventional form. *Athens Ga.: Inside/Out* (1986) uses musical performances and interviews to tell the story of a town's culture. Godfrey Reggio's *Koyaanisqatsi* (1983) is a nonfiction form in which not a single word is ever spoken throughout the entire feature film. The story is told with images on screen and the supportive music of Philip Glass. *Microcosmos* (1996) moves the sphere of its exploration to the very small, and uses extraordinary **macro photography** to bring the world of insects to the big screen.

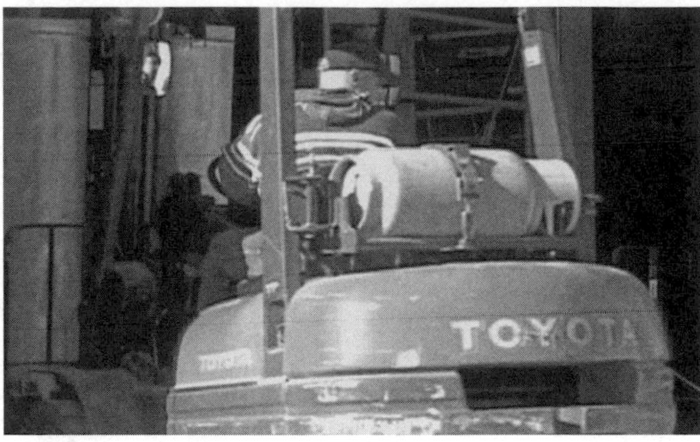

Figure 8.6 Industrial films communicate the messages of companies and their services. (Courtesy of Oliver Media Services, LLC)

Industrials

Industrial films, also known as corporate films, are produced for a business or other organization to facilitate a communication objective. Industrial films take many forms. Some are designed for **internal communication**. These programs are made for employees and cover such topics as sales training, safety, and company policies. Some industrial films are used as a motivating tool for employees and highlight achievements. Other industrial films are designed for **external communication**. They might be used to reach a client base or as a marketing tool to recruit new clients and describe what the company does.

The industrial film has roots close to advertising, public relations, and marketing. Corporate films often use the same research and analysis methods that advertising agencies use. You need to define the target audience and determine how to reach and persuade that audience to conform to the program's objectives. In effect, many industrial films are just long commercials. Industrial filmmaking is generally a well-paying form with significant opportunity in most markets, which provides many emerging video professionals with paid production opportunities.

While some industrial films are promotional in nature, others are intended to achieve specific learning objectives, as in the case of a safety training video. When the primary objective of a program is educational rather than promotional, the program is often labeled as an instructional film.

Instructional

Instructional films are a subset of both traditional documentary and industrial films. All documentaries are instructional in a sense. Documentaries are designed to inform the audience about the world. Films classified as

Figure 8.7 Instructional films are often designed to achieve specific learning objectives. (Courtesy of Troy Scott Burnette)

instructional, however, integrate specific learning objectives. These films often use methods such as explicitly stating learning goals in the beginning, using highly structured presentation of material, titles listing key points, and a review of objectives at the end of the program. Some instructional films tell a story that is designed to promote discussion after the screening. The classification of a nonfiction program as instructional is ultimately a subjective one, but many films that utilize formal teaching methods and learning objectives in a video presentation format are commonly labeled as instructional films.

Producing effective instructional films requires extensive research about the audience and instructional methodology. For example, educational programming for children must be developmentally appropriate for the targeted age group. Instructional videos must consider the audience's existing knowledge base, the specific learning objectives, strategies for maintaining viewer attention, and techniques for maximizing viewer memory and recall of the program's lessons.

Assessing the effectiveness of instructional films is an important area of research. It is the only way to know if an instructional video actually works. Such formal study began in earnest in World War II with the U.S. Army testing military training films. The Army was dismayed to learn that in many cases the intended objectives of the film were not met. Some films were misunderstood and others perceived as boring. By systematically studying the effects of the films, the Army was able to make adjustments to meet their instructional objectives (Hovland, Lumsdaine, & Sheffield, 1949). Some areas of contemporary research interest include distance education in college teaching (Jerry & Collins, 2005) and children's educational television (Uchikoshi, 2006).

News

News production is fast-paced and has fast turnaround. While a documentary or industrial film might be many weeks or months in the making, a news story is usually produced in a matter of hours from concept to screen.

The production of a local television newscast usually begins with an early morning meeting of reporters, producers, and a news director. They bring story ideas from the news wire, tips, and press releases. At the morning meeting, producers and reporters pitch their ideas and decide which stories to pursue. The space for news stories in a telecast is limited. Once you take out commercials and station identifications, a typical 30-minute newscast has about 22 minutes for news. When you factor in the recurring segments, such as weather and sports, the window for content is quite small.

News stories are short format. Most news stories run about 25 to 80 seconds. News stories that are shot in the field and edited together are called **packages**. News packages usually run between 60 and 80 seconds, but a featured segment can run two minutes or more.

A **news producer** is responsible for a particular newscast. She will select the stories to be produced for her show. The individual stories are then assigned to reporters who each work in conjunction with a photographer/editor. The reporter pursues leads to find subjects to tell the story effectively. This often begins with making a number of phone calls and setting up interviews with experts on the issue and people who have been directly affected by events.

The **reporter** conducts interviews with subjects on camera and builds a script for the story around the interview content. One of the conventions of the news format is to present both sides of a controversial issue. The reporter will therefore try to get one or more favorable and unfavorable points of view on an issue of controversy in the community. In most cases, news stories have to be researched, shot, and edited in a few hours. In other cases a reporter has more

Figure 8.8 Broadcast news tells stories on a fast production schedule. (Courtesy of WYFF-TV)

time. Perhaps he will design a feature or multipart story, and might be budgeted some extra time to gather elements. Rarely, however, will a local news team have more than a few days to produce their packages. Extended production time is most common for featured stories for the **ratings (sweeps)** periods.

Like the long-form documentary, the standard format for a news package is to record interviews with people (A-roll) on camera and then drop in relevant images (B-roll) to show elements of interest being discussed. The reporter will often add a **voice-over** to set up the story and to provide transitions between interviews and topics within it. In some circumstances the reporter introduces the story or concludes the package with a **stand-up**. When a reporter stand-up is placed in the middle of a package it is called a bridge.

The anchor in the studio reads some news stories live over images on screen. This story format is called **anchor over video**. If the story is read in part by the anchor and also contains a voice-over by a reporter, it is called a **VOSOT (voice over sound on tape)**. When news stories read by the anchor feature natural sounds rather than a reporter voice-over, the stories are sometimes called a **NATSOT (natural sound over tape)**.

News packages shot in the field are played back during a news show, which is produced in a studio setting. The television news studio has multiple cameras. Three or four cameras allow the intercutting of various shots in the live broadcast. This is achieved by having all of the cameras patched into a control room where a director can see the shots of each camera on different monitors. The director calls out shots from the script to a **technical director**, who punches the buttons and selects the camera angle that the viewer at home sees that very instant.

A call from a director might be, "Ready One." The technical director then prepares to push the button for camera No. 1. The director will then say, "Take One." At that instant the technical director punches the button for

Figure 8.9 Television studio control room.

Figure 8.10 Broadcast news studio floor.

Camera One. During the broadcast, the control room has an audio operator who handles the sound for all the microphones and different audio sources in the show. There might also be a graphics person who designs titles for the show. Overseeing all of this is the producer who keeps track of the time and makes sure everything runs on schedule. The producer can speak to the anchors in the studio through an **IFB** (interruptible feedback) earpiece. The producer can also have the **floor manager**, who is within view of the anchors, give cues to draw things out or to wrap things up to make sure that the news show is completed on time.

Reality TV

The genre of **reality television** has its modern roots in the success of Fox's television series *Cops* from the early 1990s. Other similar successful programs followed including *Rescue 911,* which introduced other dramatic elements such as reenactments. The popular success of *Cops,* in conjunction with its low production cost, attracted many imitators. Producers worked to design original concepts and an entire genre was born that now constitutes a significant portion of television content.

Cops is quite simple in its method. A camera observes events as they unfold in the field, and an officer provides commentary during the drive to a location and after a citizen encounter. Contemporary reality television is more complex in its production elements. Programs now often integrate participant interviews with the staging of games, events, and scenarios into which real people are placed. The level of reality in reality television is, however, debatable. What is consistent is that participants in semi-unscripted settings determine an outcome that is not entirely known in advance by the producers.

Many reality shows take place at fixed locations, such as large residential houses, where participants live together. The success of MTV's *The Real World*, which premiered in 1992, helped pave the way for the location-based format. In these cases, reality television integrates a combination of production techniques including field production, but also studio television elements discussed above for news broadcasts. Reality shows set at a fixed location use multiple cameras recording the action simultaneously. These signals are fed to a production center where the director monitors events and communicates with the camera operators, telling what position to take, and what shots to compose to be able to construct a dynamic scene.

With multiple cameras and microphones, one of the challenges of contemporary reality TV production is the abundance of material that needs to be reduced in editing. There can be several hours of camera footage and individual microphone feeds for each real-time hour of activity at a location.

While reality television is attractive to producers due to its relative low cost and popular appeal, programs that offer one big surprise or payoff at the end of the season, such as *The Bachelor*, are not generally suitable for syndication. Once the secret is out of who wins in the end, few will watch for an entire season to discover what they already know. Producers of the genre are increasingly looking to the self-contained episodic format (e.g., *Super Nanny* and *Wife Swap*) for long-term syndication yield from this format.

THE CONTRACT WITH THE VIEWER

Each of the formats discussed above brings a different contract with the viewer. The contract with the viewers is the understanding you have with your audience of your role, responsibility, and obligations to honor their trust. When a program claims to portray reality, there is a unique responsibility that accompanies that claim and the rules vary depending on the format.

News production carries the ideal of objectivity. When producing the news it is the production crew's obligation to present the facts from the point of view of a disinterested party. We all have personal views we'd love to share, but the news package is not the place to stand on a soapbox. The audience should be able to trust journalists and photographers to be objective, and that unwritten contract should be honored. Even as news has evolved into news/entertainment in recent years, each journalist and photographer should strive to honor objectivity. This is not always achieved, of course, and many questionable news presentations occur every day.

Research indicates that bias is a common element in news content. Hans Kepplinger (1982) talked with news camera operators and analyzed German election coverage. He found that camera angles and selective editing were often used to convey the sentiments of the journalists. The journalists never said how they felt, but by showing one candidate from low angle, indicating authority, and another juxtaposed with negative reaction shots from the crowd, the journalists made their feelings known through optical commentary. These production techniques have an impact. A study of camera angles in the news found that the audience does, in fact, judge people photographed from even a slightly low angle to be more credible and potent (Mandell & Shaw, 1973). Since broadcast news claims to be objective, there are issues of serious ethical concern when this contract with the viewer is violated.

Dear Mr. Anderson:

I write to you on behalf of Syracuse University's S.I. Newhouse School of Public Communications to inquire about potential funding from the MacArthur Foundation for the production and dissemination of a timely documentary called *The Temple North of 49.* This film tells the story of the vandalizing and ultimate burning of a Sikh temple by four Upstate New York teens who apparently interpreted the name of the temple, Gobind Sadan, to mean "Go Bin Laden" and burned it to the ground. This hate crime, committed shortly after the tragic events of September 11, made national headlines and remains a continuing regional story.

Professors Richard Breyer and David Coryell, in partnership with WPBS Public Television, Watertown, New York, have begun to chronicle this crime, its aftermath, and the culture of the community where the arson was committed. The 60-minute documentary follows a Sikh couple, a construction worker with deep roots in the community, the president of the local school board, a local minister, and one of the arsonists as they come to terms with how their lives and the life of their community have changed as a result of this hate crime.

The film will also show how the crime forced the citizens of Hastings, Palermo, and Mexico, the New York villages where the arsonists lived and grew up, to look at themselves and question how much the burning of the temple reflected who they are and what they teach their children. When neighbors and community leaders offered their churches and schools as places of worship and offered to help rebuild the temple, some began to answer this question. After the temple is rebuilt, how many more of these citizens "North of 49"—a term used by locals to describe the area—will welcome the members of Gobind Sadan into their places of worship and their homes? *The Temple North of 49* will answer this question and document a community attempting to heal itself in a post-September 11 world where only knowledge and tolerance can lessen the chances of repeating the tragedies suffered by the Sikhs, the teenagers who committed the arson, their families, and, in a larger sense, America.

The Temple North of 49's unifying story is the reconstruction of the temple by the community, including two of the arsonists. Ground breaking begins in July 2002 and the new edifice will be ready in the fall. A spokesperson for the Sikhs told an interviewer, "We feel a great loss but we believe out of the ashes will come a new building and, more importantly, a new community based on love and the spirit of forgiveness."

The Temple North of 49 combines cinema verité sequences and interviews in the style of *Brother's Keeper*, an award-winning documentary about a man accused of killing his brother, also produced in a rural, upstate New York town.

When completed *The Temple North of 49* will be broadcast nationally on Public Television Stations in the US as well as to viewers in India via the national system. It will also be distributed to universities, schools and churches through Filmaker's Library. (See enclosed letters from Filmakers, WPBS-TV and Mr. Singh).

Figure 8.11 A documentary proposal letter. (Courtesy of Richard Breyer)

Here at Syracuse University, *The Temple North of 49* will be used in the Program on the Analysis and Resolution of Conflicts of the Maxwell School and in ethics and production courses at the Newhouse School.

The cost of the production is approximately $200,000. The Newhouse School has provided a "seed" grant of $5,000 plus $5,000 in-kind support. Another anonymous donor contributed $15,000. These funds have been used to research, videotape interviews and travel to India and the upstate communities where the crime took place.

We think that this production is in keeping with the MacArthur Foundation's interest in peacekeeping and global security. A list of members of the production is attached. Should you have questions, please do not hesitate to contact me.

Best regards,

Ingrid V. McGraw, Senior Director
Foundation Relations

Figure 8.11 (continued) A documentary proposal letter. (Courtesy of Richard Breyer)

The situation is a little different for the documentary. Some documentaries are criticized for being biased, but that is not necessarily a valid criticism. Documentaries can take a point of view. The documentary with a point of view is generally more interesting than one that tries to stand on the fence. While the documentarian can take a point of view, he must be honest in his portrayal. It is okay to focus your story in a particular direction, but the content must be true in material fact.

In the case of an industrial film promoting a company, it is understood that the film is designed to portray the company in a favorable light. The filmmaker must still be honest about elements of fact, but no one in the audience believes that a promotional film is produced from an objective point of view.

Entertainment reality television is often more akin to fiction than nonfiction in its construction. Content is regularly edited out of context to heighten drama, to tease the viewer, and to accentuate humor. Many in the audience believe that what they are witnessing is edited truthfully, and this creates a dilemma for the format. It is primarily an entertainment form, but even as entertainment the reconstruction of reality is troubling to some scholars and practitioners. What do you think?

RESEARCH AND WRITING

The Proposal

The treatment is the written sales tool for a fiction film, and the proposal is the written sales tool of the documentary. Documentary proposals often contain a synopsis of the story, a description of the approach, and a pitch describing why the story and approach are important, unique, timely, and viable. Some proposals contain budget information to recruit financing, as well as reasoning on why a particular filmmaker or organization is qualified to undertake the project.

There are two primary forms documentary proposals generally take. Some proposals are formal and use section headings to outline major elements including statement of purpose, background, program description, program goals, production timeline, financial support, distribution commitments, biographies of key creative personnel, and budget. Other documentary proposals are written as correspondence to solicit support and integrate the major selling points into a narrative.

Financing

Where there is a strong desire to tell an important story, there is usually a way to assemble the resources to make it happen. One of the primary sources of documentary financing is **grants**. There are many endowments established to support the arts, nonfiction filmmaking, and specific topic areas. For example, a foundation that is dedicated to Native American issues might be interested in sponsoring a documentary that shares information central to the foundation's mission. While some foundations issue funding to individual producers for program production, many foundations only issue payment to a nonprofit organization. It is therefore valuable to have affiliation with an official nonprofit organization to expand your range of grant writing eligibility. Church groups, private investors, government-sponsored art programs, and nonprofit agencies are also sources for independent documentary financing.

It is difficult for an emerging documentary filmmaker to get **front-end financing** from a distribution outlet such as public television stations and cable networks. There is a wealth of nonfiction content out there, so broadcasters do not generally need to finance production. They can usually pick and choose from material that is already produced. If a project is funded on the front end, financing will usually go to established filmmakers with a track record of success. In some cases, filmmakers present a rough-cut or demonstration version of a program and use this demo to recruit funding for postproduction as part of a broadcast deal. In most cases, however, you need to have a final product in hand before broadcasters and distributors will take interest. We will explore distribution in more detail in chapter 11.

If you want to tell a story, do not let a lack of money stop you. Shoot the project yourself if you have to. If you act as if you are making a project, you will find that you are making a project, and often others who care about the topic will join you in the process. It is common for documentaries to be produced **on speculation (on spec)** and on low budget.

A great way to produce the stories that matter to you is to help others produce the stories that matter to them. Work out service trades with colleagues and help each other get your projects produced. Be the camera operator for a program they are producing and have them do the same for you. You will all get more accomplished and will gain experience and build a list of credits in the process. If you need cash to fund a production, then be creative. You can produce a promotional film for a friend's company and use the income from that project to fund a documentary on a topic close to your heart.

Research

Good nonfiction writing comes from good research. You can tell a story more truthfully and effectively if you are intimately familiar with the subject matter. To find good stories and good background information, survey other media. *Brother's Keeper* (1992) examines the case of a man accused of murdering his injured and frail brother. The filmmakers scanned the newspapers and saw this case unfolding. Keeping their day jobs, they traveled hundreds of miles away on weekends to record the evolution of this tale and the trial of the accused. The end result is a remarkable feature film that culminates in the announcement of the verdict.

Outlines

We introduced the outline in chapter 1. The outline is the primary developmental tool for the nonfiction filmmaker. When the real world is your subject and your story is told with interviews, it is impossible to know or totally control where your story will go, what the subjects will say, and where these interviews might steer you. While an outline spells out the major topic areas, major points, and the primary flow of the story, it also allows modification to adapt to changes during production.

As you conduct interviews and gather more information about your topic, you might find your concept evolving. Use your outline to develop your interview questions. In turn, use interview answers to adjust your outline. Use what you learn in an interview to shape the questions you ask in later interviews. Make a working model of what you expect the final program to be, but do not lock into this model at the expense of flexibility, discovery, and innovation. In many cases, the program outline changes with every interview.

Scripts

Writing a nonfiction script usually takes place after the material is shot. Documentary and news scripts are predominantly tools for editing rather than shooting. You outline your shoot and script your edit.

Some nonfiction programs, however, are highly structured and produced from a detailed script. Historical documentaries and scientific films, for example, are often told with narration and carefully planned imagery. These films sometimes utilize a formal script rather than an outline. We will explore long-form screenwriting in our next chapter.

The News Script

Once a story is assigned, scripting a news segment begins with selecting the story angle. Most news stories seek to put facts into a relevant context with a focus on people and the elements of drama. If a reporter is assigned to cover a fire in an apartment complex, the angle of the story might be the heroic acts of the firefighters, the personal story of a survivor, or perhaps the good will of the neighbors who step in to provide assistance.

The reporter usually goes into the field without a script. The reporter takes notes and the photographer/editor gathers the sound and visual elements needed to put the package together. After the story is shot, the reporter often logs the footage and makes notes of time code for relevant shots. She writes down the quotes from interviews (**sound bites**) that will be used in the package. The exact format of the reporter's script is individual and varies from person to person, but all reporters' scripts must contain the text spoken in the segment. This is needed by the photographer/editor to assemble the package and by the closed-captioning department to prepare accurate subtitles. Reporters' scripts often contain direction on building visual elements, and sometimes include time code references to the source material. The photographer/editor uses the reporter's script to assemble the package. Usually the interviews, reporter stand-ups, and reporter voice-overs are assembled first, and other images (B-roll) are added to the audio structure to complete the package.

The producer of the news show uses the reporter's script to create the formal script used in the news broadcast. The producer's script is highly structured. The director of the news broadcast uses the producer's script to execute the live telecast. It is essential that the producer's script be clear and accurate.

The formal news script is a split-page document, but unlike the audio/video split-page script used for making commercials and music videos, the news split-page contains the script in one column and the director's notes in the other. The director's notes contain elements such as when to cue titles and graphics, and when to turn the audio channels on and off. Most often the director's notes are in the left-hand column and the script content is on the right.

9/29/2005 20:14:21, USER April Blakeney - ASHEVILLE	[HQN]SHOW.ASHEVILLE.HOLD-STORIES 1 SLUG
TAKE PKG TRT: 1:32 OC: JANE DOE *CG BINTV FORENSICS TOURNAMENT CHARLOTTE NC	((TAKE PKG)) SCHOOLS FROM THE WESTERN PART OF THE STATE... INCLUDING BROWN HIGH IN GREENSBORO... RECENTLY COMPETED IN THE DISTRICT TOURNAMENT IN CHARLOTTE. ROBINS HIGH HOSTED THE TWO DAY TOURNAMENT.. WHERE STUDENTS QUALIFIED FOR THE NATIONAL COMPETITION. BROWN HIGH HAS MADE AN APPEARANCE AT NATIONALS FOR THE LAST TWO YEARS... AND THEIR FORENSICS COACH SAYS THIS YEAR SHE HAS SOME REAL CHAMPS.
TAKE SOT SOT RUNS= :05 *CG BINTV MARY SMITH BROWN HIGH FORENSICS COACH	((TAKE SOT)) "WE HAD 18 QUALIFIERS FOR THE DISTRICT TOURNAMENT. THAT'S LARGER THAN ANY OTHER TEAM IN GUILFORD COUNTY." JUST A FEW YEARS AGO THESE CHAMPIONS WERE SCARCE... MOSTLY BECAUSE THE FORENSICS LEAGUE WASN'T WELL KNOWN IN OUR AREA. BUT NOW IT'S POPULARITY IS GROWING AND SMITH IS HAVING TO ACCOMMODATE FOR THAT.
TAKE SOT SOT RUNS:08 *CG BINTV MARY SMITH BROWN HIGH FORENSICS COACH	((TAKE SOT)) "WHEN I FIRST STARTED 6 YEARS AGO, I COULD PUT THE 3 KIDS THAT QUALIFIED FOR NATIONAL IN THE BACK OF MY VAN AND WE JUST TOOK OFF. NOW I HAVE TO HAVE A BUS." THE STUDENTS AT BROWN WHO PARTICIPATE IN THE FORENSICS LEAGUE SAY COMPETING IN THE TOURNAMENT IS MORE THAN JUST WINNING AND LOSING. COMPETITIONS HELP IN BUILDING SELF-CONFIDENCE... AND THEY GET A LITTLE RECOGNITION.
TAKE SOT SOT RUNS:11 *CG BINTV CINDY SNOW NATIONAL QUALIFIER	((TAKE SOT)) "IT'S SOMETHING THAT YOU ARE GOOD AT AND YOU ALWAYS WANT TO SHOW PEOPLE WHAT YOU ARE GOOD AT. EVEN IF WE DON'T MAKE IT TO NATIONALS, WHAT WE ARE HERE FOR, WE WERE ABLE TO SHOW PEOPLE: THIS IS WHAT I CAN DO." CINDY AND THE REST OF THE BROWN HIGH FORENSICS TEAM PROVED THEY ARE EXCELLENT AT WHAT THEY DO. COMPETITORS HERE FROM BROWN PLACED IN THE TOP 3 SPOTS OF 4 DIFFERENT CATEGORIES AND NOW 5 OF THEM ARE HEADED TO NATIONALS. SO THE FOCUS OF THE BROWN HIGH FORENSICS TEAM TURNS TO SALT LAKE CITY.. AND A CHANCE AT THE NATIONAL TITLE. FOR NEWS 123 I AM JANE DOE.

Figure 8.12 News script. (Courtesy of Apryl Blakeney)

THE NONFICTION FIELD TEAM

The size of a production crew and the equipment needed varies depending on the format and scale of the project. In local news production, the field crew is generally two people: the reporter and the photographer. In small markets sometimes the reporter will go it alone and set the camera on a tripod before stepping into the shot for a stand-up. The equipment required by the news team in the field is light and loose. A shoulder-mounted camera and tripod are standard. The photographer brings a lavaliere microphone for sit-down interviews

Figure 8.13 News reporter and photographer. (Joanne Hughes)

Figure 8.14 Many documentaries opt to go light and loose without the confines of a huge crew. (Courtesy of Richard Breyer).

and a hand mic for stand-up interviews. Lighting for local news packages is usually limited to natural light or a camera-mounted light.

In long-form documentary, the crew is often larger than a news team, but not significantly so in most cases. A documentary field team is usually composed of two to six people. In addition to the producer and photographer, you might have a sound recordist who operates sound levels and engineers directing microphone placement. You might have an associate producer who works to make sure that all elements in the outline are addressed. There may be a host who appears on camera.

Some equipment often used in long-form documentary production includes a battery-operated field monitor and a unidirectional microphone on a boom pole. Documentary lighting typically includes camera-mounted lights, portable field kits, and reflector cards. These are the basics for most low and moderately budgeted projects. High-budget documentaries can go far beyond these basics and utilize the full range of technical tools and supporting personnel.

THE INTERVIEW

The interview is arguably the most important element to master for creating successful nonfiction programs. When interviewing a subject for a video program the most important work begins before the first question is asked on camera. Successful interviews begin with research. You must know the subject matter and the right questions to ask to make the most of an interview opportunity.

A valuable way to make sure you ask the right questions on camera is to conduct **preinterviews** with your subject or potential subjects. The preinterview allows the subject to speak freely and for you to explore possible lines of questioning that will prove fruitful on camera. Consider having a different person do the preinterview from the person who conducts the on-camera interview. It is difficult for most people to get equally excited to tell the same story to the same person. Often the subject will compress the story and leave out important and colorful detail when the story is told a second time to the same person. The last thing you want is to ask your central question on camera and get a response that begins, "Well, as I already told you…."

In documentary and other long-form nonfiction programs, preinterviews are often conducted by an assistant or associate producer, who then briefs the interviewer on lines of questioning to explore and specific questions to make sure to ask. This approach is standard in talk show formats for television. That is how talk show hosts often know just the right question to ask to hear a funny anecdote. Not all documentarians conduct preinterviews. Some prefer the spontaneity of approaching the topic with the camera rolling.

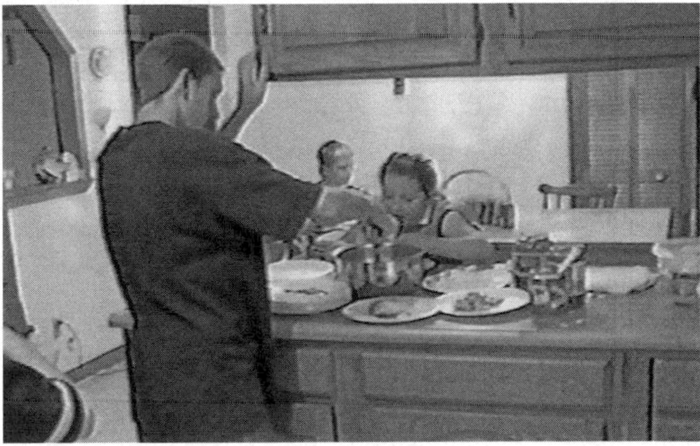

Figure 8.15 Building an interview around an event, like making dinner, is an engaging way to propel the story forward. (From *Esta Esperanza*; Courtesy of Richard Breyer)

When getting ready to shoot an interview it is helpful to consider the level of media experience that your subject has. If you are working with a spokesperson for the mayor's office, you might be able to be direct and efficient, but if you are interviewing a grandmother about her childhood, it is important that you be sensitive to the fact that your subject might be nervous and self-conscious about the process. Make the interview subject feel comfortable before the camera begins to roll.

The best way to make an interview subject feel comfortable is to let them know as much about the process as possible before a camera is pointed in their direction. Tell them the main subjects you intend to cover, but be careful about giving subjects the exact questions in advance. Sometimes this can be effective, but other times the subject works too hard to formulate a clever response and the effect is stilted. Another way to make the interview subject feel comfortable is to ask if they have any questions for you and to be honest and sensitive to their apprehensions and concerns.

There are two basic types of interview formats: sit-down and stand-up. The sit-down approach is generally more structured and well suited for longer interviews. A benefit of allowing the subject to sit down is that this gives you time to explore a comprehensive list of questions, and a subject that is seated is less likely to move around in a way that is undesirable for your composition if you want a polished look. Use a chair without wheels and one that does not swivel or rock. Unless your interview subject is experienced in granting interviews, the stress of the experience, even in a friendly context, often results in subjects rocking and rolling around in their chair to diffuse nervous energy.

Stand-up interviews might be done for practical reasons, such as limited time or awkward location. The stand-up can, however, also be a dynamic creative choice. With the stand-up interview your subject is more free and able to move in the environment more naturally. This freedom can be translated into comfort for the subject and a more natural conversation on camera.

Build events around interviews and structure interviews within events. Rather than having a subject simply talk about her participation in a civil rights march, you can bring the experience to life by retracing her steps with her through town while she tells her story.

Richard Breyer explores the lives of those affected by the El Salvador civil war in *Esta Esperanza* (1996). Rather than staging an interview in a chair with modeled lighting, Breyer talks with a mother who survived a terrible massacre in her village while she stands in her home preparing a meal. She feels more comfortable and the audience feels more like a visitor than a viewer.

Selecting the Composition

The best way to select the composition for a sit-down interview is to conduct a site visit beforehand or arrive early and explore potential options. Where should the subject sit? Can you move him away from the wall to create more

Figure 8.16 Interview compositions often integrate background elements to convey information about the subject. (Courtesy of Shalom Y'all Films)

differentiation between foreground and background and still have room for the camera? How will this angle affect what you see in the background, and how will that match up with other footage?

The interview composition, like all compositions for visual programs, is governed by the rule of thirds. While it is sometimes appropriate to center the subject in an interview composition, it is generally considered more interesting to compose your subject asymmetrically.

Here is the standard formula for a sit-down interview composition: Place the subject on one of the vertical thirds with the eyeline toward the open part of the frame. Place an element of lesser compositional weight on the other vertical third. It is often the case that this background element is selected to reinforce the elements of the story, or to tell the audience something about the person in the interview. For example, if you are interviewing a farmer about his work, it makes more sense to see his environment and farm tools in the background rather than a brick wall. When academics are interviewed, it is common to compose the shot with their bookcases behind them to visually communicate the notion of authority based on how much they have read and studied. A good

Figure 8.17 With a little innovation, a conventional interview setting can be made more interesting. (Courtesy of WYFF-TV)

rule of composing and conducting effective interviews is to put the subject in his or her world.

In addition to telling us about the interview subject, background elements can be used to tell us about the topic of the program. When interviewing a resident who is reminiscing about how clean the water used to be when she was a child, you could create a chilling effect if you show a brown, littered waterway behind her. While visuals can effectively be used to support the sound track, this is an example of how visuals can be used to contrast against the sound track to create a sense of counterpoint, contrast, and irony.

The interview subject usually makes eye contact with the interviewer, who is typically off to the side of the camera. Sometimes the interviewer sits with his head right next to the camera lens to create a camera angle that is virtually head-on. In other cases, the camera is placed far behind the interviewer and is set with a long lens to create a shallow depth of field. This can help make the subject feel more comfortable by allowing the camera to virtually disappear from view in the background.

Always explore unique ways to conduct a sit-down interview. Many professional interviewers do a masterful job of treating the interview in creative ways. Look for diverse and compelling backgrounds and consider manipulating depth of field and using diagonal lines to accentuate depth. Little variations can make all the difference. Interviewing a person sitting on a park bench can look boring, but put the camera behind the bench and have the subject turn a shoulder around to face you and you have created something much more unusual and interesting.

Miking an Interview

The lavaliere, or clip-on mic, is the most common option for a sit-down interview. Since the lavaliere mic is omnidirectional, you have flexibility in its exact placement to minimize its presence in the picture. It is important to be considerate of the subject's personal space when helping them get wired for sound. The best thing to do is to explain how you would like the microphone placed and let the subject attach the microphone himself.

As we explored in chapter 7, lavaliere microphones come in both wired and wireless versions, and there are advantages and disadvantages to each. Generally the wireless microphone is a superior option, allowing greater freedom of movement for both the subject and the camera, but it is more costly than a wired mic. Wired lavaliere microphones are less expensive, and have the technical advantage of a direct connection from the microphone to the recording device. This reduces opportunities for signal contamination.

An important caveat when working with wired lavaliere microphones in a documentary setting is the danger of the subject forgetting that he is wired and getting up and walking away after the interview is complete. More than one camera has been pulled over by a subject who forgot about the tether.

Another popular miking option for sit-down interviews is a unidirectional microphone placed outside of the frame. This mic has advantages over the lavaliere mic in that it is not visible in the frame, and it eliminates the possibility of picking up rustling if the subject moves. The unidirectional mike can be locked down out of frame on a microphone stand or held by a boom operator. Some practitioners advocate using both a lavaliere mic on the subject and a unidirectional mike on a stand out of frame to maximize options and offer insurance. These two sources can be recorded separately to each of the camera's audio tracks. When recording sound in moving situations, a camera-mounted mic, wireless lavaliere, or a unidirectional mic with a pistol grip or on a boom pole are excellent options.

Releases

News stories generally rely on **implied consent** as the basis of permission to use a subject's voice and image. The immediate nature of news, and the public interest in a free press, yields different legal requirements for news than most forms of film and video programs. The theory of implied consent is that if a person talks to a news reporter on camera, that in itself implies the granting of permission to use the material for reproduction and broadcast. It is unusual for a local news reporter to get a written release for an interview.

The rules are different for other nonfiction formats, however. In these other situations it is important to obtain consent in the form of a **performance release** (see *Appendix A* for a sample) from interview subjects. Whenever possible and appropriate, you should get a signed performance release before an interview takes place. This way the subject cannot change his mind and leave you with nothing you can use for your effort. This can happen if the interview does not go well in the subject's mind. Sometimes it is worth the risk of waiting to get a written release until after the interview takes place. This can be appropriate if there is a lack of trust on behalf of the interview subject at the beginning of the process and imposing a contract on them might risk your losing the interview altogether. If your plan is to conduct a friendly interview in which the subject is to serve as an expert or as a sympathetic character, then successfully obtaining a performance release after the interview is much more likely than if you were to ask challenging or potentially embarrassing questions.

Some practitioners prefer to obtain an **on-camera release** rather than a written release. To obtain an on-camera release, ask the subject to verbally affirm his permission to use his image and likeness. This offers significant legal protection, but it is not as legally sound as a written contract. On-camera releases are often recorded as part of the identification process at the end of an interview. Make sure to have each interview subject state and spell his name while the camera is running. It is also valuable to have the subject identify the date of the interview. This record aids in logging, editing, creating graphics, and long-term archiving.

Editorial Requests

Sometimes interview subjects want to participate in the editorial process. This request might be specific, such as a subject saying, "I don't like what I said about the closing of the restaurant. Please don't use that." Other times the subject might suggest a collaborative relationship and say something like, "I'd like to see a rough cut and give you some feedback." Unless your interview subject is your client you should be wary of allowing a subject to participate in the editorial process. As a general rule, the subject should first see the program once it is finished and released.

Asking Questions

Setting the question order for an interview should be approached with careful consideration. In virtually all interview situations the first answer that you get, whatever the question, will be comparatively stilted and awkward. Even some experienced interview subjects need one or two questions to get in sync with the interviewer and to find their rhythm. It is therefore valuable to open the interview with a friendly throwaway question. Ask something general or opinion-related loosely connected to the topic, but that is not central to the objectives of the interview. From there, develop your question order in a logical progression and make sure that you explore all the areas that need to be covered for your program. Put key questions toward the front so you make sure they get full consideration. Subjects tend to shorten their answers as they get tired. If you have a specifically challenging or confrontational question, put this in the question order after essential questions so you will have your other material recorded if the subject decides to terminate the interview upon hearing the confrontational question. Also, even if the subject does not terminate the interview, once an interview turns confrontational it is likely to stay in that tone, so plan your questions and question order accordingly.

Some interview subjects want to be polite to everyone in the room and try to make eye contact with everyone there as they address questions and tell their stories. This will confuse the audience, who will wonder why the person is looking all around. This potential problem can be eliminated quite easily. Instruct your crew not to make eye contact with the subject if the subject begins to have wandering eyes. The sound recordist should be looking at dials on the mixer. The production assistant should be taking notes and looking at a clipboard. The subject will then fully engage the interviewer.

In news reporting, it is common for interviews to be just a few minutes since the whole edited package might be just 60 seconds or less. In contrast, documentary interviews are often much longer. Consider subject fatigue, significance to the story, and access when deciding how long to schedule your interviews. Is the subject central to the story? Is she someone you can easily interview again if you need more information? How long is your program running time? Interviews range widely in their total time. For documentaries, sit-down interviews of 15 to 30 minutes are common. Forty minutes reaches the threshold of fatigue for most people, and 60 minutes is generally considered long for a single on-camera conversation without a break.

Reverse Angles: Interviewer as Subject

In news stories, the reporter is often involved in telling the story. Most newsmagazine programs, such as *Dateline* and *60 Minutes*, as well as some documentaries, also use the interviewer as part of the story. In these cases you might want to utilize a second camera to cover the interview. This second camera serves as the **reverse angle** or reverse. The reverse angle allows the editor to cut to the interviewer as he asks questions, and to cut away to the interviewer for reaction shots during the subject's answers. Having both cameras synced to the same time code makes editing easier in postproduction. You need to follow the 180-degree rule in camera placement. The axis of action passes between the interviewer and the subject, eye to eye, and both cameras must be placed on the same side of this imaginary line to maintain visual continuity and proper screen direction.

Often cameras in these two-camera setups are placed behind the subject and the interviewer, off to one side so that by changing the focal length of the lens the camera operator can get a wide range of visual compositions including medium shots, close-ups, extreme close-ups, and over-the-shoulder shots.

If two cameras are not available, the illusion of two cameras can be created by staging reverse shots of the interviewer, and even rereading the list of questions in the same tone that they were first delivered in so these shots can be cut into the program. If this technique is used, it is important to make a best effort to honestly portray the reverses and the question reading as closely as possible to the way that these elements unfolded during the actual interview. Some practitioners believe that this technique should not be used and that it is a misrepresentation of what happened. The choice of whether to stage reverses depends on the program, audience, contract with the viewer, and your own values.

Self-Contained Responses

In circumstances in which the interviewer's questions will not be used in the final program, it is important to guide the interview subject to give responses in self-contained statements. People experienced with granting media interviews are adept at doing this and will adjust to this direction quickly. For those not experienced in speaking on camera the adjustment can take some time; you might need to ask a subject to answer a question more than once.

If you ask, "Are thermal inversions a problem in this region?" and the subject responds, "Yes, they cause carbon dioxide to stay trapped in the area," the viewer would have no way of knowing that the issue was thermal inversions if only the answer is used in the program. Therefore, if your program design does not integrate the interviewer's questions, then you will need to guide the interview subject to incorporate the question into her response. Give an example and gently persist during early questions until they get the technique integrated into the conversation. A self-contained response to our example question would be, "Thermal inversions are a problem in this region because they cause carbon dioxide to stay trapped in the area."

Listen and Be Flexible

Listen to the responses of your subject and imagine how they will fit into the final program. Are you getting what you need? If not, do not be reluctant to ask different versions of the same question to get at the issues of interest to you. Also, be open to asking unscripted follow-ups. It is not possible to anticipate the direction an interview will take and the facts that will be revealed. You might find that the focus of your program changes or a new storyline evolves from what you learn during an interview. Be confident and aggressive about telling the best story possible. Have a plan going into an interview, but also be flexible and explore unanticipated opportunities and new lines of inquiry.

Really listen to your subjects. Sometimes an interviewer gets attached to the question outline and marches right through it. If you do not listen to the answers and fail to ask follow-ups to explore what is revealed, you will often miss the heart of the real story.

The interviewer is not the only one who needs to pay careful attention to the answers and the content of the conversation. The camera operator needs to use the content of the interview as a guide for shot composition. For example, if the subject is revealing a particularly personal and intense account, a slow zoom-in will increase the visual intensity as well.

Camera Coverage

A good convention for adjusting composition during an interview is as follows: Start with a medium or a medium-wide shot of the subject. Adjust the shot as the content and feel of the scene suggest. When making adjustments to the composition by changing the focal length of the lens (zooming in, for example), it is generally advisable in a nonfiction setting to make adjustments with the assumption that the move will be used in the final program. If, for example, the subject is giving a statement, do not **bang zoom** in to make a quick adjustment under the assumption that the editor can insert a cutaway. This might be a criti-

Figure 8.18 A close-up can be used to emphasize intensity during an interview. (Courtesy of WYFF-TV)

cal moment in the interview, so make on-camera composition adjustments that are appropriate for use on-screen.

The camera operator needs the confidence and discipline to speak up if something is wrong. Do not let an interview that is of poor technical quality progress. If the sound drops out in your headsets, or the interviewer is about to ask a new question and your media storage space is low, then you need to speak up. The producer is depending on your ability to create a high-quality recording and sometimes you need to interject yourself to make that happen.

Some producers develop a secret language with the camera operator so they can make coverage decisions in a discreet manner. A subject might want to ramble on about a totally irrelevant topic. A producer does not want to offend the subject, but does not want to waste a lot of recording space on this irrelevant material either. In this case, the producer might cue the camera operator to stop recording and have another cue when it is time to start recording again. Conversely, a subject might spontaneously start to offer some important information outside the context of the formal interview. The producer can cue the camera operator to capture this in a subtle way that does not make the subject self-conscious and risk losing the spontaneity of the event.

Turn Off Your Tally Light

The **tally light** is the red light on the front of the camera that signals the camera is recording. This is helpful in some situations, such as working in a television studio to let the actors or news anchors know which camera is active, but in field recording, especially nonfiction work, it is often a distraction. Turn the tally light off. If there is not a disable option, cover the light with tape.

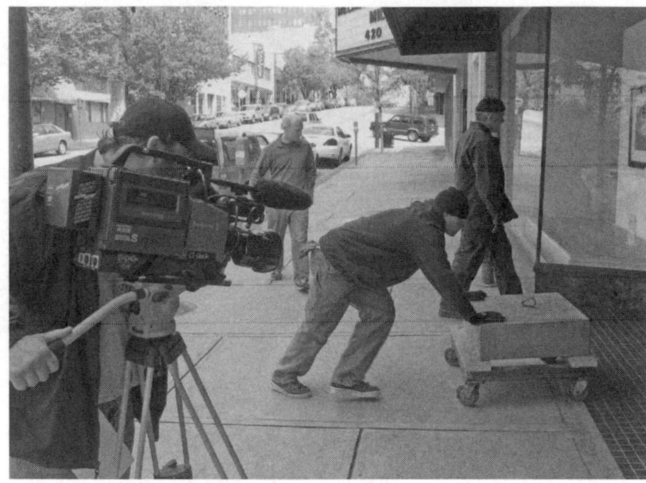

Figure 8.19 Make sure you can build a sequence. Gather all the shots you need including master shots, close-ups, and reverse angles.

Make Sure You Have It Covered

Whenever you set up for an interview on location, consider the entire location and what else you can photograph to support the interview. Build in time to record cutaways and other content at each location. What can you show the audience as a cutaway during the interview to serve as a bridge between questions? The diploma of an expert and the flag on the wall of a police officer's office tell the audience about the interview subject and provide a valuable continuity tool for the editor. If you can successfully shoot for the editor, you will be a valued professional whom producers want to work with time and again.

In many cases it works well to gather cutaways and sequence-building material (B-roll) after the interview. As the interview subject speaks, the producer and the camera operator need to imagine what will appear on the screen during each statement. If the subject is talking about developing a reading comprehension program, you might imagine seeing a tutoring session on screen. Make notes in your mind or on paper. Make sure you have all the material you need to build sequences before leaving the location. Do not just get a wide shot of a tutoring session. Get close-ups, over-the-shoulder shots, and reaction shots to build an entire scene. Make sure you have it covered.

LIGHTING THE INTERVIEW

Lighting a subject for an interview is simple in some respects, but can be challenging in others. It is simple in the sense that interview lighting can be

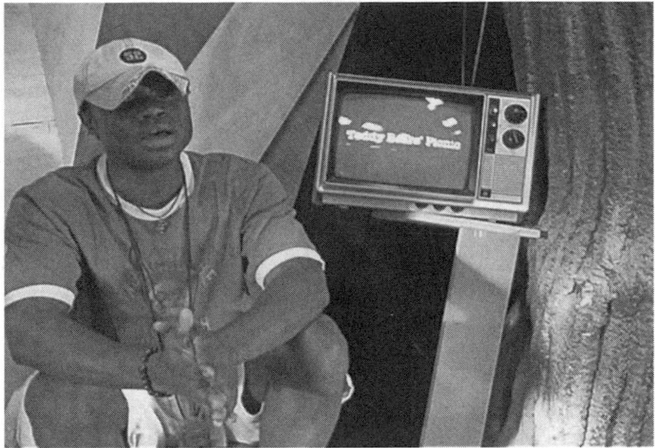

Figure 8.21 Use light to create interest in the background. (Courtesy of Troy Scott Burnette)

a model example of three- or four-point lighting. If you are working in a studio with an overhead lighting grid, you can create model lighting with great control. Lighting on location is another matter, and this is where the challenges of interview lighting really begin. On location, you need to assess the available light and how it can be used or excluded. An office window might provide a beautiful and representative background for an interview. It might also spill harsh daylight over your subject's face. You can turn fluorescent lights off, close window blinds, and hang blankets on windows out of frame. Once you decide exactly what existing light you wish to keep and work with, you can turn your attention to shaping that light with filters, reflectors, diffusion, and adding supplemental light to complete your lighting design.

Interiors

Lighting interior location interviews can be a challenge. In many cases the existing light cannot be totally controlled. In other cases you will work in a small space, such as an office or a conference room. You might find that you do not have sufficient space for the placement of instruments and that controlling the light in a small room is difficult since there is so much reflection, which causes the total effect to look flat.

Figure 8.20 Interview setup. (Chris Walker)

As in any creative lighting set-up, decide the motivation for your light. Is it the window? Is it the lamp on the desk? Is it an implied source from out of frame? Place your key light first. Most field lights are 250 to 1,000 watts, and hitting someone in the broad side of the face with direct light from one of these instruments will cause the subject to squint uncomfortably. You will generally want to work with more diffuse or reflected light. Consider bouncing the key light off of a white wall or white card, or consider using a scrim and some diffusion material.

Next, decide if your setup will allow for a back light. A back light is preferred in most situations, but is not possible in all field locations due to space, equipment, or time limitations. A primary function of the back light is to separate the subject from the background. If the subject has dark hair and is sitting in front of a dark background, a back light is important. Without effective backlighting, it might look like you are interviewing a dark wall with a face on it.

Once you have your key and back light set, you can add fill light to lessen the shadows on the non-key side of the subject's face. Select a contrast ratio for the interview and put your key and fill lights in balance.

In some settings, effective fill light can be achieved without the use of an additional lighting source. It is often possible to bounce overflow from the key to create a fill light with a bounce card. Once you find the right position for the reflector, you can either have someone hold it in place or clamp it to a grip or light stand.

Once the fill light is in place, you have all the elements of the three-point lighting formula set. You can then add a background light for a four-point variation. Experiment with lighting the background in a stylistic way. Rather than hitting the background with full illumination, have the background in the shadows providing just enough illumination to reveal the essence of its elements. Another option for background lighting is to light only part of the background. This creates a low-key background design. You can use a practical light in the background to feature elements such as family photos on a small table, or you can use barn doors and flags to sculpt your background and throw a shaft of light, which defines a targeted area of secondary interest on a bookcase or wall.

If you do not have the time, space, or equipment to fully explore the potential lighting options for an interview setup, it is valuable to know what is sometimes referred to as hit-and-run lighting. This design is fast to set up, it only requires two lights and a white card, and it looks good.

Hit-and-Run Lighting

To achieve a fast and effective interview lighting setup, start by placing one lighting instrument on the subject, opposite from the key-light side. Adjust the instrument so that the direct light passes in front of the subject's face. You do not want any direct light to hit the subject's face. The subject's face will be partially illuminated by the indirect spill light from the instrument. This soft spill light serves as the fill light. Next, bring in a white card and bounce the

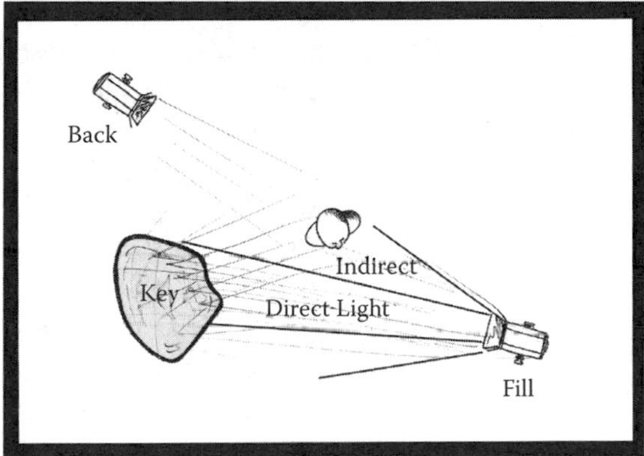

Figure 8.22 Hit-and-run lighting is a fast and effective way to create a three-point lighting design with two instruments and a reflector. (Illustration by Jesse Knight)

direct light coming across the subject's face onto the opposite side of the face. This reflected light is the key light. You can make adjustments in the intensity of the key light and change the contrast ratio by moving the lighting instrument or position of the white card. The second instrument is set up as a traditional back light. The interviews with Marc Norman on the companion DVD of this text were recorded using this lighting technique.

Camera Light

When time and efficiency are of the essence, the most basic lighting configuration for an interview (other than working with available light) is to use a camera-mounted instrument. This is fast and simple, and the position of the light eliminates most shadows. This lighting technique also offers even illumination of the subject. Using a low-intensity light or diffusing a camera light with filters can help create a more natural effect. The disadvantages of camera-mounted lights are that the background gets no lighting attention, there is no back light, and the light—while even—is also flat and uninteresting. The advantages of speed and convenience make this a preferred lighting technique for many news interview applications.

Exteriors

Shooting an interview outdoors offers its own set of challenges. The sun serves as a powerful source of illumination, but its color temperature is constantly changing. It is always moving and changing intensity as the day progresses and the cloud cover comes and goes.

Using the sun as a key light can work under some circumstances. If the conditions are right for angle and intensity, you can direct sunlight as a key light and bring in a white card to serve as a fill. The sun also lights the background very well. This allows for an effective lighting design with nothing more than a single bounce card. In many cases, however, the sun is simply too intense to serve as a key light directly on the face of a subject.

Another variation of simple exterior lighting for an interview is to use the sun as a back light to cut a rim light on the subject and pop the subject out from the background. With the use of two bounce cards you can create key and fill light for a three-point design.

Just because you are working outdoors does not mean that you cannot use artificial light here as well. The same artificial lighting designs used for interior lighting can be applied outdoors, or variations can be employed to supplement the natural light for a more sculpted image. It is not uncommon to use the sun as a back light and to have two artificial lights serving as key and fill for a

Figure 8.23 You can create a three-point lighting design outdoors using the sun and two reflectors. (Ann Grover)

sit-down interview outdoors. Just make sure to balance your artificial lights so that the color temperature matches the daylight.

In the end, the best way to light an interview is the way that looks best for the camera. There will be occasions when little or no adjustment to existing light will be required. In chapter 6 we explored controlling light. When working in nonfiction consider an approach that is centered on discovering and utilizing available light. The subject of nonfiction is reality, so use light from the real world. Documentary production is often about finding light. Put your camera and subject in position to make the most of existing light. You might go into an office for an interview with your light kit in hand and find that the overcast light coming through the picture window casts a perfect soft key light on your subject, and the natural reflection of the space gives you all the fill you need. When you open the door, the adjacent office window throws backlight right where you need it. This convergence of elements does not fall into place this perfectly often, but it does happen, and you have to take note to see it. The amateur will struggle with the light kit. The professional knows when to keep the lights in the box.

With practice you will discover what lighting instruments and techniques work best. You will be able to light your interviews faster and more successfully with experience. Practice with friends before your first shoot in the field to gain a helpful head start on field lighting for interviews.

CONCLUSIONS

The audience trusts the nonfiction filmmaker to be honest. The specific contract with the audience varies by format. The rules for news production differ from those of the promotional film, but in all cases the nonfiction filmmaker must be truthful. When you develop a documentary, consider the range of approaches you can take. For example, will you cover a topic using an approach akin to Cinema Verite or one closer to Direct Cinema?

Obtaining funding for documentaries can be a challenge. Grant opportunities provide some of the best financing options for emerging nonfiction filmmakers. Because of their fluid nature, most nonfiction programs are written using an outline, which is often adjusted as discoveries are made in the production process. A formal script is often written after the material is shot to guide the editing process.

The interview is a central part of many nonfiction programs. As you plan your interviews make sure to conduct research and preinterviews before the on-camera session. Consider the range of lighting, miking, and compositional choices available to create the most technically refined and professional interview coverage possible.

You have expanded the basic elements of production through Unit II with a study of short-form works, which use multiple scenes to construct a unified program. You have gone beyond the basic functions of the camera to conduct a comprehensive review of the tools of lighting and sound, and the options for using these tools to achieve varied creative objectives. You now have the foundation for creating works of nonfiction using an expanded range of technical and creative tools.

Video projects range in running time from less than a minute to feature-length. As the scale of a project expands, so does the complexity of the process and the number of elements that must be managed to produce the program successfully. The third and final unit of this book concentrates on advanced applications required to produce longer form works. You will explore feature-length programs and the writing, production, direction, marketing, and distribution of long-form projects. The final goal of the third unit, and of the entire text, is to provide a foundation for you to consider future study and career options. For some, your aspirations in video production might consist of gaining knowledge and skills that will serve you as a moviegoer and hobbyist filmmaker. For others, the journey through this text will expose you to new ideas, challenges, and goals that will help launch your life's work, be it to serve as a film editor for a Hollywood studio, a staff member in a corporate or government communications office, a member of a local news team, or to forge your own path as an independent producer.

SAMPLE EXERCISES

1. Conduct an informal preinterview with someone you think would make an interesting subject of a documentary. Create a program outline and on-camera question list based on this preinterview.
2. Study the local news section of your community newspaper. Choose a story you think would make a compelling news package and outline how you would tell this story on television.
3. Construct an interview setup. Choose an interesting location and background. Use the tools of lighting and sound and record your test on camera.

RECOMMENDED READINGS

Barsam, R. M. (1992). *Nonfiction Film: A Critical History.* Bloomington: Indiana University Press.

Bernard, S. C. (2004). *Documentary Storytelling for Video and Filmmakers.* Burlington, MA: Focal Press.

Keller, T., & Hawkins, S. A. (2002). *Television News: A Handbook for Writing, Reporting, Shooting, & Editing.* Scottsdale: Holcomb Hathaway.

REFERENCES

Flaherty, R. (1924). *My Eskimo Friends, "Nanook of the North."* Garden City: Doubleday, p. 126; cited in Barsam, R. M. (1992). *Nonfiction Film: A Critical History.* Bloomington: Indiana University Press, p. 50.

Hovland, C. I., Lumsdaine, A. A., & Sheffield, F. D. (1949). *Experiments on mass communication.* Princeton, NJ: Princeton University Press.

Jerry, P., & Collins, S. (2005). Web-based education in the human services: Use of web-based video clips in counseling skills training. *Journal of Technology in Human Services, 23*, 183-199.

Kepplinger, H. M. (1982). Visual bias in television campaign coverage. *Communication Research, 9,* 432-446.

Mandell, L. M., & Shaw, D. L. (1973). Judging people in the news unconsciously: Effect of camera angle and bodily activity. *Journal of Broadcasting, 17,* 353-362.

Uchikoshi, Y. (2006). Early reading in bilingual education: Can educational television help? *Scientific Studies of Reading, 10*, 89-120.

UNIT III

ADVANCED APPLICATIONS

CHAPTER 9: FEATURES AND LONG FORM
CHAPTER 10: DIRECTING
CHAPTER 11: MARKETING AND DISTRIBUTION
CHAPTER 12: PROFESSIONAL AND CAREER OPPORTUNITIES

The goal of our final unit is to explore advanced applications used to create video productions. In Unit III you will explore how large-scale projects are produced, how the entertainment industry works, and your options for advanced study and career development beyond this course.

Chapter 9 introduces the theatrical feature and other long-form program formats. You will study how a movie is made and options for participating in this exciting creative process. Chapter 10 is dedicated to the art and practice of directing. Chapter 11 examines what to do when the project is complete and how to get your program to your audience through marketing and distribution. The book concludes with chapter 12, which identifies a broad range of career options and career development strategies in video production.

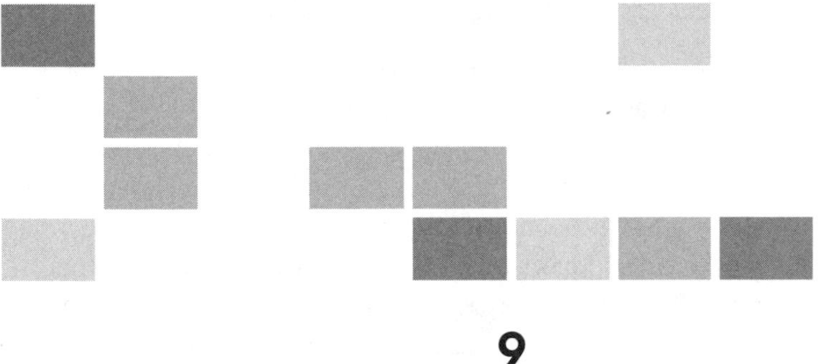

9

FEATURES AND LONG FORM

CHAPTER OBJECTIVES

As you improve your skills in video production, you can build toward the challenging process of making a feature-length program. Your career goals might include working in the studio system or you may want to forge your own path as an independent. This chapter is designed to review feature-length cinema production and related career options.

You will explore the process of making a full-length motion picture and examine the methods that professionals use to organize and implement the process. At the end of this chapter you will have a foundation of understanding how movies are made and a basis for planning your next course of study if making movies is your ultimate objective. The goals of this chapter are to:

- Examine various approaches to feature-length production;
- Introduce the structure and format of professional screenwriting;
- Explore budgeting and financing;
- Review crew positions and elements of the production process for features.

Robert Rodriguez was an undergraduate film student at the University of Texas at Austin. Early in his studies, Rodriguez decided that the best way for him to achieve his goal of making theatrical movies was to just get out there and do it. What he did was remarkable, inspiring, and innovative. Robert signed up to be a research subject in a medical study. This meant that he had to stay in a research facility for many weeks. He dedicated this sequestered time to his writing. He finished the study with a screenplay in hand and made several thousand dollars for his participation in the research.

Piecing together other modest resources, Rodriguez produced *El Mariachi* (1992) for a total budget of about $7,000. This seems impossible, but Rodriguez's approach was to put virtually every penny into film stock, processing, and film transfer to video. The film was shot on 16mm, which is a much more affordable option than the standard 35mm. Rodriguez is bilingual, an American citizen who speaks English and Spanish. *El Mariachi* was made as a Spanish language film, which was designed for export to the international marketplace. Rodriguez borrowed the camera used to make the film. His friends were cast as actors.

After production, Rodriguez had the 16mm film negative transferred to videotape so he could do a rough cut on video. His local cable company gave him access to edit in their facilities overnight when the office was closed. Rodriguez cut a trailer first. He used the trailer as a motivator to push forward with the full edit. When his rough cut was complete, Rodriguez circulated the project on videotape to potential buyers and was offered $10,000 for domestic rights to the film.

Initially Rodriguez was thrilled. He didn't expect to make a penny on the film. It was merely a practice exercise for him. He believed that his first film would not be very good, and that he would have to make several films before he would have anything in hand that was marketable. However, something seemed strange to Rodriguez about the domestic rights offer for his film: The offer was made from an overseas company, which oddly was not interested in purchasing the international rights. He had some concerns that his film might be pirated overseas.

While considering his options something amazing happened. Executives from Columbia Pictures reviewed the film and Rodriguez was paid six figures for the rights to *El Mariachi*, which was then remastered with an extensive postproduction budget, blown up to 35mm, and released theatrically. Robert Rodriguez is now an A-list director whose credits include *Desperado* (1995), *Spy Kids* (2001), and *Sin City* (2005).

The Blair Witch Project (1999) is an equally remarkable Cinderella story. This film foreshadowed the ongoing transition in the industry from working exclusively with film to electronic capture for theatrical distribution. *The Blair Witch Project* utilized an innovative structure of a simulated documentary that combined 16mm film with Hi-8 video. The budget for *The Blair Witch Project* was approximately $40,000, which is significantly more than *El Mariachi*, but quite inexpensive by industry standards.

The Blair Witch Project was screened at the Sundance Film Festival and created quite a buzz. Artisan Entertainment advanced the film's owners $1 million for distribution rights. The owners agreed and the deal was made. The transaction became the joke of Sundance. There was talk about how Artisan got ripped off. The buyers of Artisan, however, saw something that a lot of the other festival attendees did not. This was the right film at the right time with an innovative design. Based on its cost-to-gross earnings ratio, *The Blair Witch*

Figure 9.1 Director Chris Kentis and Producer Laura Lau created the theatrical feature *Open Water* (2003) with a small-format video camera and about $130,000. (Lions Gate/Photofest; © Lions Gate Films)

Project became the most profitable film in history, which has grossed more than $240 million worldwide.

With the advancement of digital video technology, the expense of working in film is not necessary to create a theatrical feature. *Open Water* (2003) was shot mostly on weekends by husband and wife team Chris Kentis and Laura Lau. *Open Water* cost approximately $130,000 to make, and the entire project was shot with a small-format digital video camera. What makes these films work is not how much they cost, but the ideas behind them and effective execution. The concept for *Open Water* was built around a true story of a couple that went scuba diving and the dive boat left them behind. Nothing was ever seen of them again. The filmmakers, who are avid divers, hypothesized what might have unfolded. *Open Water* grossed more than $30 million in its U.S. theatrical release alone.*

The Studio System

The first theatrical full-length motion picture was *The Story of the Kelly Gang,* released in 1906. In the first half of the 20th century, major studios predominantly produced theatrical features. The studios were **vertically integrated**, which meant that they had control over every aspect of the production process. The writers were on staff, directors and actors often worked under long-term contracts, the studios did their own marketing and distribution, and in many cases they also owned the theaters where the movies were shown. This type of

* The budget estimates presented for *El Mariachi* (1992), *The Blair Witch Project* (1999), and *Open Water* (2003) are based on up-front costs and do not include deferments.

closed system dominated the industry into the 1950s. Independent theaters and producers were relatively few and far between.

With the rise of television in the 1950s, the production landscape became more complex. Theatrical features faced their first real competition since their inception. People did not have to pay to go see movies in the theater when content they considered of equal entertainment value was available to them for free in their home. The early content for television was mostly old movies and live programming. Television evolved to include its own content and style including episodic programming in 30- and 60-minute lengths.

From the 1960s through the 1980s, the independent producer was a powerful force in television production. Since the 1990s, however, there has been a consolidation of ownership to five mega-companies controlling the majority of television production and distribution. The television market is currently less accessible to the independent producer than in decades past.

The Independents

In 1978, John Carpenter's *Halloween* helped change the norms of feature film production. Using simple production elements and a creative application of storytelling, Carpenter and producer Debra Hill were able to create *Halloween* on a budget of about $300,000. The film became a cultural sensation and, at that time, was the highest-grossing independent film. The success of *Halloween* sparked a number of imitators, and for much of the next decade there was an entire genre of similar films that lacked *Halloween's* innovation but still achieved moderate financial success.

In 1989, Steven Soderbergh's *Sex, Lies, and Videotape* further demonstrated the potential of the independent to succeed in the theatrical marketplace. This intellectual drama won major awards at Sundance and Cannes and was a surprise commercial hit. This opened the eyes of studios and distributors to the renewed earning potential of independent films.

In the decade that followed, Miramax and studio divisions including Fox Searchlight and Sony Pictures Classics have provided greater opportunity for independent films to obtain theatrical release. The big-budget studio film is still the core of the film industry, but low-budget independent films need not have huge attendance numbers to earn a respectable profit margin. In fact, many independent films trump the blockbusters on a **per-screen average** basis.

Video Capture for Long Form

The transition to digital video capture in production is an exciting revolution across the industry. Shooting long-form programs for distribution on digital video is not just for the small-time independent. In 2002, George Lucas redefined feature production when he produced *Star Wars: Episode II—Attack of*

Figure 9.2 George Lucas's *Star Wars: Episode II – Attack of the Clones* proved that a big-budget theatrical release could be successfully produced with high-definition video. (Luicasfilm Ltd./20thCentury Fox/Photofest; © Lucasfilm Ltd.)

the Clones in 24P high-definition video. This was a studio-sponsored, high-budget, high-profile feature for theatrical release, and it was shot on video.

There is still a place for film in the marketplace of the early 21st century. The industry as a whole is platformed with extensive investment in film technology. The resolution of film is higher than the best commercially available high-definition video capture, but film is an expensive and cumbersome technology compared to its fully digital counterpart. Technological developments are closing the resolution gap between film and digital video, which is further accelerating the adoption of video in professional production.

Just as digital video editing substantially replaced film editing in a matter of years, the same technological shift is under way for capturing images. This transition for capture is slower because of the expense to change systems, and the fact that film is still considered a superior capture medium because of its high resolution. It is just a matter of time, however, until digital video capture for theatrical productions becomes the industry standard. David Lynch shot *Inland Empire* (2006) on digital video and decided to never look back. "I started working in DV for my Web site, and I fell in love with the medium. It's unbelievable, the freedom and the incredible different possibilities it affords, in shooting and in postproduction. For me, there's no way back to film. I'm done with it" (Dawtrey, 2005, May 12, pp. 1, 62).

Television Formats

The major formats for television programming include 30- and 60-minute television episodes and made-for-television movies. In episodic television production, the executive producer is the main creative force behind the program. The executive producer of a television series is in much more creative control than the director. In fact, many TV series use contract directors based on availability and will often have different directors from episode to episode. It is the executive producer, sometimes called the **showrunner**, who oversees the process of the series production and makes sure that there is continuity in style from episode to episode.

An hour-long television episode includes approximately 44 minutes of content. The rest of the time is used for commercials and station identification. Thirty-minute television episodes contain about 22 minutes of programming. Even on public and pay television, which do not use commercials, an hour-long program is not quite an hour. The exact length of the program varies depending on the station, but station identification, station self-promotion, and trailers of upcoming events usually consume several minutes of each hour. Made-for-television movies are usually structured for a broadcast time slot of two hours. These made-for-television movies run about 90 minutes of content with the remaining half hour for commercials.

For every television series that makes it to broadcast, there are dozens that fail in the development process. Producing a television series begins with making a **pilot**. The pilot is a sample episode that is used to demonstrate the program concept and approach to potential buyers.

Most television series never make it past the pilot stage. In some cases there is simply no buyer interest. In other cases, a broadcast or cable network might order 6 to 13 episodes to test the series on the air. It is rare that a new program will be given a full order all at once, usually a season of 22 episodes. Of these series that have a sample run of a few episodes, most will be cancelled. For every 50 pilots produced, there may be one show that goes the distance to be a moderately successful series. For every 20 or so moderately successful series, there might be one that hits a so-called home run, the primary goal of television series producers. These home-run programs are the series that produce enough episodes to go into **syndication**. There is no magic number of episodes required for syndication. Generally, however, distributors want as many episodes as possible, and the preferred number is usually north of 60 episodes. This requires at least three full seasons to carry long-term commercial value. Programs such as *Seinfeld*, *The Simpsons*, and *Friends* are among the select examples of series making it to that golden level. The payoff

Figure 9.3 A pilot program is used to sell a television series. From the pilot episode of *Salsa Man*. (Courtesy of Ironwood Media Group)

for this achievement is substantial. A series can reap a profit of hundreds of millions and even more than a billion dollars over the life of the project if it is syndicated successfully.

Screenwriting

In Unit I we surveyed a number of organizing tools the screenwriter uses, including notebooks, bulletin boards, outlines, and scene outlines. You also know formats for various screenwriting applications including the split-page script, the treatment, and the news script. This section introduces the **screenplay**, sometimes called the master scene script. The **master scene script** is the screenwriter's primary document. We will explore both the structure and format of professional screenwriting. The structure includes the elements that go into the script. The format is simply how the elements are organized.

Screenplay Structure. Screenplays have a defined structure. The largest building blocks within a screenplay are the acts. Film and video projects have three acts because stories have a beginning, middle, and end. The three-act structure develops each stage of the story.

Writing a screenplay is an articulation of drama. Drama is a character's journey. You must take your character from beginning to end, from point A to point Z, through a journey and the story.

A screenplay is the writer's vehicle to take characters on a journey. Your protagonist has objectives. There are one or more antagonists and obstacles that the protagonist must overcome. Supporting characters help the protagonist through the journey. This journey is defined by the three-act structure.

In Act I, the story is established and characters are introduced and developed. The audience meets the main character and learns her objectives. Once the audience knows the context of the story, Act II introduces a major complication or confrontation. The main character must overcome a succession of complications to move forward toward her goal. Act III resolves the story. The dramatic question is answered toward the end of the third act. The main character either succeeds or fails in the dramatic quest.

The screenwriting format roughly mirrors a pace of one page per minute of screen time whether you have extensive dialogue or just description of visual elements. You can therefore use the page count of your screenplay to calculate the timing of act breaks. Assuming a feature program of two hours, you will have approximately a 120-page script.

Act I should run about 30 pages for a two-hour program. In Act I you establish the relationship between characters, flesh out the primary characteristics of your main character, introduce the audience to the main character's dramatic goals, and lay the foundation to pique the audience's interest in the main character's quest. Act I often focuses on character development. At the end of Act I, you should change the direction of the story and introduce a significant complication or conflict.

Act II constitutes the heart of your screenplay. It runs from about page 30 to about page 90, comprising an hour in the middle of a two-hour program. Act III comprises the last half hour of the film, assuming a two-hour structure. In Act III the confrontations and complications reach a crisis, the crisis is resolved, the dramatic question of the program is answered, and there is a resolution to the story.

The act breaks within a screenplay constitute points of major transition. These transitions are achieved with plot points. A **plot point** is a dramatic event in the story that points the story in a new direction. For example, if your story is about treasure hunters who find a clue to the location of a hidden key, and when they get to where the key should be they find a dead body instead, you have created a significant change in the direction of story, one that the audience probably did not anticipate.

It is essential that there be a major plot point at the end of both Acts I and II. Act breaks, however, are not the only locations of plot points in a screenplay. If there were only two twists and turns in a two-hour film, then there would be a lot of boring time in between. Screenwriters create plot points within acts as well. Where they go and how many are used depend on the specific story and program length.

While the first act of a feature-length screenplay runs about 30 minutes, it is important to get the audience involved right away, so develop an even shorter dramatic unit within the first act. Within the first 10 minutes of a feature an audience will either be hooked or disinterested, so you need to think of the first 10 minutes as a self-contained unit. *

Treat the first 10 minutes of a feature as a short film in its own right. Introduce the main character, offer a dramatic objective, take the story through complications, and have this abbreviated dramatic journey lead to a larger dramatic question. In the beginning of *Raiders of the Lost Ark* (1981), we meet Indiana Jones and follow his quest to capture a golden idol from an ancient temple. Indiana finds the idol, escapes the booby-trapped cave, gets captured by a Nazi sympathizer, and makes his escape on the skids of a seaplane. This introductory sequence throws the audience into the character of Indiana Jones, his goals and his enemies, all in a thrilling 10 minutes.

The act structure for commercial television is defined by commercial break requirements. An hour-long television drama is usually presented in four acts plus a teaser and a tag. The **teaser** segment leads the program and draws the audience in. The **tag** closes the program and serves as an **epilogue**. Each commercial break serves as an act break. It is important in television writing to build in a major plot point before each commercial break. You need to keep the

---

* Much of the information presented here on feature screenplay structure is adapted from the theories of Syd Field, whose work is considered by many to be the model of the industry. Field, S. (1994). *Screenplay: The Foundations of Screenwriting*. New York: Dell.

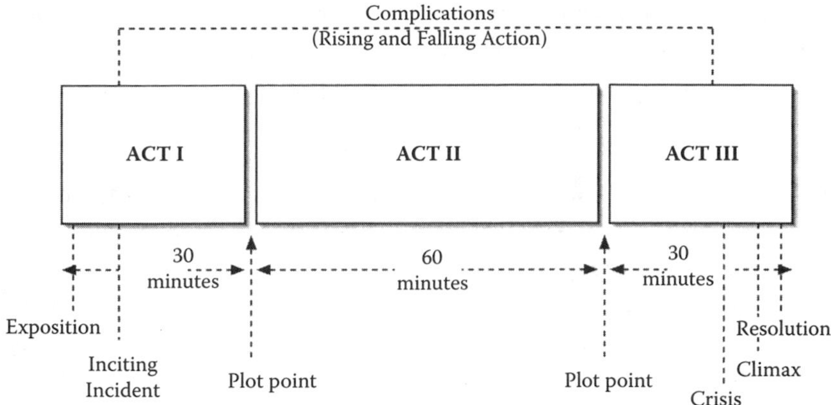

Figure 9.4 Films and video projects are generally written in a three-act structure. (Judi Rivers)

audience engaged so they stay with your show to the next segment. This is particularly important at the bottom of the hour when many viewers are inclined to see what else is on if they are not fully engaged in a show.

Television shows often integrate three plotlines. The A-story is the main plot. The B-story is a sub-plot, which usually focuses on supporting characters. The C-story is usually lighter in tone, and is often inserted in drama to provide comic relief. The C-story is called the **runner**.

Half-hour television episodes often use the same A-B-C plotline structure, but due to their shorter running time the stories are told in two acts instead of four, also with a teaser and a tag. Two-hour made-for-television movies are structured in seven acts with an epilogue.

Your screenplay will be stronger if you develop and integrate elements of backstory. **Backstory** is what happened to your characters before the story begins. It includes where your characters were born, where they went to school, what their childhood was like, and so on. Backstory can include dramatic details, such as having a character serve time in prison for murder. Developing the backstory is an important process for the writer. Even though much of this backstory will not be explicitly communicated to your audience in the screen-

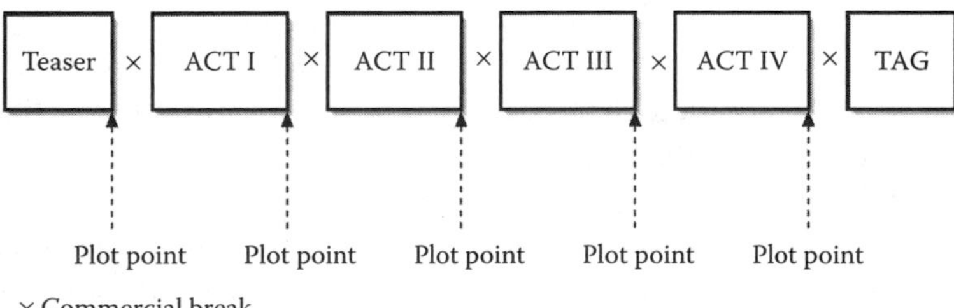

Figure 9.5 Hour-long episodic television is usually written in four acts with a teaser and a tag. (Judi Rivers)

play, it will come through in subtle ways. You might have a line of dialogue or a snide comment that is a reflection on a previous experience. Write a biography for each of your main characters. You will find that after you compose the backstory writing the screenplay becomes easier. It is easier to express what a character feels and wants to do if you know the character's personality inside-out before the story beginning. Akira Kurosawa wrote a complete dossier for each major character in *Seven Samurai* (1954) and he had the actors study these documents to prepare for their roles.

Remember that characters are action. That is why the people that portray characters on screen are called actors. Characters need to do things to move the story forward and to take their journey. It doesn't necessarily have to be predominantly physical action, although physical action is a visible and favored tool of many screenwriters and directors. Action can also be in the form of words. If a character reveals a secret to sabotage a relationship, or he makes a call to order the murder of a snitch, the character is taking action through communication.

You must always address the needs of your character. What does the character want and how badly does he want it? What will the character do to achieve those needs and how will the audience follow that journey?

We have defined the overarching structure of the screenplay, breaking it down into its various acts and exploring the main elements that carry the audience from beginning to end. The primary building block used to create a screenplay is the scene.

A scene is a component of your story unified by time, location, and theme. There is no standard length to how long a scene should be. It could be a brief moment or a long, complex interaction. The important thing in constructing scenes is that every scene should move the story forward.

Every scene in a motion picture should have an objective. There is not as much room for sidetracking and subplots in a video project as there is in a novel. Every scene should take us from point A to point B, moving us through time, space, and the story. When writing the scene, you need to know where you are going.

An effective way to write scenes is to begin at the end. Know how you want the scene to end and then work toward that point. If a scene is going to end with the main character learning that his brother stole his car, then start your creative thinking there. Consider alternative routes and twists the scene can take. Wind back to the beginning of the scene. Now you have a goal to achieve and a discovery to make through your characters.

Working from a scene outline or index cards that represent each scene will make it easier to edit the whole screenplay and allow you to build your screenplay component by component. The prospect of writing 120 pages is an overwhelming consideration for many people, but writing a series of half-page to two page scenes will propel you though the process faster than you might expect.

Screenplay Format. The screenplay, or master scene script, uses a few simple formatting rules. You begin the screenplay on page number one with the title of the project, name of the author, and from there you indicate "SCENE 1" or simply identify the number "1." Each scene is numbered sequentially. Certain identifying information is put in all-caps in a screenplay, including the identification of the scene number.

Each scene is also identified by the abbreviation "EXT." or "INT." This designates whether the scene takes place at an exterior or interior setting. This is important information for planning a shooting schedule. It is best to schedule exteriors first whenever possible, so you will have the opportunity to go inside if the weather is bad.

In the same line as the "EXT." or "INT." you also identify the location. It might say, "NEIGHBORHOOD STREET" or "MANHATTAN RESTAURANT," which lets the reader know more information about where we are. Within the same line after that, there is a dash and you identify the time of day. A full scene identification line might look like this: "EXT. PARKING DECK – NIGHT."

Master scene scripts sometimes identify the act structure and indicate where each act begins. This is particularly useful in television, where act breaks designate where commercial breaks will occur. For theatrical films and other programming without a commercial-interruption structure, identification of the act breaks does not have to be explicit in the screenplay.

Descriptive information is provided single-spaced, block left or indented five spaces, and is written in regular language to tell the reader what is going on. For example, it might say, "It is a foggy summer morning. The light announces the beginning of the day. DAVID MORRIS walks to the window and rubs the sleep from his eyes. His hangover weighs heavily on his face." Each time a new character is introduced, the character's name is put in all-caps. Technical information is also placed in all-caps. For example, the writer might indicate that there is a "FADE-IN" or that the "OPENING TITLE SEQUENCE" starts here.

Generally, however, it is not the screenwriter's job to insert extensive technical information. If a writer has a concept for something technical that is integral to the communication of the story, that can be included, but there should not be significant information about transitions, cutting points, and other shooting and editing direction. The director undertakes the visual interpretation of the screenplay.

Dialogue is written under the name of the character who says the lines. A lot of beginning screenwriters make the mistake of centering the character's name on the page. They should be indented a fixed length from the left margin so that all name identification lines match up. If centered, longer names will be further left than shorter names. Twenty-five to 30 spaces indented is the norm for character names before dialogue. The character's dialogue is written under the character's name and is also indented from the left margin, but only 10 to 15 spaces. Using these spacing conventions allows someone scanning the screenplay to easily identify descriptive information, characters, and dialogue.

```
                                                          31.

                                            (DISSOLVE TO)

36    INT.  HOSPITAL - PEDIATRICS - DAY                          36

      CAITLIN is heading down the hospital corridor.

                          TALBOT'S NARRATION
                  ...So CAITLIN plunged into her
                  duties on the board of directors
                  with the same sense of dedication.
                  The hospital was always a second
                  home, after all.  Trouble is, you
                  can't always go home again...

36A   NURSES STATION - CONTINUOUS                                36A

      CAITLIN enters the nurse's station where Delia is working.

                          DELIA
                  You're here pretty late.

                          CAITLIN
                  I know.  I've got to get out of
                  here.  We've got something on.

                          DELIA
                       (bantering)
                  Which is it this time, Versace or
                  Dior?  My heart bleeds for you,
                  child.  All those decisions.
                       (beat)
                  Tell me something, darlin'.  What
                  exactly are you doing here?

      CAITLIN looks at her.

                          CAITLIN
                  Where's Benson?

                          DELIA
                       (kidding)
                  Why?  You gonna ask for a raise?

                          CAITLIN
                  After we redo the budget.

      Delia starts out.  CAITLIN pulls out the BUDGET from her briefcase,
      as the Hospital Administrator approaches.

                          BENSON
                  Mrs.  Cory.

                          CAITLIN
                  Mr. Benson.  I've been going over
                  these figures for the fund raiser.
                          (more)

                                            (CONTINUED)
```

Figure 9.6 Screenplay formatting denotes scene identification, descriptive information, characters, and dialogue. (From *No Recourse* by Ron Cutler; courtesy of Barry Weitz)

If a scene continues onto the next page, it is identified on the right hand side of the footer as "(CONTINUED)," or it may say "(CON'T.)." Since a lot of screenplay pages are circulated loose, identifying a scene as continued allows the reader to know if the end of the page is also the end of the scene or if it continues on another page. The reader can then be sure he has all the pages for the scene in hand.

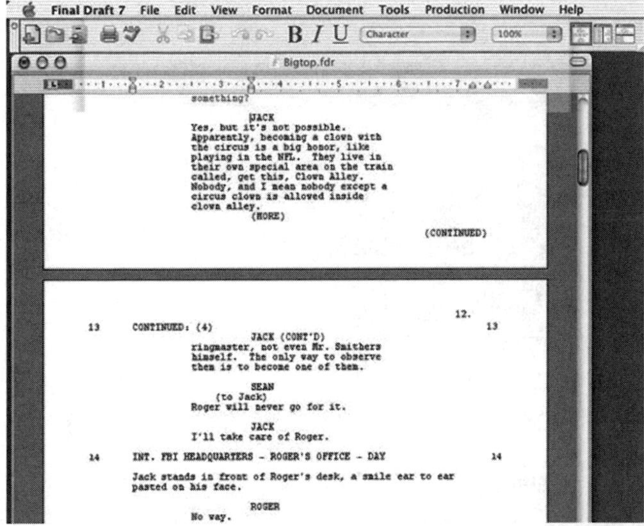

Figure 9.7 Screenwriting software makes formatting easy. (Image courtesy of Final Draft, Inc.)

Manually formatting a screenplay using a word processing program can be a bit of a challenge. It becomes quite tedious to format all the indentations, and if you make a single line change within the screenplay, the entire formatting of the document page breaks will change, thereby knocking all your "(CONTINUED)" markers out of whack.

Fortunately the solution to this challenge is simple. There is authoring software specifically for writing screenplays. This software is not expensive. With screenplay authoring software you can program your character names as function keys, and with a single keystroke you can set your indentation for dialogue. Since the software knows where the scene breaks are, if you make any changes the program automatically resets your "(CONTINUED)" markers in the correct locations.

The screenplay serves as the blueprint from which the entire production is constructed. The processes of planning and producing long-form projects are examined next.

Budgeting

Before a project can go into production, the cost must be determined. One of the first stages in the preproduction process, after approval of a screenplay, is to translate the screenplay into a list of props, actors, locations, the number of days it will take to capture all the material, and facilities needed throughout the production process. This is achieved by conducting a **script breakdown**.

A script that is composed using screenwriting software, such as Final Draft, can be imported into production planning software, such as Gorilla.

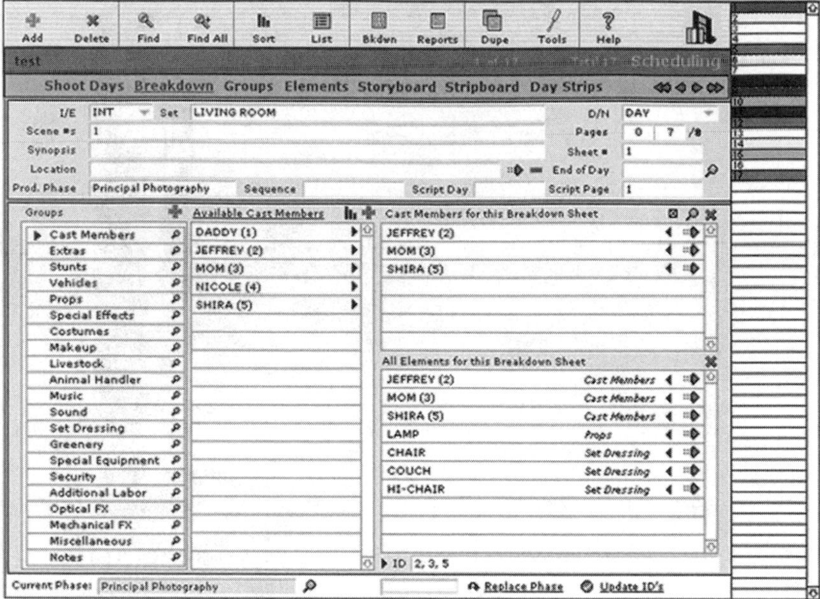

Figure 9.8 A scene breakdown created with production planning software. (Image courtesy of Jungle Software)

Locations, props, and actors needed for each scene can be tagged and broken out scene by scene. Once there is a breakdown of the script, you'll get a better sense of how much it will cost to produce the project and how much time will be needed for shooting.

An itemized budget for a feature-length program can run 20 pages or more. Budgets are broken out into two main categories: **above-the-line expenses** and **below-the-line expenses**. Above-the-line expenses are generally negotiable items, and usually include the rights to the script; salaries of the producers, director, and principal cast; travel; living expenses for the key personnel; and fringe benefits for above-the-line professionals. Above-the-line expenses can vary greatly. An unknown actor in a smaller project will have a low salary line compared to an A-list actor on a major motion picture, who can command a multimillion dollar fee.

Below-the-line expenses are essentially everything else related to the cost of a project. Below-the-line expenses are generally fixed expenses. In other words, these budget lines do not vary significantly from project to project. If you need five days of camera rental, it will generally cost the same for project A or project B. Below-the-line expenses can, however, vary from market-to-market and state to state.

Below-the-line items include camera rentals, tape and film stock, special effects, and postproduction labs. Below-the-line expenses also include the remainder of the artists and craftspeople not listed above, such as the gaffer, camera assistants, boom operator, carpenters, and so on.

THE TOHICKON CREEK

EXEC. PRODUCER: GRETCHEN WILSON
PRODUCER: EMILY HODGES
DIRECTOR: KEVIN GOSCH
WRITER: GILLIAN SLATER

SAG/DGA/WGA/NON IATSE NON TEAMSTER
LOCATION: BUCKS COUNTY, PENNSYLVANIA
SHOOT: 18 DAYS - 6 DAY WEEKS
SHOOT DATE: NOVEMBER 16, 2006

BUDGET PREPARED BY: VERNE WALTERS

BUDGET DATE: MAY 22, 2006

Acct#	Description	Page #			Total
11-00	STORY, RIGHTS, CONTINUITY	1			94,000
12-00	PRODUCERS UNIT	1			280,000
13-00	DIRECTION	1			133,200
14-00	CAST	2			449,761
15-00	TRAVEL & LIVING	3			90,850
19-00	FRINGES	4			73,781
	ABOVE THE LINE TOTAL	4			1,121,592
20-00	PRODUCTION STAFF	4			156,596
21-00	EXTRA TALENT	6			30,937
22-00	SET DESIGN	6			29,755
23-00	SET CONSTRUCTION	7			25,000
25-00	SET OPERATIONS	7			57,830
26-00	SPECIAL EFFECTS	8			3,000
27-00	SET DRESSING	8			69,945
28-00	PROPERTY	9			27,525
29-00	WARDROBE	10			56,155
30-00	PICTURE VEHICLES/ANIMALS	10			16,650
31-00	MAKEUP & HAIRDRESSING	11			24,710
32-00	LIGHTING	11			53,505
33-00	CAMERA	12			73,920
34-00	PRODUCTION SOUND	13			22,652
35-00	TRANSPORTATION	14			152,201
36-00	LOCATION	16			209,902
37-00	PRODUCTION FILM & LAB	18			95,850
42-00	CREW OVERTIME	19			20,000
43-00	FRINGES	19			91,409
	PRODUCTION PERIOD TOTAL	19			1,217,542
45-00	FILM EDITING	19			87,550
46-00	MUSIC	20			30,000
47-00	POST PRODUCTION SOUND	20			60,750
48-00	POST PROD. FILM & LAB	21			5,000
49-00	MAIN & END TITLES	21			7,500
59-00	FRINGES	21			6,569
	TOTAL POST PRODUCTION	21			197,369
67-00	INSURANCE	21			46,000
76-00	FEES AND CHARGES	21			167,500
	TOTAL OTHER	22			213,500
	TOTAL ABOVE-THE-LINE				1,121,592
	TOTAL BELOW-THE-LINE				1,628,411
	ABOVE & BELOW-THE-LINE				2,750,000
	TOTAL FRINGES				171,756

Figure 9.9 Sample summary budget for a $3 million film.

Figure 9.9 contains a sample summary budget for a $3 million film. Even though they constitute just a few items on the list, above-the-line expenses comprise nearly 40% of the budget. Figure 9.10 breaks out one of these summary line items, transportation, into its full detail to illustrate just how many individual components potentially feed into a single line item of a program's budget. *Appendix C* contains a blank summary budget template to help you develop your own budgets.

When constructing a budget, it is important to be as accurate as possible. You do not want to pad a budget or underestimate costs and run out of

Acct#	Description	Amount	Units	X	Rate	Subtotal	Total
35-00	**TRANSPORTATION**						
35-01	TRANSPORTATION COORD.						
	TYLER DAUM						
	PREP	2.5	WEEKS		1,800	4,500	
	SHOOT	3	WEEKS		1,800	5,400	
	WRAP	1	WEEK		1,800	1,800	
							11,700
35-02	TRANSPORTATION CAPT.						
	PREP	1.5	WEEKS		1,600	2,400	
	SHOOT	3	WEEKS		1,600	4,800	
	WRAP	1	WEEK		1,600	1,600	
							8,800
35-04	DRIVERS						
	GRIP	3.5	WEEKS				
	ELEC	3.5	WEEKS				
	HAIR/WDRB	4	WEEKS				
	CAMERA	3.5	WEEKS				
	2-ROOM	3	WEEKS				
	2-ROOM	3	WEEKS				
	FUEL TRUCK	5	WEEKS				
	HONEYWAGON	3.5	WEEKS				
	VAN	4	WEEKS				
	VAN	4	WEEKS				
	STAR TRAILER	3	WEEKS				
	COOK	3.3	WEEKS				
	COOK HELPER	3.3	WEEKS				
	HELPER	3.3	WEEKS				
	INSERT CAR DRIVER	5	DAYS		350	1,750	
							65,245
35-42	EQUIPMENT RENTAL						
	COORDINATOR'S CAR	6	WEEKS		300	1,800	
	HONEYWAGON	3.3	WEEKS		1,586	5,234	
	CAMERA	3.5	WEEKS		520	1,820	
	PROP	3.5	WEEKS		468	1,638	
	SET DRESSING	5	WEEKS		364	1,820	
	STAKEBED	4	WEEKS		442	1,768	
	STAKEBED	3	WEEKS		442	1,326	
	2 ROOM	3	WEEKS		936	2,808	
	2 ROOM	3	WEEKS		936	2,808	
	STAR	3	WEEKS		588	1,764	
	HAIR/WDRB	3.5	WEEKS		1,534	5,369	
	FUEL TRUCK	3.5	WEEKS		450	1,575	
	MAXI-VAN #1	4	WEEKS		300	1,200	
	MAXI-VAN #2	4	WEEKS		300	1,200	
	MINI VAN	5	WEEKS		225	1,125	
	CRANE	3	DAYS		400	1,200	

Figure 9.10 Budget detail of transportation expenses.

resources before the project is complete. One way to help avoid running over budget is to build in a 10% contingency for potential cost overruns and add this contingency amount to each budget category or the total estimated budget.

How do you know how much things are going to cost? Above-the-line items are mostly negotiable. Below-the-line items will generally be fixed in price, but by carefully shopping and getting several quotes for each line item, you can often incrementally reduce below-the-line costs. Be aware, however, of quality/cost trade-offs and how they might impact your project.

You can start getting a sense of what things are going to cost simply by doing some research, making calls, and getting quotes. A producer spends a lot of time on the phone. What will it cost to rent a camera in this town? If you need a helicopter with a pilot to record an aerial shot, call regional flight

Acct#	Description	Amount	Units	X	Rate	Subtotal	Total
35-00	**TRANSPORTATION (continued)**						
35-42	EQUIPMENT RENTAL (continued)						
	TOOL'S	4	WEEKS		200	800	
	CAPT TRUCK	5	WEEKS		250	1,250	
							36,505
35-49	OIL, GAS, OTHER						
			ALLOW		12,000	12,000	
							12,000
35-50	CAR RENTAL						
	EXEC PRODUCER CAR	9	WEEKS		205	1,845	
	PRODUCER/UPM CAR	8	WEEKS		200	1,600	
	WRITER CAR	1	WEEKS		178	178	
	DIRECTOR CAR	7	WEEKS		178	1,246	
	CAST CARS	3	WEEKS		165	1,485	
	PRODUCTION ACCT CAR	9	WEEKS		151	1,359	
	DP CAR	4	WEEKS		151	604	
	WDRB	6	WEEKS		150	900	
	1STAD	6	WEEKS		151	906	
	SET CARGO	5	WEEKS		225	1,125	
	1ST AC	3	WEEKS		151	453	
							11,701
35-76	REPAIRS AND MAINTENANCE		ALLOW		2,500	2,500	2,500
35-85	OTHER COSTS						
	BASE CAMP SUPPLYS	1			1,000	1,000	
	SEWER	1			1,000	1,000	
	INSERT CAR	1		5	350	1,750	
							3,750
					TOTAL FOR 35-00	15	152,201

Figure 9.10B

operators to find out if they have the hardware to accommodate your needs and how much it will cost if they do. *The Producer's Masterguide* is an annual publication that contains excellent guidance for creating accurate budgets. The manual provides a market-by-market breakdown of crafts and service costs for major production centers around the world.

Learning to create and manage budgets is important at every level of production, including class assignment projects. Your first student projects will likely have some real expenses including recording media, food for the crew, and gas to get to your locations. You should also budget and account for your virtual expenses when making student projects. Your school might supply cameras free of charge, but carefully plan how many days of camera time you need and how many hours of computer time you need to edit your program. Work hard to stick to budgeted hours; if you run over the allocated hours on these items, consider making adjustments when budgeting your next project. This discipline will help you to manage real budgets more effectively when overruns equal more money out of pocket.

Union and Non-Union Projects. Projects are either union or non-union. This differentiation affects the budget significantly. Union projects are generally more expensive to make. Union members have certain compensation requirements that are mandated by their organizations. The largest production centers in the United States, Los Angeles and New York, are primarily union markets. Although it costs more to produce a union project, the expense is arguably worthwhile. The most renowned practitioners in the world in every area of production are generally union members. Every area of production has a union. For example, the Directors Guild of America, the American Society of Editors, the American Society of Cinematographers, and the Screen Actors Guild are all professional unions. When composing a budget, a primary factor that will determine the personnel expenses is whether the cast and crew will be union members or not.

Independent films are often nonunion projects. In some contexts this can be a wonderful opportunity for all involved. In other contexts, the lack of union protections can result in the cast and crew being overworked and underpaid.

Tax Incentives. Budgets are also affected by tax incentives offered to filmmakers. State legislatures are increasingly implementing legislation to attract productions. When a production comes to town, a lot of money flows into the local economy. Production is an environmentally friendly business that does not use significant natural resources. For these reasons, states are in high competition to be the most attractive location for projects. Many states offer sales tax reductions and other incentives to attract production. The incentives offered by a location can result in a savings of tens of thousands of dollars on a large project.

Financing

Where does the money come from? The financing of long-form projects can be complicated and varies from project to project. In fact, almost every project is funded in a slightly different way. Complex arrangements are made in which different companies put up capital and share the risk and potential rewards. Sometimes a major studio will finance production and another studio will finance the marketing and distribution of the same project. The budget might be further supplemented with international partners who provide financing in exchange for distribution rights in regions overseas.

A detailed exploration of film and video financing is beyond the scope of this text, but it is valuable for the video production student to have a sense of how independent long-form projects are financed. Taking a script into production requires enthusiasm, confidence, and salesmanship. Your excitement about a project will be contagious. It may take some time and no one gets his or her project financed on enthusiasm alone. You must also have a strong concept, good screenplay, credible portfolio, and a viable production plan to attract investors.

Independent feature financing is largely done through private investors. Fund-raising events are a significant way to recruit financing. Potential investors are invited to an event, often a cocktail party. The event will sometimes include a draw to get people in the door. For example, if a celebrity is affiliated with the project, often an appearance by this person can help foster interest. Some fund-raising events are dedicated to informal conversation in which the producers meet the guests, explain the project, and solicit participation. Other events have a formal presentation component. Sometimes producers make a trailer or other promotional video for the project that is presented as a conversation starter.

Investors buy shares of the project. It is generally advisable to keep the share price at a level low enough that an individual investor can afford to participate, but not too low that it becomes a record-keeping nightmare, especially when it comes to paying dividends down the line. Five thousand dollars is considered a good benchmark to set as a single share price. If you wish to produce a project with the help of investors, it is important to get professional counseling from an attorney and an accountant before any fund-raising begins.

Investing in entertainment programs, particularly independent projects, is a high-risk and high-yield venture. Many independent films never make a profit and investors never see a penny of their capital returned, let alone any profit. Most investors know this and participate because of the excitement of being involved in the entertainment business, or because they want to support the arts in their community or a project with a theme or message they feel strongly about. That is the high-risk component of independent film investing.

The high-yield component is what helps keep independent filmmaking alive. When an independent film does become a hit, the rewards can be huge. The stock market averages a long-term annual return of about 8%, whereas the people who put $40,000 into *The Blair Witch Project* (1999) were quite handsomely compensated when Artisan picked up the film for distribution and advanced the filmmakers $1 million. That advance alone is an immediate return on the up-front cost of making the film of 2,500%.

You need not necessarily sell shares to secure financing for your project. You can also trade shares for services. Successful film and video financing isn't only about cash in hand, it is also about controlling cash flow. The owner of a local motel might not be able to pay $5,000 in cash to purchase a share. If you are able to trade one share, however, the hotel owner might be able to give you **service in kind** worth $5,000, or even more. For example, if the production is going to take place in the off-season, there are going to be rooms in the motel that will go unused anyway. Perhaps you can strike a deal in which you pay the motel owner for utilities so he does not take a loss. By allowing the cast and crew to stay at the motel while you work on location, you create a service trade that adds value to your production and costs the motel owner nothing.

If you are creative, you can put together a significant percentage of your budget in service trade. Perhaps a camera rental shop or a friend with a camera will be able to trade service for shares. The cast and crew might dedicate themselves to the production without pay in agreement for ownership or payment on the back end if the film is profitable. An agreement to delay payment until the project makes money is called a **deferment.** This type of arrangement can work for everyone. It makes the project financing feasible and keeps everyone motivated because they are personally invested in the project's success.

Completion Guarantee. A **completion guarantee** is a type of insurance that can be a valuable component in recruiting financing. Having a completion guarantee allows the producer to say to investors, "This project will get completed. I can guarantee that we will not get halfway through production and run out of money."

When a project purchases a completion guarantee, a representative of the insurance company monitors the progress of the production. If the production runs over budget by a set percentage, the insurance company is authorized to fire the director and bring in an in-house director who specializes in efficiently completing projects. If this occurs, it means more often than not that quality will be sacrificed. It is not a perfect solution, but it can provide peace of mind to potential investors to know that insurance underwriting is in place. Such a policy is expensive and usually reserved for moderately- to high-priced projects. It is not something you will likely encounter on a small-scale independent project.

Retaining Ownership. When you make deals, keep in mind that one of the most important things that you can do is retain ownership. You are going to have to give some share of the returns to your investors, of course, but if you can construct the financing in a way that gives you long-term control of the project, that is considered to be key.

How is it possible to retain ownership in a deal? Here is an example: Consider that you are working to produce a television movie. You have a script in hand and a major actor lined up to play the lead. You pitch the project to a television network. For the rights to broadcast the program, the network gives you a set amount of money. The network will recover their investment and more with the sale of commercial time for the broadcast. That is not quite enough money for your budget, however, so you give the network domestic rights only. The network gets exclusive rights to broadcast the program for a fixed amount of time in the U.S market.

You set up a second deal with an overseas company and give them international rights for a limited time and thus are able to package together enough revenue to cover your budget. The program is produced, broadcast, and your investors earn a profit. The key in this example is that you have only given your investors permission to air the program for a fixed period of time. You still own the project after that and everything about it. You can do the merchandising, you can go to DVD, and you can have it rebroadcast on the same network or another down the line. To own the project is to own its revenue potential in perpetuity.

Product Placement. Product placement is an increasingly significant component of program financing. Sometimes you can get companies to pay you cash without them gaining an interest in owning your program simply for integrating their product or service in your show.

Pathfinders: Exotic Journeys (1996) is a television series funded entirely by product placement. The series follows celebrities as they participate in adventure travel. Nissan financed the series, which includes establishing shots of the principals arriving in the sponsor's product. If you have passion for a good idea, work hard to recruit the resources to make it happen and never underestimate the power of creative financing options.

The Production Process for Features and Long Form

Throughout this text we have explored the components that contribute to making video programs. In chapter 5 we reviewed the process of making television commercials and other short-format projects. In chapter 8 you studied the unique elements of nonfiction. In this section we will review the process of making features and other long-form works from preproduction through postproduction. Managing this entire process is the job of the producer.

The Producer. The word **producer** can mean many things in film and video production. There are many types of producers. Some producers are **financial producers**, who deal mostly with the funding of the project and running the production from a business perspective. Other producers are **practical producers**, who oversee the day-to-day operation of the production to make sure it is running smoothly and that the creative team has what they need to do their job within the constraints of the budget.

The third type of producer is a **creative producer**. This is someone who is involved in shaping the program's concept and content in a supervisory and administrative capacity. Often a screenwriter who stays involved in the project through production will earn a producer's credit for her creative collaboration.

The role of a producer varies depending on the project. For example, the title "**executive producer**" means different things in a television movie, a television series, and a feature film. On a television movie, the executive producer is the main creative force responsible for bringing the project together. She is the one who comes up with the story idea, contracts the writing, raises the capital for the production, and packages the actors and project together. The executive producer makes the television movie.

In series television, some executive producers are involved with the financing, but other executive producers are also writers on the series. It is common for an executive producer to also be the head writer. This person oversees the continuity of the series from episode to episode and shapes the life of the entire series. David Chase, the key creative force behind *The Sopranos*, is a good example of a television series executive producer and showrunner.

In feature films, the executive producer is generally not as significant to the production process as in the case of television. Sometimes the executive producer on a film project is someone who once owned the story rights, or perhaps he had a supporting role in the genesis of the project early on. In feature film

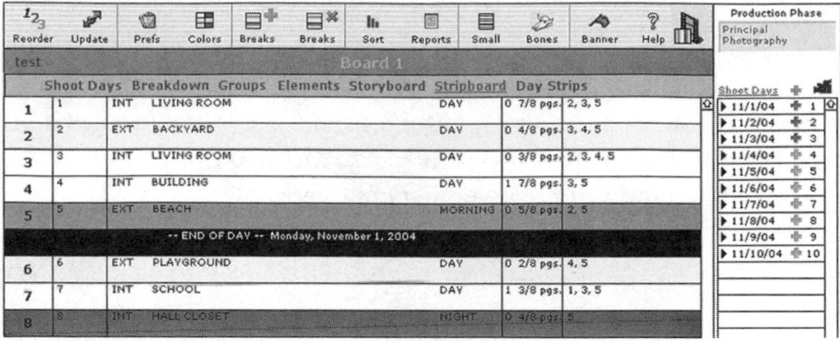

Figure 9.11 Production scheduling stripboard. (Image courtesy of Jungle Software)

Tue, Feb 22,2000 **Angel Doll** Page 1

Shooting Schedule

SCHEDULE FOR ANGEL DOLL February 22, 2000

Shoot Day #1 – Fri, Feb 25,2000

EXT - Whitey's House - Day — 6/8 Pgs.

Scene #: 25

Jerry meets Otis, goes inside

Cast Members
1. Jerry
2. Whitey
27. Otis Madger

Props
Backpacks
Blankets

Vehicles
ND Sedan (1)

Special Effects
Smoke in chimney

EXT - Whitey's House - Day — 2/8 Pgs.

Scene #: 84PT

Opening to scene as door answers

Cast Members
3. Fronia Black
6. Mary Barlow

EXT - Whitey's House - Day — 4/8 Pgs.

Scene #: 91

Whitey's family is not going to pagaent

Cast Members
1. Jerry
2. Whitey
3. Fronia Black
5. Jack Barlow
6. Mary Barlow
9. Larry

Props
License plates

Vehicles
Barlow's car

EXT - Whitey's House - Day — 2 2/8 Pgs.

Scene #: 5

Cub Scouts drop off gifts to Whitey's family

Cast Members
1. Jerry
2. Whitey
3. Fronia Black
4. Sandy
10. Mrs. Barnes
11. Billy Barnes
12. Randy Clark

Extras
Delivery boy

Props
Boxes of gifts
Canned goods, clothes
Delivery boy's bicycle
Leg braces
License plates
Littlest Angel
Newspaper bag, newspapers
Wrapping paper

Vehicles
Army jeep
Barnes' car

EXT - Whitey's House - Day — 7/8 Pgs.

Scene #: 122

Whitey not home, Jerry will look for him

Cast Members
1. Jerry
22. Somber Man

Props
JC Higgins bike

Vehicles
ND Sedan (1)

Figure 9.12 Shooting Schedule. (Courtesy of Wild Bunch Films)

production it is the producer, not the executive producer, who drives the project through to completion. This long process begins with preproduction.

Preproduction. Once the screenplay, budget, and financing are in place, the **unit production manager (UPM)** uses the script breakdown to create a **production schedule**. The production schedule builds a timeline for the program from the first days of planning to its final edit, and sometimes beyond editing through distribution. Often a production schedule is represented graphically using a **stripboard,** which allows overlapping phases of the process (e.g., shooting pick-ups and editing) to be displayed simultaneously. Stripboards are often broken out day by day or week by week, depending on the scale of the project, with separate lines for each element of the production process. This graphic plan can be mounted on a wall, which allows the production management team to eyeball how they are doing on each particular day of the process, to see what is running on or behind schedule, and what is coming up next.

The details of the production schedule and stripboard might be loose at first. For example, a project might be planned at four weeks of shooting, but that might be all that is determined at first. The details of what happens in those four weeks takes shape with the creation of the shooting schedule.

Production planning software can generate all sorts of lists, including a breakout of the interior scenes, the scenes that use the lead actors, the scenes that use a vintage car, and so on. The software can also run lists based on multiple variables. For example, production-planning software can tell you which scenes use the lead actor and live horses. This data is used to create the most efficient shooting schedule possible. The **shooting schedule** lists the scenes that will be shot on each day of production, the order of the scenes to be captured each day, and often the time allocated for shooting each scene.

A production must obtain liability insurance early in the process. If there is an accident that involves injury or loss it can ruin a project, careers, and lives. Virtually all rental houses require **replacement coverage** insurance for the equipment. A single high-end camera package alone can be worth more than $100,000. Insurance is one of the single largest expenses in independent film production.

Purchase orders (P.O.) help ensure that expenditures are authorized and accounted for. A written purchase order must be submitted to and approved by a producer before a check is cut or an authorization to spend is granted.

Studio space needs to be reserved and locations need to be scouted and confirmed. A **location scout** takes photos or video of possible locations and reports back with a list of options. In many cases, regional governmental film offices streamline the job of the location scout by providing a map and photos of locations matching the scout's needs. In the case of interior locations, a location scout will often draw floor plans with measurements.

The location scout must anticipate factors that will be important on the day of production. Is there adequate parking? What about security issues? Is there power available for all of the equipment?

PURCHASE ORDER

ANGEL DOLL PRODUCTIONS, LLC
"THE ANGEL DOLL"

PO # 1053 MS

VENDOR WILCOX SOUND
ADDRESS

PHONE 910.815.
FAX 910.3411.
CONTACT NAME DONNA
TAX ID#
INCORPORATED YES ☐ NO ☐

REQUESTED BY: H. WOODS | DEPARTMENT PROD. | DATE 2/24/00 | SET #

PURCHASE ☐
RENTAL ☐ RENTAL DATES: START 25 FEB END

TERMS:
DAILY ☐ WEEKLY ☑ MONTHLY ☐ EXTENDED ☐

QUAN.	DESCRIPTION	PER UNIT	SUBTOTAL
31	WALKIES	13/WK	403–
18	HEADSETS	5/WK	90–
4	HAND MICS	3/WK	12–
12	SINGLE BANK CHARGERS	N/C	
4	SIX-BANK CHARGERS	N/C	
	WALKIE #s: 1381, 1355, 1284, 1222, 916		
	1227, 1349, 1335, 1270, 1329,		
	2411T, 1297, 1268, 1323, 1272, 1377,		
	836, 898, 1247, 1420, 1236, 1369,		
	1256, 1312, 960, 1301, 1309, 844, 1320,		
	1332, 1351 (SPARE #1240 & #21)		
ACCOUNTING ONLY: 835-56		TAX	
VENDOR: PLEASE MAKE SURE THAT PURCHASE ORDER NUMBER IS CLEARLY MARKED ON ALL INVOICES.		TOTAL	505–

APPROVAL: Dept. Head | Finance | UPM | Producer

Figure 9.13 Purchase Order (P.O.). (Courtesy of Wild Bunch Films)

Before working on public property, the production needs to obtain the proper permits. In the case of using interior or exterior shots of private property, the production needs a **location release** from the property owner. A sample location release form is provided in *Appendix A*.

All of the production equipment must be lined up. The director coordinates with the crew to determine equipment needs and with the producers to manage equipment requests in the framework of the budget. Some of the equipment that needs to be reserved includes cameras, camera support, sound recording equipment, and lighting. Preproduction arrangements also include the coordination of transportation, lodging, and meals. The one place a production should never cut corners is on feeding the cast and crew. A well-fed crew is a happier and harder-working crew. On professional productions, the

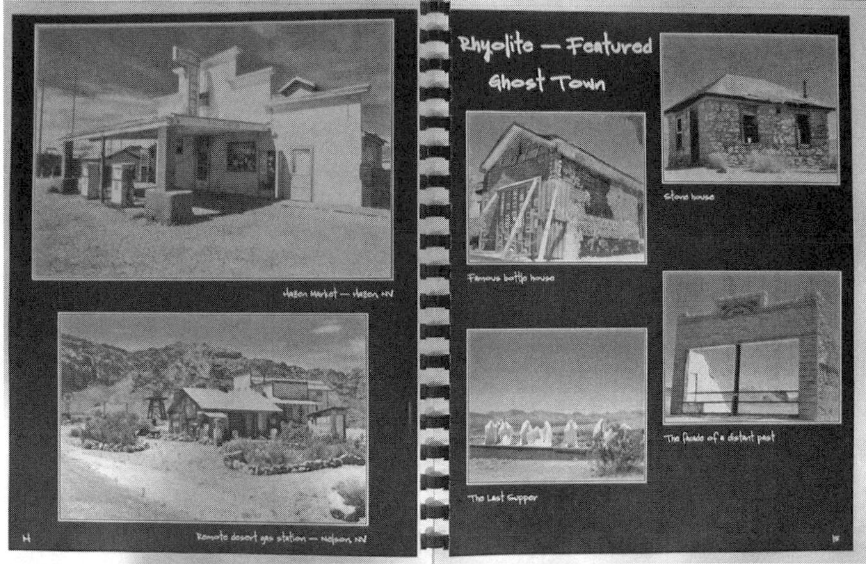

Figure 9.14 Regional film offices offer resources to assist location scouts. This manual by the Nevada Film Office illustrates locations across the state. (Courtesy of the Nevada Film Office)

rules for meals can be quite rigid. Certain mealtimes and meal resources are stipulated by contract. If there is not a set mealtime, then a banquet or catering table should be available at all times.

Production. The roles and responsibilities of each person during production vary depending on the scale of the project, and whether it is union or nonunion. On a union project, roles are specifically defined and people do not generally do things outside of their job description. In a nonunion production, people often wear many different hats and a few people may execute the roles of many.

The shooting phase of the process is intense. The day can begin at 4:00 or 5:00 a.m. for the technical crew and run until midnight until planning for the next day is complete. While many projects follow a five-day-a-week schedule, on some projects the crew works six days a week, and for tight schedules and remote location work the crew might push past 10 days straight.

The length of shooting schedules varies significantly. Hour-long episodic television can be in production for just a few days per episode. The production timeline for features typically varies from about 4 to 16 weeks. *The Little Shop of Horrors* (1960) was shot in two days, while *Arabian Knight* (1995) is reputed to have taken 28 years to complete.

Once a project goes into production, the actors bring the characters in the script to life. **Actors** can be defined by different types. **Principal actors** (or lead actors) portray the main characters in the film. **Supporting actors** have a significant role in the film but are not the primary focus of the story. **Bit**

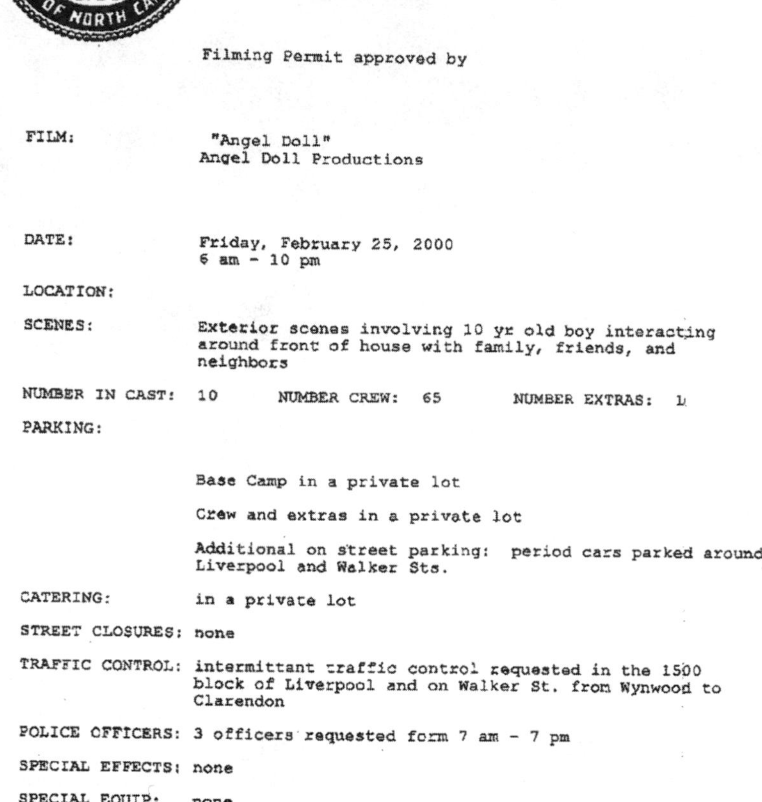

FILMING PERMIT

CITY OF WILMINGTON • PUBLIC SERVICES & FACILITIES •

Filming Permit approved by

FILM: "Angel Doll"
Angel Doll Productions

DATE: Friday, February 25, 2000
6 am - 10 pm

LOCATION:

SCENES: Exterior scenes involving 10 yr old boy interacting around front of house with family, friends, and neighbors

NUMBER IN CAST: 10 NUMBER CREW: 65 NUMBER EXTRAS: 1

PARKING:

Base Camp in a private lot

Crew and extras in a private lot

Additional on street parking: period cars parked around Liverpool and Walker Sts.

CATERING: in a private lot

STREET CLOSURES: none

TRAFFIC CONTROL: intermittant traffic control requested in the 1500 block of Liverpool and on Walker St. from Wynwood to Clarendon

POLICE OFFICERS: 3 officers requested form 7 am - 7 pm

SPECIAL EFFECTS: none

SPECIAL EQUIP: none

SPECIAL REQUEST: request permission to remove wooden fence post and chain that separates Love Grove Park from the street, and replace with a 1950's period fence. original fence will be restored upon completion of filming.

ADDITIONAL INFO: minor prep to house and neighborhood over several days prior to filming.

Figure 9.15 A filming permit is required to shoot on public property. (Courtesy of Wild Bunch Films)

players have only a few lines of dialogue. **Extras** are seen on screen but do not have spoken lines. **Stand-ins** model for lighting setup and blocking so that actors can study their lines and rest. **Stunt doubles** execute the more dangerous elements of the action.

The use of an **actor breakdown** sheet, which indicates what actors are needed for each scene, aids in the construction of the shooting schedule and the actors' schedule. An **extras breakdown** guides the casting department in the recruiting of extras for each day of production. There might be days when no extras are needed and other days when hundreds are required.

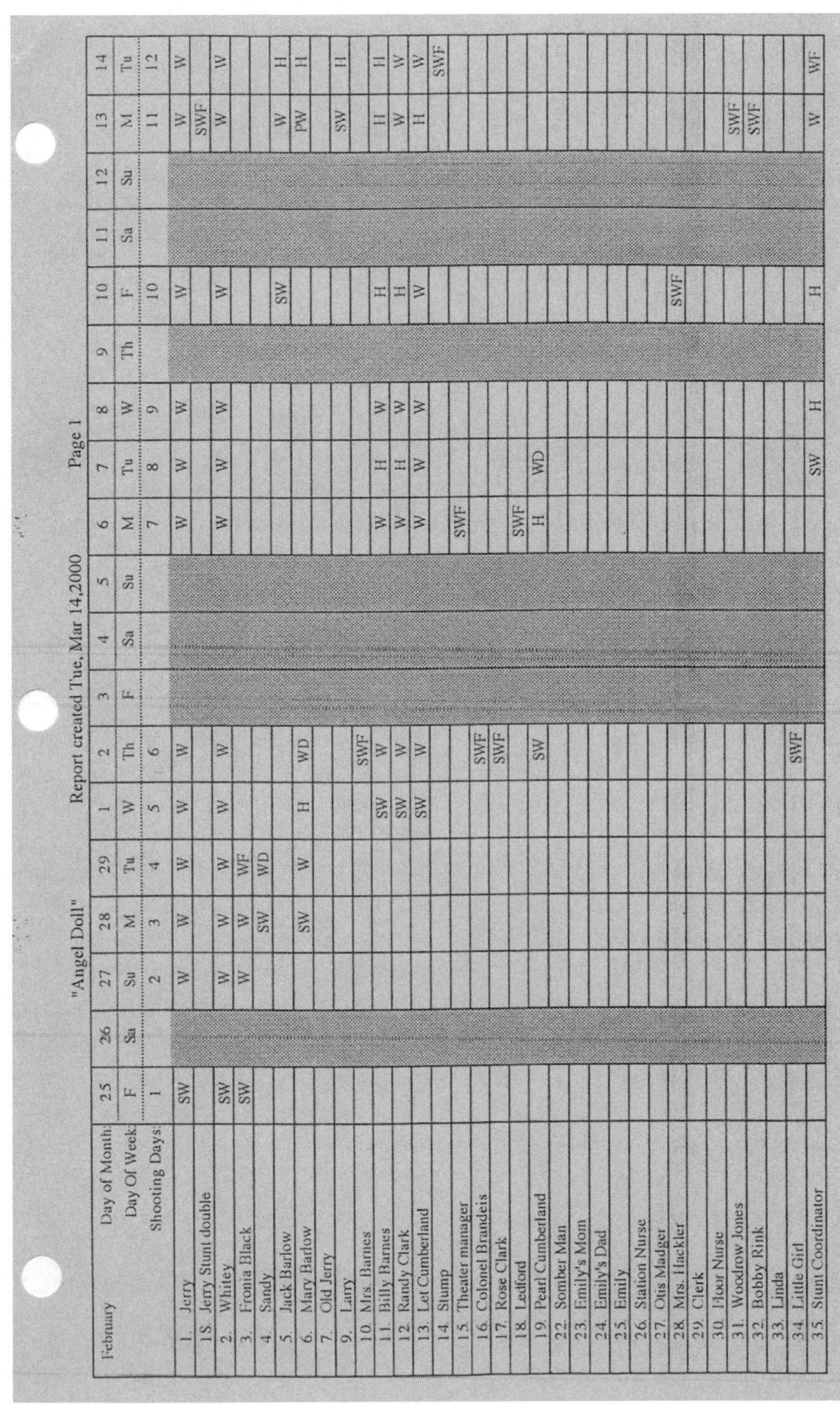

"Angel Doll" Report created Tue, Mar 14,2000 Page 1

February Day of Month:	25	26	27	28	29	1	2	3	4	5	6	7	8	9	10	11	12	13	14
Day Of Week:	F	Sa	Su	M	Tu	W	Th	F	Sa	Su	M	Tu	W	Th	F	Sa	Su	M	Tu
Shooting Days:	1		2	3	4	5	6				7	8	9		10			11	12
1. Jerry	SW		W	W	W	W	W				W	W	W		W			W	W
1S. Jerry Stunt double																		SWF	
2. Whitey	SW		W	W	W	W	W				W	W	W		W			W	W
3. Fronia Black	SW		W	W	WF														
4. Sandy				SW	WD														
5. Jack Barlow															SW			W	H
6. Mary Barlow				SW	W	H	WD											PW	H
7. Old Jerry																			
9. Larry																		SW	H
10. Mrs. Barnes							SWF												
11. Billy Barnes						SW	W				W	H	W		H			H	H
12. Randy Clark						SW	W				W	H	W		H			W	W
13. Let Cumberland						SW	W				W	W	W		W			H	W
14. Stump																			SWF
15. Theater manager											SWF								
16. Colonel Brandeis							SWF												
17. Rose Clark							SWF												
18. Ledford											SWF								
19. Pearl Cumberland							SW				H	WD							
22. Somber Man																			
23. Emily's Mom																			
24. Emily's Dad																			
25. Emily																			
26. Station Nurse																			
27. Otis Madger																			
28. Mrs. Hackler															SWF				
29. Clerk																			
30. Floor Nurse																			
31. Woodrow Jones																		SWF	
32. Bobby Rink																		SWF	
33. Linda																			
34. Little Girl							SWF												
35. Stunt Coordinator												SW	H		H			W	WF

Figure 9.16 Actor Breakdown. (Courtesy of Wild Bunch Films)

Angel Doll Productions
Extras Breakdown2/14/00

1

Fri 2/25	Shoot Day	#1	Ext Whitey's House 1 (w) older delivery boy	
				1
Sun 2/27		#2	Int Whitey's House	
Mon 2/28		#3	Int Whitey's House	
Tues 2/29		#4	Int Whitey's House	
Wed 3/1		#5	Ext Army Camp 2(w) mp's 15(w) fatique (1 capt ; 1lieut) 2 drivers (transpo) 7(w) patients(children) 3(b)patients (children) 3(w) nurses	
				28+2=30
Thurs 3/2		#6	Ext Cumberland House 1 (b)jobbing gardner 2(b) women neighbors Int Army Colonel's Office 1(w)mp 1(w) husband	
				5
Sun 3/5		#7	Ext Thomasville (Parade) 9(w) band 4(w) clowns 1(w) Santa 3(w) elves 9(w) teen boys w/ reindeer antlers 1(w) Miss America 50 spectators -30(w) 20(b)-	
				77
Mon 3/6		#8	Int Movie Theatre 4(b) boy 6(w) boy Int Ledford's Store 1(b)woman 3(w) women 1(w)teen girl 1(b) teen boy 2(w) men	18

Figure 9.17 Extras Breakdown. (Courtesy of Wild Bunch Films)

Once the production gets under way, the producer is often the person who administratively manages the execution of the project. The **line producer** is the producer's eyes and ears on the set, and she reports back to the producer with day-to-day progress and updates. The unit production manager (UPM) manages the budget and handles the planning and logistics in the trenches of production. If a camera dolly is absent when it is needed, it is often the unit production manager who will spring into action to solve the problem, and then determine what went wrong in the first place. The UPM is also the one responsible for generating and distributing call sheets that announce what will be achieved each day and for creating a **daily production report**, which documents the day's progress compared to goals. The **daily hot cost** report itemizes funds expended each day compared to budgeted allocations.

Angel Doll Productions, LLC

Daily Hot Cost

Date: 2/25/00

To:
FR:

Day 1 of 18

Start Date 2/25/00
Finish Date 3/21/00

BUDGETED DIRECT COSTS	(OVER)/UNDER TO DATE	ESTIMATED FINAL COST

Crew Call: 630am Lunch Out: 1230 Lunch in: 1300 Wrap: 1803 Last Out: 1900

	BUDGETED	ACTUAL	(OVER)/UNDER	NOTES
Crew Overtime	771	30.02	$740.98	
Cast Overtime	357	165.69	$191.31	
Catered Meals	97	95	$22.00	
Rawstock	5000	4770	$82.80	
B Camera Stock	1500	N/A		
Film Developed	5000	1490	$193.70	
Misc.				

Today's Variance $1,230.79

Cumulative Variance

Special Notes:

UPM Acknowledgment ______________________

Figure 9.18 Daily Hot Cost. Note that some budgeted and actual categories, such as catered meals, are recorded in units and not dollars. (Courtesy of Wild Bunch Films)

The **script supervisor** is in charge of continuity. She watches everything that unfolds during the shoot with an eagle eye, taking careful notes about the specific position of people and objects in a scene so that these elements can be matched up in subsequent setups. The costuming department keeps their own continuity book to make sure that clothes, accessories, and how they are worn match from shot to shot and day to day.

The director of photography supervises the creative photographic process, camera crew, and lighting crew. The sound recordist captures the audio, while the boom operator positions the microphone for each shot. When everyone is in place, sound and camera roll.

Postproduction. Professional editors utilize computer-based editing systems that are very similar to those used by student filmmakers, but the postproduc-

COSTUME BREAKDOWNS -

PRODUCTION			ACTOR	Actor Keith
			CHARACTER	old Jerry
CHANGE	**SCENE**	**DESCRIPTION**	**COSTUME**	
1	1+2	Int. Jerrys House 2000 christmas Eve DAY	Shirt - (Christoper Hayes) Burgundy, blue, gold, green purple plaid, B/F, B/O collar 4s *open + untucked T-neck - (Duofold) Navy 4s *Tucked in pants - (GAP) Drk. blue denim 5 pocket jeans Belt - (Structure) Brown w/ pewter buckle + Dbl. loops sox - brown dress shoes - (Rockport) Brown brushed leather w/ ridge toe, lace-up Accessories - watch (A/O) - pewter + wht. L wrist	
CHANGE	**SCENE**	**DESCRIPTION**	**COSTUME**	
1			same as 1+2 only shirt tucked in top 2 buttons open	
1+	137 139	Ext. Secret place " " 2000	JKT - (structure) Drk. Olive w/ Faux wool collar Zip + button Front *open	
or 1−			or No top shirt (plaid) T-neck + JKT	

Figure 9.19 The art department often maintains a continuity book for costuming to make sure that everything matches up from one setup to the next. (Courtesy of Wild Bunch Films)

Figure 9.20 Postproduction sound design session. (Courtesy of ProComm Studio Services)

Figure 9.21 Video postproduction labs can generate virtually any visual effect required for a production. (Walt Bost)

tion of a major feature utilizes a whole range of tools and facilities beyond the editing computer.

The material recorded in production is imported into a computer editing system, often in draft mode. This material is time code matched to the original film negative or high-resolution video. If the material was filmed using a double-system method (separate sound and image recording) then the sync sound must be imported into the computer separately and put back into sync with the picture shot by shot. This is achieved with the aid of time code and the scene slate.

The editor then organizes the material into bins, and builds the program in the timeline. The creative methods used by editors vary considerably. Some editors build a program scene by scene, sticking with a scene until it is finely tuned. Other editors start by assembling the raw footage of an entire program in the timeline and refine it all together draft by draft.

The editor might work with one or more assistants to help in the huge process of taking hours of material and sculpting it into a streamlined program. The director consults with the editor throughout the assembly process.

Once the visual images and sync sound elements are refined and finalized, the director locks the program. Once the project is **locked**, no more shot changes are made. It is important that the program stay in the exact order and running time once it is locked.

After the film it locked it is spotted. **Spotting** a film is the process of selecting where music and sound effects go. Spotting sheets include time cues and are used by the artists contributing to the sound design to build their elements.

This locked and spotted cut of the project is exported and used by several postproduction facilities. A copy is sent to the project's composer, who scores the film and directs the musicians recording the score to match the images. A copy of the edit goes to the automated dialogue replacement (ADR) facilities, where actors come back and replace lines of dialogue that are not clean or do not have the correct presence and perspective. Yet another copy goes to the sound effects designers and editors, who work to layer in all of the subtle and dramatic sound elements that bring the full aural experience to life.

A sound mixing facility takes the sync sound, original musical score, prerecorded music (such as vintage or popular songs), and sound effects, and brings these elements together in a final mix that puts everything in balance. This mix requires balancing the relative volume of each of the elements, as well as balancing the distribution of sounds across each of the speakers in a multiple speaker mix (e.g., stereo, surround sound).

Shots that require visual manipulation are sent to the visual effects lab, which creates visual special effects to match requirements of the script. The visual effects lab imports high-resolution source material into their systems for manipulation. For example, there might be a scene where a character changes into a horrible monster. The visual effects lab creates this transformation. After the source images are manipulated to create the effect, the new shot is exported from the lab's facilities in the exact length needed to match the placeholder in the locked version of the program.

The final picture and sound mix are then married together and the program is exported to a **master** for mass reproduction and distribution. We explore the processes of marketing and distribution in chapter 11.

CONCLUSIONS

It is a mammoth undertaking to bring a major program from concept to script, through financing, production, and finally to the screen. With the shift toward video capture for professional long-form works, greater opportunities exist for the independent producer to participate in the feature-length production process.

Try converting your story ideas into a three-act structure using the proper screenwriting form. Using screenwriting and production planning software will aid in the translation of your screenplay into a budget and other planning documents. When making a budget do so as accurately as possible and build in a 10% contingency for potential cost overages.

Use your budget as the framework to raise financing. There are many creative models of film and video financing, but all projects involving investors are inherently complex business arrangements and require the counsel of an attorney and an accountant. Creative funding models, such as service trades, deferments, and product placement, can make project financing more feasible.

The production process for features requires careful planning, meticulous record keeping, and the coordination of many professionals to bring it all together. The director is the architect and leader of this process. There are numerous strategies and tools that help the director successfully complete the production journey. Whether the director is creating an epic feature or a five-minute short, many of the strategies for success are the same. We will explore the role of the director in the next chapter.

SAMPLE EXERCISES

1. You are given $1 million to create a feature. How will you budget this money to get the job done?
2. Outline a feature-length project. Make the first 10 minutes of your feature a stand-alone dramatic journey, as well as an introduction to the larger questions of your story. Script the first 10 minutes of this feature using the formal screenwriting format.
3. Produce a short test program based on the 10-minute script you composed for Exercise #2.

RECOMMENDED READINGS

Bension, S. (annual). *The Producer's Masterguide: The International Production Manual for Motion Picture, Broadcast Television, Commercials, Cable/Satellite, Digital & Videotape Industries*. New York: Producer's Masterguide.

Field, S. (1994). *Screenplay: The Foundations of Screenwriting*. New York: Dell.

Rodriguez, R. (1996). *Rebel Without a Crew: Or How a 23-Year-Old Filmmaker With $7,000 Became a Hollywood Player.* New York: Penguin Books.

REFERENCES

Dawtrey, A. (2005, May 12). Lynch invades an "Empire:" Digital pic details a mystery. *Cannes Daily Variety,* pp. 1, 62.

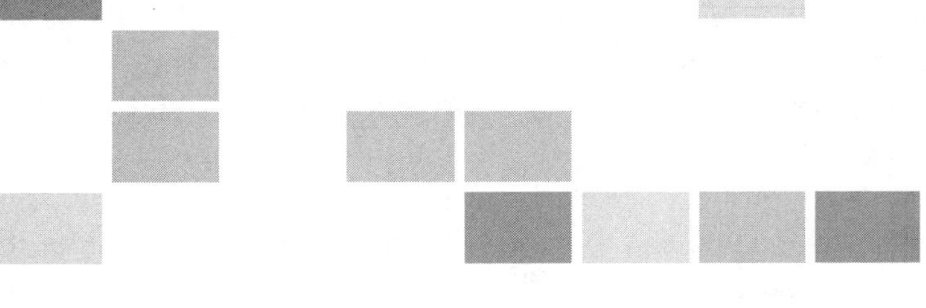

10

DIRECTING

CHAPTER OBJECTIVES

"The best films are best because of nobody but the director" (Halliwell, 1990, p. 346). There is truth in this observation by Academy Award-winning director Roman Polanski. A successful production needs a leader. Trenton McDevitt sees filmmaking as analogous to going to war. There is a definitive chain of command and the director is the five-star general. Everything that matters in the process is under his control. Burt Lancaster pushes the metaphor of the director's power even further, claiming, "It's the best job in the picture business because when you're a director, you're God" (Halliwell, 1990, p. 346). While some directors might feel this way, the reality is a little more down to earth. Directing is a grueling challenge with tremendous responsibility and unparalleled creative rewards. The goals of this chapter are to:

- Review directorial style choices;
- Examine the elements of directing;
- Foster an understanding of the actor's process;
- Survey strategies for working effectively with the cast and crew.

"Just what is a director?" asks François Truffaut. "A director is someone who is constantly asked questions. Questions about everything. Sometimes he has the answers, but not always." In *Day for Night* (1973), Truffaut presents an account based on his life experience working as a film director. The main character in the film, played by Truffaut, is a director who experiences virtually every possible challenge and reward one might face in a career. He scrambles when the producers demand the production be moved to a tighter schedule. The money runs short and things constantly go wrong on the set.

Truffaut shares the internal turmoil of a director as he reaches the midpoint of production. "Before filming begins I always hope above all to make a beautiful film. Then as the first difficulties arise I lower my sights and I'm satisfied simply to get the film completed." The ultimate message of the film, however, is one of great reward. We see that despite all the challenges, everything comes together in the end and the result is magical. Truffaut confides in his lead actor: "There's more harmony in films than in life. No traffic jams; no dead periods. Films keep going on, you know, like trains in the night. People like you, like me, are only happy in our work, making films" (Truffaut, 1973).

The **director** is the boss on the set and the ultimate authority responsible for all creative dimensions of a production. There are few people the director must answer to. The director is accountable to the **producer**, who is in charge of making sure that everything runs on budget and on schedule. In some cases the producer has to say no to a director's request because of cost or other practical limitations. For this reason, some directors prefer to also act as producer, thereby giving them both administrative and creative control over the project. Other directors prefer to leave the bookkeeping and management to someone else so that they can concentrate on creative vision. Having a separate producer also builds in a safety net for the project by not placing too much power in the hands of one single person.

The director is also accountable to the financiers. Ultimately, the people paying for the project have the final say. In most cases the financial backers afford as much latitude to the director as possible and do not interfere with the creative process. If it is clear that a project is going astray, however, the executives can step in and reorient the director, or, in extreme cases, replace the director to save a production. Other than reporting to these few people, however, the film director is usually in total control. Everyone else on the project ultimately reports to and is accountable to him.

Directorial Style

Directors vary significantly in their approach to the creative process. Some directors are people oriented, concentrating on interacting with the crew and collaborating with the actors to evoke the best performance possible. Directors such as Clint Eastwood are calm on the set and build a performance through conversation with the actors and creative team. Eastwood does not usually yell, "Action!" at the beginning of a **take**, but rather quietly queues the technicians to roll the equipment, and often says to the performers, "Begin." Eastwood is known for **tail-slating** shots, which means that he brings in the clapperboard that records the identifying information into the shot at the end rather than at the beginning. This further reduces distractions for the actors at the beginning of their performance. Tom Savini also dispels with the director's lingo, and prefers to say to his actors, "Whenever you're ready." It is noteworthy that both

Figure 10.1 Director Tom Anton checks the composition of a shot during the production of *At Last.* (Courtesy of RiverDream Productions)

Eastwood and Savini were actors before they became directors. They employ a sympathetic approach which enhances the actor's process.

Other directors, such as George Lucas, are more technology-centered. Lucas is known for seeing the filmmaking process as a technical craft and he dedicates much of his attention as a director to designing and executing remarkable special effects.

Some directors are highly structured and follow a carefully laid out plan. Hitchcock is best known for this approach. Other directors, such as Dennis Hopper, are loose in their style, allowing improvisation and discovery during rehearsals and shooting. Much of *Easy Rider* (1969) was created through improvisation.

Directing styles can further vary in how detail oriented a director chooses to be. Some directors micromanage the production process and double-check virtually every creative choice made by the crew. Other directors are global in their thinking with a primary focus on communicating broad statements and allowing significant latitude in how that direction is realized by the cast and crew.

Some directors are known for their collaborative spirit. Mike Leigh (*Topsy Turvy*, 1999; *Vera Drake*, 2004) spends weeks in rehearsals and is open to working with actors to adapt lines and make script changes in the process. Sidney Pollack (*Out of Africa*, 1985; *The Firm*, 1993) is an accomplished director and actor; he is frequently called an actor's director for his ability to get into sync with his cast and to foster an effective and rewarding work environment.

Working effectively with actors sometimes means adopting a stern approach. While shooting *The Wild Bunch* (1969), the principal actors fell into a lazy posture early in the production by showing up for work completely unprepared. The director, Sam Peckinpah, put an end to that with a single ultimatum. He gave the actors 20 minutes to learn their lines for the day and threatened to replace anyone who was not prepared when the time expired. The actors scrambled to find a quiet location to study their lines and every actor was prepared for work from that moment forward.

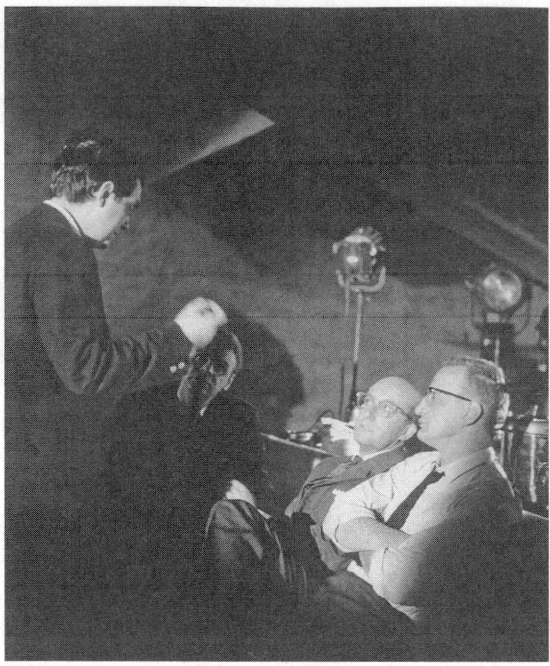

Figure 10.2 Stanley Kubrick (left) discusses a scene with Peter Sellers (center) and George C. Scott on the set of *Dr. Strangelove* (1964). (Columbia Pictures/Photofest; © Columbia Pictures)

A few directors are masterful at every element of production. Stanley Kubrick was known as a genius of technical craft, obsessively detail-oriented, and emotionally engaged with his actors. He allowed extensive improvisation as well as demanded repeated takes to hit marks and deliver a scene perfectly. Kubrick never settled for good enough. Kubrick spent more than two years in production on *Eyes Wide Shut* (1999) to explore everything there was to be discovered in the material. On the production of *Paths of Glory* (1957), Kubrick recorded 68 takes of a last meal of condemned prisoners, using a new roast duck for virtually every attempt.

Directing styles can differ from artist to artist and project to project. A director who is assigned a 30-second commercial on a one-day schedule is going to take a different approach from a documentary director working on a two-month schedule for public television. The commercial requires a more controlled approach and limited deviation from scripted materials. However, that same director might use the PBS documentary platform as an opportunity to give more creative latitude to the crew and to take more chances with exploration and discovery.

There is not a single correct way to direct video projects. Start by following your gut and give straightforward direction to make things happen. What you will find is that some of these choices work very well. Your approach in these cases will click and you will return to successful methods time and again.

For other directorial choices, you will find things do not work out the way you had intended. For example, you might decide to let your videographer have wide freedom in composing shots. That might work out well or you might be disappointed. How the experience plays out will guide your approach the next day.

Your own directorial style will emerge from your personality and experience. Like everything in production, and most things in life, learning to be a good director comes through observation and practice. The choices you make while working with people and equipment will ultimately shape the product on screen. Many projects are identifiable by director in the way shots are composed, recurring symbols that are used, the pacing, and the tone of the acting.

The Elements of Directing

Directing is coordination, interpretation, and evoking performance. On any scale project, the director is the one responsible for realizing an aesthetic vision. Many people assist with this process, of course, but ultimately the director is the one who has to make sure that all the creative elements fit together.

Coordination. First and foremost, directing is the practical process of coordination. Consider the logistics required to shoot a single battle sequence. There may be hundreds of people on a mock battlefield. Before the scene can be shot, the battlefield has to be prepared to look authentic. Special effects are put in place, and all the action of the characters, technical coordination for lighting, cinematography for multiple angles, and sound recording have to be planned and put in place. The director must make sure all of this comes together, but cannot possibly supervise each element personally or else the process would take much too long to complete.

For this reason, the director has assistants. The director will most likely concentrate on rehearsing the scene with the principal actors. She will also coordinate with the leaders of each creative unit to make sure all is coming together for the big shoot. The director of photography will brief the director on the status of camera positions and how the changing sun might affect the scene. The art director will provide an update on the positioning of effects, props, and costuming progress.

The director often relies on a **first assistant director** (first A.D.) to make sure everything is set up and in place when it is time to record the scene. As director/producer Trenton McDevitt puts it, "The first assistant director on the set makes sure the film gets done, and the director makes sure the film gets done right."

The first assistant director is the one who keeps things moving. He is often the bad cop in the process, riding people to keep on schedule, often yelling and giving orders. Not all first assistant directors are this aggressive, but the first A.D. must be prepared to step in with authority. The first assistant director

Figure 10.3 The director must coordinate the simultaneous actions of many people. (Courtesy of RiverDream Productions)

serves as the lightning rod for all major problems and many consider this role to be the toughest job on the set.

Often there is also a second assistant director. The second assistant director is usually charged with managing the actors. This responsibility includes keeping track of the principal actors and making sure that they are in position when needed. The second assistant director also manages the supporting actors, bit players, and extras. When a complex scene requires the coordinated action of dozens of extras, it is usually the second assistant director that designs their placement and movements. During the recording of the shot, the second A.D. is often the one to cue the extras, too.

In a production there is a well-defined chain of command. Sometimes the reporting relationships are specific. In union production, which includes most major motion pictures, the second assistant director reports to the first assistant director, and first assistant director reports to the director. If the second assistant director were to bypass the first A.D. and go right to the director, there would be a violation of the chain of command and the first assistant director might be quite upset.

On other projects, particularly smaller-scale and independent features, there is a hierarchy, but there may be more direct reporting and consultation with the director. George A. Romero is known for his openness and receptiveness to input from every member of the crew. Romero's crewmembers describe the set as a family environment. Regardless of the rigidity of the chain of command, the director must never lose sight that he or she is ultimately responsible for the final decision on every creative choice.

While many directors seek extensive input from the professionals on their team, video projects cannot be efficiently created through a democratic voting process. Decisions in production come fast and furious across a range of challenges and the director has to be prepared to make numerous calls quickly. Some will be made as instantaneous snap decisions. Sometimes these decisions can utilize input, but other times there is simply not the opportunity or time. A director who goes around saying, "Well, what do you think?" for every decision will most likely not be very successful. Directing is coordination.

Interpretation. Directing is also interpretation. A visual program starts out as ideas on paper. It is the director's job to interpret what the words mean and to translate words into images and sounds. When you read a scene, it might be obvious to you how it would best be portrayed on-screen. This intuitive response to the material comes from your own aesthetics and assumptions. If the script were given to 10 different people, you would probably get 10 dramatically different interpretations of the content.

In translating material from paper to the big screen, the director deals not only with the text, but also (more importantly) the subtext. The question must be asked, "What is really going on behind the lines of dialogue?" When a character says, "I look forward to seeing you tomorrow," the director must decide if that statement is a genuine expression of wanting to get together again, or a mere social courtesy and deep down the character really hates the person. If it is the latter, the director must choose how to communicate the tension to the audience. Will it be in the inflection of the dialogue, in the camera position, or in the actor's body language? These are all elements of interpretation.

When the director is also the screenwriter, there is an inherent understanding of both the text and subtext. Even in these cases, however, a director might change an interpretation as the process evolves. Every script is open to multiple layers of interpretation. Exploring what the material means and designing the mechanisms that will communicate meaning to the audience are among the most rewarding parts of the directing process.

When a director is also the screenwriter (and sometimes the producer), he is often referred to as an **auteur**, the French word for author. These directors

Figure 10.4 Sofia Coppola (left) produces, writes, and directs. Her work has a distinct style and the marks of an auteur. Shown here with Kirsten Dunst in production of *The Virgin Suicides*. (Paramount/Photofest; © Paramount Pictures)

often portray more unity of vision and individual style. Directors who have been described as auteurs include Orson Welles, Stanley Kubrick, and Woody Allen.

Evoking Performance. The third role of the director, evoking performance, is perhaps the most important. Arguably, it is the actors' performances that make a program come to life. It requires skill and empathy to evoke performance effectively. For beginning filmmakers, working with the technical side of production is so challenging and consuming that new directors sometimes neglect the importance of working with people, particularly actors. To guide actors effectively you need to understand the actor's process.

Understanding the Actor's Process

Directing is not only interpreting and translating ideas to the screen, but also communicating these ideas through another person's behavior. That is a complex and difficult task to achieve.

A director cannot work with an actor effectively if she does not understand the actor's process. Regardless of the scale of your project, you need to know how an actor approaches his work and be able to address questions that an actor asks about his character. An actor wants to know:

1. Who am I?
2. What do I want?
3. How do I get what I want?

Characters have objectives. Actors facilitate their character's journey by knowing what they are. Be prepared to tell your actor his character's objectives and motivation.

Each actor's process varies. You might be familiar with the phrase **method acting**. This term comes from a number of acting styles derived from a system of acting training pioneered in Russia by Konstantin Stanislavski at the beginning of the 20th century.

The techniques pioneered by Stanislavski at the Moscow Art Theatre were studied and embraced by New York City's Group Theater, founded in 1931 by Harold Clurman, Cheryl Crawford, and Lee Strasberg. The founders and members of the group splintered and formed their own acting schools that placed emphasis on particular methods of acting. The common thread between these schools was the intent to create human realism in an actor's performance.

Lee Strasberg joined The Actor's Studio in New York City in 1949. A few of Strasberg's students include Al Pacino, Robert DeNiro, and Jane Fonda. The Strasberg method of acting relies heavily on utilizing **sense memory**. If a character is sad in a scene, the actor using the method of sense memory will evoke a personal memory that is extremely painful, such as the death of a beloved family pet. The actor focuses on the pain of that memory and projects that pain as a realistic bridge into the experience of the character. This can often result

Figure 10.5 Robert DeNiro studied method acting under Lee Strasberg at The Actor's Studio. From Martin Scorsese's *Taxi Driver.* (Columbia Pictures/Photofest; © Columbia Pictures

in highly realistic performances and actual tears. Critics of the sense memory method claim it is an unhealthy psychological practice for the actor.

Stella Adler put the emphasis in actor training on the power of imagination and imaginative circumstances. Rather that evoking a memory of personal pain, the actor using Adler's method will imagine himself in the circumstances of the character. An Adler method actor is likely to desire extensive background and context from the director to help guide the imaginative process. Marlon Brando studied under Adler.

Sanford Meisner created a style of acting training known as the Meisner Technique. Meisner's methods focus on reacting and having the actor take the emphasis off herself. Meisner exercises often integrate repeating what is said. For beginning actors, for instance, if one actor says to another, "Your shirt is blue." The Meisner actor is likely to reply, "Your shirt is blue." As this is repeated over and over, the actors begin to personalize the dialogue and add observations. Initial training in the Meisner Technique is dedicated to eliminating the prescriptive aspects of conversation and having the actor take the emphasis off oneself. Untrained actors can be so self-absorbed that they miss a lot of what is actually going on around them. It is through such simple exercises that the actor develops a greater sensitivity to her fellow actors and the environment, which Meisner argues opens the actor's range and the creative process. Robert Duvall and Diane Keaton studied under Meisner.

There are many other noteworthy schools of acting and each utilizes slightly different training methods. Yale, Julliard, and New York University are among the top institutions for actor training.

Have a conversation with your actors to determine the methods they find most productive and useful in their own work. If you understand the process of each of your actors, you will be able to offer much more effective direction, which will ease communication and result in a performance that better captures your vision.

Directing Actors

The core guidelines for effectively directing actors are actually quite simple. There are just a few techniques and rules to follow and the rest will come out naturally in a relationship with your actors.

The most important rule is the most difficult one for beginning directors to follow. When working with actors it is essential to be process-oriented rather than result-oriented. This is a challenge because you often know the result you are seeking and it can be tempting to articulate that directly. For example, a director might be inclined to tell an actor, "Speed it up" or "I need you to cry in this scene." While this is clear to the director, it is devoid of motivation and context for the actor.

It is easy to translate these two outcomes into process-oriented direction. Instead of telling your actor to speed it up, let your actor know that his character is in a state of urgency. The acceleration of the pace of the scene will come naturally through the actor's feeling the urgency of his character. The outcome will also be more realistic. Instead of simply telling an actor to cry, work on finding something the character is experiencing that the actor can relate to. Describe how the character is feeling. Explain what happened to the character.

Another excellent way to give concise direction is to tell the actor in a sentence or two about the journey through the scene. Include what the character wants and how he gets it. Describe the scene and the character's motivation. The director might say, "You are extremely frustrated in your inability to make your point to your husband. You just want to scream, but you are afraid to do so."

Never read an actor's lines for her. If you feel the actor is not getting at the performance you envision, try offering more direction. Elaborate or give direction from a slightly different perspective. The director might have to say, "Your frustration is contained. You are fighting not to show it. You do not want your husband to know you are frustrated. You are trying to project calm, but you are burning inside." The worst thing you can do, according to actors, is to read their lines for them.

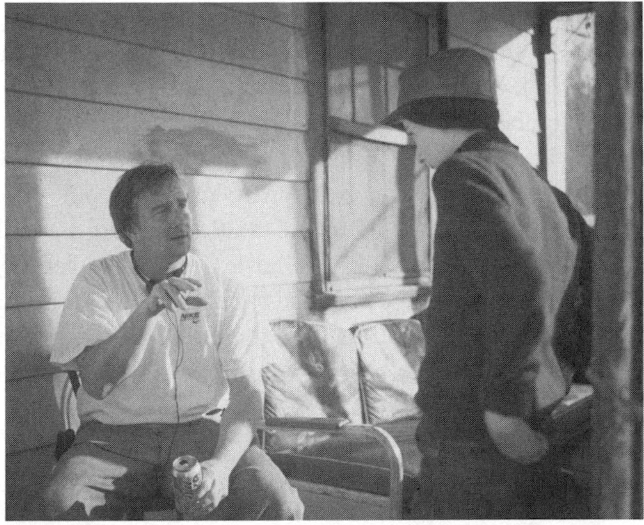

Figure 10.6 Sandy Johnston (left) was known for his ability to work with actors of all ages. Shown here directing Michael Welch on the set of *The Angel Doll.* (Photo by Jim Bridges; Courtesy of Wild Bunch Films)

As a director, you will sometimes encounter a discrepancy between your and the actor's interpretation of a scene. This can be a challenge. If time and the context permit, it is valuable to let an actor argue for his or her interpretation. Directors are often inspired to change their own view when an actor provides an insight they had not considered.

Another issue that sometimes emerges is the actor's substitution of phrasing and lines from the script. There are directors who want the script read exactly as written. There are other directors who are open to the substitution of a word or phrase. Some directors take the substitution concept even further and allow the general concepts of the dialogue to be translated through improvisation. The director develops an understanding with the actors of what level of line substitution is an acceptable part of the process.

As a director, it is likely that you will have frustration with an actor not performing the way you imagined the scene realized, despite all your efforts to provide motivation, context, and direction. There are times when it just does not flow. In some cases it is best to take a break and try again after a short time to gather some distance and perspective. In other cases you must face the reality that it is not going to get any better and the shooting day is slipping away. You might have to make the call that what you have is good enough for this scene and move on. In other cases, the disconnection between the director's vision and the actor's performance is so great it cannot be overlooked. In these circumstances you can try to return to the setup on another day and try again. Kubrick often solved this problem by pushing through with even more takes. His goal was to wear away the actor's preconceptions of the scene until a new plateau of discovery was reached.

Despite the rigorous auditioning process, sometimes a project goes into production before the director recognizes the hard reality that an actor is simply wrong for a part. In extreme cases actors have been removed from principal roles after production begins. Harvey Keitel was originally cast to play the lead role of Willard in Francis Ford Coppola's *Apocalypse Now* (1979). It wasn't until the entire production was on location in the Philippines and principal photography began that Coppola screened the **dailies** and made the decision that Keitel was not going to work as Willard. Coppola replaced Keitel with Martin Sheen. Fortunately such occurrences are rare. Generally, auditions and rehearsals flag these problems in time, and the collaborative process of creating an effective performance is highly rewarding for the actor and director.

The Production Process for the Director

With a script in hand and a budget on the table, one of the first things the director does is assemble the team of professionals to help realize her vision. In some circumstances the director has to work with a crew assembled by the producers, but often the director hires those she wants for all major creative positions. Directors who have had success with certain artists, be it cinematography, sound design, or editing, will return to these people time and again. With a trusted crew in place, the director can begin confidently delegating responsibility.

The production designer reports to the director. She leads the art department to create the elements that appear in front of the camera. The production designer usually starts by drafting sketches of sets and costumes. Once approved by the director, the full scale of the art department goes into high gear making costumes, building sets, and acquiring properties. The art department also handles miniatures and special effects.

The director of photography also reports to the director, and often is a close collaborator on visually interpreting the script. In some cases the director collaborates with the sound designer early in preproduction, especially if the program involves significant sound effects or is based largely on musical elements.

Casting. In some cases a director is brought onto a project with principal casting decisions already made by the producers. This can happen when a film is packaged. Sometimes negotiations are made for financing that are contingent on getting a particular actor or actors to agree to come on board. This packaging of actors can sometimes occur before the choice of director is even made. In most situations, however, the director usually makes the final casting decisions.

Often casting is achieved with the support of a **casting agency** and a **casting director**. A casting agency is a company that specializes in distilling the most appropriate actors for various production needs and the casting director leads this process. Casting agencies and directors have ongoing relationships

Figure 10.7 Screen tests are recordings of auditions used to make casting decisions. (Courtesy of William Olsen)

with actors and their agents. When various projects come up, they produce a short list of potential actors for the director to audition.

In other cases the casting agency has an **open casting call** where anyone that fits the basic physical description of the character can show up and read for the part. Sometimes a scene is provided to the actors reporting to an open casting call ahead of time; sometimes it is given to them at the location to study while they wait to be seen; and in other cases the casting meeting is more of an improvisation and interview than the execution of a formal scene.

In most cases casting directors can tell quickly if an actor is a viable candidate for a role. Sometimes hundreds of interested actors reply to an open casting call. It is the casting director's job to reduce this pool to a handful of finalists. Sometimes the director participates in the wider casting call or sends a representative to the preliminary casting sessions. In other cases the director relies upon the professional judgment of the casting agency to make these early decisions.

Casting usually takes place in rounds. After the first round a few hundred applicants might be reduced to 50. These 50 will be invited for a callback. This is an exciting development for an actor. The number of callbacks varies. In some cases there are no callbacks for a part at all. The director might be struck with an actor on the first read and announce, "You're hired."

As the pool of candidates is narrowed, later auditions are videotaped or recorded on film. These recorded auditions are called **screen tests**, which provide a record for casting professionals to use in making decisions, to gain a sense of how well an actor performs in front of the camera, and to see how the actor looks on camera. When making movies it doesn't matter what a performance looks like in the room. It is the translation to the screen that is the most important thing.

Rehearsals. Once casting decisions are made, the director leads rehearsals. The first step of the rehearsal process is often a **table read**. During a table read, all the principal actors of the film or television episode sit around a conference table and read their lines directly from the script. The objective here is not to hone a performance, but rather to get the actors familiar with the content and speaking the dialogue out loud.

After the table read, the rehearsal process varies significantly in format and structure depending on the project. A situation comedy might have three days of rehearsals in which the script is practiced in large blocks. Long-format film projects are usually rehearsed scene by scene. Sometimes rehearsals last for weeks before going into production. In other cases rehearsals last only a few minutes before a scene is shot. Building in time for rehearsals to iron out creative choices can be valuable in saving expensive time on the set.

On the Set. Generally it is good to start early and to allow ample time for setup, but the director should only summon the people he needs. Beginning directors often make the mistake of having their entire cast and crew show up at 7:00 a.m. only to spend two hours planning technical elements while the actors sit and wait, growing tired and frustrated. Be efficient with people's time. Give breaks to personnel when you do not need them, but keep them available and in communication so you will not lose time when you do need them.

The cast and crew start the day with a call sheet in hand. The first people to arrive for the day are usually those who coordinate technical setup. Sometimes setting up equipment and decorating the sets can take many hours before actors arrive.

Often the on-set rehearsal process begins with the director and actors working alone on the set for the first rehearsal. This is a time when the rest of crew takes a break to free the director and actors from additional distractions. Once the director and actors are satisfied with the performance elements, the director collaborates with the director of photography to determine how the

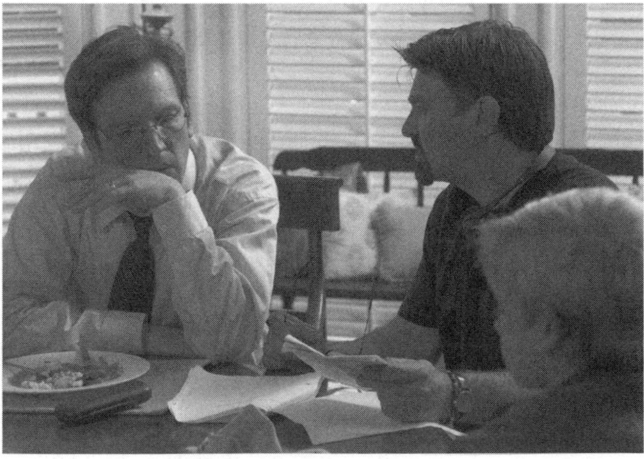

Figure 10.8 The director and actors work without the full crew during the first rehearsal. (Courtesy of RiverDream Productions)

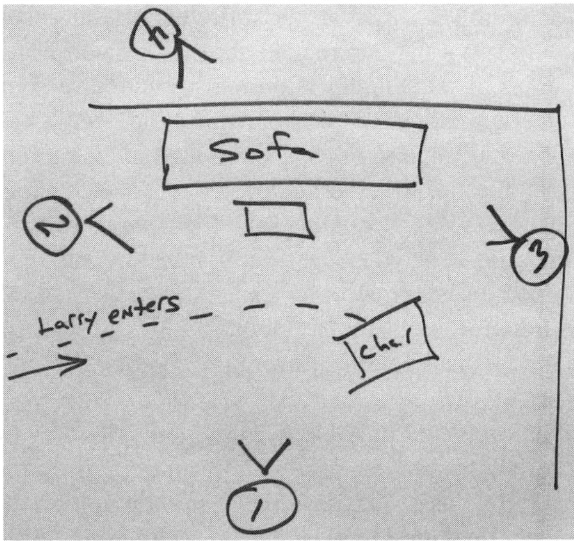

Figure 10.9 Planning the placement and movement of actors, props, and equipment is called blocking.

scene will be shot. The rest of the crew is called back for a **technical rehearsal** and marks for cameras and actors are made. When the technical rehearsal is complete the actors are sent for wardrobe, hair, and makeup while the crew sets the lights using stand-ins. When the set is ready, the actors are brought back and, if necessary, one more rehearsal is done before filming.

When directing your own scenes there are a few technical tips that will make the process smoother. In addition to rehearsing with the actors, study the lighting and set design. Make sure you are satisfied with these elements. Check the video monitor to verify how the shot looks on camera. With this foundation in place, bring the actors on the set and do a technical rehearsal, which integrates all actor movements and equipment moves. The process of planning the placement and movement of actors and equipment is called **blocking**. Practice the scene and all technical moves before recording.

When all is in place, cue the camera operator to start recording. After receiving verification that the camera is rolling, pause a moment and cue the performance to begin. Pay attention to cutting points in long sequences in case there is a mistake. Considering where a shot will be edited allows retaking only part of a long take to work around an error.

Study the actor's performance. The tone of the actor's voice and inflection are crucial to the quality of a work. The pauses and spaces between words are important and add power. The director focuses not only on what the actor says and how she says it, but also on how the actor moves. How is each actor's body positioned? How should they move for best effect? There is much more communication to be realized through movement than the obvious direction dictated by the script.

Before wrapping any location make sure you have it covered. Reference your storyboards and shot list and make sure that everything you intended to capture was recorded. This includes making sure you have your master shots, reverse angles, reaction shots, and various cut-ins and cutaways. Give your editor options. Before **striking** and moving on to the next location it is best to do what you can to make sure that the material is of solid technical quality. For digital video production this is simple. Take the time to watch select takes or spot check the material in playback. Listen to the audio and review the picture carefully. Make sure that the microphones are working correctly and that the camera is recording image and sound. Once you are satisfied that the scene is captured, you can give the cue to capture room tone, then strike and move on to the next location.

In film production its not possible to immediately review the film, so one thing directors do for insurance is to give a command to the director of photography to "check the gate." The director of photography will then have the first assistant camera operator open the camera and physically inspect the gate where film exposure takes place. If there is not any hair or dust in the gate, chances are better that the film was captured correctly. It can be hours or even a day or two before a director is able to screen material that has been shot on film. This material, rushed each day from the lab, is called the dailies or **rushes**.

One of the most important skills of a director on the set is time management. There almost never seems to be enough time. The director has to oversee all creative aspects of production and pace all modules of a project so that it is not sidetracked on a minor detail at the expense of more important efforts.

While in production, a director works with the clock virtually 24 hours a day. After the last setup of the day, the director reviews footage shot that day (or the prior day in the case of film, which needs to be processed). He then plans for the next day's shoot. During production, the director is working when he is not sleeping. Some directors sleep four hours or less per night in the heat of production. Learn how to manage time effectively and you have tackled one of the major challenges of effective directing.

Collaborating With the Cast and Crew

A director who is a clear and effective interpersonal communicator will have greater success translating his internal vision into one for the screen. The collaborative process of production means that the director relies on dozens of people to execute complicated tasks simultaneously.

The director is always fielding questions from the cast and crew. Every individual working on a project believes that his or her specific role is important. Each crewmember also wants to make sure they do a good job, and in cases where there are several options they often want to review these choices with the director. With a barrage of questions and a million things to do on limited time, the director has to be aware that his reaction matters. Guidance and direction should be clear and unambiguous even if they must be brief. Speed in addressing some concerns is often necessary. Looking a collaborator in the eye, however, and making sure that they are satisfied with their concerns can go a long way.

A director must be a psychologist. Production is a creative process, infused with creativity, invested with ego and feeling. Something that might be a minor or even irrelevant issue for the director might be extremely important to someone else on the project. Respect the contribution and input of every cast and crewmember.

Becoming a Director

Earning the opportunity to direct large-scale projects is usually achieved through one of three approaches: apprenticeship, lateral entry, and independent filmmaking. In the apprenticeship approach, the aspiring director must get into an environment that provides the opportunity to advance toward the goal of working as a director.

Getting a position with a casting agency, casting department, script continuity, or as a production assistant to one of the assistant directors are all ways to get yourself on the directing pathway. From one of these entry-level positions, you work to advance toward the role of a third or second assistant director, then to first assistant director, and then with a combination of skill and golden opportunity a directorial debut.

The role of assistant director is also an excellent training ground to become a producer, since the job is largely centered on logistics, managing the crew, and managing time.

Often working as an assistant director is not enough to demonstrate that you are qualified to be the principal director, which is a quantum leap in responsibility. Along with service under a director, aspiring assistant directors need to direct their own projects and share these projects with the people who have the authority to offer a directing opportunity. This type of career nurturing often takes years. An aspiring director needs to get her reel of independent directing efforts into the hands of producers and principal directors. Hopefully this will lead to constructive feedback and the opportunity to talk at greater length with senior executives. It is this kind of presence that can put a young assistant director on the short list for directing an upcoming project.

Some professionals earn the opportunity for a directorial debut through a lateral process. Based on years of competent service and loyalty, a cinematographer or a special-effects artist who has worked with a particular producer or director for years might be given the chance to demonstrate what he can do in the top role.

A third way to enter as a director is through carving your own path and proving you have what it takes. Independent filmmakers who make a successful low-budget feature can bypass the entire apprenticeship process and be brought on board at this supreme level. This is an unusual entry strategy, which

Figure 10.10 Spike Lee (right) demonstrates remarkable directorial range. A well-established director of fiction films (*Do the Right Thing; Jungle Fever*), Lee also directed *When the Levees Broke: A Requiem in Four Acts*, a documentary exploring the aftermath of Hurricane Katrina. (HBO/Photofest; © HBO Photographer: David Lee)

fails for most who try it, but it can happen (see the case of Robert Rodriguez described in the introduction to Chapter 9).

Anyone interested in directing big-budget features has to recognize that very few people ever make it to this level. The odds are against you going this far, but you need not be discouraged. There are many directing roles in entertainment, advertising, government, education, and industry. If your dream is to be a director, pursue it. Seek an entry-level position that allows collaboration with directors. Consider opportunities in independent filmmaking. The tools for directing your own digital video shorts and features are right within your grasp.

CONCLUSIONS

The mystique of the director is a powerful one in film and video production, but the reality of directing is one of hard work to achieve success. There is no single correct way to direct a visual program. Directors vary significantly in both creative style and approach to working with their cast and crew. With all creative responsibility set on the director's shoulders, he must excel in a range of tasks to coordinate the efforts of the cast and crew, interpret the script, and evoke effective performances from the actors.

Beginning directors often overlook the importance of collaborating with actors. Understanding the actor's process can greatly enhance communication and the quality of performances. Actors differ in their methods, and the director needs to understand the methods each actor uses. The director should respect the contribution of every member of the cast and crew and nurture the creative process.

Achieving the role of director for a major motion picture is difficult, but it is possible through apprenticeship, lateral entry, and proving yourself by creating your own independent films. While directing theatrical features is an achievement obtained by only a few, everyone can direct their own projects and pursue opportunities to experience this role of unparalleled creative force in production.

SAMPLE EXERCISES

1. Select a scene from a script. Apply your interpretation, cast actors for the roles, and direct the scene without production equipment. Concentrate on evoking an effective performance.
2. Volunteer to be an actor in one of your friend's projects. One of the best ways to become an effective director is to understand the actor's experience.
3. Write a scene that includes dialogue between two characters. Include character objectives and obstacles in your scene. Produce the scene on video. Strive to make your scene professional in every respect.

RECOMMENDED READINGS

Brestoff, R. (1995). *The Great Acting Teachers and Their Methods.* Lyme, NH: Smith and Kraus.

Kingdon, T. (2004). *Total Directing: Integrating Camera and Performance in Film and Television.* Los Angeles: Silman-James Press.

Rabiger, M. (2003). *Directing: Film Techniques and Aesthetics.* Oxford: Focal Press.

REFERENCES

Halliwell, L. (1990). *Halliwell's Filmgoer's and Video Viewer's Companion* (9th ed.). New York: Harper & Row, p. 346.

Truffaut, F. (1973). *Day for Night* (video recording). Burbank, CA: Warner Home Video.

11

MARKETING AND DISTRIBUTION

CHAPTER OBJECTIVES

Producing a good project is only half the battle. The target audience needs to know the project is out there and have a means to view it. Marketing is defined in the MSN Encarta Dictionary as *the business activity of presenting products or services to potential customers in such a way as to make them eager to buy. Marketing includes such matters as the pricing and packaging of the product and the creation of demand by advertising and sales campaigns.*

Successful marketing includes effective distribution. Distribution strategies and channels, many unique to the entertainment industry, will be given special attention in the latter part of this chapter. Marketing lets the public know about your project and distribution makes it available to them. We will explore the techniques used to support the release of major motion pictures and identify options that are particularly useful for small-scale programs and independent producers. The goals of this chapter are to:

- Examine the tools used to market video programs;
- Explore the importance of good press relations;
- Review different channels for film and video distribution;
- Identify distribution strategies that maximize revenue.

Marketing

Marketing is the creative and strategic process of making the public aware of a film or video program. The goal is to create interest in seeing the program and to purchase the program's ancillary products. You are a target of film and video marketing all the time, including the preliminary trailers shown during the first 10 to 20 minutes of theatrical releases.

Theatrical Trailers. The **theatrical trailer** is one of the core promotional tools in the movie business. This is often how the movie-going public first learns of an impending project release. It is not uncommon for a theatrical trailer to be screened in theaters six months or more in advance of a film's release. Full-length theatrical trailers run approximately two minutes. **Teaser trailers** can be a minute long or less.

Often teaser trailers are used long in advance of a project's release to plant the seed of recognition and stimulate conversation about the upcoming film. A teaser trailer might reveal only a shot or two from the film or use only titles and a logo set to music and narration. Sometimes a minimalist approach is necessary because the teaser trailer is distributed before production even begins.

A full-length trailer is generally distributed closer to a film's release date. If you pay attention, you will notice that theatrical trailers are packaged carefully. Trailers screened before a feature frequently match the genre, style, and target audience of the film the audience has paid to see. This way the distributor maximizes the potential impact of the trailer by reaching an audience that is most interested in the type of film being promoted.

In most cases the final cut of a film is not complete when the theatrical trailer is produced. There are companies that specialize in making movie trailers, and they often work from raw footage provided by the studio. You might remember cases when you have seen a shot in a trailer that does not end up in the final film. This happens sometimes when the final editing decisions have not been made for the film by the time the trailer is needed, and the people producing the trailer can only guess what will make the final cut. In other cases trailers contain material produced specifically for advertising purposes.

The style of trailers varies by market. There are often different versions of a trailer for domestic release and overseas release. American trailers are generally quicker in their cutting pace and put more attention on special effects and action than do overseas trailers for the same film. Overseas trailers generally use a slower editing pace with more emphasis on characters than action.

Trailers usually begin with logos of the companies that have produced and will distribute the film. The trailer then gives a strategic summary of the film, sometimes with the guidance of a narrator and/or a montage.

The primary objective of the theatrical trailer is to pique the audience's interest so they will invest their time and money to attend the film when it is released. For this reason, trailers strive to reveal enough about the film so that the audience wants to know more, but a trailer does not reveal so much that the audience feels they already know the essence of the story or its outcome. All trailers are designed to tease the audience and to invite them to come back for more.

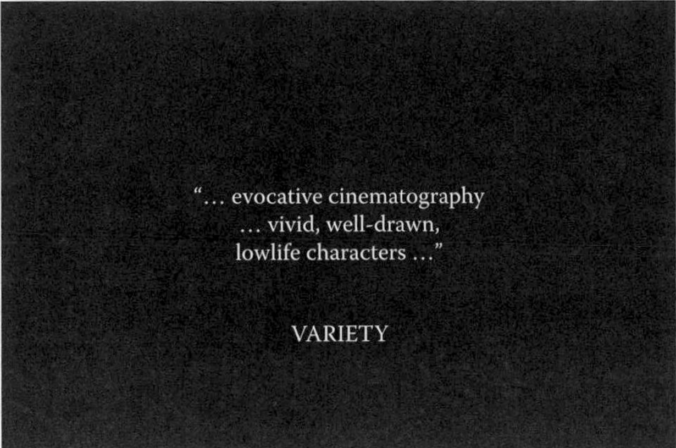

Figure 11.1 Trailers are a core component of film promotion. (Courtesy of Paul Schattel)

The end of a trailer sometimes indicates a release date or approximate time of release. For example, it may say, "Opening Christmas Day," or, "Coming This Summer."

Trailers are often produced with the aid of market research. If a focus group or sample audience does not like a film, sometimes a trailer will be used to reframe the general image of an upcoming film to make it appear more appealing. For example, a bittersweet drama about a divorced parent might not be well received by test audiences because it is too depressing. In this case, the theatrical trailer and accompanying television spots might highlight some of the film's upbeat and funny moments to frame the feature as a comedy. When an advertising campaign has to portray a film in a form other than its true genre, that usually spells box office disaster for the project. The objective of the marketing team, however, is to do the best that they can with tools available and the product at hand.

Trailers are also used as previews at the beginning of DVDs. These announce future DVD releases that match the genre of the title and also support an upcoming theatrical release. Since many films do not receive theatrical distribution and go straight to DVD release, DVD trailers are valuable for promoting future DVD titles. A trailer is also a valuable marketing tool for independent filmmakers seeking a distributor or financing to complete the postproduction of a project.

Most trailers are constructed for a general audience but this need not always be the case. If a trailer is bundled with like-rated content, such as an R-rated DVD, or if the trailer is used in some other restricted audience context, the trailer can contain restricted elements.

Thirty-Second Television Ads. The marketing campaign for the release of a major motion picture often includes the strategic placement of one or more 30-second television spots in advance of a film's release. Sometimes a television advertising campaign extends beyond the initial release of a film, particularly if the film finds an unexpected audience or if it wins major awards, which often creates a new wave of interest.

Thirty-second television ads, like the trailer, are designed to intrigue the audience without revealing the film's outcome. The ads must be tailored with content appropriate for the distribution channel. Broadcast television has standards that require certain limitations in the content used.

Both the theatrical trailer and 30-second spot are ideal methods for promoting a program through the Internet. If you cannot afford the media buys for television broadcast time, the Internet can make your promotional materials available to a wide audience.

Internet Promotion. The Internet is one of the most cost-effective and powerful resources in film and video promotion. Producers and distributors often set up domains dedicated to each individual project. These sites provide exclusive information about the film, help create advance interest in the program before its release, and are effective for long-term support of the project by promoting DVD sales. Web site traffic can be enhanced with contests, promotions, and discussion forums.

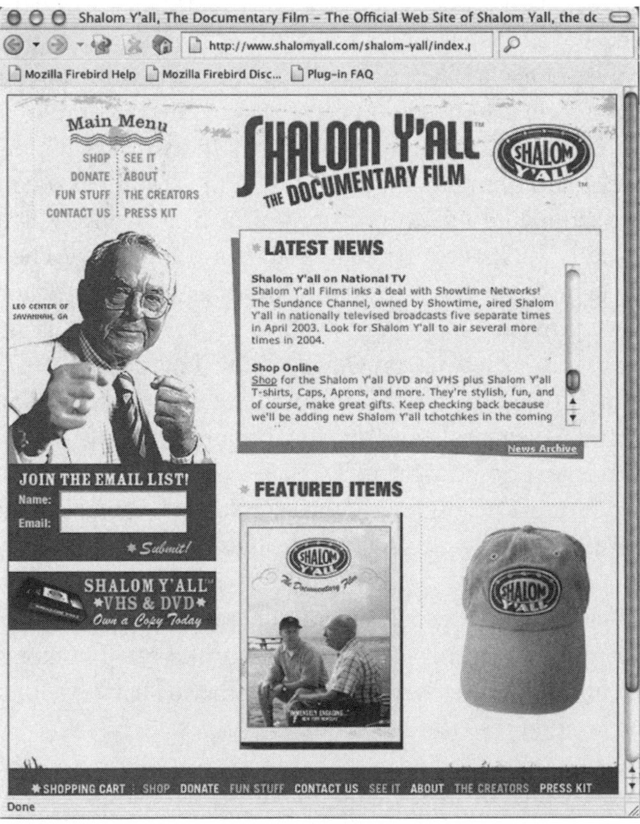

Figure 11.2 Internet promotion can be cost-effective and reach a wide audience. (Courtesy of Shalom Y'all Films)

In advance of the release of George A. Romero's fourth zombie epic, *Land of the Dead* (2005), NBC/Universal established a fan site and recruited members for its zombie army. Fans received points for returning to the Web site and answering trivia questions that required research about the film. Fans could redeem their points for promotional merchandise.

The trivia questions were changed regularly so fans returned for multiple visits. The points fans earned were ordered by rank, with the top earners' scores published on the main page. Fans could see their ranking among all users every time they logged on. This scoring system helped keep fans involved and active. Discussion boards and news links further kept the salience of the film and its release in the foreground.

Internet distribution of your promotional materials can be virtually free. Word-of-mouth communication and message boards can go a long way in getting the word out about your project's Web site. Major film releases support their programs' Internet sites with complex marketing plans including the use of search engine placement and banner ads on high-traffic sites and portals.

Print Materials. Promoting your project can also be enhanced with print materials. The marketing plans for films often include print advertisements in newspapers, magazines, and other print distribution channels such as postcards mailed to a targeted audience and handbills distributed at locations of interest to the target audience. Promotional posters are another popular option. Posters used in the promotion of a film are called **one sheets**. The most popular size one sheet is 27 by 41 inches. Small 8 1/2 by 11 inch or 11 by 14 inch versions are called mini one sheets, which are a good option for the independent filmmaker on a limited budget.

Press Relations. Reaching the audience directly is a valuable component in marketing a project, but getting the press to publish stories about your project for you is even better. Studios and distributors hire advertising and publicity agencies, which work with the media to disseminate information about a film and its release.

There are publicity Web sites designed exclusively for media writers and film reviewers. These sites are generally password-protected and only members of the press are given access. The sites contain electronic press releases with background information about the film and downloadable high-resolution images for publication to enhance articles that promote a film. These resources make the job of the press much easier, which results in more articles published.

While some smaller production companies use a printed portfolio with information about the film to facilitate promotion, the **portfolio press kit** is mostly a thing of the past for major film releases. Virtually all promotion for major motion pictures is done through the distributors' Web sites and through the distribution of **electronic press kits (EPKs)**. The electronic press kit is generally distributed as Internet files or on Beta-SP videotape, which is readily

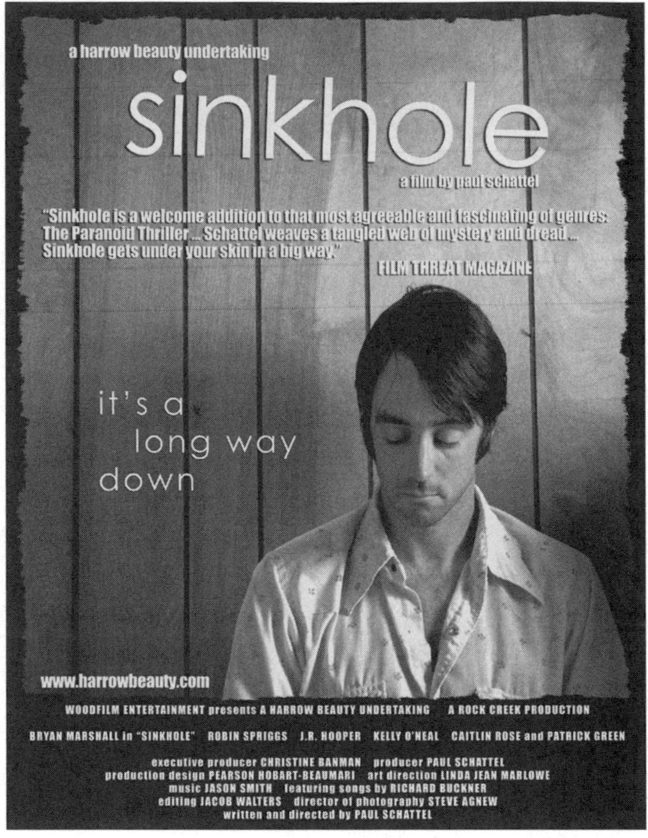

Figure 11.3 One sheet. (Courtesy of Paul Schattel)

Figure 11.4 A portfolio press kit and an electronic press kit (EPK) on Beta-SP videotape.

compatible with the editing facilities of most television stations. This allows broadcast reviewers to insert clips from a film into film review programs and news segments. The EPK also provides easily accessible background information for print writers and reviewers. An EPK will generally run about 30 to 45 minutes and contain clips from the film, interviews with the actors and crew, and a comprehensive set of the film's trailers and television spots.

Press Junkets. A **press junket** is a block of time set aside for massive media exposure to promote a project. A suite of conference space is reserved and the actors are brought in to conduct an intense series of interviews. A junket can run three days or more, and in that time each actor (and sometimes the director) gives dozens of interviews to reporters from all across the country.

Each actor is set in a specific space with the lighting preset and the background designed to further promote the film. Often a promotional poster for the project fills the background. The press is well cared for and fed in a separate wing of the conference center or hotel. Press participants include network news anchors and small town newspaper reporters. Security is tight at press junkets. Often there can be several top-name actors participating and access to them is strictly controlled. Closed-circuit television is in place and the interviews are monitored. Sometimes an interview turns into a personal attack on a celebrity rather than a discussion of the project. If this happens, a producer will usually interrupt the interview and politely but firmly let the reporter know that his time is up.

In many cases the video cameras for recording the interviews are provided for the media but sometimes major media outlets, such as nationally syndicated news programs, will set up their own equipment.

A press junket can be mind-numbing for the actors and the director. They are sometimes asked the same questions over and over and must work to make each telling of the tale as fresh as the first. For the actor, this might be the 50th time they told a story, but for the television audience in Cleveland, for example, it is the only insight they will get into the making of the film.

Never underestimate the importance of good press relations. It can cost a fortune to buy television commercial time and newspaper ad space, but when the media writes stories and positive reviews about your film, all of this golden publicity is essentially free.

Program Ratings. Film and television ratings affect the composition of the audience. As the audience changes, so do marketing and distribution strategies. If a film is not rated, most theaters will not exhibit it. Television content rated "TVMA," for mature audiences, is limited to certain time blocks in most cases.

The movie rating system is a voluntary industry effort governed by The Motion Picture Association of America (MPAA). A panel of industry peers reviews each film and makes its rating assessment based on objective criteria, such as specific language used and instances of nudity and violence. Subjective criteria are also used, such as an assessment of the context of the language or other restricted elements. Nudity in a serious hospital scene is likely to be treated differently than in a comic or sexual context.

Sometimes a film includes a single swear word or a brief flash of nudity, which results in a more restrictive rating. Paradoxically, a more restrictive rating sometimes draws a larger audience. In one study, 56 boys aged 10 to 14 were asked to read a program description and indicate if they would like to watch the program. Fifty percent wanted to see the film when they were told it was rated R, but not a single person (0.0%) said they wanted to see it when it was rated G (Cantor & Harrison, 1996). Film marketers know this and there was a significant scandal in 2000 when it was discovered that a film studio contracted a market research firm that used children as young as 9 years old to test R-rated films.

The MPAA rating system uses the following categories: G (General Audiences: All ages admitted), PG (Parental Guidance Suggested: Some material may not be suitable for children), PG-13 (Parents Strongly Cautioned: Some material may be inappropriate for children under 13), R (Restricted: Under 17 requires accompanying parent or adult guardian), and NC-17 (No One 17 and Under Admitted).

Film producers have the option to appeal a rating assigned by the MPAA. In some cases an appealed rating is changed without edits. In other cases the film producer alters the content of the film to meet the requirements of the MPAA to achieve a desired rating.

Broadcast television ratings are also based on a voluntary industry system. Since there is so much television content, an independent ratings board in not practical. Television programmers rate their own content and this rating is indicated in the margin of the screen, which can be used in conjunction with parental control features such as the V-Chip. Television uses both age- and content-based ratings. The age-based ratings include TVY (all children), TVY7 (directed to older children), TVG (general audience), TVPG (parental guidance suggested), TV14 (parents strongly cautioned), and TVMA (mature audiences only).

Critics considered this system lacking in context, so a content-based system was added, which indicates programs that contain violence (V), sex (S), offensive language (L), sexually suggestive dialogue (D), and fantasy or cartoon violence (FV). News and sports are not rated and cable television has its own systems of program advisories. Ratings are an important part of program marketing because they impact audience composition.

Cross-Promotion. In a **cross-promotion** a distributor teams up with another type of business that shares the same target audience. This creates a **synergy** and streamlines the expense of advertising and promotion for both companies. For example, a film release might be tied in to a soft drink maker. The soft drink advertisements utilize imagery from the movie, and the movie promotional items direct fans to purchase the soft drink for a chance to win a contest. Cross-promotion is often coordinated with product placement in a film. Since

Figure 11.5 Cross-promotion creates a synergy and benefits both companies. (Courtesy of Wild Bunch Films and Carolina Beverage Company)

these are not competing but compatible businesses, both companies gain by utilizing a cross-promotion.

Merchandising. The marketing of a film is often integrated with ancillary product merchandising. The production company need not get directly involved in the manufacturing of toys and T-shirts. The program's characters and images are often licensed to companies that specialize in making these products. Having toys and video games that mirror the content of a film creates a synergy of cross-promotion, a wider income base, and a diversification of revenue streams.

The Marketing Campaign. Effective marketing of a film or television series includes many elements converging together. The marketing techniques discussed above are combined with publicity tours in which the people involved

Figure 11.6 Merchandising enhances promotion and offers additional revenue. (Courtesy of Shalom Y'all Films)

in making the program, particularly the actors, are sent on the talk show circuit and other publicity events around the country. Publicity events are often combined with contests to get the public involved. Contest prizes are designed to further enhance promotion. By giving away T-shirts and hats with the program's title and logo, the promoters are basically recruiting people to walk around as living billboards.

Marketing is creative and coordinated selling. In some cases the budget for marketing exceeds the budget for production. Marketing is that important. Utilize marketing to promote your own work. It is a challenge to sell anything, but if you are selling something that you are proud of, the process can be rewarding. Recruit an audience for your programs and seek a return on your hard work. Marketing puts your work in the audience's mind, and distribution puts your work before their eyes.

Distribution

While marketing is the process of informing the audience about the existence of a program, distribution is the mechanism of actually making the content available to the audience. Distribution channels take many forms including movie theaters, broadcast television, cable television, DVDs, VHS, the Internet, cell phones, personal digital assistants (PDAs), and mini players.

Theatrical Distribution. Theatrical distribution is extremely competitive. There are a limited number of screens available. If a film does not test well with research audiences after its completion, it might not see theatrical distribution at all. If a film is released theatrically and does not do well its opening weekend, it is not uncommon for the feature to be pulled from theaters within a couple weeks. The opening weekend returns are absolutely critical to the theatrical life of a film. This was not always the case. It used to be more common that a film was given time to find its audience, but this model began to change after the summer of 1975. When *Jaws* was released it was expected to be a routine summer diversion movie—hopefully a successful one. Surprisingly, it blew away all earnings estimates, raking in $21 million in its first week alone, and by the end of its phenomenal run it had earned over $470 million. *Jaws* only cost about $12 million to make. This was the birth of the modern summer **blockbuster**, which helped change the way studios modeled distribution. The current studio distribution model puts paramount emphasis on the opening weekend. Films that lag are quickly pulled. Why is this the case? In part, this approach is due to the relationship between the distributors and the movie theaters. During the first two weeks of a film's release the movie theater usually keeps only 10% of the ticket sales. This ratio changes over time. The theater can earn as much as 80% of the ticket sales at the end of a run. When a distributor has a strong opening they earn more than if the same ticket sales are strung out over the course of two months.

Theatrical distribution comes in both first- and second-run. First-run theaters get films upon initial release and charge a premium price for admission. The second-run theaters get films after their first-run potential has been exhausted. Second-run theaters make films available at a later time for a reduced cost.

The means of theatrical distribution is usually the physical delivery of a 35mm print of the film. The distributor coordinates with the production

Figure 11.7 35mm physical prints are large and expensive. Video downloads are certain to play a larger role in theatrical distribution models in the future. (Ann Grover)

studio and processing laboratory to produce multiple prints, which are then shipped to theaters across the country. It is not uncommon for thousands of prints to be distributed for a major film's opening-day release. This is a substantial investment. It can cost millions of dollars simply for the production of prints.

Because of the tremendous cost of producing physical prints of films, strategies that allow electronic delivery of features to the theaters are in development. One viable option is to deliver programs to theaters through an encoded satellite downlink, which is exhibited through high-definition video projection.

While the distribution landscape for studio motion pictures is competitive, the situation for the independent filmmaker is even more challenging. Theatrical self-distribution of independent films is sometimes limited to individual arrangements with independent theaters on a one-by-one basis. For the independent film producer to be successful in these negotiations, however, an unknown film usually needs to have some sort of unique draw for patrons of the theater. If all or part of a film was shot in the same town of the theater, or if the director, producer, or lead actors have family roots in the community, there is a stronger chance that an independent theater will give the film an opportunity for exhibition.

The independent filmmaker should be prepared for the reality that success in theatrical self-distribution usually means one or two screenings at any single theater. It is not realistic to expect a theater to give up an entire week for an unknown film when that same screen time could be dedicated to a major release. Achieving theatrical distribution as an independent, beyond one or two screenings in a few cities, generally requires representation by a distribution company.

Distribution of independent films is mostly arranged on a percentage basis. The terms of each deal vary, but generally a distributor offers a film producer a percentage of revenue for the rights to distribute the film. Sometimes the cut for the film production company might be less than 10%. In other cases it can be 60% or more. The percentages can also change over time. A distribution deal might assign 10% of the receipts to the production company at the film's opening, but the terms could increase this percentage after a certain period of time or after the film's revenue hits the break-even point for the distributor.

Many distribution deals include a cash **advance**. An advance is used to make the deal more attractive to the film production company by offering an immediate payment upon signing. Some advances are modest, while other advances reach into the multimillions.

The production company must be vigilant in cutting the best deal possible. The best deal is not simply the fattest advance. The best deal often includes terms specifying the distributor's support of the project and a larger percentage of earnings. It can be better to sign a deal with a distributor that offers less cash up front, but with a guarantee that the film will be given a certain level of advertising support. This advertising can make the project go further in the marketplace and equal more dollars in the long run.

Sometimes the film production company pays the distribution company to release a film. This happens in cases when the distributor perceives a film as too risky an investment. A production company that feels strongly about their film, and has the money to spend, can enter a **service deal** in which they finance distribution. A service deal often results in a larger percentage of earnings going to the production company since they shoulder most of the risk. Even a limited theatrical release can greatly enhance DVD sales and the marketability of a film for cable and broadcast television. It also makes the film eligible for Academy Awards. For these reasons, some production companies pay for the privilege of distribution.

There is a tremendous amount of independent content out there and very little room on the slate of a theatrical distributor. For this reason, getting a distributor to even look at your material can be extremely difficult. The primary inroad for consideration by a distributor, outside of a personal contact on the inside, is film festivals.

Film Festivals. Major film festivals serve as markets for making film distribution deals. Film festivals streamline the job of the distributor. The format of film festivals is to have a committee of judges review films submitted to the festival and only the best, particularly in a major festival, are exhibited. This narrows the field for the distributor tremendously. While the distributors' representatives at the festival cannot attend every screening, discussions and buzz at the festival point the acquiring agents in the direction of films that should be reviewed.

Figure 11.8 Film festivals serve as forums for making distribution deals.

Further aiding the review process for the distributor is the awarding of prizes and special recognitions at festivals. Award-winning films at major festivals are particularly attractive for distribution consideration.

Television Distribution. While theatrical screens are greatly limited, television, by contrast, is a hungry animal. Consider that there are more than 120 broadcast, cable, and satellite channels available. If each channel runs 24 hours of content a day, that is a programming window of at least 2,880 hours *per day* that needs content. While film festivals serve as a primary deal-making platform for theatrical motion pictures, the National Association of Television Programming Executives (NATPE) annual convention is one of the primary brokerage forums for television programming. At the NATPE convention, program producers and distributors come together to make deals that put television shows on the air.

A few corporate groups control most television production and distribution. The independent television producer has a relatively small voice in today's market, but there can be opportunities. While it is not likely that an independent producer's first television series will be picked up for network broadcast, a niche cable channel with targeted content is more likely to take an interest in the creative work of the independent.

The independent television producer must often shoulder significant **front-end risk**. Distributors are not likely to pay for the production of a television series by an emerging producer based on a pitch or a pilot episode. They will often require a series of completed episodes before making a deal. This can require significant investment on behalf of the production company with no guarantee a buyer will be found. With innovation, creativity, good production

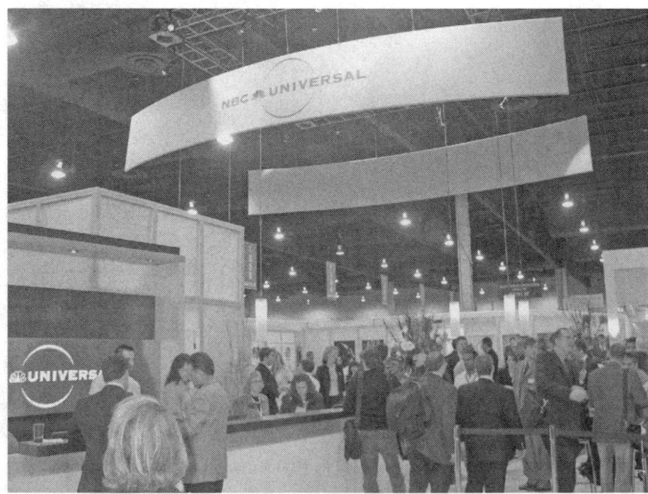

Figure 11.9 The National Association of Television Programming Executives (NATPE) convention is a primary forum for the buying and selling of television content.

Figure 11.10 Niche programming for targeted interests can help the independent enter the television market.

values, and content of interest to the audience, however, the independent can crack the nut of television distribution.

Television distribution channels are differentiated by type. There are the major broadcast networks and their affiliate stations. These include ABC, CBS, CW, Fox, and NBC. Public television stations are supported by public funds, viewer donations, and corporate sponsorship. Cable and satellite services include several tiers of programming. Some cable and satellite networks are predominantly advertiser-supported and are offered without a premium charge to subscribers. These networks include ESPN, CNN, HGTV, and MTV. Other cable and satellite networks are considered to be premium channels. Many are offered without advertising and subscribers pay a monthly fee for access. These channels include HBO, Cinemax, and Starz. Yet other channels provide content on a pay-per-view basis. The wide range of channels and funding models offers a number of options to the content producer for distribution.

The actual delivery of television content to the originating station is generally achieved through satellite transfer. Television networks feed their content to affiliate stations as the programs air. Syndicated content purchased for broadcast on television is also delivered by satellite, but this is generally not done simultaneously with public broadcast since different stations schedule content in different time slots. The **master control room** at a television affiliate station might be fed a half-hour game show every day at 4:00 p.m. The station has its equipment set to record this content for broadcast later that same evening.

Cable networks also deliver their content to each community's cable company via satellite. Direct broadcast satellite (DBS) television is sent by satellite to each consumer's home.

Figure 11.11 Master control room of a television station. (Joanne Hughes)

DVD. DVD is a popular and profitable distribution option for programs ranging from feature films to independent shorts. Features that never make it to theatrical distribution can often turn a profit on DVD sales alone. The DVD market for some theatrically released films can outperform the box office revenues. One way that studios increase DVD sales is to include bonus material that can only be acquired on DVD. The inclusion of interviews, extras, and behind-the-scenes footage makes the DVD more attractive, particularly to dedicated fans of the film and collectors. The predominant industry philosophy of DVD releases is to give the consumer something more than just a movie. For the independent film producer, DVD pressing is accessible and affordable, sometimes less than $1 per disc to press, making DVD a viable format for self-distribution.

To achieve wide availability, a DVD generally needs a distributor. Unless your DVD is in the catalog of a professional distributor it is difficult to get your program into mainstream resale sources including retail chain stores, major video stores, and major online retailers. Large retail companies do not have the time or inclination to deal with independent producers on a one-on-one basis. These companies work with distributors to build their retail product line.

The potential for an independent project to be picked up for DVD distribution is much more promising than theatrical distribution. Whereas theatrical distribution requires a commitment of a physical space, which is quite limited, DVD distribution is simply a matter of adding the product to the catalog and agreeing to represent the film to potential buyers for a commission. Distributors have to be selective in the films they represent. They do not want to be known as the company that handles a lot of substandard product, but a DVD

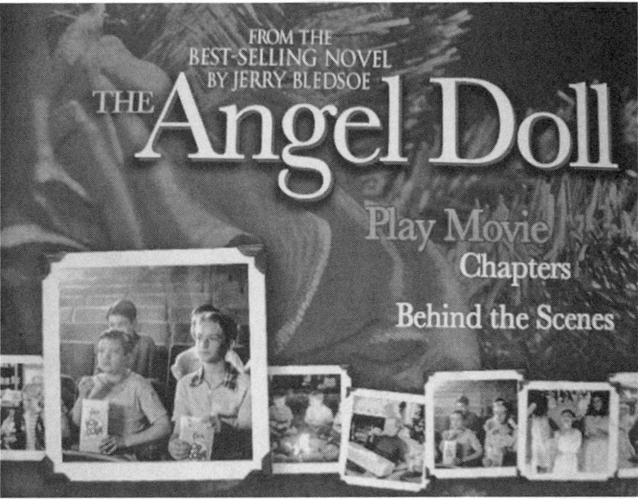

Figure 11.12 DVD menu design and bonus features are important value-added elements. (Courtesy of Wild Bunch Films)

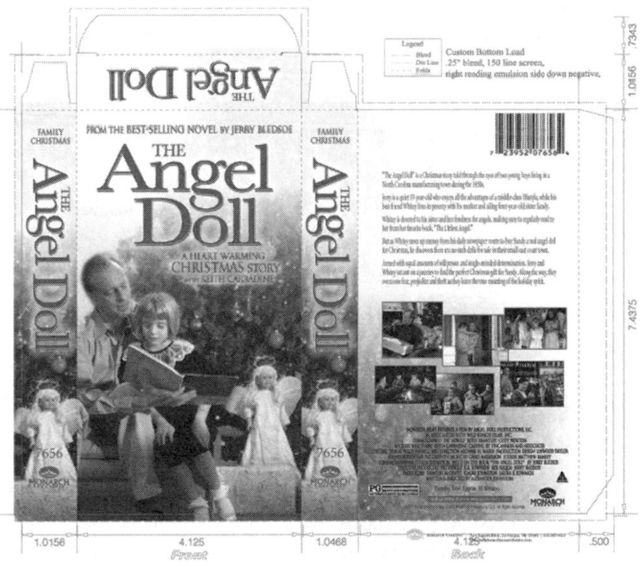

Figure 11.13 DVD and VHS box designs are critical for catching the customer's attention at the point of sale. (Courtesy of Wild Bunch Films)

distributor need not turn away a good film that fits its product profile because of space limitations.

Bonus features and graphic layout are important components of DVD authoring. How the menu looks, how it works, and what special features are included add significant value to the product. Applications such as DVD Studio Pro make professional DVD design accessible to virtually anyone with a personal computer and modest supporting hardware.

The **box art** is another important element in DVD design and distribution. Insert material is a value-added feature often included with a DVD. A foldout that provides a detailed description of the chapter contents, production stills, biographies of actors, trivia, and facts about the production is another attractive component for the consumer.

DVDs can be successfully self-distributed. With aggressive marketing at festivals, special events, word of mouth, and a presence on the Web, small independents can realize income from their productions.

DVD distribution is defined by region. DVDs are often encoded for playback only on machines in certain parts of the world. This allows control of different versions of a film to appeal to different cultural norms and helps control distribution in the world marketplace.

Some DVD releases retain the original aspect ratio and **letterbox** the image. These versions are identified as widescreen. Other DVD releases are modified to fill the screen of a standard television. These versions are referred to as full frame.

DVDs can be protected from unauthorized reproduction with the integration of copy protection encoding. This process adds to the cost of DVD manufacturing, but it helps preserve the market value of the program by reducing illegal copies in circulation.

VHS. VHS tapes are another means of program distribution. VHS manufacturing is more expensive than DVD and VHS tapes cost more to ship than DVDs. The market share for VHS is steadily eroding. VHS is also lower technical quality than DVD, and its linear form makes elements such as bonus materials impractical to include in most cases. For these reasons, many producers and distributors bypass the VHS market entirely, while others make this option available to reach consumers still using home videotape players as their primary system.

Stair-Stepping Distribution. We have explored a number of distribution channels that can be used to deliver a program to the audience. Most programs, however, do not select one single means of distribution at the exclusion of others. Distribution is often managed in stair-stepping manner. A feature film enters the market at the highest level possible. Theatrical distribution comes first. Theatrical release is then generally followed by DVD distribution, pay-per-view, and pay-television services. After those revenue streams are exhausted, the film is contracted for advertising-supported broadcast television. The film's distribution life can continue with sales to second-tier cable and repeated showing on broadcast television. Later there might be an anniversary edition that is theatrically released with new material, or perhaps an anniversary-edition DVD. A successful feature will exhaust every distribution option and revenue potential available. Keep in mind that this stair-stepping process is not a one-dimensional line. In addition to the domestic market, these various distribution channels are utilized in other regions around the world. The overarching marketing and distribution strategies for a major program are complex and can last for decades. It is not uncommon for a long-forgotten film to reemerge as a 10th, 20th, or 25th anniversary edition.

Piracy is an increasing concern affecting distribution strategy. Once a popular program is released in theaters it is often intercepted and illegally distributed. This hurts the revenue potential of the film, particularly for latter distribution channels such as DVD sales. Solutions to this problem are elusive. One solution strategy is a **uniform release date**, whereby a film is made available in multiple distribution channels simultaneously. If the consumer wants to go to the theater, they can. If the consumer wants to buy the DVD through the mail, that option is available at the same time. It will also be on pay-per-view. This uniform release approach has not been generally realized, but it is an emerging market strategy.

Internet and Small-Screen Distribution Channels. The Internet is an important channel for content distribution. **Webcasting** is the process of delivering streaming, compressed content. Webcasting can be done in real-time, in which case the entire audience views the program at a fixed time. Web-delivered content can also be stored on a server for the customer to retrieve any time. **Video-on-demand (VOD)** can be structured for download or as streaming content.

Compression technology and media storage capacity are continually evolving toward higher efficiency and lower cost. The result of this evolution is the migration of many traditional media outlets to online content delivery. Watching whatever happens to be on television is a thing of the past. Huge content databases offer consumers a virtually limitless menu of content options, which can be summoned for viewing on demand. Systems are in place, and others in development, that allow the permanent archiving and access-on-demand of all network broadcasts. Powerful search engines targeted specifically for audio and video files direct consumers to the enormous and growing databank of video programming accessible through the Internet. Blinkx is a leader in this area, with major portals Google and Yahoo following with the advent of Google Video and Yahoo Video. Anyone can publish video content and gain access to a mass audience through services such as YouTube.

Cellular phones, personal digital assistants (PDA), and compact entertainment tools such as Apple's iPod are expanding the horizons of program delivery. These channels are carving a significant market share of content distribution. Program producers need to be attentive to the needs of the consumer using a cell phone, PDA, or mini player with a small screen and unique user patterns. It is not reasonable to expect that large segments of your potential audience will want to watch a feature film on his or her cell phone, but on-demand movie reviews and news delivery are attractive content options for the commuter riding a train and looking to make constructive use of the time. A student learning to kayak can now watch an instructional video saved to

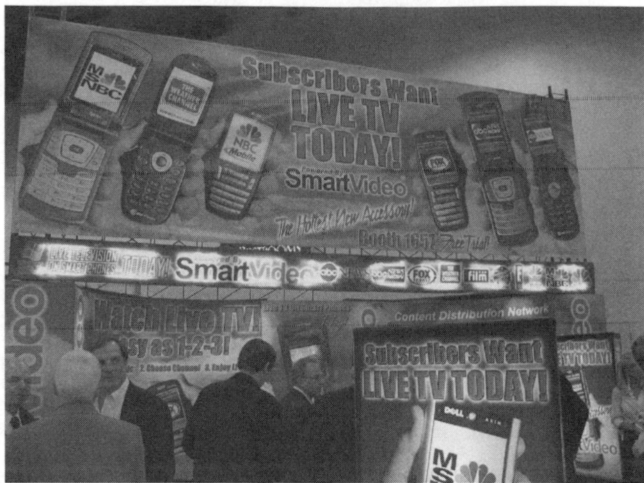

Figure 11.14 Industry attention is increasingly focused on small-screen distribution channels such as cell phones, personal digital assistants (PDAs), and mini players.

an iPod on the riverbank when the review is needed most. The channels for content distribution are wider in range now than ever before and this spells opportunity for producers.

CONCLUSIONS

We have dedicated the majority of our attention in this text to the elements of creating video productions. You now have a better understanding of how to market and distribute these programs.

There are many effective advertising tools used to market film and video productions. The theatrical trailer is a mainstay of the industry. The 30-second TV spot is also popular for supporting major releases. You can use these tools to promote your own programs by posting a trailer or 30-second spot on the Internet. The Internet can also be used for promotional Web sites that contain trivia, contests, interviews, DVD ordering information, and other exclusive content to attract an audience and support a project. Print materials used in film and television marketing include posters (one sheets), postcards, and handbills.

Never underestimate the importance of good press relations. Advertising space is expensive, so do what you can to facilitate the job of the press so they write stories about your project. Develop a Web site for press access and produce a portfolio press kit or an EPK.

Consider how a program rating will affect your marketing strategy and distribution options, and make sure to target your content to obtain the rating that fits your marketing and distribution model. Consider cross-promotion opportunities early in preproduction and integrate product placement during production to enhance a cross-promotion, if appropriate.

Merchandising can be as big or small as the market demands. Some programs generate more revenue in ancillary toy and game sales than in ticket sales. Virtually any scale entertainment program can utilize hats and T-shirts to spread the word of the project and generate additional income. When planning your marketing, think in terms of an overarching strategy and how you can effectively integrate various marketing elements to promote your project.

There are many distribution channels available. Consider how you can feasibly deliver your program to an audience. Film festivals provide a valuable forum for long-form program producers and distributors to make deals, but theatrical distribution is difficult to achieve.

A few large companies predominantly control television production and distribution, but there are opportunities for the independent producer in niche cable and satellite networks. DVD is a large market for content distribution and highly accessible to the independent. You can effectively pursue self-distribution on DVD and VHS. Keep your eyes on the horizon for developments in newer distribution channels. The Internet, cell phones, PDAs, and mini players are increasing market share and providing unique distribution opportunities for the innovative producer.

SAMPLE EXERCISES

1. Outline a complete marketing and distribution strategy for a program you have made or one that you would like to make.
2. Select one of your favorite films. If you were hired to design a cross-promotion for this film in partnership with another company, what company would you choose and why? Develop a cross-promotion strategy for this partnership.
3. Take one of the projects you have created and develop a plan to put it into distribution. Design the methods for delivering your program to your audience. You can host a public screening, press DVDs, and post your project on the Internet. Can you develop other distribution options for your project? How will you cover your expenses? Can you turn your program into profit?

RECOMMENDED READINGS

Bosko, M. S. (2003). *The Complete Independent Movie Marketing Handbook: Promote, Distribute and Sell Your Film or Video.* Studio City, CA: M. Weise Productions.

Cones, J. (1997). *The Feature Film Distribution Deal: A Critical Analysis of the Single Most Important Film Industry Agreement.* Carbondale, IL: Southern Illinois University Press.

Purcell, L. (2004). *Making DVDs: A Practical Guide to Creating and Authoring Your Own Disks.* New York: McGraw-Hill.

REFERENCES

Cantor, J. & Harrison, K. S. (1996). Ratings and advisories for television programming. In *National Television Violence Study.* Vol. 1 (pp. 361-410). Thousand Oaks, CA: Sage Publications.

12

PROFESSIONAL AND CAREER OPPORTUNITIES

CHAPTER OBJECTIVES

As you continue your study of video production keep an eye toward the horizon and build a foundation for your long-term career objectives. There are a number of tried and tested strategies that will benefit your professional development and enhance your career opportunities. Our final chapter explores these strategic options. The goals of this chapter are to:

- Examine internship opportunities;
- Introduce the power of networking and building personal contacts;
- Review the process of creating a professional show reel;
- Discuss film festival participation for student and independent filmmakers;
- Explore some hidden career opportunities in video production.

Congratulations! You now have an understanding of how to produce video projects across a range of formats and styles for varied applications. The final topic that we will explore is planning your course of action from here. The most important thing to advance your skills in production is to practice. Take advantage of advanced coursework in your area of interest. Make sure to explore some related electives outside of your major.

When young filmmakers are asked what they want to do, they often say, "I want to direct," or "I want to be an editor." However, when asked what they are doing to prepare for their objective, many students do not know what to say next. One error that some aspiring filmmakers make is to wait for something to happen to them, but that is not how you will get where you want to be. If you want to direct visual programs, then direct them. You might not be able to start with a high-budget feature, but you can make shorts on a regular basis.

Always be doing something. Always work toward your objectives, even on a small scale, and always put yourself in a position where you can expand your range of experience and opportunities. You should continually have a project in the works. Doing will get you there more than anything else. One of the best ways to enhance your skills and to gain practice is through a professional or academic internship.

Internships

Internships are one of the most valuable college experiences you can have. Potential employers are more impressed with someone who has been in a real work environment than someone who has not. All things being equal, a job opening will go to the candidate who has had an internship. Sometimes internships lead directly to full-time jobs. If an entry-level position becomes available at the company where you are interning, you have a tremendous advantage over external candidates. You are already in the door and know the people who make the hiring decisions.

Work hard during your internship. The executives with the power to hire know which interns come in late and which stay after hours. They know which interns talk on the phone with friends and the ones who ask, "Is there anything else I can do?"

There is often a great deal of turnover of entry-level employees in large organizations. In many cases, interns fill these positions. There might be, however, only one or two positions that become available in a large company and 10 to 20 interns at any given time. The positions are going to go to the best people. You need to work hard and put in long hours in an internship to open the door to greater opportunity. Your supervisor has contacts at many different companies and organizations, and will do his best to help you in your job search if you do a good job for him.

Internships vary in type in two main ways: unpaid versus paid, and academic credit versus no credit. Not surprisingly, the best internships are usually unpaid. The companies with popular internship opportunities, such as New York television headquarters and California film studios, do not need to offer compensation to attract interns. It is a tremendous opportunity in itself to intern at these organizations.

Some companies sweeten the pot to attract strong candidates. The companies that offer paid internships are often smaller operations. These businesses sometimes have limited resources and staff and utilize interns as a significant part of their work force. Since a paid intern costs a company less than a salaried full-time employee, the strategy of offering paid internships can be a viable economic model for some companies.

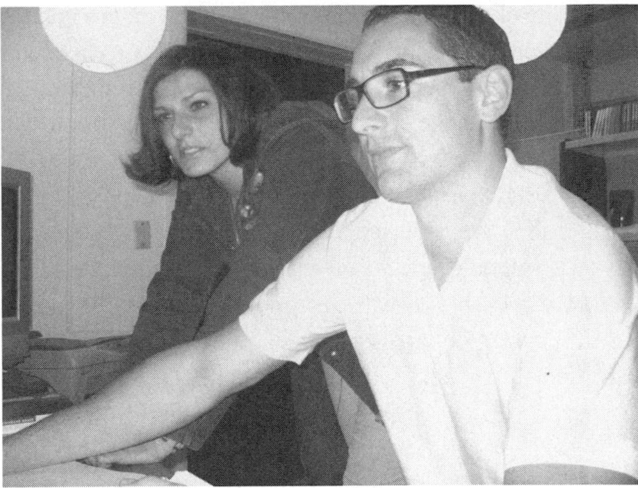

Figure 12.1 Internships offer opportunities for developing production skills and making professional contacts. (Jennie Picarella)

The size of an organization is not necessarily a predictor of the quality of an internship experience. Many large companies have excellent internship programs. Some large companies, however, allow interns to get lost in the big system. In a small company you will often find the opportunity to participate in a wide range of company functions and experience close mentoring. In other small companies, however, you will find people who exploit the free labor of an intern.

Remember that an internship is supposed to be a learning experience. You will be expected to work, but you should look for an internship opportunity where you will get mentoring and the chance to explore the range of what the company does. The best internships balance time for contributing to the company, observation, and mentoring.

Some college and university departments offer academic credit for student internships. This allows you to make progress toward your degree while obtaining a valuable professional experience. Internship programs at some companies are only available to students who participate for academic credit. This is done, in part, to stop people from using an internship as an excuse to gain access to a company solely for employment seeking rather than a comprehensive learning experience. While some companies require that their applicants participate for academic credit, many internship opportunities do not. Even if your academic department does not offer credit for an internship, it is still strongly advised that you allocate time for an internship experience in the course of your studies.

There are many schools of thought on when to take your internship. Sophomore year is the absolute earliest. Some advocate taking an internship later (junior year) so you have an even stronger technical skill and knowledge base at the beginning of the experience. Others suggest that your senior year is best because if an entry-level position becomes available, you are in a better position to be able to give an employment starting date as your graduation approaches.

An internship is a great way to test whether or not something you think you want to do is really something that you want to do. Many interns come away saying, "I've found my calling. I love this!" While others say, "I'm ready to change my major." Seek an internship that best fits what you think you want to do. You might find that the experience fits perfectly with your expectations or you may find that it opens doors to other opportunities. One student was sure she wanted to be a director, and was disappointed when her internship assignment was with the casting department instead of the directing unit. By the end of the internship, however, she was thrilled with the challenging process of casting, and found herself on a career path she had not even considered before.

Networking

While some job opportunities in video production are advertised in newspapers and trade publications, many are not. A large number of employment opportunities are discovered through networking. **Networking** is the process of cultivating personal contacts to help you in your job search. Do not keep your job search a secret. Let everyone know what you want to do and when you plan to be available. Networking works by utilizing the power of math. Say you know 30 people that can help you in your job search. If each of these people mentions your availability to four others, you now have a network of

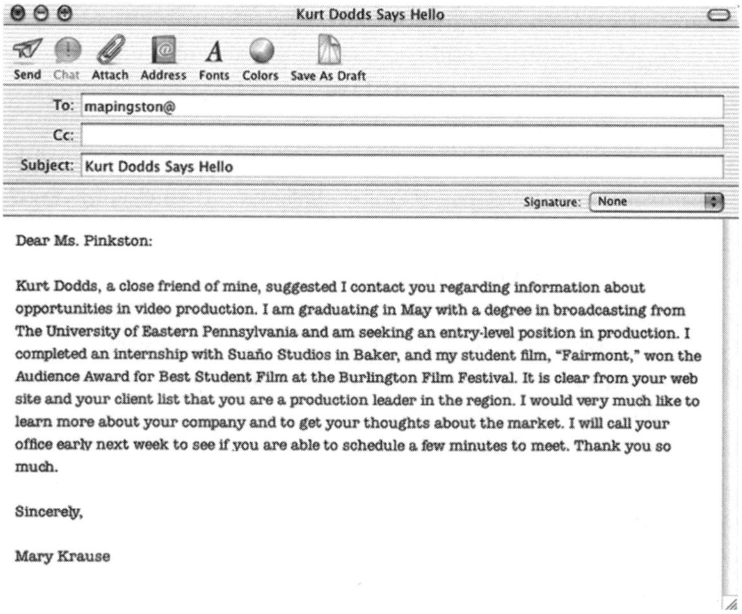

Kurt Dodds Says Hello

Send Chat Attach Address Fonts Colors Save As Draft

To: mapingston@

Cc:

Subject: Kurt Dodds Says Hello

Signature: None

Dear Ms. Pinkston:

Kurt Dodds, a close friend of mine, suggested I contact you regarding information about opportunities in video production. I am graduating in May with a degree in broadcasting from The University of Eastern Pennsylvania and am seeking an entry-level position in production. I completed an internship with Suaño Studios in Baker, and my student film, "Fairmont," won the Audience Award for Best Student Film at the Burlington Film Festival. It is clear from your web site and your client list that you are a production leader in the region. I would very much like to learn more about your company and to get your thoughts about the market. I will call your office early next week to see if you are able to schedule a few minutes to meet. Thank you so much.

Sincerely,

Mary Krause

Figure 12.2 Sample networking e-mail.

150 people. Carry the contacts out one more level and you are up to 750 people who are aware of you and your job search.

Often the attractive positions are never advertised because when a need arises within a company, it is often filled privately with an intern or through a networking contact. Get out there and make contacts.

Networking meetings are as important as job interviews. Use your contacts to set up brief meetings with the people who have the power to hire in the companies that interest you. Arrive at the meetings prepared with questions and make sure to ask your host if there is anyone whom she recommends you talk to. Ask if it is okay to use that person's name when you make future contacts. This is how your network grows. The ultimate goal of networking is to put you in communication with an employer that has a current or emerging need you can fill. Sometimes a networking meeting can itself create a job opportunity. There are cases of employers being so impressed with a job seeker during a networking meeting that they have created a position for them. More frequently, a potential employer will come back to you when a future need arises, but do not wait for the phone to ring. You need to make the follow-up. Organize your networking contacts into a notebook. Tape business cards that you have collected to the pages of your job search notebook. Make notes including the date of the meeting and important topics and job search ideas that were discussed. Follow up with each of your networking contacts every three months to let them know you are still on the market and to ask if they are aware of any new opportunities. This type of persistence is what lands many excellent positions. Do not discourage easily. Dig in for the search and try to enjoy and learn from the process.

Show Reels

Your show reel is your most important tool in job hunting and client recruitment. You are only as good as your last project and people want to see what you have done. Anyone can talk about video production, but to demonstrate what you have done in the past is the best indicator to others of what you will be able to do in the future.

While there is no single fixed format for the show reel, there are three general categories. Some show reels take a montage approach, utilizing a quick succession of images to show the candidate's range of experiences. Sometimes a montage is set to the project's original sound or to music. The construction of a montage show reel serves as a demonstration of the applicant's ability to edit.

Other show reels take a segment approach. These use fewer examples but take more time to put each example in context. While a montage show reel might show 30 or 40 different shots in just a couple of minutes, a segment show reel might only show clips from two to four projects, with each clip running longer. The viewer gets a better sense of the original project's context and pacing.

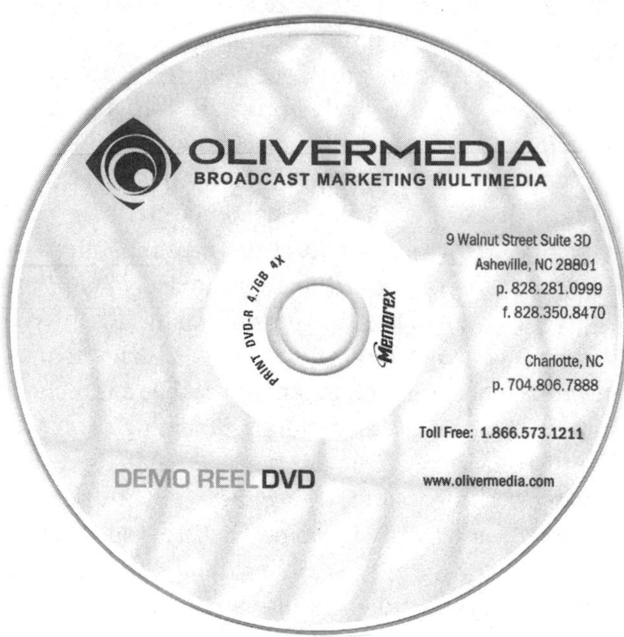

Figure 12.3 Your show reel is your calling card. Make sure you identify your contact information clearly. (Courtesy of Oliver Media Services, LLC)

The third general strategy for show reels is to combine these two approaches to create a hybrid. A hybrid show reel opens and/or concludes with a brief montage and includes a few program segments in greater context for the body of the reel.

It is often valuable to identify some key elements of your work within your show reel. It is common to use on-screen titles at the beginning of a segment to identify elements such as the project title, the name of the client (if it is a contracted work), the program's release date, and your role in the project.

Some people take a jack-of-all-trades approach in their show reel and seek to illustrate that they can do a variety of jobs. Others make their show reel more targeted and demonstrate their work in one area, such as editing or cinematography. There are trade-offs to each of these approaches. Which one will be more effective comes down to what the employer is seeking. A small company might be impressed with someone who can shoot and edit effectively, whereas a larger company looking specifically for an editor might be more drawn to the candidate who is framing her editorial talents exclusively.

A professional show reel usually runs about two to six minutes. At least two minutes is generally required to give a range of examples and to show that you have a significant body of work. A show reel over six minutes is too much for the reviewer's needs in many cases. There can be over 100 applications for a position in a production house and each applicant submits a reel. You need to get the employer's attention and make a good impression quickly.

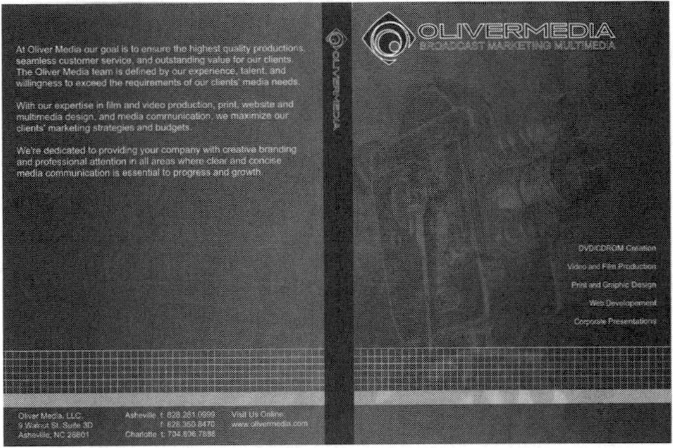

Figure 12.4 Show reel box art design should be clean and professional. (Courtesy of Oliver Media Services, LLC)

Make sure to identify the running time on the reel itself and on the storage case. If your reel concludes with your strongest material, then you want the viewer to know that your show reel is three-and-a-half minutes long. Otherwise they might feel they have a good sense of your work at the three-minute mark and miss your big conclusion.

Also identify the disk and storage case with your name and contact information. You want to make it as easy as possible for an employer to contact you. Many people lead their show reel with their name and contact information as titles. It is also valuable to close the show reel with this information as a final impression.

The exact style of your show reel is a personal choice. Some show reels are cut fast, while others are melodic. Some are set to music, while others make extensive use of audio tracks from their projects. Take the programs you have created into the editing room and see what catches your attention as you watch your projects again. You might find that the assembly of your show reel is a natural and organic process. Share your show reel draft with trusted friends and colleagues. Let them know you want their honest assessment so you can make your show reel even better. Your show reel should be considered an evolving work in progress. Whenever you do something new and outstanding make sure you update your reel. Most show reels are distributed on DVD, but VHS is requested in some cases. You might want to have some of each format available. Carry your show reel with you if you visit a film festival. You never know whom you might meet.

Film Festivals

We discussed film festivals as a tool used for the marketing and distribution of professional films in chapter 11. Film festivals are also an excellent platform for student and emerging filmmakers as well. Your first student projects will not be screened at Sundance or Cannes, but as your work matures in quality you are likely to find a forum for competitive public exhibition.

There are hundreds of film festivals in the United States each year. Film-festivals.com has a searchable database by location and date. It is possible to visit a film festival every weekend of the year in the United States. You are certain to find a film festival within driving distance of your home. Many film festivals have student divisions, and many strive to support regional filmmaking and student filmmaking. Entry fees for student works, in many cases, are less than $30.

Because there are entry fees associated with most film festival participation, you will have to be selective in which festivals you choose to enter. A benefit of entry fees is that it keeps aggressive self-promoters from blanketing every festival, and this provides a greater opportunity to have your work screened at the festival of your choice.

Carefully read the rules of each film festival you are considering. Some only accept work that was shot on film, others only projects shot on video. Some festivals require that your work be produced within the last 12 months, not yet been submitted to a festival, or only submitted to a limited number of festivals.

You can research individual festivals and submit entries one at a time or by using a consolidation service. Many professional and student filmmakers use the online network Without a Box (http://www.withoutabox.com) to streamline the festival entry process. Filmmakers submit one standardized entry form, one copy of their project, and one press kit. They can submit multiple entries from a selection of over 1,000 unique festivals around the world using Without a Box's interface.

If your work is accepted into a film festival and you are able to attend, you will have the opportunity to personally present your work and receive feedback in discussions with audience members, peers, and film professionals. Film fes-

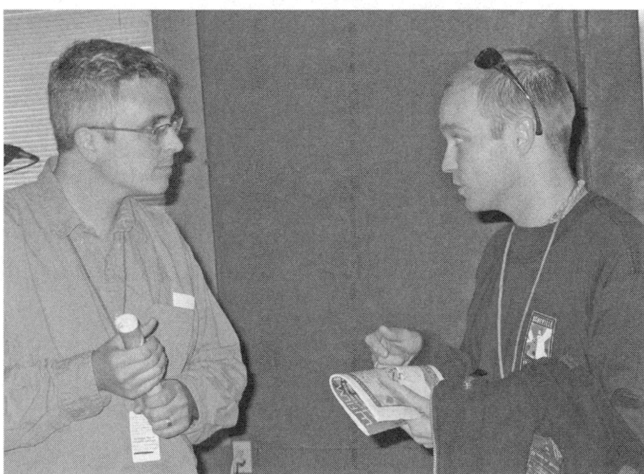

Figure 12.5 Film festivals allow student filmmakers to meet potential collaborators and are dynamic learning environments.

tivals are dynamic networking opportunities. Collaborations are established at festivals as filmmakers exchange business cards and say, "We should do something together." In other cases a filmmaker meets a producer who says, "I like what you do. Let's see if we can work on something down the line."

Winning a prize at a film festival is a great boost for any filmmaker and the life of a project, but is not necessary to obtain significant recognition. If your project is selected for screening, such selection and screening is itself recognized as a meaningful accomplishment. A screening committee watches every work submitted and makes their selections before the final slate of films is presented to the audience and festival judges. A large percentage of submitted projects are rejected.

Since potential employers and clients do not have the ability to watch the full-length version of everyone's work, having your work screened in a film festival signals potential employers that your work has already gone through a rigorous competitive process and has been judged. There is a lot of junk circulating out there. If your work is festival-screened, it is more likely to get an employer's attention.

Opportunities in Video Production

There are many professional opportunities in film and video production. We have explored many of these opportunities throughout the text including working with local television stations, advertising companies, production houses, as well as major film and television studios. The employment opportunities list also includes positions in industry, state and federal government, nonprofit organizations, religious organizations, academia, health service organizations, and self-employment.

Most large corporations, such as IBM and General Motors, have in-house video production facilities and staff to create internal and external communication programs. Hospitals are another potential employer with needs ranging from education to community relations programs. Universities often have in-house production departments to serve the academic needs of the campus and produce material for external communications. Web design studios often generate full-motion content within banner ads and stand-alone video content for Web sites. These design studios need artists with the video production skills to make motion pictures come to life for Internet delivery.

While animation studios create their programs with drawings and computer programs, the storytelling methods and visual design elements are the same as those we have studied here. This is also the case for video games, which are more like films than ever before. The visual design, virtual camera moves, and narrative structure of video games often follow the core principles of film and video production. The video game industry provides another opportunity to apply your visual storytelling skills.

Figure 12.6 The same principles of the visual language used in live-action also apply to animation and video games. From the animated short *Nightlite.* (Greg Bliss)

How far you can go in production depends on a lot of factors including skill, timing, persistence, and a little bit of luck. There are several markets that are centers for film and television production. New York City; Wilmington, NC; and Orlando, FL are relatively large production centers. Vancouver and Toronto enjoy significant production activity due to cost advantages. If, however, you want to get into the heart and soul of the industry, insiders advise that it is best to move to Los Angeles.

Every year untold thousands of aspiring film and video production artists make the migration to Southern California. A lot of them find they do not have the drive or skill necessary to make it, but if you have the passion you can find opportunities in L.A. The classic entertainment industry tale still holds true today: Head out west, share an apartment, take on part-time jobs, and always be networking and knocking on doors. Don't be discouraged easily in any job search. It can take weeks just to get a viable interview and many months before an offer for employment happens.

There is a joke that every waiter in Los Angeles is also an actor. That holds some truth. Those looking to break into the industry often work in restaurants, as message couriers, and as production assistants. Here is the secret to these jobs: Newcomers to Hollywood do not work in restaurants just to pay the bills. There is a strategic reason for serving tables. The key is to work at the *right* restaurants, where the executives have their meetings. It does not go over well to give your resume to a director who is trying to eat dinner. There can be an occasion, however, when friendly conversation between server and patron leads to an opportunity.

Message couriers also have a great inroad. Their job is to travel to studios and executive suites to deliver packages and documents. A lot of these packages are sensitive materials and designated to be hand-delivered to an industry insider. Once again, it is the personal contact that might lead to something bigger.

Working as a production assistant can also open doors. There is the legend of the production assistant who was asked by a gaffer to move a cable for him because he was precariously hanging from a ladder. The production assistant says, "I can't touch it. I'm not in the union." The gaffer, in danger of falling, responds, "Grab the cable and I'll get you in the union." While the reality is not as simple as this legend suggests, the general principle applies. Being on a production set yields opportunities.

There was a young kid who gained access to the Universal Studios lot and made friends with the right people. He was quiet and observant at the right times, drinking up all he could learn like a sponge. He also spoke up at the right times, letting the people at the studio know he was an original and creative thinker. The kid was Steven Spielberg, who later directed *Jaws* (1975) for Universal at the age of 28. If you have talent, drive, creativity, and persistence, you can break into the Hollywood system.

Once in a while there is a revolutionary change within the industry that opens up tremendous opportunity. In the early 1990s there was a transition from linear editing to nonlinear computer-based editing. There were so few people trained with the skills to do this at the time that the studios were actually scrambling to employ competent nonlinear editors. If you were in Hollywood at the time and knew computer-based editing, you could have written your own ticket into a major studio.

It is impossible to predict when the next revolution like this will occur. Be alert to industry happenings and trends. Monitor trade publications and be willing to adapt and act quickly so that you are on the leading edge as new technologies and techniques emerge.

Going Independent

Going into business for yourself offers flexibility and total self-direction. As an independent you can choose the kind of work that you want to do and can operate from virtually any location. Many freelancers get started by buying basic production and editing equipment, but this is not necessary. You can get started by renting equipment as needed on a project-by-project basis.

There are significant production needs of businesses and consumers in every market. The freelancer or independent can step in to offer these production services. Using your show reel, you can enter a bid with an advertising agency to produce a commercial. With some additional study and practice in advertising design, you can approach clients directly and produce television ads in your community. Producing industrial videos for businesses in your region is another needed service that independent filmmakers can provide.

Do not overlook the direct consumer-services market. Wedding videographers work primarily on weekends and can make upwards of several thousand dollars per event. The creative practitioner finds opportunities beyond obvious consumer services. One video producer approached a local church. It turned out that for special church events, such as the annual Christmas play, parents overran the floor scrambling to take home movies. The producer offered a solution. She would be the official videographer for the congregation, thereby

a

b

Figure 12.7 Production opportunities for the independent range from (a) direct consumer services to (b) big budget features. ([a] Zygmunt Knochowski; [b] Photo by Jim Bridges, courtesy of Wild Bunch Films)

having only one unobtrusive camera during the event. Parishioners could buy a copy of the program for a nominal fee and the church got a free copy for their archives. The parents could enjoy the events without worrying about taking pictures. Everybody won, and the videographer expanded the service to other area churches.

As an independent producer, you can certainly think bigger than the boundaries of your community. Be looking for the next innovative program concept and big moneymaker. A top-selling program one Christmas season was a fireplace video. People who did not have a fireplace in their home could play a real-time image of a fire on their television for several hours. Needless to say, this program was extremely inexpensive to produce, but the simple concept ended up making a lot of money.

One of the greatest success stories of a simple concept going big is the story of The Baby Einstein Company. Julie Aigner-Clark and her husband, Bill Clark, created a video for small children called *Baby Einstein* (1999). The program showed images of toys, which were accompanied by music and voice-overs of words, numbers, and stories. The elegance of the project was in its simple design. The program was sold to parents though a regional retail chain and it was so popular it went national. The Baby Einstein Company grew into a multimillion-dollar business from that one simple project and was eventually sold to The Walt Disney Company.

The Internet allows anyone to develop a marketing campaign for his or her independently produced product. With creative use of **meta tags** and a modest investment for advertising placement, you can have access to a global market for your productions.

Business Forms

If you decide to go into business, it is important to consider the many forms your business can take. Once someone pays you for your production services then you are in business. The most simple business form is the **sole proprietorship**. You generally do not need to file any paperwork to establish a business as a sole proprietor, but you might need to register your business name. As the name suggests, a sole proprietor is personally responsible for all profits, losses, and legal liability. If you operate in the same manner but with the collaboration of one or more other people, then you are engaged in a **general partnership**. This form also includes personal liability of each partner. While formal action is usually not required to establish a general partnership, the drafting of agreements with the aid of an attorney is advisable.

More complex business forms include the **limited partnership**, the **limited liability partnership (LLP)**, and the **limited liability company (LLC)**. These forms offer specific liability limits and protections for the owners. A **corporation** is a legal entity that is distinct from those who form it, and it is distinct from its shareholders. Each of these more complex business forms requires the filing of specific legal paperwork for establishment. The definitions and registration procedures for each of the business forms discussed here (and others not listed) vary by state law. If you decide to go into business, make sure to research the laws of your state and employ the aid of an attorney and an accountant to make sure everything is done correctly.

CONCLUSIONS

There are opportunities for making money in video production. It is wonderful to be able to earn a living doing something you love. Building toward a career does not have to be the only objective for advanced study of digital video production. Filmmaking is an art form—a means of self-expression. You now have the skill base and tools to put forth ideas that are important to you in a form that has the potential to reach a wide audience.

Understanding how to make motion pictures also equips you to better appreciate motion pictures. When you view movies you will pick up more of the nuances, subtleties, style, and techniques used. Before this course you spoke the language of the audience. Now you also know the language of the filmmaker.

Close this book and go see a good film. If you are a true filmmaker at heart, the experience of watching a good film will inspire the next step—to pick up your camera, put your eye to the viewfinder, and your vision to the world.

SAMPLE EXERCISES

1. Research the internship policies of your academic program and conduct a search to find internship opportunities that interest you.
2. Use your contacts to set up an informational networking meeting with a production company or mass communication organization in your community.
3. Create a show reel. Update the reel regularly and always have a new project in the works.

SUGGESTED READINGS

Baber, A., & Waymon, L. (2002). *Make Your Contacts Count: Networking Know-How for Business and Career Success.* New York: Amacom.

Gore, C. (2004). *The Ultimate Film Festival Survival Guide.* Hollywood, CA: Long Eagle.

Morgan, B. J., & Palmisano, J. M. (2004). *Film and Video Career Directory: A Practical, One-Stop Guide to Getting a Job in Film and Video.* Detroit: Gale Research, Inc.

APPENDIX A

SAMPLE RELEASE FORMS

Music Rights Agreement
Performance Release
Location Contract

MUSIC RIGHTS AGREEMENT

This Synchronization License Agreement (hereinafter "Agreement") is made and entered into this the ____ day of __________, 20___, by and between _______________ (hereinafter referred to as "Licensor") and __________ _____________, its successors, assigns, licensees and designees (hereinafter collectively referred to as "Filmmaker") .

In consideration of mutual covenants and conditions contained herein, the parties hereby agree as follows:

Licensor grants to Filmmaker the nonexclusive, irrevocable right, license, privilege and authority to arrange, use and record the musical composition(s) and recording(s) entitled ____________________________________ composed by ______________________________(hereinafter the "Musical Composition") in synchronization or timed relation with the film production tentatively titled ________________________________ (hereinafter the "Film").

Licensor authorizes Filmmaker to use or cause to be used the Musical Composition in conjunction with the Film in any manner Filmmaker deems fit, including, but not limited to, the exhibition, promotion, advertising, exploitation, and/or publicizing of the Film and the right to license the Musical Composition in conjunction with the Film throughout the world on any medium or forum, whether now known or hereafter devised. In addition, this License constitutes a direct license of any and all performance rights which may become payable in connection with such permitted uses and Filmmaker need not make any payments or obtain performance rights society licenses in connection therewith.

In consideration of the rights granted hereunder, Filmmaker shall accord credit to the composer(s) and publisher(s) of the Musical Composition, provided that the manner, form, and frequency of such credit shall be determined by Licensee in its sole discretion.

The term of this license shall commence upon the date set forth above and shall continue in perpetuity. The territory of the License is worldwide.

Without limiting the generality of the terms set forth above, Filmmaker shall have the right to alter, expand, adapt, edit, add to, subtract from, remix, combine with other material, and make any arrangements and/or derivative works of the Musical Composition, and Filmmaker will have the sole right to determine whether and in what manner the Musical Composition will be advertised, publicized, performed, or exploited, if at all. In connection therewith, Licensor irrevocably waives its so-called "moral rights."

Licensor hereby represents and warrants that he/she/it has the full and exclusive legal right, power, and authority to enter into this Agreement and to make and grant the representations, warranties, and agreements contained herein and that the consent of no third party is required for Filmmaker to fully exercise his/her/its rights hereunder. Licensor warrants, represents, and agrees that Licensor will obtain in writing all requisite consents and permissions of labor organizations, the copyright owners and the Artist (if applicable) whose performances are embodied in the Musical Composition and that Licensor will pay all re-use payments, fees, royalties, and other sums required to be paid for such consents and permission, in connection with Filmmaker's use of the Musical Composition.

Licensor hereby indemnifies and agrees to hold harmless Filmmaker from any and all claims, liabilities, demands, causes of action, losses, costs, fees, damages, or obligations of any kind (including attorneys' fees), which Filmmaker may suffer or incur or become liable for, directly or indirectly, arising from any breach of Licensor's warranties, representations, or covenants under this license, or in any way arising from, related to, or concerning Filmmaker's use of the Musical Composition.

Accepted and Agreed To:

Licensor

By: ____

Its: ____

Address: ____

____

Telephone: ______________________________________

Filmmaker

____

Address: ____

____

Telephone: ______________________________________

For illustrative purposes only: Not intended as legal advice

PERFORMANCE RELEASE

I, the undersigned, on behalf of myself, my heirs, executors, and administrators, do hereby grant to ______________________________, its successors, assigns, licensees, and designees (hereinafter collectively referred to as "Filmmaker") the right to photograph me and to record my voice, performances, actions, poses, and appearances, and to use my voice, picture, photograph, silhouette, and other reproductions of my physical likeness in connection with the motion picture tentatively entitled ______________________________ (hereinafter referred to as the "Film").

I hereby grant to Filmmaker the perpetual right to use, at Filmmaker's sole discretion, my name, biographical material, and any and all still and motion pictures, sound track recordings, and records which Filmmaker may make of me or my voice, in or in connection with the Film, including, but not limited to the exhibition, promotion, advertising, exploitation, and/or publicizing of the Film throughout the world. I further grant to Filmmaker the right to reproduce in any manner whatsoever any recordings, including all instrumental, musical, or other sound effects produced by me, in connection with the production and/or postproduction of the Film. I specifically waive any right to compensation I may have for any of the foregoing.

I hereby indemnify and agree to hold harmless Filmmaker from any and all claims, liabilities, demands, causes of action, losses, costs, fees, damages, or obligations of any kind (including attorneys' fees), which Filmmaker may suffer or incur or become liable for, directly or indirectly, arising from, related to, or concerning or the use of my name, biographical information, physical likeness, voice, and sound in the Film as herein provided.

I certify and represent that I am over 18 years of age and have read the foregoing and fully understand the meaning and effect thereof.

Name: ______________________________

Address: ______________________________

____

Telephone: ______________________________

Signature: ______________________________

Date: ______________________________

Name of Character: ______________________________

For illustrative purposes only: Not intended as legal advice

LOCATION CONTRACT

Permission is hereby granted to ______________________, its successors, assigns, licensees, and designees (hereinafter collectively referred to as "Filmmaker") by _________________________ (hereinafter referred to as "Owner/Agent") to use the property located at ___________________ __________ (hereinafter referred to as the "Property"), for the purpose of photographing and recording scenes (interior and/or exterior) for motion pictures, with the right to exhibit all or any part of said scenes in motion pictures throughout the world, at the Filmmaker's sole discretion. The Filmmaker shall own all rights in and to any and all photographs and recordings made in or on the Property forever and for all purposes. The Filmmaker shall have no obligation to pay any fee or other consideration for the exercise of the rights granted under this contract. The permission granted herein includes the right to bring personnel, equipment, props, and temporary sets onto the Property, and to remove same after the completion of filming.

The above permission to use the Property is granted for a period of ___ Days & Weeks, beginning on ____________________________ (Day & Date) and ending on ______________________________ (Day & Date).

The Owner/Agent does hereby warrant and represent that the Owner/Agent has full right and authority to enter into this contract, and that the permission of no other person, firm, or corporation is necessary to enable Filmmaker to enjoy full rights to the use of the Property as granted herein. The Owner/Agent does hereby indemnify and agree to hold harmless Filmmaker from any claims, liabilities, demands, causes of action, losses, costs, fees, damages, or obligations of any kind (including attorneys' fees), which Filmmaker may suffer or incur or become liable for, directly or indirectly, arising from, related to, or concerning a breach of this warranty.

No addition to, or modification of, any terms or provisions of this contract shall be effective unless set forth in writing and signed by the parties.

Date: ____________________________________

____

Filmmaker

____

Owner/Agent

____

Printed Name of Owner/Agent

Address: ____________________________________

____

Telephone: ____________________________________

For illustrative purposes only: Not intended as legal advice

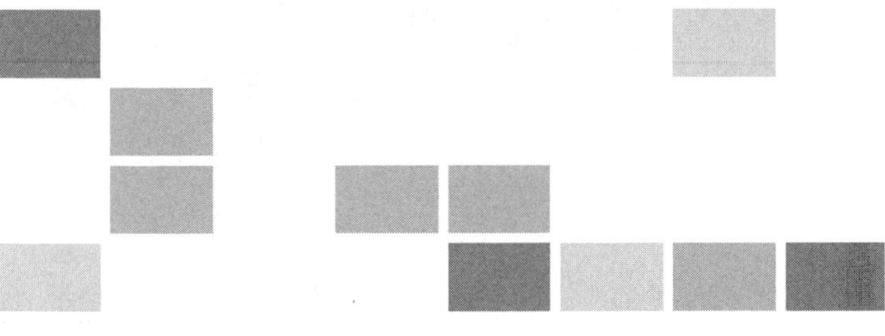

APPENDIX B

STORYBOARD TEMPLATES
4:3
16:9

(4:3)

(16:9)

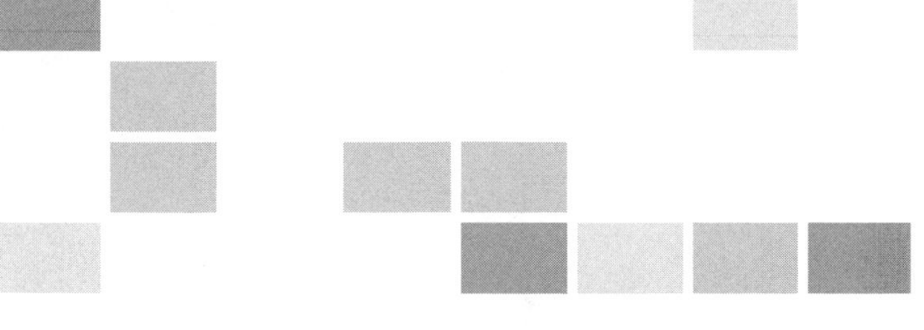

APPENDIX C

SUMMARY BUDGET TEMPLATE

PROJECT TITLE:________________________________

PRODUCER:
DIRECTOR:
WRITER:

LOCATION:
SHOOT:
SHOOT DATE:

BUDGET PREPARED BY:

BUDGET DATE:

Acct#	Description	Page #			Total
	STORY, RIGHTS, CONTINUITY				
	PRODUCERS UNIT				
	DIRECTION				
	CAST				
	TRAVEL & LIVING				
	FRINGES				
	ABOVE THE LINE TOTAL				
	PRODUCTION STAFF				
	EXTRA TALENT				
	SET DESIGN				
	SET CONSTRUCTION				
	SET OPERATIONS				
	SPECIAL EFFECTS				
	SET DRESSING				
	PROPERTY				
	WARDROBE				
	PICTURE VEHICLES/ANIMALS				
	MAKEUP & HAIRDRESSING				
	LIGHTING				
	CAMERA				
	PRODUCTION SOUND				
	TRANSPORTATION				
	LOCATION				
	PRODUCTION LAB				
	CREW OVERTIME				
	FRINGES				
	PRODUCTION PERIOD TOTAL				
	EDITING				
	MUSIC				
	POST PRODUCTION SOUND				
	POST PROD. LAB				
	MAIN & END TITLES				
	FRINGES				
	TOTAL POST PRODUCTION				
	INSURANCE				
	FEES AND CHARGES				
	TOTAL OTHER				
	TOTAL ABOVE-THE-LINE				
	TOTAL BELOW-THE-LINE				
	ABOVE & BELOW-THE-LINE				
	TOTAL FRINGES				

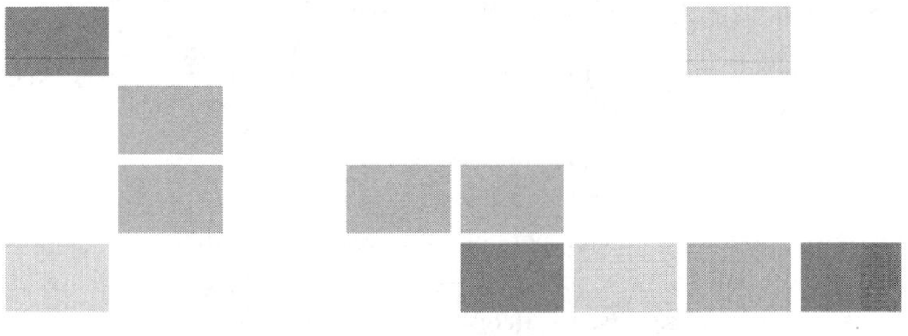

GLOSSARY

180-degree rule — A principle of shooting and editing that allows a camera to take any position on one side of an imaginary line. Application of this rule helps maintain *spatial continuity* while violating the rule can easily disorient the viewer.

above-the-line expenses — Budget categories that include story rights and salaries and benefits for the producer's unit, *director,* and *actors*; generally negotiable expenses.

Academy Flat — A popular *aspect ratio* for *widescreen* motion pictures; the ratio of the width of the screen by its height is 1.85:1.

act — A structural unit of screenwriting and production; a major unit of a story. There are generally three acts in films. The act structure for television varies depending on the program length.

actor breakdown — A planning document that lists which *actors* are needed on each day of a production.

actors — The performers who portray the *characters.*

adaptation — The translation of a story from literature, theater, or other medium into one for the screen.

additive color — The process by which colors are created with light. Mixing variations of the three *primary colors* of light together (red, green, and blue) can create virtually any color possible.

ADR — See automated dialogue replacement.

advance — A prepayment that is offset against royalties or future earnings; often used by distributors to entice a production company into signing a distribution deal by offering an immediate cash payment.

advertising copy — The text of a television commercial or other advertisement.

AGC — See automatic gain control.

amplitude — The height of a sound wave from crest to trough; a measure of the loudness of a sound.

analog — A signal that corresponds to the phenomenon it represents in a continuous manner; usually represented by waves that vary in *amplitude* as the characteristics of a sound or video source vary. Analog signals contain significant noise and degenerate when copied.

analytic editing — Starting with a whole idea and then breaking that idea down into its component parts; often implemented visually through the use of *deductive scene construction.*

anchor over video — A news story in which the anchor reads a script to prerecorded video during a live news telecast.

angle — The direction from which a camera is pointed toward a subject.

antagonist — The villain in a story; the one who creates obstacles for the *protagonist.*

aperture — The adjustable opening in the camera body or lens that regulates the amount of light reaching the imaging surface.

aperture control — A camera setting that regulates the amount of light that reaches the imaging surface.

aperture ring — A control on camera lenses that can be turned to regulate the amount of light passing through the lens.

A-roll — The primary footage shot in a *documentary* interview.

aspect ratio — The relationship of the width of a film or video screen compared to its height.

atmospheric track — A sound recording of an environment used to maintain continuity in sound editing; often exterior environments. Compare *room tone.*

audio limiter — A control that sets a maximum recording level of an audio signal; generally used to prevent overmodulation and distortion.

audio mixer — A device used to control audio levels and to combine several audio sources into one or more composite signals; also the person who operates this device.

auteur — French for "author"; used to describe directors with a commanding style and unity of vision.

auto focus — A camera control option that uses an infrared signal or other sensor system to judge the distance of objects from the camera to set the focus.

automated dialogue replacement (ADR) — The process of replacing lines of *dialogue* in *postproduction* by rerecording them while the performer watches a playback of the scene on a screen; also called "looping."

automatic gain control (AGC) — A recording control that automatically adjusts the audio levels to achieve full saturation; also a camera setting to boost the *video gain control* automatically to the ideal level for image reproduction in low light conditions.

available light — Light that exists in an environment without adding any additional artificial lighting.

axis of action — An imaginary line that defines where camera positions can be set to maintain proper screen direction. When two *characters* are interacting, the axis of action usually connects them along their line of sight.

back light — A light that is pointed toward the back of a subject; used to provide definition and to separate the subject from the background.

background light — A light that is pointed toward the background to illuminate what is behind a subject.

backlight setting — A camera control that overrides the automatic *aperture control* to let in more light; often used in amateur videography to achieve proper foreground exposure when people are standing in front of windows.

backstory — The imagined history of *characters* that happened before the story begins; used to guide *screenwriters* and *actors* in creating more realistic portrayals.

ballast box — A regulator used to control the amount of current flowing to an electrical device; often used with *HMI* lights.

bang zoom — A fast zoom; often achieved in manual mode.

barn doors — Metal flaps on a light housing that can be positioned to exclude light from certain parts of a set.

base illumination — The amount of overall, even light in an environment that is in place before creative lighting elements are added.

below-the-line expenses — Budget categories that include most every expense of a production other than story rights and salaries and benefits of the producer's unit, *director* and *actors*; generally fixed expenses.

best boy — The *gaffer* or *key grip's* first assistant.

bin — Folder in a nonlinear editing system used to organize and store audio and video clips.

binaural — Hearing that utilizes two ears for stereophonic perception.

bit player — An *acto*r who has a few lines of *dialogue* but not a prominent role in a project.

blanket license — A license agreement, often used with music, sound effects, and stock video footage, that allows the license holder to use the resources for an unlimited number of projects in exchange for the payment of a single license fee.

blimp — A sound-dampening cover used to reduce film camera noise.

blockbuster — A film that attracts a large audience and produces huge gross earnings.

blocking — Planning the placement of *actors*, *props*, and equipment on a set, and the movement of *actors* and the camera.

boom operator — A member of the sound team who positions the *microphone* with a *boom pole*.

boom pole — A long pole used to hold a *microphone* out of the camera's field of view.

bounce card — A portable flat surface used to reflect light; often made of foam core or synthetic material mounted on a wire frame.

boundary microphone — A specialized *microphone* that is used to record indirect sounds.

box art — The design elements of DVD and VHS packaging.

breakdown — A translation of the script into various components and categories (*actors*, *props*, locations, etc.); often cross-referenced by scene to facilitate scheduling and production planning.

B-roll — Secondary footage; shots used to add visual variety and to exemplify the topic in *documentary* and news interviews.

call sheet — A document circulated in advance of a shoot that provides essential information for the cast and crew such as the location, time to report, and objectives for the day.

camera crane — See crane.

camera operator — The crewmember who does the actual recording with a film or video camera.

capacitor microphone — A microphone that uses an electrically charged plate as the pick-up element; generally less rugged and more expensive than a *dynamic microphone*, but also more sensitive.

captured — See digitized.

cardioid microphone — A directional *microphone* with a heart-shaped pick-up pattern.

casting agency — A company that specializes in matching available roles with appropriate *actors*.

casting director — The primary person who selects the *actors* for a project.

CCD — See charge-coupled device.

characters — The people or other beings who populate a story; often classified as *major characters* (the main focus of the story) and *supporting characters.*

charge-coupled device (CCD) — An imaging surface made of an array of light-sensitive capacitors; used in digital photography and videography.

CinemaScope — A widescreen format that was popular in the 1950s and 60s with an *aspect ratio* of 2.35:1.

cinematographer — An artist who creates images with a motion picture camera.

Cinema Verite — French meaning "true cinema"; a documentary style that originated in France in the 1960s; known for using interviews to uncover a deeper reality that is normally hidden.

circumaural headset — Audio *headphones* that completely cover the ears.

clapper/loader — The crew member who is responsible for loading film magazines and holding the scene *slate*, or *clapperboard*, in front of the camera to identify each shot.

clapperboard — See *slate.*

climax — The dramatic peak of a story; the moment when the *dramatic question* is answered.

clip — A contiguous segment of sound or video in a nonlinear editing program.

close-up (CU) — A *shot* that isolates details of objects; composition of a human subject that includes the head and shoulders.

CMOS — See complementary metal-oxide-semiconductor.

CND — See cumulative noise damage.

color constancy — A human perceptual phenomenon that allows us to perceive objects as staying the same color even though various lighting conditions actually cause the color of objects to change quite a bit.

color correction — The process of using filters to change the color characteristics of light to match the needs of a situation; often used in mixed lighting situations to standardize light sources to emit the same *color temperature.*

color temperature — A method for defining the color of light using a numerical scale; reported in degrees Kelvin.

complementary colors — Any two colors that produce a shade of gray when mixed together; the opposite color of a *primary color.* Using a colored filter will reduce or exclude the complementary color.

complementary metal-oxide-semiconductor (CMOS) — An imaging sensor first introduced to digital video in 2005; easier and less expensive to produce than *charge-coupled devices.*

completion guarantee — An insurance policy that guarantees a project will not be halted due to budgetary overruns; often used as an incentive to secure financing.

complication — An obstacle faced by the *protagonist.*

composite character — A fictional person used to represent the combined traits and experiences of two or more actual people.

composition — The arrangement of elements within a frame.

compound lens — See zoom lens.

concept — The main elements of a story; often described in a sentence or two. Similar to *log line.*

continuity — Having the elements of a scene match up correctly from one shot to the next.

continuity error — A mistake caused by editing shots together that do not match.

contrast range — The range of brightness that can be handled by a medium between its rendering pure white and pure black.

contrast ratio — The ratio of varying brightness levels within a *composition*.

copyright notice — Legal copyright protection enacted by publishing the word "copyright" or the copyright symbol (©) followed by the year of publication and the name of the person or company that owns the work.

copyrighted work — A form of intellectual property that is protected by law; cannot be reproduced or otherwise infringed upon without permission of the copyright owner.

corporation — A legal entity that exists separately from its board members, employees, shareholders, and founders.

crane — A support system that can raise a camera into the air for dramatic vertical camera moves.

crawl — Credits or other titles that move across the screen.

creative producer — A *producer* who participates in the creative development or execution of a project; often a *screenwriter* who collaborates beyond the submission of the script.

crisis — The main confrontation between the *protagonist* and the *antagonist*; the scene in which the *dramatic question* will be answered.

cropping — Changing a *composition* by cutting along the edges and making the *frame* smaller.

cross-fade — An audio or video transition in which one element *fades out* while another *fades in*; also called a *dissolve* in the case of video.

cross-promotion — An arrangement between a program *producer* or *distributor* and another company that shares the same target audience to implement a coordinated marketing campaign that promotes both companies.

CU — See close-up.

cucoloris — A metal template placed in front of a lighting source that is used to create a patterned lighting effect.

cumulative noise damage (CND) — A loss of hearing resulting from long-term exposure to loud noise that affects both frequency range and perceived loudness.

cut — One *shot* immediately following another.

cutaway — A *shot* that shows an object or detail that is outside of the main action of a *scene*.

cut-in — A *shot* that reveals details within a *scene*.

dailies — The footage shot each day; often screened by the director later that same day or the next.

daily hot cost — A daily report that details the budgeted and actual expenditures of recurring expenses.

daily production report — A document produced by the *unit production manager* (UPM) that reports daily progress on a project compared to the day's goals; often used to keep producers and investors informed of progress.

day for night — The process of simulating nighttime shots that are actually filmed during the day; often achieved with a combination of filter use and exposure control; can also be added as a computer effect in *postproduction*.

deductive scene construction — A form of editing that starts with a wide field of view and then moves in to show relevant details; the primary approach used in the *master scene method*.

deferment — An agreement to delay receipt of payment until after a project is completed and revenue comes in. Can be based on a flat rate and/or a percentage basis.

demonstration format — An advertising style that shows how a product works; often-linked with elements of ease and convenience.

depth of field — The range of distance from the camera in which elements appear to be in focus.

destructive editing — An editing system that erases or irreversibly alters the original source material once an editing modification has been made.

dialogue — Spoken words in a video program; a conversation between two characters.

diffused light — Light that is softened; indirect light.

diffusion filters — Filters used to soften light and to make it less direct; often made of frosty plastic materials or sheets of spun synthetics.

digital — A method of transmitting or storing information that uses discrete numbers or other symbols to represent data.

digital zoom — A method of magnifying a portion of an image by electronically processing the signal. The result is often a grainy and pixilated image.

digitize — Importing material into a nonlinear editing system.

Direct Cinema — A *documentary* style that originated in the United States in the 1960s that values noninterference with the subject and editing in chronology.

direction arrows — *Storyboard* notations to indicate *character* or object movements in a shot.

director — The leading creative artist on a project.

director of photography (DP) — The artist in charge of creating the visual elements of a project; often supervisor of the camera, lighting, and *grip* units.

disk-based audio recorder — A field recording unit that captures sound information directly to a computer hard drive.

dissolve — A video editing effect in which one shot *fades out* while another shot simultaneously *fades in*. Also called a *cross-fade*.

documentary — Nonfiction works that present factual information in an informative manner.

dolly — A wheeled support system that allows the camera to be moved smoothly.

dolly grip — The crew member responsible for placement and movement of a wheeled camera support used for moving shots.

dots — Small disks, often mounted on wire rods, used to block light from hitting areas of a set or subject; used for discrete control of limited areas.

double scrim — A *scrim* that reduces light intensity by one *f-stop*.

double-system — Recording sound and image using separate equipment and putting the elements in sync in *postproduction*.

DP — See director of photography.

draft mode — Editing in low resolution to save storage space. See *off-line editing*.

dramatic question — Will the *protagonist* succeed in his or her objective?

dramatic structure — A formula for telling stories which often includes exposition, inciting incident, complications, crisis, climax, and resolution.

dramatic time — The measure of time according to the events of a story; often accelerated or condensed to compress long periods of time for dramatic effect.

dynamic microphone — A magnetic induction microphone that uses a moving coil to register sound information; generally more rugged and less expensive than a *capacitor microphone*, but also less sensitive.

ECU — See extreme close-up.

edge numbers — A numerical coding system integrated into the margin of film stock that allows the creative decisions made in a computer-based editing system to be matched up with the camera negative.

edit decision list (EDL) — A log of the creative editing decisions made during the *off-line editing* process (draft mode), which is used to conform the material in the *on-line editing* phase (high-quality mastering).

EDL — See edit decision list.

EI — See exposure index.

electronic press kit (EPK) — A publicity package containing press releases, publicity photos, project facts, video clips, and interviews that is distributed to the media through Internet access, videotape, or other electronic delivery. Compare *portfolio press kit.*

ensemble cast — A group of *actors* of comparable status who portray a set of *characters* with equivalent significance to the story.

epilogue — The final segment of a television *episode,* also called the *tag,* which is often used to set up the next episode; a brief postscript that occurs after the formal resolution to a story.

episode — A unit of measurement in television to define each individual program within a *series.*

EPK — See electronic press kit.

EQ — See equalizer.

equalizer (EQ) — A sound-processing device that can increase or decrease the *amplitude* of specific frequency ranges.

establishing shot — A *shot* used to define the location where a *scene* takes place; often a wide shot that occurs at the beginning of a scene.

executive producer — A *producer* involved in financing a production or a person who makes a valuable creative or administrative contribution to getting a project off the ground.

exposition — The background information that the audience needs to join the story; often revealed in the beginning of a program.

exposure index (EI) — The light sensitivity rating of a medium; reported as a numerical value.

exterior shot — A shot recorded outside.

external communication — A message designed for an audience outside of the organization that produced it.

extra — An *actor* who appears on camera for a brief peripheral role without any lines of *dialogue.*

extras breakdown — A listing of how many *extras* are needed for each day of a production and their demographic characteristics.

extreme close-up (ECU) — A *shot* that isolates intimate details of an object; an extreme close-up of a person often features the subject's eyes.

eye light — A discrete light used to highlight a person's eyes.

eyeline — An imaginary line that follows a person's line of sight.

eyepiece focus — A setting on the camera used to adjust the viewfinder for individual eyesight variations.

fade-in — A video-editing effect in which the screen starts out black and an image gradually emerges; the same can be achieved in audio by gradually going from silence to sound.

fade-out — A video-editing effect in which the screen gradually goes from an image to black; the same can be achieved in audio by gradually going from sound to silence.

feature — A long-form project with a running time of 70 to 80 minutes or more.

festival release — A legal release by a copyright owner to allow a filmmaker to use music or other material for the purposes of entering a project in film and video festivals only; also a legal release granting permission to have a work screened in a *film festival.*

field mixer — A small, portable *audio mixer.*

field monitor — An external video monitor connected to the camera that is used to review material during *production*; often used by the *director* to supervise the image during the shooting process.

fill light — A light used to fill in the shadows created by the *key light.*

filter factor — A numerical value used to rate camera filters based on the amount of light they absorb; used to make *aperture* corrections for proper exposure.

filter frames — An external frame on a lighting instrument or camera lens that allows filters to be attached and changed quickly.

financial producer — A *producer* whose participation on a project is centered on providing funding or managing the project from a business and accounting perspective.

first assistant director — The *director's* primary assistant; often in charge of keeping the crew on task and on schedule.

fish eye — An extreme *wide-angle lens*; often distorts objects close to the lens and elements around the edges.

flag — A piece of black material mounted in a wire frame that is used to block light.

flicker fusion rate — The frequency at which an intermittent image appears to be a constant image.

flood setting — A control position that sets a lighting instrument to casts a wide beam over a large area.

floor manager — The person who coordinates and the activities on a television studio set on behalf of the *producer* or *director.*

fluid head — A *tripod* mechanism that is in contact with the camera and filled with a viscous oil to allow smooth *pans* and *tilts.*

focal length — The distance from the center of the lens to the *focal point*; also the level of magnification of a lens.

focal plane — The location, as indicated on the outside of the camera body, of the imaging device within the camera.

focal point — The fixed point at which light passing through a lens will converge with maximum sharpness.

focus group — A market research method that tests advertising concepts and products with actual consumers.

focus puller — The camera crew member responsible for changing the focus setting on the camera during a *shot* to accommodate for moving camera, moving subjects, or to shift the viewer's attention.

Foley — The craft of creating *sound effects* in a studio using *props* to achieve various effects.

footcandle — The amount of light that is evenly cast on one square foot by a light source of one candlepower from a distance of one foot.

frame — The boundaries that define the edge of an image; also a single image of motion picture within a series.

Fresnel lens — A lens used in lighting instruments that is made with concentric circles of glass rather than a single convex surface to reduce its size and weight.

front-end financing — Funding that is paid or committed before a project is produced.

front-end risk — An investing arrangement in which one or more parities put their money into a project up front and assume liability for loss if the project is not successful.

frost material — Filter material that looks like a frosty window which is used to diffuse a light source.

f-stop — A numerical value used to indicate the amount of light passing though an *aperture*; a mathematical ratio of the size of the optical hole in a lens and the *focal length* of the lens.

gaffer tape — Tape used by the lighting and *grip* crews to secure objects and cables; looks like duct tape but is made of cloth and does not leave a sticky residue.

gaffer — The head of the electrical department; supervisor of setting lights.

gator grip — Spring clamp with teeth used to attach lighting and *grip* equipment to stands or other surfaces.

general partnership — A business formed by two or more persons. The partners are personally responsible for all profits, losses, and liabilities.

graduated filter — A camera filter that changes its level or quality of filtering from one side to the other.

grant — A funding resource opportunity often provided by nonprofit agencies, governmental units, and private endowments.

grip — A lighting and rigging technician; also equipment used by members of the grip crew to rig equipment.

grip stands — Metal stands used to hold lighting accessories.

half scrim — A *scrim* that covers only half of the lighting instrument.

hard effects — *Sound effects* that are in sync with the picture.

HDTV — See high-definition television.

headphones — Compact speaker system worn over the ears to monitor sound during the recording process and to check recorded sound in playback.

headroom — The space between the top of a person's head and the top of the motion picture frame.

head-to-head method — Positioning two *microphones* with their pick-up elements right next to each other; used to avoid *phasing* when mixing two microphones down to a single channel.

Hertz — A measurement of cycles per second; often used in audio to define the frequency of a sound.

high-angle shot — A shot looking down on a subject; often conveys a sense of submission and weakness.

High-Definition Television (HDTV) — A television broadcasting and display standard that is of significantly higher quality than *standard television*. HDTV operates in 1,080 lines of horizontal *resolution* and a 16:9 *aspect ratio*.

high-key lighting — Bright overall illumination; often used in comedy and happy scenes.

HMI light — Hydrogen medium-arc-length iodide. A lighting instrument that uses an arc of electricity between two contacts instead of a filament; highly efficient lighting that is balanced for daylight.

holistic continuity — A psychological approach to *continuity* that puts the emphasis on viewer perception and consistency within the syntax of a particular project rather than a set of predetermined rules.

Hollywood style of editing — See master scene method.

hook — An element of interest in a script or program designed to get the audience engaged.

Hypercardioid — A directional *microphone* with a pick-up pattern that is more narrowly focused than a *supercardioid* microphone, but not as narrow as an *ultracardioid* microphone.

IFB — An interruptible feedback earpiece. A device worn in the ear of news anchors to allow them to hear instructions from the *producer* in the control room.

image stabilizer — A camera setting that electronically processes the video signal to remove small variations of camera movement from the image. Not generally used by professionals because it reduces image quality and the effect often looks unnatural.

implied consent — The agreement to use ones image and likeness in a news interview that is assumed by virtue of agreeing to talk to the *reporter* on camera.

import log — A planning list of shots used to *digitize* material into an editing system; often created by the *editor* while reviewing *window dubs.*

in-camera effect — Any signal processing that is achieved by the camera before the image is recorded. Some cameras allow the use of fades, dissolves, and rudimentary titles. Generally intended for amateurs and home video use.

incident light — Light that is coming toward a surface or subject.

incident light meter — An instrument designed to measure the amount of light falling onto a subject or a set.

inciting incident — An event that places the *dramatic question* of the story into motion.

inductive scene construction — An approach to editing that presents a scene in various *close-ups.* The context of the situation is created in the mind of the viewer though a synthesis of the *shots,* like building a puzzle.

industrial film — Training or promotional video produced for a business.

in-point — The starting frame of an edit.

instructional film — A nonfiction program that seeks to achieve specific learning objective; often presents material in a highly structured form.

interior shot — A *shot* that takes place indoors.

interlace scanning — The process used by standard video cameras and monitors by capturing or displaying information on the odd-numbered horizontal lines, then the even-numbered horizontal lines, and then back to the odd lines in recurring succession. Compare *progressive scanning.*

internal communication — A message that is designed for an audience within the organization that produced it.

inverse square rule — A principle of lighting intensity: Each time you increase the distance between a light source and a subject by twofold, you decrease the intensity of the light on the subject by fourfold.

iris — See aperture.

jib arm — A camera support system that includes a pole asymmetrically mounted on a tripod. A camera is placed on the long end of the pole and counterbalancing weights on the other; used for vertical camera moves of moderate range.

jump cut — A *continuity error* in which objects change position from one shot to the next.

juxtaposition — To put next to; to place side by side.

key frame — A frame of a *clip*, often the first frame or one that is selected by the editor, which is displayed as a thumbnail image in a computer-based editing system.

key grip — The head of the *grip* crew.

key light — The light that is used as the main source of illumination.

key out — Removing an area of a particular color or brightness level from a shot to allow the insertion of other content; the process used in creating *matte effects.*

kicker light — A small light used to increase the illumination on a specific, limited part of a set.

lap dissolve — Short for "overlap dissolve." See *dissolve.*

lavaliere microphone — A small *omnidirectional microphone* that is usually attached to a person's shirt.

leadroom — The open area in a composition in front of a moving person or object.

lens hood — A protective cover of a camera lens, which also helps reduce *light flares.*

letterboxing — The process of masking the unused portion of a frame with black bars to present *widescreen* content on standard screens without *cropping* the original image.

light flare — A streak of light appearing in an image from sunlight or other light sources entering the lens at a severe angle.

light meter — A tool used to measure the amount of light in an environment to aid in proper *aperture* setting.

limited liability company (LLC) — A business form offering limited liability to its owners; a popular option for small businesses.

limited liability partnership (LLP) — A business form offering limited liability to the partners; a popular option for companies in which all partners wish to have an active role in the management of the company.

limited partnership — A business form that contains both general partners, who actively manage the company, and limited partners, who serve as investors and receive dividends. The limited partners do not participate in the day-to-day operations and have reduced liability.

line level signals — Audio signals that are amplified and often used for transfer between various components such as cameras, mixing boards, and CD players.

line producer — The *producer's* representative on the set; often manages the budget and reports back to financial and administrative producers with updates and areas needing intervention.

linear editing system — Equipment that manipulates film, videotape, or other media that is in roll or cassette form; requires accessing the exact physical location on the original source material for each element needed. Compare *nonlinear editing (NLE).*

linear media — Recording media that store their information in a line (roll or cassette forms are common). Film, videotape, and audiocassettes are examples of linear media.

LLC — See limited liability company.

LLP — See limited liability partnership.

location release — A legal contract granting permission to use private property and images and sound gathered at that property.

location scout — The crewmember who travels to potential shooting sites in advance of a production to plan where filming should take place.

locked — A version of a film or video edit that the *director* has determined is in its final shot sequencing and final running time; a necessary step before all *sound effects*, *musical scoring*, and *visual effects* can be added since these elements require conforming to a determined running time.

log line — A brief articulation of the main elements of a story; a single-sentence project description used for promotion.

long shot (LS) — A composition that frames a subject from a distance and often puts a subject in context of the surroundings.

low-angle shot — A shot filmed from a low camera position; often coveys a sense of dominance and power.

low-key lighting — Overall dark and high contrast lighting; often used in horror and suspense scenes.

LS — See long shot.

lux — A unit of illuminance; there are approximately 10.75 *lux* in a *footcandle*.

lyrical editing — A form of editing that varies shot length in a sophisticated pattern like a symphonic progression.

macro photography — Extreme close-up recording that is achieved by using a lens in the *macro setting*.

macro setting — A control that allows the lens to focus on objects very close to the camera.

magic hour — The time of day after sunset but before nightfall.

magic lantern — A tabletop unit that projects hand-painted glass slides or photo reproductions onto a screen using a lens and lamplight; introduced in the West in the late 17th century and a popular entertainment device until the end of the 19th century.

master — The original version of a completed video project; also an abbreviation for *master shot*.

master control room — The "nerve center" of a television station where content is played back from tapes and drives, satellite feeds are managed, commercials are inserted, and the television signal is calibrated and transmitted to the public.

master scene cut-in — See master scene method.

master scene method — A standard technique for editing scenes that uses a wide shot containing all of the relevant action and inserts of various *cut-ins* and *cutaways* to direct the audience's attention to details as the scene progresses.

master scene script — The screenplay.

master shot — The main shot containing all of the relevant action which is used in the *master scene method*.

matte box — A camera lens cover that accepts filters and patterned templates.

matte effects — Compositing two or more images together with the aid of computer processing and a special background; often a blue or green screen.

maximum sharpness setting — The aperture setting of a lens that will render the point of focus with the greatest clarity possible; usually one or two f-stops down from wide open.

MCU — See medium close-up.

media buys — The process of purchasing television broadcast time or other media access to run an advertisement.

medium close-up (MCU) — A composition with a scale between a *medium shot* and a *close-up.*

medium long shot (MLS) — A composition with a scale between a *medium shot* and a *long shot.*

medium shot (MS) — A popular composition that frames human subjects from about chest up.

meta tags — Data placed in the head section of an HTML document which helps search engines identify the document correctly.

method acting — A style of acting that utilizes memory and imagination to evoke performances.

metric editing — An approach to editing that uses *shots* of equal length.

mic — Abbreviation for *microphone.*

microphone — A mechanical device that converts sound pressure into an electric signal for sound amplification and recording.

microphone-level signal — An audio signal that is not amplified; the type and strength of audio signal generated by a *microphone.*

mike — Verb meaning to position a *microphone.*

mini-plug — A 1/8" audio connector; often used to connect personal *headphones.*

MLS — See medium long shot.

mono — A single-channel audio signal.

montage — A sequence of *shots* that is often used to condense events, expand an idea, show events happening in different locations simultaneously, or to convey the internal thoughts of a *character.*

motivating light — The process of justifying artificial lighting by implying a *practical source* such as a streetlamp or campfire.

moving storyboards — Rudimentary video recordings of people or models designed to illustrate how a scene works in its pacing and *blocking* before a project goes into production.

Moviola — A machine used it edit motion picture film.

MS — See medium shot.

musical formats — An advertising style that features music as the central element of interest.

nanometer — A measurement of length; often used to define electromagnetic spectrum.

narrative commercial — An advertising style that treats a commercial like a miniature film complete with elements of the dramatic structure.

narrator — The voice that carries the audience through the story; often achieved through *voice-over.*

NATSOT (natural sound over tape) — A news package containing natural sounds that is *voiced over* by the news anchor during a live news telecast.

negative conformer — A film editor who takes the creative editing decisions made in a computer or with a *work print* and carefully cuts the original camera negative to match.

networking — Using personal contacts and systematic interpersonal communication strategies to find a job.

neutral density — A filter that reduces the intensity of light without altering other characteristics.

news producer — A person responsible for the content and administration of a news telecast.

NLE — See nonlinear editing.

non-destructive editing — An editing system that allows the user to alter *clips* without erasing or altering the original data files. Compare *destructive editing.*

nonlinear editing (NLE) — A computer-based editing system; an editing system in which data and files can be randomly accessed.

noseroom — The open space in the frame in front a person who is in full or partial profile.

NTSC — Standard television in the Americas and select territories. Based on 525 lines of horizontal resolution; named for the body that adopted the standard: National Television Systems Committee.

objective perspective — A *shot* that implies the point of view of a detached observer.

off-axis — Recording an audio source with the *microphone* pointed in a direction other than directly at the audio source.

off-line editing — Low-resolution editing process used to make creative decisions without the use of expensive high-resolution equipment or need to use extensive data storage space.

omnidirectional microphones — A *microphone* that records sound from all directions with equal strength.

on speculation — A business venture that is undertaken with the anticipation of future earnings but without a commitment of payment or sales in advance.

on-axis — Recording an audio source with the *microphone* pointed directly at the sound source.

on-camera release — Giving permission to use one's image and likeness by stating so on camera.

one sheet — A promotional poster for a film or video project.

on-line editing — High-resolution editing system for mastering a final program in distribution-quality.

open casting call — A casting session in which the general public is invited to audition.

open light — A light that does not use a lens or glass enclosure.

outline — A writing format using hierarchical lists and brief descriptions of each topic area.

out-point — The ending frame of an edit.

overhead shot — A high-angle shot pointing straight down; often called the "point of view of God," and sometimes used to foreshadow tragic events.

overlap dissolve — See dissolve.

overlapping action — The process of recording the same action from multiple angles to give the editor more options in *postproduction.*

over-the-shoulder shot — A camera angle often used to record conversations or to show what a *character* sees; recorded from behind the character, usually with his or her shoulder partially in *frame.*

packages — Broadcast news stores that are edited together before the live telecast.

PAL (phase-alternating line) — Standard television system used in much of Europe, Asia, Africa, and South America; based on 625 lines of horizontal resolution.

pan — Moving the camera from side to side on a *tripod* head or other fixed camera support to scan a landscape or change the point of attention.

pan drag — A *tripod* control that regulates the amount of resistance in side-to-side movements; used to create smoother camera moves.

pan lock — A *tripod* control that prevents side-to-side camera movements; used to lock down the camera for laterally stationary recording.

panhandle — A small rod extending from a *tripod* head used to move the camera to execute *pan* and *tilt* shots; allows greater leverage and smoother camera moves.

parabolic microphone — A *microphone* assembly that uses a parabolic reflector to gather sounds for quality recording from a significant distance.

parallel construction — An editing approach that portrays events happening simultaneously in two or more locations.

parametric equalizer — An *equalizer* that allows the user to select an exact frequency range for manipulation.

pedestal — A vertical post in a *tripod* that can be raised or lowered to adjust the camera height; also a video calibration control that sets the darkness level.

pedestal crank — A geared mechanism in the body of a *tripod* that is used to raise the tripod head higher or lower to accommodate a desired camera position.

pedestal lock — A control that prevents movement of the *pedestal crank*.

per screen average — A measure of a project's success based on the revenue generated for each theater screen used; often reported on a daily, weekly, or cumulative basis.

per use license — A type of permission to use a resource (music, sound effect, stock video footage) in which as fee is negotiated for a single usage.

performance release — A legal agreement to allow the use of a person's image and likeness in a film or video production.

persistence of vision — The brief retention of an image in the mind after the physical stimulus is removed.

perspective lines — Angular lines that will eventually converge at a point outside of the frame (*the vanishing point)*; used in two-dimensional design to create an illusion of depth.

phantom power — Electric power provided to a *capacitor microphone* by an external source (mixing board, video camera) over the microphone cable.

phasing — A reduction of stereo imaging and loudness that can occur when the signals of two *microphones* recording the same sound are combined.

phono plug — 1/4" audio connector.

physical continuity — Consistency in matching the location and posture of physical objects from one *shot* to the next.

pick-up — A shot recorded after the main production phase, often with a reduced crew, which is used to replace original material of poor technical quality, or to capture new material needed to complete the editing process.

pistol grip — A *microphone* support device that is designed for handheld use.

pitch — A brief oral presentation designed to sell a program idea to a *producer* or a potential client.

plot point — A turning point in a story; a major event in a screenplay.

point-of-view shot — A shot with a *subjective perspective*; the audience sees what the character sees.

polarizing filter — A filter than only transmits light from a specific angle; good for eliminating glare.

pools of light — A tool for creating the illusion of depth in videography by building areas of brightness and shadow at various depths in a composition.

pop filter — A spongy cover placed over a *microphone* pickup element to reduce interference from wind and breath; helpful for protecting against distortion from hard sounds such as words that begin with the letter "p."

portfolio press kit — A printed promotional packet for a film for video project that is distributed to the media and potential distributors; often contains press releases, fact sheets, and publicity photos.

position jump — A *continuity error* in which a slight change in camera *angle* or *focal length* makes it appear as though people or objects jump from one part of the *frame* to another.

postproduction — The phase of the filmmaking process that takes place after *principal photography*; the editing phase.

practical producers — *Producers* who are involved in the day-to-day implementation of making a film or video project.

practical sources — Lighting sources that are part of the environment including windows, table lamps, and overhead lighting.

preinterviews — An informal conversation with an interview subject used to plan the question list for an on-camera interview.

preproduction — The phase of the filmmaking process that takes place before *principal photography*; the planning phase.

presentation storyboards — Illustrations on poster board or PowerPoint designed to *pitch* an advertising concept to a client.

press junket — An intense and coordinated publicity effort usually timed just before the release of a project; includes interview opportunities for media outlets with the *principal cast* and *director.*

preview window — A monitor used to display a video source in an editing suite; also a monitor for displaying the material queued for broadcast in a television station control room.

primary color — A color that can be mixed with other primary colors of the same set to create any hue in the visual spectrum. The primary colors used in video production are red, green, and blue, which are *additive colors.*

prime lens — A lens with a fixed *focal length*; cannot change its level of magnification.

principal actors — The primary cast; the people portraying the main *characters.*

principal photography — The shooting phase of *production*; the time when the cast and crew do the actual filming.

problem/solution format — An advertising style that establishes a problem shared by the audience and then shows how the product solves that problem.

producer — A person who administers the making of a film or video project from a supervisory, executive, or senior managerial position.

production — The time period when the cast and crew actually film the project; also called *principal photography.*

production schedule — A timeline of the entire production process.

production storyboards — Illustrations used to guide the shooting process.

program — A complete video or film project.

progressive scanning — Recording or presenting video information one horizontal line at a time, from top to bottom.

properties — Objects used by the actors or to decorate a set; also called props.

props — See properties.

prosumer — A combination of "professional" and "consumer"; used to define a class of mid-priced production gear that is utilized by both markets.

protagonist — The hero of the story; the main *character* whose journey the audience follows.

proximity effect — A form of distortion that occurs when a *microphone* is placed close to a sound source causing an increase in low-frequency sensitivity.

PSA — See public service announcement.

public domain — A class of intellectual property that is available for public use without charge or need to obtain permission.

public relations campaign — A coordinated plan designed to extend a message or a public image to an external audience; often includes public information strategies using multiple media outlets.

public service announcement (PSA) — A commercial used to promote a nonprofit organization or to increase awareness of an issue of social significance.

public service campaign — An information campaign, often conducted by a nonprofit agency, designed to disseminate information for the betterment of public health or quality of life.

purchase order — An accounting document that authorizes and records expenditures.

quick-release plate — Mounting hardware used to attach a camera to a *tripod* that allows instant removal of the camera with the push of a button.

ratings — A scientific measure of television viewership that is used to set advertising rates; also the time periods when rating measurements take place.

RCA cable — A common cable used for transferring audio *line-level signals* between components; also used for consumer-quality video signals.

reaction shot — A view of a character's reaction to events happening in a scene.

reality television — A class of entertainment programming that follows real people in semiscripted or unscripted situations.

record deck — A videotape deck that builds a program in a *linear editing system* or a deck used for mastering a project in a *nonlinear editing system.*

reference tone — A tone of fixed frequency that is used to calibrate audio components and to set audio recording and amplification levels.

reflected light meter — An instrument designed to measure the amount of light reflected off of a subject.

reflector boards — See bounce card.

render — The process of creating a new data file to represent an effect or transition in *nonlinear editing.*

replacement coverage — An insurance policy that guarantees payout equal to the cost to replace production equipment if the equipment is lost or damaged.

reporter — The person who goes out into the field to research and cover stories in broadcast news production.

request for proposal (RFP) — A public announcement inviting qualified candidates to bid on a project by submitting a written portfolio meeting the specifications of the call.

resolution — The amount of detail in a video image; a measure of image quality; also the end of a story.

reverse angle — A point of view opposite the current angle in a scene.

rhythmic editing — A sequence that is defined by a recurring pattern of shot length. For example, there might be a short-short-long or long-long-short pattern.

rising and falling action — The tempo and rhythm of a story that is created by the protagonist's mastering of successive *complications*.

rocker switch — A bidirectional button used to control two operations; often used on video cameras to change the magnification power of *zoom lenses* up or down.

room tone — An audio recording of an interior environment used to bridge audio elements and to maintain audio continuity in editing.

rough cut — A draft of an edit; a version of an edit that does not contain all of the final elements in polished form.

rule of thirds — An approach to visual composition that divides a frame into nine parts, like a tic-tac-toe board. Elements of interest are best placed on these lines. The four points where the lines intersect are considered to be the most dynamic parts of the frame.

runner — A minor plotline in a television episode which is often comic in nature; also called the C-story.

rushes — See dailies.

scene — A series of *shots* that are unified in time, location, and theme.

scene outline — A writing format that contains a list of all the *scenes* in a program with a brief description of each.

screen test — A filmed or videotaped audition to help determine how an *actor* will appear in a role.

screen time — The actual running time of a video project regardless of the time frame of events in the story.

screenplay — The script; the story of a film or television program in written form.

scrim — A wire screen placed over a lighting instrument used to reduce the overall intensity of light without changing its quality.

script breakdown — A list of *actors*, *props*, locations and other elements required by the script to realize a story on screen; used for budgeting and scheduling.

script supervisor — The crewmember responsible for observing and maintaining *continuity*.

season — A collection of 6 to 26 television episodes that are designed to be broadcast in succession for part of a year.

second unit — A small camera team responsible for gathering additional shots needed for a production.

sense memory — A tool of *method acting* in which an actor evokes a personal memory matching the experience of a character to feel the emotions of the character.

sequence — A collection of *shots* that is often unified in time and theme, but not location. A chase sequence, for example, takes the audience to a number of different places in the shot series.

series — The total collection of television *episodes* for a particular project.

series photography — A set of still photographs taken in rapid succession to analyze movement; a step in the evolution of motion pictures.

service deal — A distribution arrangement in which a production company shoulders the financial risk of distribution rather than the distribution company. The production company, in effect, pays to have the distribution company represent them.

service in kind — A product or service that is accepted as payment instead of cash.

servo motor — A mechanism that allows discrete mechanical control from a remote distance; often used with camera and other equipment controls in film and video production.

shafts of light — Narrow beams of light sculpted across surfaces; used to add interest and depth.

shock mounts — A support that suspends a *microphone* in a network of rubber bands to reduce the potential of contaminating sounds from jarring movements.

shooting ratio — The ratio of footage shot to footage used in the final program.

shooting schedule — The plan of *scenes* to be shot on each day and the locations of those *scenes.*

shot — A unit of film or video that is uninterrupted from the time the camera starts to the time it stops; also an uninterrupted segment of film or video in the final program.

shot list — A document created by the *director* to plan the best shooting order for maximum efficiency and to make sure no required shots are omitted during the hectic production process.

shot log — A record of descriptive information made during the shooting process to document the content and quality of each *shot.*

shotgun microphone — Any *microphone* in the directional class; often a *microphone* that has a long interference tube and includes *supercardioid*, *hypercardioid*, and *ultracardioid* types.

show reel — A collection of video clips highlighting examples of past production work used by companies and individuals to demonstrate their qualifications to potential clients and employers.

showrunner — An executive *producer* in television who is the creative force behind a series; often the head writer of the series as well.

shutter speed — The amount of time that the camera exposes each image to light; often given in fractions of a second such as 1/60; 1/125; 1/500.

side rejection — The ability to exclude or reduce the sensitivity and recording strength on the side of a *microphone.*

signal-to-noise ratio — The relationship of the strength of a sound to the inherent background noise in the system. Low signal-to-noise ratios cause hiss when the signal is amplified.

silk spun — Filtering material composed of a loose weave of fibers placed over a lighting instrument to partially diffuse the light while retaining some incident unfiltered light.

simultaneous brightness contrast — Seeing pure black is only possible when an area of brightness is within the same field of view; a principle of human visual perception.

single scrim — A *scrim* that reduces light intensity by half an f-stop.

single-system — A recording method in which image and sound are captured in sync on the same medium.

slate — A tool used in traditional film production and other *double-system* recording methods to allow picture and sound to be matched up in *postproduction*; also called a clapperboard.

snoots — A tube placed over a lighting instrument to limit its coverage to a narrow beam with well-defined edges.

soft effects — *Sound effects* that are not in sync with the picture.

sole proprietorship — A business that is functionally equivalent to the individual running it. The owner is personally responsible for all profits, losses, and liabilities.

sound bites — Brief statements by an interview subject that are used in broadcast news stories.

sound effects — Sound elements other than voice and music that add to the aural experience.

sound recordist — The crew member whose primary responsibility is the clean capture of audio during *production*.

sound stage — A controlled studio environment that is protected from outside sound contamination.

source deck — The playback deck in a linear videotape editing system.

spatial continuity — Keeping the audience geographically oriented from one *shot* to the next.

special effects color filter — A lighting or camera filter designed to alter the color of light for creative effect.

special effects filters — A camera filter used to modify the light in a creative manner; includes starburst and fog filters.

speech bump — An increase in *microphone* sensitivity in the vocal range (approximately 300 to 3,000 Hz).

spill — Light that falls onto an area of the set other than its intended location.

split-page script — A scripting format often used in producing commercials and other short projects which lists the visual information in one column and the sound elements in the other. News scripts list the script text in one column and the director's notes in the other.

spokesperson — An advertising style that uses a recognized personality, often a celebrity or trusted public figure, to endorse and promote a product.

spot check — The process of reviewing sound and image recordings to make sure that there are no technical problems.

spot meter — A light meter that measures the reflected illumination of a very small part of a set.

spot setting — A control position that sets a lighting instrument to cast a narrow beam over a small area.

spotting — Deciding where *sound effects* and music will be inserted into a project; often done after the project is *locked*.

spreader — A *tripod* accessory that is set on the ground and used to hold each of the three legs in place for greater stability and control.

spring head — A type of *tripod* head that uses the resistance of spring mechanisms to regulate camera movement. Generally these are low-quality designs, which are not appropriate for professional use.

stand-ins — People used to set lighting and to plan *blocking* so the *actors* can rehearse or rest.

stand-up — A segment in a broadcast news story when a *reporter* talks to the camera.

static shot — A *shot* in which the camera does not move.

Steadycam — A proprietary camera stabilizing system designed for smooth handheld operation.

stereo mix — A two-channel audio recording designed for playback on systems with a left and right speaker.

stereoscopic — Vision with two eyes; viewing system allowing three-dimensional spatial perception.
storyboards — A series of *shot* illustrations used for production planning.
striking — Taking down a set and putting equipment away after a shoot.
stripboard — A graphical presentation of a *production schedule* or *shooting schedule.*
stunt doubles — Specially trained professionals who undertake the dangerous scenes for the *actors.*
subjective perspective — Putting the camera in the *point of view* of a character.
subtractive color — The approach to color-mixing used with paint and printers' ink. Mixing variations of the three *primary colors* of pigment together (yellow, cyan, and magenta) can create virtually any color possible.
supercardioid — A directional *microphone* that is more narrowly focused than the standard cardioid *microphone.*
supporting actors — *Actors* who have a significant role in a program, but who do not portray the main character(s) of the story.
supporting character — A minor *character* who helps the *protagonist* in his or her dramatic journey.
surround sound — A sophisticated recording, mixing, and playback system for audio that is designed to produce realistic sound from multiple directions, including from behind the listener.
sweeps — The *ratings* periods.
symbolism — An advertising style that incorporates objects or other elements that are designed to convey symbolic meaning rather than straight descriptive information.
sync sound — See synchronous sound.
synchronous sound — Sound that matches picture.
syndication — The sale of rights to broadcast television content; often negotiated for each program on a market-by-market basis. Many distributors and station groups purchase the rights to broadcast a television series in multiple markets as part of a syndication deal.
synergy — An effect of two or more forces working together that creates a product greater than the simple sum of individual efforts.
synthetic editing — Building a concept though the accumulation of details; often implemented visually using *inductive scene construction.*
table read — A reading of the script by all of the principal *actors* in a casual setting; often the first stage of the rehearsal process.
tag — The last brief segment of a television program; also called the *epilogue.*
tail-slating — Identifying a shot with the scene *slate* at the end rather than at the beginning; often done to avoid distracting the actors or for practical issues of *blocking.*
take — An attempt to record a *shot.*
tally light — The red light on the front of a camera that indicates the camera is recording.
target audience — The people whom a commercial or other video project is intended to reach.
t-axis — The dimension of time in film and video.
TCB — See time code break.
teaser — The first segment of a television program, which is designed to *hook* the audience.

teaser trailers — A short promotional clip for a film designed to create advance buzz and interest long before the release of a project; often 30 to 60 seconds in length.

technical director — The person in a television studio control room who punches the buttons to select the active camera in a multicamera setup.

technical rehearsal — Practicing a scene with all camera moves and other technical elements in effect; often the last rehearsal before shooting.

telephoto lens — A lens with a high level of magnification.

temporal continuity — Maintaining a logical and consistent flow of time in a *scene* or in a program.

testimonials — An advertising style that features satisfied customers sharing their experience and success with a product.

thaumatrope — A paper disk with illustrations on each side set between two pieces of string. When the strings are twirled the two images appear to merge into one.

the line — The imaginary line used in the application of the *180-degree rule* to maintain *spatial continuity.*

theatrical trailer — A promotional advertisement of about two minutes for a film primarily intended for movie theater distribution. DVD and the Internet are also popular distribution channels.

three-act structure — An approach to screenwriting that breaks a film or video project into three main units. The application of this formula gives dimension and pacing to a program and facilities the elements of the *dramatic structure.*

three-shot — A *shot* composed to include three people in the *frame.*

tilt — Moving the camera up or down while it is mounted on a *tripod* head to shift the viewer's attention to objects above or below the current field of view.

tilt drag — A *tripod* control that regulates the amount of resistance in up and down movements; used to create smoother camera moves.

tilt lock — A *tripod* control that prevents up and down camera movements; used to lock down the camera for vertically stationary recording.

time code — A method of cataloging audio and video recordings; assigns each frame of video a fixed numerical identification value.

time code break (TCB) — An interruption in continuous time code recording that results when a time code generator defaults to zero because of a gap on a videotape between recorded shots; can cause difficulty in logging and editing.

time-lapse — The process of accelerating time on screen by recording *frames* at intermittent intervals or by accelerating video footage in the computer during *postproduction.*

timeline — The interface in a computer-based editing system used to build a video project; often contains areas for composing multiple channels of video, audio, titles, and transitions.

tracking — Moving a camera sideways to keep up with people who are walking or to follow other moving objects.

treatment — A written narrative version of a story idea designed to sell a project to producers and clients.

trilogy — A series of three films or video programs with a unified theme.

tripod — A camera support system with three legs.

tripod plate — Mounting hardware that is attached to a camera, which allows the camera to be locked into place on a *tripod* head.

trucking — See tracking.

t-stop — Similar in function to *f-stops*, but t-stops adjust for light absorbed within a lens, and are based on the actual amount of light transmitted to the imaging device; t-stops are a more accurate basis for *aperture* setting than *f-stops*.

two-shot — A shot composed to include two people in the frame.

ultracardioid — The most narrowly focused *cardioid* option available; a highly directional shotgun *microphone*.

ultraviolet filter — See UV Filter.

umbrellas — An umbrella-shaped reflective surface used to diffuse light; often used in enclosed spaces.

unidirectional microphones — A class of *microphones* with more sensitivity in one particular direction; includes all varieties of *cardioid microphones*.

uniform release date — A marketing model in which all potential channels of distribution are utilized simultaneously.

unit production manager — The crewmember responsible for the on-site administration of a film or video project.

universal housing — A protective camera casing designed to be used with many different camera models.

UV filter — A camera filter that reduces the amount of ultraviolet light reaching the imaging surface; often used to reduce haze and fog.

vanishing point — The point at which two converging *perspective lines* eventually meet.

vectorscope — A instrument used to calibrate the color in a video signal by graphically representing color bars and plotting the ideal color settings.

vehicle mount — A camera support system used to attach a camera to a car or other vehicle.

vertically integrated — A business model in which a single company or conglomerate controls all aspects of a product from design to distribution.

video gain control — A camera function that changes the effective sensitivity of the imaging device to allow recording in low-light situations. Use of video gain adds significant noise to the image.

videographer — The crewmember who operates the camera in video production.

video-on-demand — A service in which consumers can order a program to begin at any time of their choosing. Primary distribution channels include cable television and the Internet.

view screen — A small video display window that is usually flipped out from the side of a camera.

viewfinder — The small eyepiece-sized viewing monitor located on the back of a camera.

visible light — The range of electromagnetic spectrum that can be translated by the human brain into visual experience.

voice-over — A vocal recording that is generally set to a series of images and often recorded in a sound studio rather than on location.

volume units — A unit of measurement uniquely utilized by a VU meter, which is the most common device for displaying audio recording levels in video production equipment.

VOSOT (voice-over sound on tape) — A news package that contains vocal segments by a *reporter* that also has segments read by a news anchor during a live news telecast.

VU — See volume units.

walk and talk — A technique for recording conversations in which the *characters* and the camera keep in motion to produce a ever-changing background.

waveform monitor — An instrument that displays the luminance (brightness) information of the video signal in graph form; used for calibration.

webcasting — Distribution of content over the Internet.

white balance — A camera control that sets the imaging system to a white reference for accurate color reproduction.

wide-angle lens — A lens with a wide field of view.

widescreen — Any *aspect ratio* in which the width of the screen is significantly greater than 1.33 times its height.

wild track — Original audio, including natural sound and sound effects, that is gathered separately from picture.

window dub — A copy of footage that has time code information displayed on the screen; used to log the footage and to make preliminary editing decisions.

windscreen — See pop filter.

wipe — An editing transition in which one image slides across another and replaces it.

work print — A copy of motion picture film that an editor cuts on a *Moviola.*

x-axis — The horizontal dimension.

XLR — A three-poled *microphone* cable or connector; a high-quality mono cable used to transmit audio signals.

y-axis — The vertical dimension.

z-axis — The dimension of depth.

zoetrope — A small cylinder with viewing slits that is mounted on a stand. When the cylinder is rotated there is an illusion of motion created by the images on the inside of the device.

zone metering system — A camera light metering system that uses more than one data point for calculating correct exposure; a metering system that allows the user to select the area of the frame used to take the light meter reading.

zoom lens — A lens containing many glass elements, which can be moved within the lens housing to control focus and magnification level.

zoom shot—An optical effect produced by a camera lens that magnifies a part of an image during a shot (zoom-in). The effect can also be reversed to reveal the context of an object (zoom-out).

INDEX

B

C

D

E

F

G

H

I

J

K

L

M

N

O

P

Q

R

S